Programming with UNIX Threads

Charles J. Northrup

John Wiley & Sons, Inc.

New York · Chichester · Brisbane · Toronto · Singapore

Publisher: Katherine Schowalter
Senior Editor: Diane D. Cerra
Managing Editor: Mark Hayden
Text Design & Composition: Charles Northrup

Designations used by companies to distinguish their products are often claimed as trademarks. In all instances where John Wiley & Sons, Inc. is aware of a claim, the product names appear in initial capital letters. Readers, however, should contact the appropriate companies for more complete information regarding trademarks and registration.

This text is printed on acid-free paper.

This publication is designed to provide accurate and authoratative information in regard to the subject matter covered. It is sold with the understanding that the publisher is not engaged in renderling legal, accounting, or other professional service. If legal advice or other expert assistance is required, the services of a competent professional person should be sought.

Library of Congress Cataloging-in-Publication Data:
Northrup, Charles J., 1962 -
   Programming with UNIX Threads / Charles J. Northrup.
   p. cm.
   Includes index.
   ISBN 0-471-13751-0 (pbk : alk. paper)
   1. UNIX (Computer file) 2. Operating systems (Computers)
 I. Title.
 QA76.76.063N674 1996
 005. 1--dc20   95-
35799
                  CIP

Printed in the United States of America
10 9 8 7 6 5 4 3 2 1

In Memory of Rose M. Triola

Contents

viii

Preface

Major technical breakthroughs, like the transistor, are rare events. These breakthroughs have far-reaching effects on science, business, and at times society. The UNIX operating system is such a breakthrough.
R.L. Martin [Mart84]

The second most exciting breakthrough in computing science, following only the invention of multiple execution threads, is the incredibly clever way these multiple threads interact and interrelate within a single process to efficiently share the limited resources of today's single-threaded multiprocessor architectures.
S. Gibson [Gibs92]

This book presents the UNIX Threads Interface in a way that is understandable for application programmers already familiar with the C programming language and the UNIX operating system, but unfamiliar with the concepts of parallel execution paths and the synchronization issues they impose. This book does not address the detailed design of implementing a threads library, nor the design of the operating system supporting threads. Instead, it focuses on discussions of the application programming interface. In this sense, the book is for those programmers who require more information and better examples than can be found in the manual pages accompanying the Software Developers Toolkit for the UnixWare 2.x and Solaris 2.x operating systems. This book does not address the POSIX 1003.1c Threads Interface.

Portability

The UNIX Threads Interface is based on the UNIX International MPWG specifications for multithreading. It is a subset of the IEEE POSIX 1003.1c Threads Interface, known as the pthreads Interface. The UNIX SVR4.2 MP UNIX Threads Interface specification varies slightly from that offered on the Solaris 2.x operating system. An attempt is made to highlight the differences where appropriate.

The Solaris 2.x UNIX Threads Interface and the UnixWare 2.x UNIX Threads Interface are similar, although the details of the implementations are different. Neither interface conforms to the pthreads Interface described by the POSIX 1003.1c standard. The pthreads Interface can be supported on both operation systems through a user-level library.

Organization of the Book

This book is divided into three parts:

1 UNIX Threads	Describes the UNIX Threads model (Chapter 1), The UNIX Process Model (Chapter 2), and the UNIX Threads Interface (Chapter 3).
2 Synchronization	Describes the synchronization primitives available through the UNIX Threads Interface (Chapter 4) with detailed descriptions of Mutex Locks (Chapter 5), Condition Variables (Chapter 6), Semaphores (Chapter 7), Recursive Mutex Locks (Chapter 8), Reader Writer Locks (Chapter 9), Barrier Locks (Chapter 10)
3 Advanced Topics	Thread Signal Handling (Chapter 11) and Scheduling (Chapter 12) are described in this section. The concepts described in this book are all tied together in creating the ADAM software utility (Chapter 13). ADAM provides a higher-level view for parallelism within your application.

Examples

All examples included in this book are in the C Programming Language. Perhaps the most difficult aspect of preparing this book lies in the examples. Examples are easy to contrive, but useful, concise examples serve a better purpose. The examples are intended to provide a foundation for a repository of useful functions that can easily be reused.

The synchronization examples were designed following a modular approach. In this sense, a software module contains one or more functions available for your application programming needs. The module may also contain one or more functions local to the module itself. Each software module has a corresponding data structure with pointers to the available functions. This extra layer of indirection, although having a potential impact on performance, provides a well-structured method for using the examples.

The Software Development Environment

The examples presented in this book were developed and tested on the UnixWare 2.0 operating system (Beta Copy TLP/5).

Acknowledgments

Writing this book has been an experience for my family. I am indebted to my wife Camille, for her love and support throughout this entire process, and to my daughter Breanna for being patient with me while I worked on weekends to complete this book.

I would like to thank Dr. W. Cox of the Novell Corporation, for his useful comments on the organization and presentation of this material during its early stages. I gratefully acknowledge permission granted by Unix System Laboratories, Inc. to reproduce and include excerpts taken from UNIX System V Release for ES/MP Multi Processing Detailed Specifications. Each excerpt is annotated with the footnote " [1] Printed with Permission of Unix Systems Laboratories, Inc. All Rights Reserved."

The technical assistance of A. Josey, A. Protin, J. Veech, G. Vitovitch, and S. Young of the Novell Corporation was a pleasant experience. I am also grateful for the comments provided by the reviewers: Mark Beardon, Robin Chen, Shu-Wei Chen, Emden Gansner, Yennun Huang, Chandra Kintala, Dave Korn, Jeff Korn, John Mocenigo, Steve North, John Pokrapinski, Valerie Torrez, and Ryan Wallach.

Background

The UNIX operating system originated in 1969 at AT&T Bell Laboratories[1] as a multiuser computing environment through which several people can be running programs at the same time. The operating system multiplexes the programs onto an available processor for execution. Although the UNIX operating system itself has undergone considerable change over the years, the underlying process model has remained intact. The process model represents the high-level view of a process within the UNIX operating system and incorporates the process control mechanisms.

This book introduces the UNIX Threads Application Programming Interface for multithreaded application development. Basic terminology is introduced with definitions as used throughout this text. The UNIX Threads Interface permits multiple execution paths within a single UNIX process.

---

[1] D. Ritchie, K. Thompson, M. McIllroy, and J. Ossanna were involved in the beginnings of the UNIX operating system. R. Cannaday was briefly involved in the UNIX file system design.

The need to provide concurrent processing in the UNIX operating system is not a new concept. Many projects have been driven to use several processes to perform a task that logically required only one process. These projects had to turn to inefficient IPC mechanisms [Ritc78].

The term multiprocessing, as used in this book, describes the ability of the operating system to manage multiple processors for the execution of processes [Davi83] [JoJo91c] [SunM92]. Many variations on the definition of this term are found throughout the literature, with the simplest being:

> to get a computer to do more work, or to do the same amount of work faster, add more CPUs. [CaVa92]

[Deit90] adds clarity to the definition by describing multiprocessing as the ability to execute discrete portions of a computation on multiple processors truly simultaneously. These concurrent processes display physical concurrency [Gosc91]. Processes are considered concurrent when their execution overlaps in time [Atwo76] [Thom79] [WeSm83].

There are two basic hardware architectures for designing multiprocessors: an *asymmetric* architecture and the *symmetric* architecture. In an asymmetric multiprocessor each CPU has its own memory. In a symmetric multiprocessor each CPU shares common memory. The symmetric multiprocessors are known as *shared memory multiprocessors* [Beck84] [Test86].

Multiprocessors have been around for more then two decades but were extremely expensive and beyond the means of many businesses. The operating systems running on these multiprocessors were generally proprietary and offered unique methods for providing the parallel processing.

The software technologies used in the operating systems were primitive in their support for multiprocessing. The operating systems were required to maintain information on two or more processors. The measure of this extra work is the *multiprocessing overhead*, or simply the MP overhead. It includes system activities such as context switching, kernel lock spinning, and scheduling [DiIy91].

The initial designs were characterized as coarse-grained multiprocessing operating systems. They provided additional CPU capabilities without requiring changes to the application programs. The operating systems managed the execution of multiple applications on several CPUs, thus providing physical concurrency. The applications did not know which CPU they were executing on, nor did they care. The concurrent processes execute independently of each other, or they could be asynchronous, requiring some form of synchronization [ChMi81]. The latter case includes concurrent processes using the shared memory interprocess communication facilities.

Although the individual processes executing on a coarse-grained multiprocessor do not execute any faster than they would on a uniprocessor, the overall throughput is effectively increased. The actual throughput gains, however, were less than expected, due largely in part to the lack of operating system support for parallel processing.

A driving force in the proliferation of multiprocessor computer systems for today's environment is the realization that they can be manufactured with existing hardware, and as such can exploit the plethora of existing software. Such a system would not only provide the computing power necessary for advanced applications, but would also reduce the cost in comparison to purchasing several computing systems. This is possible, since the applications executing on the multiple CPUs share the common peripheral devices such as the hard drives.

As the hardware costs continue to decrease, the trend has clearly been toward lightweight processes and parallel processing [Lamp77] [Shat84] [MuTa85] [Schn85] [MKOI85] [Fren86]. There are some in the literature who suggest multithreading is a necessity to realize the continuing gains in performance experienced during the prior two decades, while others see it as a method simply to take advantage of a computer's power. Applications that must handle asynchronous events are easier to design with multiple threads of control [McSw89]. Multithreading will permit programmers to produce highly structured programs that may be smaller in size [Phil78] than equivalent sequential structured programs.

In providing a UNIX parallel programming model, [Bart87] raises two concerns: the communication between the independent processes, and the cost of managing the processes of an application. The MP overhead of creating, terminating, blocking, unblocking, scheduling, and performing context switches can have a serious impact on performance.

[BeOl87] describes seven main goals in providing a parallel abstraction for computer programming.

1. Real performance improvements over uniprocessor implementations
2. Support shared memory parallel programs
3. Provide the foundation for support of higher-level abstractions such as multitasking, microtasking, and other parallel language run time support
4. Permit single process applications to easily be extended into parallel versions
5. Extend the conceptual view of a single process program, not replace it; the new interfaces must be intuitive extension of existing interfaces
6. All new facilities should be consistent with the UNIX style of programming
7. The implementation must be efficient

[GaPe] identifies four methods for obtaining higher performance. The first looks to faster circuitry and improving the synchronization primitives. This falls into hardware technology, including faster CPUs, faster bus capabilities, and the technology used in connecting multiple CPUs into a single system. The second method emphasizes vectorizing compilers to recognize parallelism, such as with several Fortran compilers and various C compilers. The third method looks for new parallel algorithms, while the fourth emphasizes new approaches such as data flow models.

The UNIX Threads Interface falls into the third category. It provides the means for a single program to overlap computation and I/O on a uniprocessor, thus increasing the performance of the application. On a multiprocessor computer, it provides the foundation for exploiting the processing power available in all CPUs. To take advantage of this processing power requires the use of parallel processing techniques.

[SunM91] notes the benefits of parallel processing as:

- Increasing job throughput by permitting independent tasks to be handled by separate processors
- Sharing computing resources, such as memory and storage media with multiple CPUs, lowers the overall cost of computing
- Better coordination and faster interaction between related tasks though a high-speed interconnect between the multiple CPUs
- Employing software partioning practices in the architecture of the application

[GeNa90] reasons that concurrent programming is desirable for:

- The notational convenience and conceptual elegance in writing systems with parallelism
- Efficiently exploiting a multiprocessor computer's capabilities
- Permitting a reduction in process execution time
- Enhancing the ability of programmers to derive concurrent solutions for complex problems

[Birr89] provides additional benefits of using concurrency as:

- As an extension to the process model, applications would no longer need to consist of multiple separate processes, each running in a separate address space
- For driving slow I/O devices, such as disks, networks, and printers
- To provide the mechanisms for multiple simultaneous human interactions
- For use in a distributed system a server could easily be extended to service requests from multiple clients
- Deferring evaluations even on a uniprocessor, which could reduce latency

During 1990, UNIX System Laboratories, NCR, Olivetti, Unisys, and the Intel Corporation sponsored the Intel Consortium as a joint effort to design and implement a multiprocessor version of the UNIX System V Release 4.0 operating system. In this release, the operating system was broken down into subsystems that can execute concurrently on any of the available processors [CBBC91].

An interesting facet of the first implementation is that it centered on the existing process model. The early multiprocessing systems were concerned with executing entire processes on the available

CPUs and are characterized as *coarse-grained* multiprocessing implementations, although the operating system itself was in a sense more *medium-grained*. The process model was described as *heavy-weight* since its startup time, and time for context switch was considered expensive.

The next level of parallelism is often referred to as *medium-grained*. With this level of parallelism, the process startup time and the context switching time are less expensive. To use this model, the programmer decides which parts of a single application can execute in parallel. By dividing a program into multiple execution paths, called *threads*, an application may require less run time than that of the more serial approach taken above. The ability to divide the application into these discrete parts, however, is not obvious to those of us who have always been thinking in terms of a single process.

The final level of parallelism is called *fine-grained* parallelism.[2] With this approach, a compiler or interpreter determines those instructions that could be executed in parallel. Some examples of this include the current Fortran compilers that provide parallelism within iteration constructs.

The UNIX Threads Definition

Features from the UNIX SVR4 Release 4.0 and the UNIX SVR4.1 Enhanced Security were merged to produce the UNIX SVR4.1 Enhanced Security/386 porting base.[3] The UNIX SVR4.2 Enhanced Security Release with Multiprocessing Features (MPF) was then built from this base.[4] This newer operating system provides the multiprocessing capabilities of the earlier UNIX SVR4 MP release and also provides for the multithreaded capabilities at the application level. The 4th Edition of the UNIX System V Interface Definition, as provided by UNIX Systems Laboratories, Inc., describes the multiprocessing features.

The Solaris 2.x operating system also provides a multithreaded capability. The threads interface available on the Solaris 2.x and the UnixWare 2.x operating systems were influenced by [PKBS91].

---

[2] A middle-of-the-road approach to parallelism is given by [ARAL89] who introduced the conceptual *variable-weight* process for the UNIX operating system to provide simple concurrent extensions.

[3] Unix Systems Laboratories, Inc. marketed this product as the UnixWare Release 1.0.

[4] The UnixWare 2.x operating system is derived from the UNIX SVR4.2 ES/MP.

1

The UNIX Threads Model

The UNIX Threads Interface is an extension of the traditional UNIX process model. This chapter presents a high-level description of the UNIX Threads Application Programming Interface.

1.1 Introduction to Threads

A *thread* is simply an execution stream through a process. In the traditional UNIX process model, a single thread of execution starts with the first instruction of the function `main()` and follows the logic of the application until the process terminates. The traditional process model incorporates the address space into the process such that every process executes in a disjoint address space. This offers a boundary protection scheme to ensure a process cannot interfere with another process's execution. The traditional process model also includes the process's resources (*see Figure 1.1*).

| EXECUTION STREAM | RESOURCES | ADDRESS SPACE |

Figure 1.1   Components of the traditional UNIX process.

With the UNIX Threads Interface, an application now has one or more execution streams within the same UNIX process (*Figure 1.2*). Each execution stream is a *thread of control*, or simply a *thread*. A UNIX process with a single *thread* can create additional threads within the same process address space.

A thread separates the process's sequential execution stream from its other resources [Rash86] [ABLL91] [StSh92] [Muel93]. The resources are shared between the multiple execution streams. On a multiprocessor computer system, two or more threads of the same UNIX process can execute concurrently on different processors. The threads execute as concurrent execution streams sharing the same address space performing tasks associated with the desired services [CoDo88].

1

To support the separate execution streams, each thread requires a piece of executable code with a stack and data [Gosc91]. The user-level stack provides for per-thread local variable administration [PKBS91]. From the operating system's perspective, each of the executing threads must have a separate kernel stack and process context [CGT88]. This will allow each thread to execute system calls, and to service interrupts and page faults independently [EKBF92] [McSw89].

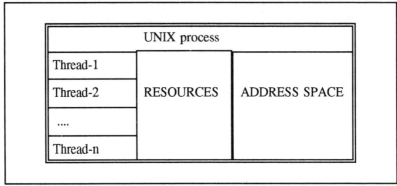

Figure 1.2   Components of a multithreaded UNIX process.

In this book, a thread is an execution stream with its own stack, local variables, and program counter, sharing resources with other threads executing in the same address space. Collectively, all threads executing in the same address space are called *sibling* threads. The relevance of the term *sibling* is that it does not imply a parent and child correlation, as with UNIX processes, but a peer relationship.

Listing 1.1 provides an example of a multithreaded application. The main thread creates a sibling whose execution begins at function printThread. The UNIX process now has two execution streams executing in parallel. The main thread will call the thr_exit function to complete its execution. The UNIX process will not terminate until the sibling thread completes its execution.

Listing 1.1   *hello.c* -- Hello World Example Program.

```
1   #include <thread.h>
2   #include <stdio.h>
3   #include <unistd.h>
4   static void *     printThread(void *);
5
6   void *
7   main(void)
8   {
9         thr_create( NULL, 0, printThread, NULL, 0, NULL);
10        thr_exit((void *)0);
11  }
```

Listing 1.1   *continued.*

```
12   static void *
13   printThread(void *arg)
14   {
15         printf("hello, world from thread %d\n", thr_self());
16         thr_exit((void *)0);
17   }
```

1.2 Thread Implementations

Threads are implemented as a kernel-level abstraction, a user-level abstraction, or a combination of the two. *Kernel-supported* threads, as the name implies, require kernel data structures, such as a process table entry and user table entry to represent the thread. *User-level* threads are represented by data structures within a process's own address space.

User-level threads do not require direct support from the operating system. A user-level thread, however, has the potential to execute only when associated with a kernel process.   The implementation must therefore *multiplex* a user-level thread onto the kernel process for execution, and later preempt it in favor of running a sibling thread (*see Figure 1.3*).

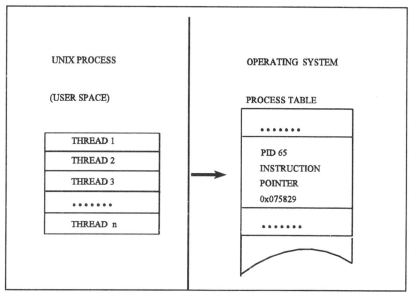

Figure 1.3   Multiplexing user-level threads onto a single UNIX
process for execution.

An advantage of this implementation is that most thread operations do not require a change from user mode to kernel mode [ABLL91] [MSLM91]. This can permit thread creation, scheduling, and eventual termination to complete with better performance than an equivalent kernel-supported thread implementation. A secondary advantage is that user-level threads are extensible. Additional functionality can be added in user space without requiring a new release of the operating system.

In a kernel-supported threads model, each thread has its own context, including the private storage area, volatile registers, and a stack. A kernel-supported threads model has the disadvantage that the kernel size will increase with each thread added to any process. Another disadvantage is that the operating system designers must anticipate a broad range of uses for the threads to ensure proper support. If a particular application requirement cannot be implemented through the kernel-supported thread control API, then the application must incorporate some form of workaround. By providing for every possible use of the kernel-supported threads, however, the size and complexity of the kernel-supported threads implementation increases.

Some implementations use one kernel thread per user-level thread (*see Figure 1.4*). The kernel thread is a *lightweight* process, or LWP for short. The user-level thread is *bound* (a one-to-one mapping) to the kernel LWP. System scheduling, dispatching, and execution of kernel LWPs will result in the execution of the *bound* user-level thread. The disadvantage here is that each user-level thread requires the creation of a kernel LWP, thus consuming kernel processing time. Similarly, when a user-level thread must terminate, the corresponding kernel LWP must also terminate. A kernel LWP has the disadvantage that it cannot do any other work once blocked (i.e., due to synchronization) until the synchronization is complete.

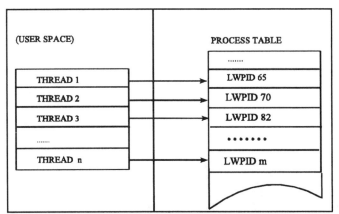

Figure 1.4   User-level threads bound to kernel LWPs.

Other implementations offer both *multiplexed* user-level threads and *bound* threads. The number of kernel LWPs available for the *multiplexed* threads can be tuned by the implementation, or manually adjusted by the application.

1.3 Thread Bindings

The UNIX Threads Interface provides for *multiplexed* and *bound* threads.[5] Multiplexed threads are a user-level abstraction and therefore have no direct representation in the UNIX kernel. Bound threads, conversely, require direct kernel support. A bound thread has a user-level representation, but requires a one-to-one mapping with an LWP. The thread bindings apply for uniprocessor or multiprocessor computer systems.

The default thread creation action assumes a multiplexed thread and allocates a data structure in the process's user address space to represent the newly created thread.[6] User-level scheduling of the multiplexed threads will map a thread onto an available kernel LWP for execution. The operating system will schedule the kernel LWP based on the characteristics of the mapped thread. Some implementations will maintain a set of kernel LWPs for this purpose. This set is called the *multiplexing* LWP *pool*, or more simply, *the pool*.

With multiplexed threads implemented at the user-level, a UNIX process may have more user-level threads than kernel LWPs in the pool. The UNIX threads implementation will multiplex the threads to the kernel LWPs following the scheduling policy and priority of the multiplexed threads. This action occurs at the user level.

Alternatively, the thread creation method allocates a unique kernel LWP for the user-level thread. In this instance, the thread is bound to its kernel LWP. A bound thread cannot execute using an LWP from the pool. Similarly, the implementation will not map a multiplexed thread to a bound thread's LWP.

The relationship between threads and kernel LWPs is shown in Table 1.1. A traditional UNIX process has one thread and one kernel LWP (a 1-to-1 binding relationship). When there are M threads and only one kernel LWP, the implementation must alternate the mapping of threads to the kernel LWP.

The third line of Table 1.1 shows only one thread and N lightweight processes. This binding relationship has no benefit to the application and is therefore not generally supported. Having N light-weight processes with only one thread does not increase the performance of the application. Certain implementations will temporarily permit this situation to occur, and then silently remove any unused kernel LWPs.

---

[5] The UNIX Threads Interface does not define the implementation. Certain systems may provide only bound threads, while others will provide both multiplexed and bound threads.

[6] If the implementation does not provide multiplexed threads, then thread creation will always assume a bound thread.

Table 1.1   Thread and kernel LWP Bindings.

THREADS	LIGHT-WEIGHT PROCESSES	BINDING RELATIONSHIP
1	1	1-to-1
M	1	*M*-to-1
1	*N*	*unused*
M	*N*	*M*-to-*N*

The final line of Table 1.1 shows *M* threads and *N* lightweight processes. When the number of kernel LWPs exceeds the number of multiplexed threads, the UNIX threads implementation may quietly discard the extra kernel LWPs. Most application designs will use the *M*-to-*N* bindings, and a smaller percentage of 1-to-1 bindings. In a client-server application, for example, the primary server routine can execute as a separate bound thread. When the client requests a particular service, then the primary server routine can start a new thread to service the client. This newly allocated thread will be multiplexed onto an available LWP from the pool.

Attributes can be applied to describe characteristics of the thread. Both multiplexed and bound threads can have attributes. The two attributes currently supported are the `daemon` and `detached` attributes. The `daemon` attribute modifies how the process termination occurs, while the `detached` attribute modifies the availability of the thread's termination status.

A UNIX process will terminate when the last thread exits, or if the UNIX process voluntarily terminates, such as with an `exit()` system call. The `daemon` attribute affects the first situation, and permits a UNIX process to terminate after the last *non-daemon* thread exits. When the last *non-daemon* thread terminates, the UNIX threads implementation will silently terminate any remaining `daemon` threads.

The `detached` attribute indicates that the application program does not require the exit status of the thread. Normally, when a thread exits, a sibling can request the exit status of the terminated thread.

1.4 Thread Resources

Sibling threads share certain resources associated with the UNIX process. Some obvious resources shared between sibling threads include global memory, file descriptors, and the process identifier. Sibling threads executing in the same address space are not afforded any boundary protection between them. When a thread modifies the value of a global variable, the new value is immediately visible to all siblings. Similarly, when one thread issues a `chdir` system call, all threads effectively have changed their current working directory.

1.4.1   Thread-Private Data

Sibling threads cannot share certain resources. Each thread, for example, must have a unique identifier within the scope of the UNIX process. Data that cannot be shared between sibling threads is called *thread-private data*. Other examples of thread-private data include the virtual time interval timers, signal stacks, registers, instruction pointer, signal mask, and the errno variable.[7] The thread-private data is determined by the implementation. Table 1.2 details the resources shared between sibling threads and those resources that are private to a thread.

Table 1.2   Shared and Private Thread Resources [1]

Shared Resources	Private Resources
Global Memory	Thread Identifier
Current Working Directory	Interval Timers
User Identification	Signal Mask
File Descriptors	Registers
Shell Environment	Errno
Umask	Instruction Pointer

1.4.2   Thread-Specific Data

Sibling threads can have their own view of data items identified as *thread -specific data*. A UNIX process's threads, for example, should not share application-specific error variables. Thread-specific data is different from thread-private data. The UNIX threads implementation defines the thread-private data, while the application defines the thread-specific data.

An application designed with multiple threads can use a thread-specific global error variable to report error conditions. Consider, for example, an application using a database API that provides a dberror global variable (*see Listing 1.2*). When a database access error occurs, this variable

---

[7] On certain compilation systems, errno will be interpreted as a cpp macro reference when the _REENTRANT macro is defined (see the errno.h include file for details).

[1] Printed with Permission of UNIX Systems Laboratories, Inc. All Rights Reserved.

will be set to the type of error encountered. This sample code fragment shows two functions to query the database.

Listing 1.2   Sample code fragment using an application-specific global error variable.

```
1   extern      db_t    database;
2   extern      error_t     dberror;
3
4   int
5   queryEmployeeRecords( char *name)
6   {
7         record_t    *empRec;
8
9         empRec = dbQuery( database, EMP_RECORDS, name );
10        if( dberror )
11              return(-1);
12        .....
13  }
14
15  int
16  queryDepartmentRecords( char *department )
17  {
18        record_t    *deptRec;
19
20        deptRec=dbQuery(database,DEPT_RECORDS, department);
21        if( dberror )
22              return(-1);
23        ....
24  }
```

In this example, a thread executing the queryEmployeeRecords function could inadvertently report an error condition caused by a sibling thread executing the queryDepartmentRecords function. Suppose, for example, that thread T1 is executing the dbQuery statement (*line 9*) of the queryEmployeeRecords function.   On a multiprocessor, a sibling thread T2, is concurrently executing the dbQuery statement (*line 19*) of the queryDepartmentRecords function.   If either query fails, the dberror variable will be set to indicate the type of error condition.   The challenge then becomes that both T1 and T2 have the same view of the dberror variable, and both queries will report a failure although only one experienced the failure.   To prevent this, the dberror variable must be identified as a thread-specific datum and referenced through a key-value mechanism available with the threads API.

1.5 Thread Execution

A process's threads execute in a single UNIX process environment. In this environment are all of the resources shared by the sibling threads and one or more thread execution environments. A thread execution environment describes the scheduling policy and priority value for a thread, and the disposition of signals (*see Figure 1.5*).

From the operating system's perspective, the process has one or more kernel LWPs that provide the execution vehicle for the threads. The threads are multiplexed onto an available kernel LWP from the pool, or can be bound to a specific kernel LWP until the thread terminates.

Multiplexed threads can execute only when mapped to a UNIX process's LWP. The mapping service offered by the implementation will propagate the characteristics of the thread to the kernel LWP. The operating system uses these characteristics to schedule and subsequently dispatch the kernel LWP for execution.

When the kernel LWP issues a kernel call on behalf of the multiplexed thread, the thread remains bound to the kernel LWP until the kernel call completes. If the kernel call blocks, the multiplexed thread along with its kernel LWP will also block. In the following statement, the kernel LWP and the multiplexed thread will block, waiting for the read(2) request to complete execution.

```
read(fd, buffer, BUFSIZ);
```

If a kernel LWP from the pool is preempted by the operating system, or if it voluntarily gives up the processor, the state of the thread is saved in the UNIX process's user address space. A new thread can then be mapped to the kernel LWP.

Through the UNIX Threads Interface, a thread can suspend the execution of a sibling thread. The suspended thread remains associated with the UNIX process. A sibling thread can subsequently request the suspended thread to resume execution.

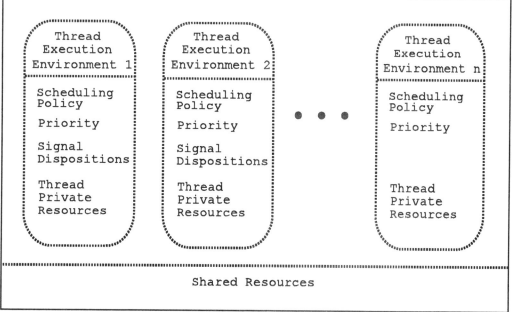

Figure 1.5   The UNIX process environment.

1.5.1   Execution States and Transitions

A user-level thread state value represents the current disposition of a thread. The state transitions for multiplexed threads appear in Figure 1.6. Bound threads have different state transitions (*see Figure 1.7*). The thread creation function will create a multiplexed thread and initialize the thread to the RUNNABLE state. If the request was to create a suspended thread, then the new thread immediately transitions to the SUSPENDED state. The multiplexed thread transitions from the RUNNABLE state to the ON PROCESSOR state once mapped to a kernel LWP from the pool. The kernel will subsequently dispatch the LWP for execution.

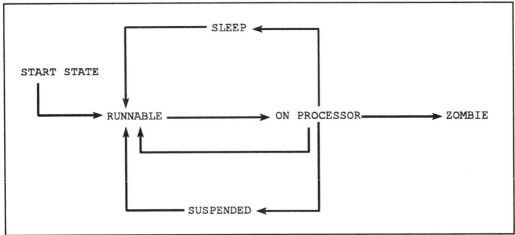

Figure 1.6   Multiplexed thread state transitions. [¶]

While executing, a thread may block waiting for a synchronization event. The multiplexed thread transitions from the ON PROCESSOR state to the SLEEP state. While in the SLEEP state, the thread does not have a kernel LWP associated with it. When the thread receives a wake-up signal, it will transition back to the RUNNABLE state. The thread will eventually be mapped to a kernel LWP from the pool and will transition from the RUNNABLE state to the ON PROCESSOR state.

The UNIX Threads Interface provides signal-based scheduling and may preempt a multiplexed thread in the ON PROCESSOR state if a thread with a higher priority enters the RUNNABLE state. When preempted, the thread transitions from the ON PROCESSOR state to the RUNNABLE state.

The UNIX Threads Interface provides a function to temporarily suspend and subsequently resume a sibling thread. A multiplexed thread can transition to the SUSPENDED state only from the ON PROCESSOR state. If a thread is currently in the SLEEP state, then the function call to suspend this thread will cause the thread to first transition to the RUNNABLE state. Once dispatched, the multiplexed thread will see the pending suspension and can perform any operations required by the implementation to ensure it can safely be suspended (i.e., *the thread does not hold any synchronization locks*). The thread will then suspend itself. A multiplexed thread remains in the SUSPENDED state until a sibling thread resumes its execution. Once resumed, the multiplexed thread transitions from the SUSPENDED state to the RUNNABLE state.

When a multiplexed thread is to terminate, it transitions from the ON PROCESSOR state to the ZOMBIE state. Upon entering the ZOMBIE state, the thread releases most of its resources. The thread remains in the ZOMBIE state until a sibling thread calls the thread wait function. The UNIX Threads Interface will then remove the ZOMBIE thread from the UNIX process. If the terminating thread has a DETACHED attribute, the UNIX Threads Interface will immediately remove the ZOMBIE thread from the UNIX process.

The difference in the state transitions for a multiplexed thread versus a bound thread is that the latter remains bound to a kernel LWP. Therefore, a bound thread will never be in the RUNNABLE state. Similarly, a bound thread cannot enter the user-level SLEEP state. A bound thread will block at the kernel level, and this can neither be recognized nor represented by the user-level thread states.

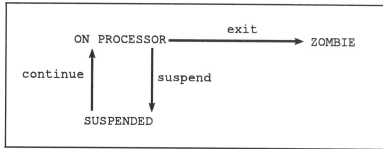

Figure 1.7   Bound thread state transitions. ¶

1.5.2   Signal Handling

The UNIX Threads Interface provides a two-tier approach to signal handling and management. The first tier provides UNIX-process-to-UNIX-process signaling. In the traditional UNIX process model, signal handling would be tier one. The second tier provides for signals between sibling threads. Chapter 11 describes signal handling and management.

1.5.3   Priorities and Scheduling

In prior releases of the UNIX operating system, a UNIX process could follow one of several scheduling policies. Each UNIX process had an associated priority influenced by the scheduling policy. The UNIX Threads Interface enhances the semantics of scheduling policies and priorities.

Each UNIX thread has its own thread priority value and associated scheduling policy. Although multiplexed threads are limited to the Time Shared scheduling policy, bound threads can belong to any of the available scheduling policies.

1.6 A UNIX Threads Library

The UNIX Threads Interface can be provided by a threads library [StSh92], or through lower-level system calls. There are several advantages and disadvantages to each approach, depending on the UNIX operating system implementation and the underlying hardware. This section describes a basic implementation of the UNIX Threads Interface provided through a user-level UNIX threads library. An advantage of providing the threads interface through a user-level library is that the implementation can offer additional features. The UNIX threads library provided by the Novell Corporation, for example, provides administrative tasks for managing user-level stacks.

1.6.1   Working with Stacks

A UNIX thread requires a user-level stack to maintain and administer local variables. During thread creation, a user-level stack is assigned to the thread. The application program can allocate a stack, or have the stack allocated by the UNIX threads library. An application-allocated user-level stack must be equal to or greater than a system-imposed minimum stack size. The UNIX threads library will allocate a number of user-level stacks of a default size for use by the application. The default size is system-imposed.

Upon the first request for a default user-level stack, the UNIX threads library allocates several of these stacks and will place them on a free list. The actual number of stacks added to the free list is implementation-dependent. When all of the stacks are in use, an additional number of stacks will again be allocated and added to the free list. When a thread terminates, the library will reclaim the stack if it was allocated as a default user-level stack. If the stack size does not equal the default size, the library will release the memory associated with the default stack. There are a predetermined number of default user-level stacks maintained in the free list. The library will release the memory associated with additional default stacks.

For most applications, the default stacks offered through the UNIX threads library will be sufficient and will save the application from maintaining its own allocated user-level stack free list. The disadvantage, however, is that the user-level stack management is not defined in the UNIX SVID. The significance here is that management of user-level stacks is essential for performance considerations when your application will create many threads. An application may therefore gain performance by allocating and managing several user-level stacks similar to the actions provided by the UNIX threads library.

1.6.2   A Housekeeper Thread

A UNIX threads library may provide a *housekeeper* thread for various thread administrative functions for the application. The housekeeper thread, for example, can manage the size of the kernel LWP multiplexing pool. The number of multiplexing LWPs in the pool can be adjusted upward or downward by the housekeeper, depending on the number of multiplexed threads currently in use. This prevents the application from needing to administer this information.

Another advantage of the housekeeper strategy is that it will create the kernel LWPs to be added to the pool. When a thread executes the thread creation function, the requesting thread can specify that an additional kernel LWP is to be added to the pool. The thread creation function, however, does not create the kernel LWP. Instead, it increments a requested concurrency counter maintained as part of the threads implementation. The concurrency counter is examined by the housekeeper thread. If the concurrency request is adjusted upward, the housekeeper will allocate the kernel LWP for the pool. The housekeeper thread will silently ignore any errors in the LWP creation request. In this sense, the concurrency request is only a hint to the implementation and may not result in an error condition being returned to the requesting thread.

When the housekeeper thread creates a new kernel LWP for the pool, it also creates a special idle thread for the LWP. The housekeeper will map the idle thread to the LWP whenever the LWP is unoccupied by a sibling multiplexed thread. Thus, the LWP always has a thread mapped to it. The idle thread is a special case of a thread and is provided only for the purpose of occupying an LWP. The idle thread does not consume any processing resources.

An advantage of this implementation is that it provides a consistent method for kernel LWP creation. The created kernel LWPs will inherit the same set of resources from the housekeeper thread's LWP. This results in a predictable, consistent set of LWPs in the pool.

1.6.3   Dynamic Concurrency Control

The housekeeper thread will ensure a minimum level of concurrency for the UNIX process by dynamically adjusting the number of kernel LWPs in the pool. This precludes the need for the concurrency level to be manually adjusted by the application process.

As part of this dynamic adjustment, the UNIX threads library can provide an aging mechanism for the kernel LWPs in the pool. A kernel LWP from the pool with a mapped idle thread will be silently discarded upon the expiration of a predefined aging interval. This permits a downward adjustment of concurrency when the number of kernel LWPs in the pool exceeds the available multiplexed threads.

The UNIX threads library can provide an upward adjustment of concurrency. The kernel LWPs from the pool (along with their mapped thread) can block waiting for a kernel call to complete. Other multiplexed threads in the RUNNABLE state become starved for CPU time. When the housekeeper thread notices this situation, it can create additional LWPs for the pool.

Certain applications, however, may require a finer granularity of control over the concurrency level. An application can adjust the concurrency level through the UNIX Threads Interface. It should be noted, however, that the UNIX SVID does not require the concurrency level to be adjusted by these functions. Instead, the requested value is only a hint to the implementation.

2

The UNIX Process Model

The UNIX operating system originated in 1969 at AT&T Bell Laboratories[8] as a multiuser computing environment through which several people can be running programs at the same time. The operating system multiplexes the programs onto an available processor for execution. Although the UNIX operating system itself has undergone considerable change over the years, the underlying process model has remained intact. The process model represents the high-level view of a process within the UNIX operating system and incorporates the process control mechanisms.

This chapter introduces process control offered by the UNIX operating system. We begin with a brief description of the UNIX process model, and then discuss the UNIX process creation, execution, and termination.

2.1 The UNIX Process Environment

Early in the UNIX operating system development the concept of an *image* was used to define the process execution environment [Ritc78]. The *image* includes the instruction set to execute, the memory image, the general register values, the open file descriptors, and other resources. A *process* is the execution of the image.

The notion of an image provides the foundation for what has become the traditional UNIX process model. A process incorporates the program instruction set being executed, a memory image of its address space, and various *resources*. Collectively, the components of a process constitute the process's environment.

The traditional process model has been with the UNIX operating system for more than two decades and has remained intact, although the control mechanisms have undergone considerable change [Ritc84]. In the traditional UNIX process model, a process is the serial execution of sequential instructions [Gosc91] [ATT86a].

---

[8] D. Ritchie, K. Thompson, M. McIllroy, and J. Ossanna were involved in the beginnings of the UNIX operating system. R. Cannaday was briefly involved in the UNIX file system design.

From a programmer's perspective, the traditional process model is defined by the *environment*. This does not simply refer to the current instruction pointer and register contents, but other available resources as well, including the address space. The incorporation of the address space into the process environment prevents a process from interfering with another process's environment.

The only exception to this *private environment* rule is the fork system call. When a process issues a `fork`, a copy of the current process is made. The original process is considered the `parent` and the new process is called the `child`. Each process must have a unique process ID (`PID`), and thus, the child process must be given a different `PID`. A relationship is maintained between the child and parent process through a parent process ID reference, called the `PPID`.

The child process will inherit the parent process's file descriptors. Although the child will have its own copy of the parent's open file descriptors, the parent and child's descriptors will have the same file pointer. Therefore, a parent may write to the file and the change in the file pointer offset will be seen immediately by the child. A parent may close the file descriptor, but the child's file descriptor will remain open.

This private nature of a process's resources is not conducive for concurrent processing. The traditional `UNIX` process model was originally designed for a uniprocessor computer system with a timesharing environment, which is the wrong model needed for concurrent programming `[ABDGLS89]` `[BaWa88]`. The model also suffers performance penalties from its high overhead in scheduling.

This heavyweight process paradigm is considered too inefficient for general-purpose parallel programming, as it can handle only coarse-grained parallelism `[CGT88]`. Operating systems, such as this, use a one-to-one correspondence between the virtual address space and the threads, thus making it difficult to design applications handling asynchronous events `[McSw89]`. These limitations motivated the evolution toward threads.

2.1.1   Loading a Process

The `UNIX` operating system begins the execution of a process with a special *startup* function loaded when the `C` program is compiled. This function results in various internal data structures being allocated for the `UNIX` process, such as the process table, user table, and file table entries. The startup routine is also responsible for establishing the argument count `argc` and the argument vector `argv[]`. The environment pointer `envp[]` is also set by the startup routine in certain implementations.[9] Upon completion of this initialization, the `main` function of the `C` program is then called.

---

[9]ANSI C specifies only two arguments to the `main()` function.

2.1.2   The Process Resources

Every process within the UNIX operating system has certain resources associated with it. These resources can be categorized either as inherited, private, or shared.[10] Certain of these resources can be modified by the UNIX process during execution, while others, from the UNIX process perspective, are READ ONLY. A process, for example, is given a unique, nonnegative process identification number called its PID. This is a private resource, since each process is guaranteed a unique PID. The PID is considered read only in that the UNIX process cannot alter its value.

2.1.3   Execution Environment

In 1978 Ken Thompson noted that a user executes programs in a computer execution environment called the *user process* [Thom78]. The execution environment represents the current state of a pseudocomputer [Ritc78]. The user process will eventually request special system services, and as a result the process will be switched from the user execution environment to the system execution environment.[11] Here, the kernel executes the desired system service for the user process.

The user process itself will block, waiting for the system service to complete. While blocked, we say that the user process is executing in kernel mode, as this follows the flow of control. The time required to perform the service is charged, for accounting purposes, against the user process requesting the services. Upon completion of the system service request, the process will be switched back to the user execution environment. The notion of an *execution environment* permits the distinction between the system services offered through the operating system kernel, and the services available in the application domain.

2.1.4   The Process Context

When a process is executing, the system is said to be executing in the context of the process [Bach86]. The context of a process includes global registers, stacks, the memory map, and other details. In preempting the process, the operating system must remember the state of the process such that the state can be restored later when the process is rescheduled. The sequence of events in changing from one process to another is called a *context switch*. (*A change from the user mode to kernel mode is a change in execution environments, not a context switch.*)

---

[10]A memory mapped area is a resource potentially shared between unrelated processes.

[11] Since the time when these terms were first introduced, various other terms have been used to denote the distinction between the system service execution environment and the user execution environment. The term *mode*, for example, is now used in place of execution environment. Thus, a process may be executing in user mode, or system mode. Others may use the term *space*, as in user space, versus system space. Throughout this book, the terms *user mode* and *system mode* will be used only when necessary to distinguish the execution environment.

During a context switch, the state information associated with the prior process, such as registers, mode, and memory management information, is saved so that it can later be restored. The state information of the new process must then be loaded. A context switch can occur when a process receives an interrupt signal, or when a system service must be invoked. Context switching can be an expensive operation. The required state information associated with the process influences the time required to perform the context switch.

2.1.5   The Process Memory Layout

The UNIX process memory configuration includes the text segment, data segment, and the stack segment. The text segment represents the program code. In the earliest version of the UNIX operating system, the text segment was loaded into memory when the program was executed. In subsequent releases, this segment is marked as READ ONLY and can be shared by multiple instantiations of the process. This segment typically has a fixed size.

The data segment holds the process's local data and is considered the private read/write memory of the process. Other processes cannot access or alter this memory. The data segment size can be increased or decreased by the sbrk system call. This segment contains the initialized and the uninitialized data for the process. In the binary executable, the entire initialized data is represented, whereas only the size of the uninitialized data is maintained. Upon execution of the binary executable, the system will know the size of the data segment by reading the initialized data and the uninitialized data size. The allocated memory for the uninitialized data will be initialized to zeros. This precludes the binary executable from having to commit excessive disk storage for data whose values will initially be zero. Historically, the data segment is also called the bss segment.

The stack segment represents the process's local stack and is used for subroutine linkage and automatic variable storage. This segment is private to the process. The stack can grow automatically as required by the process, avoiding the need to predetermine its size.

2.2 Process Creation

Two steps are required to run a new program. The first is to invoke the fork system call to create a new process. The second is to invoke the exec system call to load and execute the new program.

2.2.1   Creating a Process

The `fork` system call creates a new process called the *child process*.[12] The process issuing the `fork` system call is the `parent process`. Every process in the UNIX operating system *(except the init process)* has a parent process. To create the child process, the kernel allocates a new entry in the process table, assigns a unique `PID`, and establishes the context for the child process. The final step is to return the child process identifier to the parent process, and a zero value to the child.

The fork System Call

The UNIX Threads Interface provides three variations to the `fork` family of functions *(Figure 2.1)*. These are the `fork`, the `fork1`, and `forkall` functions. Each of these will create a new process, but the semantics is slightly different.

```
NAME:
        fork, fork1, forkall - Create a new process.

SYNOPSIS:
        #include      <sys/types.h>
        #include      <unistd.h>

        pid_t fork(void)
        pid_t fork1(void)
        pid_t forkall(void)
```

Figure 2.1   `fork()` synopsis. [¶]

The new process is created by duplicating the parent process's address space, stack, and open file descriptors. To save time, the child process maintains a `COPY ON WRITE` view of the address space.[13]

In all variations of the `fork` system call, the request will return the child `PID` to the parent and a value of zero to the child. After the `fork` completes, both the parent and the child are ready for execution. The order of execution for the parent and child processes is not guaranteed. Both the parent and the child return from the `fork` and continue with the next instruction. The

---

[12] As a historical reference, the UNIX process creation model, namely the `fork` operation, was originally derived from the GENIE time sharing system [Ritc78] [Ritc84].

[13] Available on most implementations.

[¶] Printed with Permission of UNIX Systems Laboratories, Inc. All Rights Reserved.

application code should examine the return code from the `fork` to distinguish the parent from the child. The child process will inherit some resources associated with the parent process, while others will be unique to the child. Table 2.1 details the list of inherited resources. The resources that are private to the child appear in Table 2.2.

Table 2.1   Inherited Process Resources [1]

Real user ID	Real group ID
Effective user ID	Effective group ID
The environment	Close on exec flags
Signal handling settings	Supplementary group ID
Set user ID mode bit	Set group ID mode bit
Profiling On/Off status	The nice() value
Scheduler class	All attached shared memory segments
Process group ID	Session ID
Current working directory	Root directory
File mode creation mask	Resource limits
Controlling tty	

THREAD-RELATED ISSUES:

The `fork` system call creates a process with a single thread of control (and one lightweight process). The child process is created as a copy of the thread that called the `fork` along with its entire address space. This may include critical resources such as lock states. The child process should avoid using unsafe operations until it can issue an `exec` system call.

The `fork1` system call creates the child process with one kernel LWP. This LWP is a copy of the parent's LWP that executed the `fork`. If the parent process has other sibling LWPs, they are unaffected in the parent, and do not exist for the child. The advantage of using the `fork1` call is that the process creation time is lower. The disadvantage of using the `fork1` function is that any lock held by other sibling LWPs of the parent cannot be unlocked in the child, since those LWPs do not exist in the child. The `fork1` call should be used when the newly created process will immediately execute another command.

[1] Printed with Permission of UNIX Systems Laboratories, Inc. All Rights Reserved.

The forkall system call creates a child process with the same set of kernel LWPs and threads as the parent process. The UNIX operating system Release 4 Application Binary Interface defines the fork system call as forkall.

Table 2.2   Private Process Resources [1]

The child process has a unique process ID (PID)
The child process has a different parent process ID (PPID) which is set to the PID of the calling process
The child process has its own copy of the parent's open file descriptors
Process locks, text locks, and data locks of the parent process are not inherited
The time left until an alarm signal is reset to zero
The set of signals pending for the child process is reset to the empty set
Record locks set by the parent process are not inherited by the child process

EXAMPLE:

Listing 2.1   *simpfork1.c* -- Simple fork example.

```
1   #include <stdio.h>
2   #include <sys/types.h>
3   #include <unistd.h>
4   #include <wait.h>
5
6   int
7   main(void)
8   {
9           pid_t pid;
10          pid = fork1();     /* create the new process here */
11          if ( pid < 0 )     /* check for error condition    */
12                  perror("Simple fork1() example\n");
13          else if ( pid == 0 )    /* child has pid equal to zero */
14                  printf("This is the child process\n");
15          else                    /* we must be the parent.   */
16                  printf("This is the parent process\n");
17                  printf("child process has PID: %d\n", pid);
18                  pid = wait(NULL);
19          }
20          return(0);
21  }
```

The vfork Function

During the early days of UNIX, the cost of creating a process was considered significant. When a process issued a `fork` function call, the entire process was copied to create the child. After the `fork` completed, the child process would usually execute an `exec` function call to load and execute an entirely different program. The solution was to offer a COPY ON WRITE capability. The `vfork` function provides this solution (*see Figure 2.2*).

With `vfork`, both the parent and the child processes share the same image until the memory location must be modified. The write operation is detected by the operating system, and a separate copy of that memory page is then created. This, however, increases the work of the operating system and adds overhead in the form of new system tables.

```
NAME:
      vfork - A modified fork.

SYNOPSIS:
      #include <unistd.h>

      pid_t vfork(void)
```

Figure 2.2   `vfork()` synopsis. [1]

BSD UNIX introduced `vfork`, which essentially just referenced the address space of the parent process. This avoids having to copy page table information to the child process, and reduces the administrative overhead required by the kernel. The challenge with using `vfork()` is that the parent and the child process both execute in the same address space, and thus the child process must be careful not to modify the parent's data or stack.

In calling `vfork`, the parent process is suspended until the child process issues an `exec` or `exit` function call. The child process begins execution within the same address space of the parent. After the child process issues the `exec` or `exit`, the parent resumes execution.

The disadvantage of using `vfork` is that the parent process is suspended while the child process is executing in the same address space. While this provides the ability for multiple processes to execute in the same address space, it does not address the issue of physical concurrency.[14]

---

[14] The UNIX Threads Interface Definition from UNIX System Laboratories notes that the `vfork()` function will eventually be replaced with the `fork1()` function in a future release of the operating system.

[1] Printed with Permission of UNIX Systems Laboratories, Inc. All Rights Reserved.

2.2.2   Executing a Process

An exec system creates a new process image for the calling process (*see Figure 2.3*). An application will typically `fork` a new process and have the child `exec` a different program. A successful `exec` does not return to the calling process, as that process image is overlaid with the new image.

In the first four variations of the `exec` function, the program to execute is given as `path`. This can be specified as an absolute path name, or as a path name relative to the current working directory. In the two remaining variations, the program to execute is given as `file`. If the `file` parameter is specified without a path component (*i.e., file does not contain a slash "/"*) then the directories specified in the shell `PATH` variable will be searched to locate the `file`. The shell `PATH` variable contains a list of directories to search. The directories are separated by a colon. When, for example, the `PATH` variable's value is given as:

        PATH=/bin:/usr/bin:/usr/addon/bin:$HOME/bin

then the four directories specified would be searched to locate `file`. The search order is given as left to right, and thus `/bin` would be searched prior to `/usr/bin`.

The program to execute can be an object file or a data file to be processed by an interpreter. An object file is simply loaded into memory for execution. On some implementations, if the `file` contains:

        #!ipath [arg]

on the first line, then it is assumed to be a data file to be processed by the interpreter specified as `ipath`. The system will execute the interpreter and use the `ipath` as arg_0. If there was an argument specified in the data file, then it is passed to the interpreter as arg_1. Any arguments passed to the `exec` function will be passed to the interpreter as well.

If the file to execute is neither an object file, nor a data file with the semantics defined above, then the `execlp` and `execvp` will use the contents of the file as standard input to the `SHELL`. The other variations of the exec function call do not provide this capability.

The `execl`, `execle`, and `execlp` permit one or more arguments to be specified individually as arg_0 through arg_n. The arguments are character strings. While multiple arguments are optional, arg_0 should always be specified. The character string given as arg is the name displayed through the `ps` command.[15] The other variations of the `exec` function can pass parameters through the argument vector `argv`, an array of character pointers to strings representing the arguments for the new process. A minimum of `argv[0]` must be specified.

---

[15] This feature is available on most implementations.

NAME:
```
exec - Execute a file.
```

SYNOPSIS:
```
#include <unistd.h>

int execl(const char* path,  const char *arg₀,  ...,
          const char *argₙ,  (char *)0)

int execv(const char *path,  const char *argv)

int execle(const char *path,  const char *arg₀,  ...,
     Const char *argₙ,  (char *)0, const char *envp)

int execve(const char *path,  const char *argv,
     const char *envp)

int execlp(const char *file,  const char *arg₀,  ...,
     const char *argₙ,  (char *) 0)

int execvp(const char *file,  const char *argv)
```

Figure 2.3   exec() synopsis. [1]

The process to execute will have its own user environment. The environment contains `name=value` pairs. Normally, a new process will inherit the user environment of its calling process. There are situations, however, in which it is desirable for the new process to have a unique environment.

A user environment for the new process image can be specified through the `execle` function. The `envp` is an array of character pointers to `NULL` terminated character strings. These strings are normally specified as `name=value` pairs. The use of `execle` provides a convenient mechanism to establish the user environment of the new process.

The new process inherits certain attributes of the calling process. Table 2.3 lists the inherited attributes. The new process will also inherit the open file descriptors of the calling process except those marked with the `CLOSE ON EXEC` flag. These file descriptors will be closed in the new process. All shared memory segments attached to the old image will be detached in the new process image.

---

[1] Printed with Permission of UNIX Systems Laboratories, Inc. All Rights Reserved.

Table 2.3   Resources Inherited From `exec` Calling Process [1]

Nice value	Scheduler class and priorities
Process ID	Parent process ID
Process group ID	Supplementary group ID
Semadj values	Session ID
Trace flag	Time left until an alarm clock signal
Current working directory	Root directory
File mode creation mask	Resource limits
Utime, stime, cutime, and cstime	File locks
Controlling terminal	Process signal mask
Pending signals	

When the program to execute has the `set-user ID` flag set on the program file, the effective user ID of the new process is set to the owner of the program file. The program file may also have the `set-group ID` flag resulting in the effective group being set to the group ID of the program file. These flags modify only the effective user ID and have no influence on the real user ID or the real group ID.

If the program to execute (specified as *path*) is not valid or is not found, an error condition results and control remains with the calling process. Otherwise, a new process image is created, overlaying the existing image.

EXAMPLE:

As an example of creating a new process, Listing 2.2 shows a main program creating a child process. After the child is created, the parent process waits for the child to complete execution. The listings show two new function calls, `wait` and `exit`. These are discussed in more detail in the next section.

Listing 2.2   *forkexec.c* -- fork and exec a child process.

```
1  #include <stdio.h>
2  #include <unistd.h>
3  #include <wait.h>
4  #include <sys/types.h>
5
6  void
7  main(void)
8  {
9       pid_t childPid;
10      int   childStatus;
11                          /* Only parent can return from the
12                           * forkAndExec() function. The child,
13                           * if created, will be in different
14                           * address space.                    */
15      childPid = forkAndExec("/bin/ls",NULL);
16
17      if( childPid != -1 ) {
18                          /* Check that child was created. A -1
19                           * return means that an error
20                           * condition occurred.          */
21          printf("This is the parent process\n");
22          printf("child process has PID: %d\n", childPid);
23                          /* We call the wait() function to wait
24                           * for  the child process to complete
25                           * its execution.                */
26
27          if(wait((int *)&childStatus) == -1 )
28                perror("forkexec.c");
29          else
30                printf("child has terminated\n");
31      }
32      return(0);
33  }
34
35  pid_t
36  forkAndExec(char *path, char *argumentVector[])
37  {
38      pid_t pid;
39
40      pid = fork();
```

Listing 2.2   *continued.*

```
41      if ( pid < 0 )
42              perror("forkexec.c");
43
44      else if (pid == 0 )      /* child execs the program */
45              if( execv(path, argumentVector))
46                      perror("forkexec.c");
47      return(pid);
48  }
```

2.3 Process Termination

2.3.1   Waiting for Process Termination

A parent process can wait for the termination of a child by calling the wait function (*see Figure 2.4*). This function will suspend the calling process until one of its immediate children terminates, or an interrupt signal is received. The wait function call will also return to the calling process if a child process is being traced and its execution is suspended by the receipt of a signal. If all child processes have already terminated, the wait function will return immediately. When the status of the child process is available, the wait function returns the PID number for that child.

NAME:

      wait - Wait for a child process to stop or terminate.

SYNOPSIS:

```
#include <sys/types.h>
#include <sys/wait.h>

pid_t wait(int *stat_loc)
```

Figure 2.4   wait() synopsis. [¶]

The wait function will store status information about the child at the location pointed to by the stat_loc parameter. If the stat_loc has a NULL value, then no status information is stored. The status may be examined through a series of macros, as defined in wstat(5). Table 2.4

[¶] Printed with Permission of UNIX Systems Laboratories, Inc. All Rights Reserved.

illustrates several of these macros. The parent process can examine the status returned in
stat_loc to determine if the child is really terminated or simply suspended.

Table 2.4   Macros to Determine Status of Terminated Child Process [1]

WIFEXITED(s)	If the child process terminated normally and a status is available for it, then this macro evaluates to a nonzero value.
WEXITSTATUS(s)	If the WIFEXITED(s) macro evaluates to a nonzero, then this macro will evaluate to the exit code of the child process. The exit code of the child is the value passed to the exit() function, the _exit() function, or the value that the child process returned from main().
WIFSIGNALED(s)	If the child process terminated due to the receipt of a signal, and the status is available for this child, then this macro will evaluate to a nonzero value.
WTERMSIG(s)	If the WIFSIGNALED(s) macro evaluates to a nonzero value, then this macro will evaluate to the numeric value of signal that terminated the child process.
WCOREDUMP(s)	If the WIFSIGNALED(s) macro evaluates to a nonzero value, and a core image of the child process was created, then this macro will evaluate to a nonzero value.

EXAMPLE:

Listing 2.3   *waitany.c* -- Wait for any child process to terminate.

```
 1   #include <sys/types.h>
 2   #include <sys/wait.h>
 3
 4   pid_t
 5   waitForAnyChild(void)
 6   {
 7         int    childStatus;
 8         pid_t childPid;
 9
10         childPid = 0;
```

Listing 2.3 *continued.*

```
11      do      {
12              childPid=wait((int *)&childStatus);
13              if( childPid == -1)
14                      perror("waitForAnyChild()");
15              else if( !WIFEXITED(childStatus) )
16                      childPid = 0;
17      } while(childPid == 0 );
18      return(childPid);
19 }
```

The alternative is to use the `waitpid` function call to specify a particular child process to wait for. The `waitpid` function (*Figure 2.5*) will suspend the calling process until one of its children changes state. If a child process changed state prior to calling `waitpid`, the return is immediate.

```
NAME:
        waitpid - Wait for a child process to change state.

SYNOPSIS:
        #include <sys/types.h>
        #include <sys/wait.h>

        pid_t waitpid(pid_t pid, int *stat_loc, int options)
```

Figure 2.5   `waitpid()` synopsis. [1]

The `pid` parameter specifies a set of child processes for which the status is requested. If `pid` is equal to `(pid_t) -1`, then the status is requested for any child process. If `pid` is greater than `(pid_t) 0`, it specifies the process ID of the child process for which the status is requested. When `pid` is equal to `(pid_t) 0`, then the status is requested for any child process whose process group ID is equal to that of the calling process. A `pid` value of less than `(pid_t) -1` signifies that the status is requested for any child process whose process group ID is the absolute value of `pid`. The `options` parameter is the bitwise OR of zero or more of the flags appearing in Table 2.5.

[1] Printed with Permission of UNIX Systems Laboratories, Inc. All Rights Reserved.

Table 2.5   The `waitpid` Option Flags [1]

WNOHANG	The `waitpid()` function will return immediately even if the status is not available for any of the child processes specified by parameter pid.
WNOWAIT	The `waitpid()` function will keep the process whose status is returned in `stat_loc` in a waitable state. The process may be waited for again with identical results.
WEXITED	The `waitpid()` function will wait for the process(es) to exit.

The `waitpid` function will return the process ID of the child process for which the status is available. When the `waitpid` function returns due to the delivery of a signal to the calling process, a value of -1 is returned and `errno` is set to EINTR.

EXAMPLE:

Listing 2.4   waitchild.c -- Wait for specific child process to terminate.

```
1   #include <sys/types.h>
2   #include <sys/wait.h>
3   pid_t
4   waitForChild(pid_t childPid)
5   {
6          int    status;
7          pid_t pid;
8
9          pid=waitpid(childPid,(int *) &status, WEXITED);
10         if( pid == -1 )
11                 perror("waitForChild");
12         return(pid);
13  }
```

2.3.2   Exiting a Process

A process can be terminated by one of three basic activities: The process completes the `main` function, the process calls `exit` (*Figure 2.6*), or the process terminates abnormally. In the first two cases, the process is considered to have terminated normally. An abnormal termination results from the receipt of a signal, or from calling the `abort` function.

NAME:
> `exit` - Terminate a process.

SYNOPSIS:
> ```
> #include <stdlib.h>
> void exit(int status)
>
> #include <unistd.h>
> void _exit(int status)
> ```

Figure 2.6   `exit()` synopsis. [1]

EXAMPLE:

In Listing 2.5, the `main` function will call `printf` to write a character string to standard output. After the `printf` completes, the `main` function terminates. The startup routines from the standard C library will call `exit` on completion of the `main` function. Thus, an implied call to the `exit` is made.

Listing 2.5   *vhello.c* -- A simple hello.

```
1   #include <stdio.h>
2
3   void
4   main(void)
5   {
6         printf("Hello to all\n");
7   }
```

---

[1] Printed with Permission of UNIX Systems Laboratories, Inc. All Rights Reserved.

Issuing a C language `return` statement from the `main` function will also terminate the process. The use of return in this context is equivalent to calling the `exit` function. In Listing 2.6, the `main` function is declared as type integer and thus can specify the exit status as an integer value.

Listing 2.6   *ihello.c -- A simple hello with a return value.*

```
1  #include <stdio.h>
2
3  int
4  main(void)
5  {
6          int     errorCondition = 0;
7
8          errorCondition =  printf("Hello to all\n");
9          return(errorCondition);
10 }
```

The primary distinction between the `exit` and the `_exit` functions is that the former will invoke all functions registered through the `atexit` function call (*Figure 2.7*) in the reverse order of their registration. The `exit` function will also ensure all standard I/O buffers have been flushed. The `_exit` function does not provide this capability. After calling the exit handlers, the `_exit` function is then called.

The `_exit` function will close all file descriptors, directory streams, and message catalog descriptors of the calling process. The function will also perform certain cleanup operations on any interprocess communication mechanisms used by the application. Shared memory segments, for example, will be detached. This will also decrement the `shm_nattach` in the data structures associated with the shared memory identifier. The kernel will also examine the process to determine if it has any outstanding semaphore adjustments. If so, the value is added to the `semval` of the specified semaphore.

> **NAME:**
>   `atexit` - Add a program termination function.
>
> **SYNOPSIS:**
>   `#include <stdlib.h>`
>
>   `int atexit(void (*func)(void) )`

Figure 2.7   `atexit()` synopsis. [1]

When the process that is exiting is a controlling process (*i.e., a process group leader or a session leader*), then a `SIGHUP` signal will be sent to the foreground process group of its controlling

---

[1] Printed with Permission of UNIX Systems Laboratories, Inc. All Rights Reserved.

terminal, and the controlling terminal will be deallocated. If the process holds a process, text, or data lock, then an unlock operation is performed for each lock type. When the exiting process has one or more stopped children whose process group will be orphaned by the exiting of this process, or if the calling process is a member of a process group that will be orphaned when the calling process exits, then the process group will be sent a SIGHUP and a SIGCONT signal. There is also an accounting record written on the accounting file if the system's accounting routine is enabled.

THREAD-RELATED ISSUES:

The exit function call will terminate the process and call the exit handlers even if one or more light-weight processes are in a suspended state. The suspended lightweight processes will silently vanish with the process.

EXAMPLE:

The process exit status value may be supplied as either the constant EXIT_SUCCESS or EXIT_FAILURE, as defined in the <stdlib.h> header file. Listing 2.7 provides an example of their use. The program examines the argument count, and if more than one argument was specified, an error condition is raised. Otherwise, the process completes with an EXIT_SUCCESS status value.

Listing 2.7   *exit.c* -- A program calling the exit() function.

```
1   #include <stdio.h>
2   #include <stdlib.h>
3   int
4   main(int argc, char *argv[])
5   {
6        if( argc != 1 ) {
7             printf("USAGE: uniprocess\n");
8             exit(EXIT_FAILURE);
9        }
10
11       printf("process was called with no parameters\n");
12       exit(EXIT_SUCCESS);
13  }
```

The exit function call will result in the nonshared component of the process's image being deallocated while the process structure itself is retained until the parent issues a wait function call [ATT91a]. If the calling process's parent process has not specified the SA_NOCLDWAIT flag, then the calling process is transformed into a zombie process. A SIGCHLD signal is then sent to the parent process.

When a process terminates and the parent has not yet issued the wait function call, the process is said to be a *zombie* process. A ps command will show the process as having state "Z". The terminating process structure will be retained until the parent issues a wait function call. This is necessary since the parent process may be busy, or not currently scheduled for execution, and thus will not immediately issue the wait function call. When the parent eventually does issue the wait function call, then the status of the child must be available.

PROGRAMMER'S NOTE:

If the parent process terminates prior to a child, then the init system process will become the parent for the orphaned child. This ensures that all zombie processes will eventually be waited for.

EXAMPLE:

As noted, a process may register specific functions to be called when the process terminates with an exit function call. These functions are referred to as *exit handlers*. Each exit handler is called without any arguments. Listing 2.8 provides an example of using exit handlers.

Listing 2.8   *atexit.c* -- Using exit handlers.

```
1   #include <stdio.h>
2   #include <stdlib.h>
3   static void exitHandler1(void);
4   status void exitHandler2(void);
5
6   int
7   main(int argc, char *argv[], char *envp[])
8   {
9        if( atexit(exitHandler1) != 0 ) {
10              perror("failed to register exitHandler 1");
11              _exit(EXIT_FAILURE);
12       }
13       if( atexit(exitHandler2) != 0 ) {
14              perror("failed to register exitHandler 2");
15              _exit(EXIT_FAILURE);
16       }
17       printf("All exit handlers have been registered\n");
18       exit(EXIT_SUCCESS);
19  }
```

Listing 2.8 *continued.*

```
20  void
21  exitHandler1(void)
22  {
23          printf("executing exit handler 1\n");
24  }
25
26  void
27  exitHandler2(void)
28  {
29          printf("executing exit handler 2\n");
30  }
```

2.4 Extending the Process Model

The UNIX Threads Interface model provides an interface for concurrency within the application process. The term *concurrent processes* describes processes whose executions overlap in time. The term *logical concurrency* is used to describe two or more processes that are ready for execution, but whose actual execution may be mutually exclusive. On a uniprocessor computer, for example, two or more processes could be ready for execution, but only one will be actually executing at any given time. The term *physical concurrency* is used to describe two or more processes, each of which is executing on an available processor.

The weight of a process is determined by two factors. The first is the amount of information needed to context switch the process for execution. When large quantities of information are required, then the context switch time increases. The second factor is the degree of shared memory [Gosc91].

There are three generally accepted categories of weight used to describe process models.[16] The first is the *heavyweight* model of which the traditional UNIX process model is an example.[17] The second is the *medium-weight* model, and the last is the *lightweight* model. For the purposes of this book, the UNIX Threads Interface follows the *medium-weight* process model.

---

[16]A *variable-weight* process model [ABDGLS89] was proposed to express homogeneous threads sharing all resources, to heterogeneous threads sharing some resources, down to heavyweight processes that share no resources.

[17]Various implementations of the UNIX operating system have offered diverse strategies to provide a parallel programming model through which processes may share a certain amount of resources. In the *share groups* model proposed by [BaWa88], logically related resources may be grouped into a resource group. Two or more processes may then share this resource group. Unfortunately, however, the *share group* model does not offer a solution for the process weight problem.

Heavyweight Process

The traditional UNIX process is considered heavyweight, in that it does not readily share resources with other processes (*except through the use of the shared memory IPC*). This model uses a sequential execution stream, in that there is only one thread. Each heavyweight process executes in its own address space, and is represented by a unique process structure.

Medium-Weight Process

In a mediumweight process model, there are several threads of control. Each thread has its own user-level stack. This will result in better interthread protection than between threads in lightweight processes, while still allowing efficient communication.

Lightweight Process

In a lightweight process model, the time to create a process, or to execute a context switch is significantly decreased. [Gosc91] defines a lightweight process as one that contains multiple threads all using the same text, data, and stacks, noting that the lightweight processes are sometimes referred to as threads. The thread creation, context switching, and synchronization are extremely inexpensive. The performance of lightweight processes is largely dependent on the performance of the primitives used to denote concurrency and to control the extent of parallelism within the application [ABLL91].

3

The UNIX Threads Interface

This chapter introduces the UNIX threads application programming interface. The topics covered in this chapter include thread creation, thread termination, thread concurrency, and thread-specific data.

3.1 Creating a Thread

The UNIX process startup routine will create the first thread.[18] This first thread is called the *initial*, or *main*, thread. A thread of a UNIX process can create a sibling thread by calling the thr_create function.

```
NAME:
      thr_create - Create a sibling thread.

SYNOPSIS:
      #include <thread.h>

      int
      thr_create(void *stack_address, size_t stack_size, void
            *(start_routine)(void *arg), void *arg, long flags,
            thread_t *new_thread)
```
Figure 3.1   thr_create() synopsis. [¶]

In calling the thr_create function (*Figure 3.1*), the invoking thread must specify a user-level stack for the newly created thread. The stack_address parameter identifies the stack area.

---

[18] Implementations supporting multiplexed threads will generally create the first thread as a multiplexed thread type. Other implementations will create the first thread as a BOUND thread.

The calling thread can request the `thr_create` function to provide a default user-level stack, or can specify a stack area allocated by the application. For most applications, the default stack will suffice and may provide better performance. By calling the `thr_create` function with `stack_address` set to `NULL`, `thr_create` will allocate a user-level stack for the new thread. The size of this stack is determined by the `stack_size` parameter.

A `stack_size` of zero will result in an implementation-specific stack size being allocated. A specific stack size can be requested by specifying the `stack_size` as a nonzero positive value. In either case, the stack is allocated and initialized by the `thr_create` function. Eventually, when the thread has finished execution, the cleanup process will deallocate the stack.

When using a predefined stack, the application must allocate sufficient memory for the new stack. In this instance, the `stack_address` parameter points to the allocated stack, and the `stack_size` parameter identifies the number of bytes allocated. The `thr_create` function uses this information to initialize the stack area. It is therefore inappropriate to add values to the stack prior to calling `thr_create` in an attempt to pass the values to the thread's `start_routine`.

In specifying a specific size for the stack, it must satisfy the minimum stack size required by the implementation. This is true weather using a default, or an application-defined stack is used. The stack size specified must be equal to or greater than the minimum stack size required, or the `thr_create` function call will fail with an `EINVAL` error condition.

PROGRAMMER'S NOTE:

Selection of the stack size is critical to avoid segmentation violations. In most cases, the default stack allocation will suffice. If a thread receives a `SIGSEGV` signal, try increasing the stack size to resolve the problem. Note, however, an improper pointer reference could be masked by an increased stack size and will remain a latent bug in your application.

Table 3.1 illustrates the relationship between the `stack_address` and the `stack_size` parameters. If the `stack_address` and `stack_size` relationship does not match one of the three entries appearing in this table, then the `thr_create` function call will fail with an `EINVAL` error condition and the sibling thread is not created.

The created thread will begin its execution with the function specified as `start_routine`. The function is called with parameter `arg`. The logical view of creating a new thread is different from the model used by the `fork` system call. With the `fork` system call, both the parent UNIX process and the child UNIX process continue execution with the instruction following the `fork` call.

Table 3.1   Interpreting `stack_address` and `stack_size` Parameters ¶

STACK ADDRESS	STACK SIZE	RESULTS
NULL	0	A default stack allocation will be used and the stack will have a default size.
NULL	> THR_MIN_STACK	A default stack allocation will be used to create a stack with the minimum size required by the implementation.
<address>	0, >=THR_MIN_STACK	The stack for the new thread begins at address and is greater than or equal to the minimum stack size required by the implementation.

Consider, for example, the following code fragment. After the `fork` system call completes, both the parent and the child UNIX process will continue their execution, starting with the instruction on line 3. UNIX threads behave differently. A new thread begins its execution stream at a user-defined function. The comparison of execution streams between the thread creation versus the UNIX process creation is subtle but important to understand.

```
    ....
    pid=fork();
    if( pid == -1 )
         perror(string);
    else if (pid == 0 )
         /* child process */
    else
    ....
```

The default action of the `thr_create` function is to create a multiplexed thread and to transition the thread to the RUNNABLE state.[19] This default behavior can be modified through the `flags` parameter, which is a bitwise OR of zero or more of the flags in Table 3.2.

---

[19]Implementations not supporting multiplexed threads will transition the created thread to the ON PROCESSOR state.

¶ Printed with Permission of UNIX Systems Laboratories, Inc. All Rights Reserved.

Specifying the THR_BOUND flag,[20] for example, will result in the new thread being permanently mapped to a kernel LWP allocated for the thread. If a kernel LWP cannot be allocated, the thr_create function will fail, returning an EAGAIN error indication value. Upon creating the bound thread, the thr_create function transitions the thread to the ON PROCESSOR state.

Table 3.2   Binding Relationships Flags for thr_create() [1]

THR_SUSPENDED	When the thread is created, it enters the RUNNABLE state by default. With this flag set, the new thread will enter the SUSPENDED state. The thread will not begin execution until an explicit call to thr_continue( ) is made by a sibling thread. Creating a thread in the SUSPENDED state permits the application to modify the scheduling parameters and other resources associated with the new thread prior to the execution of the start_routine.
THR_DETACHED	The exit status of the created thread will not be available to the sibling threads. This permits the UNIX threads library to reuse the thread's resource after the thread terminates.
THR_INC_CONC	In addition to creating the new thread, a new LWP is to be created and added to the pool of available lightweight processes.
THR_BOUND	The thread is bound to a new kernel LWP. Both the thread and the kernel LWP will be created as a result of the call. The thread will be bound only to this LWP and cannot execute on other LWPs. Similarly, the LWP will execute only this thread. The thread is said to be permanently bound to this LWP.
THR_DAEMON	The created thread is a daemon thread. A UNIX process will not exit until either all nondaemon threads have terminated, exit() has been called, or the initial thread completes without calling thr_exit(). The UNIX threads library will cause a process to exit if the only remaining threads are daemon threads.

---

[20]This flag has no effect for implementations not supporting multiplexed threads.

[1] Printed with Permission of UNIX Systems Laboratories, Inc. All Rights Reserved.

The THR_INC_CONC flag[21] is used to request an increase in the concurrency level. That is to say, the THR_INC_CONC flag is a hint to the UNIX threads implementation that the number of kernel LWPs in the pool should be increased.[22] The thr_create function does not actually create the kernel LWP for the pool, but merely notes that an increase in the pool size has been requested. Thus, if a kernel LWP cannot be created due to memory limitations or system imposed limitations, an error condition may not be returned to the calling thread. A complete discussion on concurrency is provided in a later section. Specifying both the THR_BOUND and the THR_INC_CONC flags can result in two new kernel LWPs being created. One kernel LWP is allocated for the bound thread, and one is allocated for the pool.

PROGRAMMER'S NOTE:

The THR_INC_CONC (or THR_NEW_LWP) flag explicitly requests an increase in the concurrency level for the application. When the thread terminates, the concurrency level is not adjusted downward. An application creating numerous short-lived threads with this flag set will quickly exceed system resources. See thr_setconcurrency for details on concurrency levels.

PROGRAMMER'S NOTE:

A multithreaded process should use default-allocated user-level stacks for THR_DAEMON-type threads. This will permit the implementation to administer the allocation and deallocation of the stack. There are no simple mechanisms available for the application to provide the administration of stacks for THR_DAEMON-type threads.

When a new thread has successfully been created, its thread identifier will be stored in the location pointed at by the new_thread parameter. If the new_thread parameter was specified as a NULL value, then the new thread identifier is not returned to the calling thread. Thread private resources are listed in Table 3.3, and shared resources are given in Table 3.4.

---

[21] Certain implementations use the THR_NEW_LWP in place of THR_INC_CONC. Solaris 2.4 also uses the THR_NEW_LWP flag.

[22] The Solaris 2.4 implementation will fail with error code EAGAIN if the kernel LWP cannot be allocated. The UNIX Threads Interface states that the THR_INC_CONC flag is only a hint to the implementation and thus certain implementations may not report the EAGAIN error condition.

Table 3.3. Thread Private Resources ¶

· Scheduling context
· Kernel stack
· Signal stack
· Real time, virtual time, and profile timers
· Thread identifiers
· LWP identifiers (if configured)
· Virtual time interval timers

Table 3.4. Resources Shared between Sibling Threads ¶

· Process address space[23]
· Process identifier
· Parent process identifier
· Process group identifier
· Session identifier
· Accounting information
· Credentials[24]
· Maximum privilege set
· Working privilege set
· Mandatory Access Control labels (if configured)
· Root and working directories
· All file descriptors
· All file and record locks
· All IPC descriptors
· Resource limits
· The file creation mode mask (umask)

---

[23] With the possible exception of a per-processor page or a per LWP register.

[24] Credentials include user and group IDs, as well as working and maximum privilege sets, MAC labels, and other information.¶

¶ Printed with Permission of UNIX Systems Laboratories, Inc. All Rights Reserved.

EXAMPLE:

As an example of using the `thr_create` function, consider the program `mkpath` in Listings 3.1 and 3.2. Program `mkpath` accepts one or more arguments as directory path names to create. A path name can be absolute or relative to the current directory. For each path name specified on the command line, the `main` function creates a thread of control to execute the `mkpath` function.

Compile mkpath program:

```
cc -c -D_REENTRANT makepath.c
cc -c -D_REENTRANT mkpath.c
cc -o -D_REENTRANT mkpath makepath.o mkpath.o -lthread
```

Listing 3.1   *makepath.c* -- The `makePath` utility.

```
1   #include <thread.h>
2   #include <stdio.h>
3   #include <unistd.h>
4   #include <string.h>
5   #include <stdlib.h>
6
7   extern void *mkpath(void *);
8
9   /***********************************************************************
10   *   PROGRAM: mkpath [dir [dir [...]]]
11   *
12   *   Program mkpath will create the directories given as command line
13   *   arguments.  For each argument, create a mkpath thread to create
14   *   the directory.
15   ***********************************************************************/
16  void *
17  main(int argc, char **argv)
18  {
19          int          numpaths;
20          int          index;
21
22          numpaths = argc -1;
23          for( index=0; index < numpaths; ++index )
24                  thr_create(NULL, 0, mkpath, argv[index+1], 0, NULL);
25          thr_exit((void *)0);
26  }
```

The `thr_create` function call specifies that a default stack allocation of a default size is to be provided by `thr_create`. The third parameter is the address of the `mkpath` function.

The next parameter is the address of the character string representing a command-line argument. This will in turn become the parameter to the `makepath` function.

Listing 3.2   *mkpath.c* -- The `mkpath` thread.

```
1   #include <sys/types.h>
2   #include <sys/stat.h>
3   #include <string.h>
4   #include <errno.h>
5   #include <thread.h>
6
7   /*****************************************************************
8    *   THREAD mkpath
9    *   Create the directory given by the argument arg. If the named
10   *   argument contains a "/", then ensure each directory component
11   *   exists or can be created.
12   *****************************************************************/
13  void *
14  mkpath(void *arg)
15  {
16          char   *endOfComponent;
17
18          if( arg == NULL )
19                  thr_exit((void *)0);
20          endOfComponent  = (char *) arg;
21          while( *endOfComponent != '\0' ) {
22                  endOfComponent = strchr(endOfComponent, '/');
23                  if( endOfComponent )
24                          *endOfComponent = '\0';
25                  if( mkdir((char *)arg,S_IRWXU) && errno != EEXIST )
26                          thr_exit((void *) 0);
27                  if( endOfComponent ) {
28                          *endOfComponent = '/';
29                          ++endOfComponent;
30                  }
31          }
32          thr_exit(arg);
33  }
```

An important point of this example is that function `main` does not have a `return` statement. Instead, it uses the `thr_exit` function call. The `thr_exit` call ensures that all sibling (*nondetached*) threads have completed prior to exiting the `main` function. If the initial thread issues a `return`, then the UNIX process will terminate, thus forcing all sibling threads to be terminated.

PROGRAMMER'S NOTE:

Certain implementations will increase the size of the multiplexing LWP pool if the THR_NEW_LWP flag is set when calling the `thr_create` function. The multiplexing LWP pool size is not automatically adjusted downward upon thread termination. See `thr_setconcurrency`.

3.2 Minimum Stack Requirements

The minimum stack size required for a new thread is influenced by the size of the internal thread data structure and thread private data required by the implementation. This size can be determined by calling the `thr_min_stack` function (*Figure 3.2*).

NAME:
        `thr_min_stack` - Report the minimum stack size required.

SYNOPSIS:
        `#include <thread.h>`

        `size_t thr_min_stack(void)`

Figure 3.2   `thr_min_stack()` synopsis. [1]

For most multithreaded applications, the default stack size provided by the implementation will suffice. Certain application designs, however, require a larger stack size and should specify the stack size as `thr_min_stack` function plus the application-specific size (2048, for example). In `makepath`, for example, the `thr_create` function call can be specified as:

```
. . . .

    thr_create(NULL,thr_min_stack()+ 2048,mkpath,NULL,0,NULL);

. . . .
```

3.3 Identifying Threads

Every thread within a UNIX process has a unique identifier referred to as the *thread ID*, or simply the TID. The TID is an integral value whose type is specified as (thread_t). The assigned value for TID is not guaranteed to be unique in comparison to the UNIX process's

---

[1] Printed with Permission of UNIX Systems Laboratories, Inc. All Rights Reserved.

lightweight process identifiers, or the process identifier. No assumptions can be made regarding the relationships between process IDs, LWP IDs, or thread IDs.

The thread identifiers can be reused within the same UNIX process. Consider an application that creates numerous short-lived threads. Each thread created within the UNIX process is guaranteed to have an identifier that is unique while the thread remains in existence. Once the thread terminates, however, the thread identifier can be reused within the same UNIX process.

Thread identifiers are not usable outside the scope of their associated UNIX process. With the threads being provided in user space, the kernel has no knowledge of their existence, and thus thread identifiers are not maintained in a global name space. The maximum number of threads available to a UNIX process is determined by the size of thread_t.[25]

```
NAME:
        thr_self - Returns the requesting thread's thread identifier.

SYNOPSIS:

        #include <thread.h>

        thread_t thr_self(void)
```

Figure 3.3   thr_self() synopsis. [¶]

The UNIX Threads Interface provides the thr_self function (*Figure 3.3*) to determine a thread identifier value. On some systems, this may be implemented as a macro, while on others it will be a function call. A common use for the thr_self function is to identify a thread issuing a diagnostic message. Consider, for example, the code fragment below in which the thread issuing an *Out of memory* error message also reports its thread identifier.

```
...
fprintf(stderr,"Error.  Thread %d.  Out of memory\n", thr_self());
...
```

---

[25] On some implementations, the thread identifier is composed of two parts. The low-order 16 bits represent the index into the thread array maintained by the UNIX threads library. The high-order 16 bits represent the number of times this array element has been reused. The actual implementation is not of grave consequences for the application programmer, except to note the lower-order index that may be referenced during debugging.

[¶]   Printed with Permission of UNIX Systems Laboratories, Inc. All Rights Reserved.

3.4 Thread Termination and Join

3.4.1 Waiting for Thread Termination

A thread calls the `thr_join` function to wait on the normal termination of a sibling thread. The `thr_join` function is similar in concept to the `wait` system call. When a thread requests to be joined with a sibling thread's execution stream, the requesting thread will wait for the sibling thread to terminate. After the sibling thread terminates, the execution streams are said to be joined and the calling thread resumes its execution. Only threads created without the `THR_DETACHED` flag can be joined.

NAME:

      `thr_join` - Join with a thread execution stream.

SYNOPSIS:

```
#include <thread.h>

int thr_join(thread_t wait_for, thread_t
*departed_thread,
            void **status)
```

Figure 3.4   `thr_join()` synopsis. [1]

The calling thread can specify a particular sibling is to be joined, or any available sibling thread. When a particular sibling thread is to be joined, its thread identifier is passed as parameter `wait_for` to the `thr_join` function (*Figure 3.4*). The calling thread will block until the two execution streams are joined. A zero `wait_for` value causes the `thr_join` function to return upon the next joinable sibling thread to issue a `thr_exit`. If `wait_for` is a nonzero value, the `thr_join` function returns `ESRCH` if the thread exists but is not joinable.

PROGRAMMER'S NOTE:

A `thr_join` function call will continue even if a signal is received by the corresponding kernel `LWP`. After processing the signal, the `thr_join` function call will continue.

---

[1] Printed with Permission of UNIX Systems Laboratories, Inc. All Rights Reserved.

The terminating thread's identifier is returned in the location pointed to by the departed_thread parameter. The departed_thread parameter may be specified as NULL, in which case departed_thread has no meaning. The exiting status of the joined thread is returned in the location pointed to by the status parameter.

When several threads call the thr_join function at the same time, only one thread will return successfully due to the termination of departed_thread. Suppose, for example, that we have three threads identified as TID-1, TID-2 and TID-3. If thread TID-1 and TID-2, both call the thr_join function and specify that they both wish to thr_join with thread TID-3, only one of the calls will complete successfully. The other will return with an ESRCH error condition.

3.4.2   Terminating a Thread

A UNIX thread can have a voluntary or involuntary termination. A UNIX thread is considered to have voluntarily terminated by returning from the thread's start routine, or by calling the thr_exit function. Although these are functionally equivalent, it is considered good programming practice to always use the thr_exit function to terminate a thread. Involuntary thread termination is the result of the UNIX process terminating. Regardless if the UNIX process terminated by returning from the main function, calling the exit function, or as the result of an exception handling routine, the UNIX threads associated with the process are considered to have involuntarily terminated.

NAME:
>   thr_exit - Terminate a requesting thread.

SYNOPSIS:
>   #include <thread.h>
>
>   void thr_exit(void *status)

Figure 3.5   thr_exit() synopsis. [1]

The distinction between voluntary and involuntary thread termination is significant with respect to the thread's termination status. When a nondetached thread voluntarily terminates, a sibling thread can examine the exiting thread's termination status. With involuntary termination, however, the thread's termination status has no significance. Only the value specified in calling the exit or _exit function has significance, and to that end, only at the UNIX process level.

All thread-specific data bindings are deleted during the termination process. If the exiting thread was created with a user-defined stack, then it is the application's responsibility to free this memory or to reuse it as appropriate. Default user-level stacks are reclaimed by the UNIX threads library.

[1] Printed with Permission of UNIX Systems Laboratories, Inc. All Rights Reserved.

In the case of a voluntary thread termination, the `thr_exit` function transitions the exiting thread from the ON PROCESSOR state to the ZOMBIE state. The UNIX threads library retains minimal information regarding the thread, such as its thread identifier and its termination status value. If the terminating thread has a DETACHED attribute, then all information regarding the thread is released.

When a nondetached thread calls the `thr_exit` function, or terminates by returning from its start routine, and a sibling thread is waiting on this termination, then the sibling thread will complete its `thr_join` function call.

The exiting thread can specify an exit status by setting parameter `status`. This `status` will then be returned to the thread calling the `thr_join` function. A thread returning from its start routine without an explicit call to `thr_exit` will have its exiting status set to the value returned by the `start_routine`. The last (*nondetached*) thread to terminate causes the UNIX process to terminate. The exiting status of this thread is passed to the `exit` function as the status value for the terminating UNIX process.

PROGRAMMER'S NOTE:

The terminating thread and the sibling issuing the `thr_join` call should always use status as a pointer. ANSI C does not guarantee that an integer, for example, typecast to `(void *)` and then back to integer will preserve all information. [1]

EXAMPLE:

Program `dirlist` (*Listing 3.3 through Listing 3.5*) generates a listing of the contents of directories specified as command-line parameters. In determining the functions to execute as separate threads, we must first categorize the role of the particular functions. The `loadDirContents` function is a logical candidate to be executed as a separate thread. A benefit of multithreading is the ability to overlap I/O and computation. Thus, having multiple threads for the `loadDirContents` function is reasonable.

The `printDirContents` function, however, generates the directory content listing on standard output. If separate threads are created to generate the listing for each directory, the output could be unreadable, as multiple threads write their data concurrently to standard output. Thus the `printDirContents` function does not make sense as a separate thread.

The `unloadDirContents` function releases the memory allocated by the `loadDirContents` function. The cost of creating the thread to step through the `dircontent_t` data structures freeing memory could become more than the cost of executing the functions sequentially.

---

[1] Printed with Permission of UNIX Systems Laboratories, Inc. All Rights Reserved.

Now that we have settled on the `loadDirContents` function being executed as a separate thread, we turn our attention to the `main` function shown in Listing 3.3. For each directory specified on the command line, a separate thread is created to execute the `loadDirContent` function. The thread identifiers of these newly created threads are then stored in the `tidArray[]`.

After all threads have been created, the `main` function enters another loop, sequentially issuing a `thr_join` call for each sibling thread. The `main` function examines the status value returned by the departing thread. The `printDirContents` function is called if the status value is `nonNULL` to generate the listing, and the `unloadDirContents` function is called to release the memory.

The `loadDirContents` function issues a `thr_exit` call to terminate the thread. The exiting status for the thread is a pointer to a `directory_t` type data structure allocated for the directory given as parameter `arg`. Although a `return` call could have been used here, the `thr_exit` explicitly identifies that the function is to be executed as a separate thread. This contrasts with the `printDirContent` function, which simply executes a `return`.

Compile dirlist program:

```
cc -c -D_REENTRANT dirlist.c
cc -c -D_REENTRANT dircontent.c
cc -o dirlist dirlist.o dircontent.o -lthread
```

Listing 3.3   *dirlist.c* -- A directory listing utility.

```
1   #include <thread.h>
2   #include <stdio.h>
3   #include <unistd.h>
4   #include <string.h>
5   #include <stdlib.h>
6   #include <dirent.h>
7   #include "dircontent.h"
8
9   /*******************************************************************
10   *   PROGRAM dirlist [dir [dir [...]]
11   *
12   * This program will list the contents of the directories specified
13   * as. For each directory command-line argument, we create an
14   * arguments thread to execute the loadDirContents().  After all
15   * threads have been created, we join their execution streams, and
16   * print the results. Finally, we release the memory associated
17   * with the dynamically allocated data structures.
18   *******************************************************************/
```

Listing 3.3   *continued.*

```
19  void *
20  main(int argc, char **argv)
21  {
22          thread_t      *tidArray;
23          int            error = 0;
24          int            numpaths;
25          int            index;
26          void          *status = NULL;
27
28          numpaths = argc -1;
29          tidArray = (thread_t *)malloc(sizeof(thread_t)*numpaths);
30          memset(tidArray,'\0',sizeof(thread_t)*numpaths);
31
32          for( index=0; index < numpaths; ++index )
33                  thr_create( NULL, 0, loadDirContents, argv[index+1], 0,
34                              &tidArray[index]);
35
36          for( index=0; index< numpaths; ++index) {
37                  status = NULL;
38                  error = thr_join(tidArray[index],NULL, &status);
39                  if( ! error && status != NULL ) {
40                          printDirContents( stdout, status );
41                          unloadDirContents(status);
42                  }
43          }
44
45          thr_exit((void *)0);
46  }
```

Listing 3.4   *dircontent.h* -- The `dircontent` header file.

```
1   typedef struct  _directory {
2        char                    *path;
3        struct _dircontent      *content;
4   } directory_t;
5
6   typedef struct    _direntry   {
7        char                    *name;
8        ino_t                    inode;
9   } direntry_t;
10
11  typedef struct    _dircontent {
12       direntry_t              direntry;
13       struct _dircontent      *next;
14  } dircontent_t;
```

Listing 3.4   *continued.*

```
15   void    *loadDirContents( void *);
16   void    *unloadDirContents( directory_t *);
17   void    *printDirContents(const FILE *, const directory_t *);
```

Listing 3.5   *dircontent.c* -- The directory content functions.

```
1    #include <stdio.h>
2    #include <dirent.h>
3    #include <stdlib.h>
4    #include <string.h>
5    #include <thread.h>
6    #include "dircontent.h"
7    /*******************************************************************
8     *   THREAD loadDirContents
9     *
10    *   This thread will open the directory named by arg and read the
11    *   contents of the directory.  Upon success, a pointer to the
12    *   directory_t structure is returned; otherwise, NULL is returned.
13    *******************************************************************/
14   void *
15   loadDirContents( void *arg )
16   {
17        DIR             *dirStream;
18        struct  dirent      *dirent;
19        directory_t         *directory = NULL;
20        dircontent_t        **current   = NULL;
21        if( (arg == NULL) || (dirStream=opendir((char *)arg))==NULL)
22               thr_exit(NULL);
23
24        if( (directory = malloc(sizeof(directory_t))) == NULL ||
25             (directory->path=malloc(strlen((char *)arg)+1)) == NULL)
26        {
27               unloadDirContents(directory);
28               closedir(arg);
29               thr_exit(NULL);
30        }
31
32        strcpy( directory->path, (char *) arg);
33        current = &(directory->content);
34
35        while( (dirent = readdir(dirStream)) != NULL )
36               {
```

Listing 3.5   *continued.*

```
37              *current = malloc(sizeof(dircontent_t));
38                      /*********************************************
39                       * If the malloc() fails, then we call
40                       * unloadDirContents to release whatever we
41                       * loaded into the directory structure.  Then
42                       * return NULL.
43                       *********************************************/
44              if( *current == NULL ) {
45                      unloadDirContents(directory);
46                      closedir(dirStream);
47                      thr_exit(NULL);
48              }
49              memset(*current,'\0',sizeof(dircontent_t));
50              (*current)->direntry.inode = dirent->d_ino;
51              (*current)->direntry.name=malloc(strlen(dirent->d_name)+
52      1);
53              if( (*current)->direntry.name ==  NULL ) {
54                      unloadDirContents(directory);
55                      closedir(dirStream);
56                      thr_exit(NULL);
57              }
58              strcpy( (*current)->direntry.name, dirent->d_name);
59              current = &(*current)->next;
60      }
61      closedir( dirStream);
62      thr_exit( (void *)directory );
63  }
64
65  /****************************************************************
66   *  FUNCTION:  printDirContents
67   *
68   *  This function will print the path name of the directory, and the
69   *  entries found in this directory.
70   ****************************************************************/
71  void *
72  printDirContents(FILE *fstream, struct _directory *directory)
73  {
74      dircontent_t      *content;
75
76      if(  fstream == NULL  || directory == NULL)
77              return(NULL);
78      fprintf((FILE *)fstream,"%s\n", directory->path);
79      content = directory->content;
```

Listing 3.5   *continued.*

```
80          while( content != NULL )
81          {
82                  fprintf((FILE *)fstream,"%s\n", content->direntry.name);
83                  content=content->next;
84          }
85          return( (void *)directory);
86  }
87
88  /*******************************************************************
89   *   FUNCTION:  unloadDirContents
90   *
91   *   This function will release the resources from the directory
92   *   structure, and then free the memory associated with the
93   *   structure itself.
94   *******************************************************************/
95  void *
96  unloadDirContents( directory_t *directory)
97  {
98          dircontent_t *current;
99          dircontent_t *next;
100
101         if( directory==NULL)
102                 return(NULL);
103         current=directory->content;
104         while( current != NULL )
105         {
106                 next = current->next;
107                 free(current->direntry.name);
108                 free(current);
109
110
111                 current = next;
112         }
113         free(directory->path);
114         free(directory);
115         return(NULL);
116 }
```

3.5 Concurrency Control

In the extended process model, the concurrency level of a UNIX process is determined by the number of kernel-level LWPs in the multiplexing pool, plus the number of bound threads. Together, this represents the maximum number of threads having the potential to execute concurrently for the UNIX process. If there are additional multiplexing threads in the same

UNIX process, these threads will remain in the RUNNABLE state until a multiplexing LWP from the pool is available.

A UNIX process with a concurrency level equal to the number of available processors will seldom, if ever, have all of its threads executing concurrently. The UNIX operating system is multitasking, and thus there is a high probability that other processes in the system will be executing. There are two functions provided with the UNIX Threads Interface to control a process's concurrency level. The thr_getconcurrency returns the current requested concurrency level. The second, thr_setconcurrency, is used to request a change to the concurrency level.

3.5.1   Examining the Concurrency Level

The thr_getconcurrency function (*Figure 3.6*) call returns the minimum number of kernel level LWPs in the multiplexing LWP pool. If the thr_setconcurrency function has not previously been called to set this value, then a zero value is returned to denote that concurrency is being controlled automatically by the UNIX threads library.[26] If the concurrency level has been explicitly adjusted by the application, then the current value will be returned.[27]

NAME:

　　　thr_getconcurrency - Returns the application-requested concurrency level.

SYNOPSIS:
```
#include <thread.h>

int thr_getconcurrency(void)
```

Figure 3.6   thr_getconcurrency() synopsis. [1]

3.5.2   Setting the Concurrency Level

The thr_setconcurrency function (*Figure 3.7*) adjusts the minimum concurrency level required by the application. This function registers a request and does not directly change the

---

[26] The Solaris 2.4 implementations of threads increments the concurrency level when the THR_NEW_LWP flag is set on the thr_create() function call. Automatic concurrency control is not provided with certain implementations.

[27] Concurrency levels adjustments are explicitly requested through the thr_setconcurrency() function, and through the use of the THR_INC_CONC (or THR_NEW_LWP) flag in a thr_create() call.

[1] Printed with Permission of UNIX Systems Laboratories, Inc. All Rights Reserved.

size of the multiplexing LWP pool itself.[28] The thr_setconcurrency function simply sets
the minimum number of multiplexing LWPs requested by the application, and returns from the
function.

The default or automatic concurrency control is used when new_level is given as zero.
The current default (*the minimum*) is one multiplexing light-weight process. Specifying a
nonzero value for the concurrency level does not necessarily guarantee that the exact
concurrency level will be realized. If the requested size would cause the number of lightweight processes for the user to exceed the system limit, then new light-weight processes would
be created only up to that limit. Alternatively, if the requested size is greater then the number
of user-level threads, the size of the light-weight process pool could diminish over time to be
less than or equal to the number of user-level threads.

On the other extreme, if the requested size would be below the number of user-level threads
in the RUNNABLE state, then the UNIX threads library will lower the number of kernel-level
LWPsin the multiplexing LWP pool to that value. The size of the multiplexing LWP pool could
be subsequently lowered to the application-requested size by the UNIX threads library due to
aging of the LWPs.

NAME:
> thr_setconcurrency - Request a change in the concurrency level.

SYNOPSIS:
> ```
> #include <thread.h>
>
> int
> thr_setconcurrency(int new_level)
> ```

Figure 3.7   thr_setconcurrency() synopsis. [1]

---

[28] Certain implementations, such as the Solaris 2.4 UNIX threads, return an EAGAIN error
condition if the requested value exceeds a system-imposed limit for LWPs. The UNIX
Threads Interface, however, defines this function as providing a hint to the level of
desired concurrency.

[1] Printed with Permission of UNIX Systems Laboratories, Inc. All Rights Reserved.

EXAMPLE:

In Listing 3.6, the `checkConcurrency` function will request an additional level of concurrency for every fifth multiplexed thread created.

Compile utility function checkConcurrency:

```
cc -c -D_REENTRANT checkconc.c
```

Listing 3.6   *checkconc.c* -- An example use of `thr_getconcurrency`.

```
 1  void
 2  checkConcurrency(int threadCount)
 3  {
 4         if( threadCount && (threadCount % 5) == 0 ) {
 5                concurrencyLevel = thr_getconcurrency();
 6                ++concurrencyLevel;
 7                thr_setconcurrency(concurrencyLevel);
 8         }
 9         return;
10  }
```

3.6 Controlling Thread Execution

The execution of a UNIX thread can be suspended and subsequently resumed by sibling threads of the UNIX process. The UNIX Threads Interface provides the `thr_suspend` and the `thr_continue` functions for controlling a thread's execution.

3.6.1   Suspending Threads

There are two methods available for suspending a thread's potential for execution. When the thread is first created, the THR_SUSPENDED flag may be specified to immediately transition the new thread to the SUSPENDED state. Alternatively, the `thr_suspend` function can be called to suspend the execution of an existing thread. In either case the thread will remain associated with the UNIX process but will not execute.

In using the `thr_suspend` function (*Figure 3.8*), the parameter `target_thread` is the thread identifier of the sibling thread to be suspended. The `thr_suspend` function will not return control to the calling thread until the `target_thread` has successfully been suspended, or if an error condition occurs.

NAME:

thr_suspend - Suspend a thread of the UNIX process.

SYNOPSIS:

```
#include <thread.h>

int
thr_suspend(thread_t target_thread)
```

Figure 3.8   thr_suspend() synopsis. [¶]

Some implementations of the UNIX Threads Interface use a notification schema to alert the target thread of a pending suspension. The requesting thread does not directly suspend the target thread. Instead, it notifies the target thread that a suspension is pending. The requesting thread will then wait for the target thread to execute. When the target thread transitions to the ON_PROCESSOR state, it will see the pending suspension request and will release any critical implementation-dependent resources it is holding.[29] The target thread will suspend itself, and will transition from the ON_PROCESSOR state to the SUSPENDED state. Although the implementation is not of grave consequence, the technique should be well understood.

A multithreaded application can have several threads attempting to suspend the same target thread. The implementation of the UNIX threads library permits only one of the requesting threads to actually send the suspension request to the target thread. The other requesting threads will recognize the suspension is in progress and will not reissue the suspension. Instead, the other thread will simply wait for the suspension of the target thread to complete.

When this happens, each of the threads will block until the target thread is suspended. The target thread will realize it has a pending suspension request, and should release any critical resources it may be holding. After releasing these resources, the target thread will suspend itself and send a signal to all threads waiting on the suspension. Again, this ensures that all threads requesting the suspension will block until the target thread is suspended. There is the potential, however, for the target thread to complete its initial suspension, be resumed by another sibling thread, and subsequently be suspended before all waiting threads are notified.

It must be pointed out that a bound thread is suspended through the kernel-level LWP functions. This is done since the LWP is not used for any other thread, and thus cannot perform any

---

[29] The critical resources are released by the implementation of thr_suspend(). The application has no knowledge of these critical resources, or that they have been released. When the target thread resumes execution, the implementation will ensure the thread reacquires the resources.

[¶] Printed with Permission of UNIX Systems Laboratories, Inc. All Rights Reserved.

useful work when its thread is suspended. A bound thread will transition from the ON PROCESSOR state to the SUSPENDED state.

If the target thread is a multiplexed thread, then the target thread must first transition to the ON PROCESSOR state before it can be transitioned to the SUSPENDED state. Thus, if the target thread is currently in the SLEEP state, it must first transition to the RUNNABLE state, and then to the ON PROCESSOR state before transitioning to the SUSPENDED state. Unlike a bound thread, the multiplexing LWP from the pool will then be made available for another multiplexed thread.

3.6.2   Resuming Suspended Threads

The thr_continue function resumes the execution of a suspended sibling thread (*see Figure 3.9*). The parameter target_thread is the thread ID of the thread to be continued. If the target thread is not in the suspended state, then this function has no effect.

When the target thread is a multiplexed thread type, then a successful call to thr_continue will transition the thread from the SUSPENDED to the RUNNABLE state. Depending on the implementation, the thread may immediately transition to the ON PROCESSOR state. A bound thread, however, will always transition from the SUSPENDED to the ON PROCESSOR state.

It is strongly recommended not to use the thr_suspend and thr_continue functions for synchronization. The ordering of concurrent thr_suspend and thr_continue pairs is undefined.

NAME:

thr_continue - Resume the execution of a suspended thread.

SYNOPSIS:
```
#include <thread.h>

int
thr_continue(thread_t target_thread)
```

Figure 3.9   thr_continue() synopsis. [1]

3.6.3   Yielding a Thread's Execution

A thread can yield its execution in favor of running another thread by calling the thr_yield function. The detailed workings of the thr_yield function (*Figure 3.10*) are implementation-dependent, as the UNIX Threads Interface states only that this is a *hint* to the implementation.

NAME:

> `thr_yield` - Yield the processor.

SYNOPSIS:

> `#include <thread.h>`
>
> `void`
> `thr_yield(void)`

Figure 3.10   `thr_yield()` synopsis. [1]

PROGRAMMER'S NOTE:

The thread calling `thr_yield` can be rescheduled immediately if it has an equal or higher priority than sibling threads.

When a bound thread issues the `thr_yield` function, a typical response would be for the thread, and its associated LWP, to yield the processor to another thread with equal or higher priority (*thread priority values are described in Chapter 12, Scheduling and Priorities*). For multiplexed threads the implementation may simply yield the thread from its multiplexing LWP in favor of executing another multiplexed thread of equal or higher priority.

EXAMPLE:

The `dbio` program, in Listing 3.7, copies the contents of file `testFile` to the standard output. A typical sequential approach using the stream `I/O` functions is shown in Listing 3.8, while a raw `I/O` version is provided in Listing 3.9.

Program `dbio's` initial thread creates the `fillbuffers` thread, which is responsible for reading one block of data at a time from the `testFile`. The initial thread will iteratively copy the next character from the buffer to the standard output. When the end of the buffer is reached, the `nextc` function switches to an alternative buffer and marks the first buffer as needing a refresh. The `fillbuffers` thread will read the next block of data into the buffer needing to be refreshed. When the alternate buffer is emptied, the `nextc` function will switch to the first buffer and mark the alternate buffer as needing a refresh. This process continues until the *end of file* is reached.

The design of `dbio` permits the initial thread to copy the characters to the standard output while the `fillbuffers` thread refreshes the previous buffer. If the program was designed with a single buffer, then the execution of the initial thread and the `fillbuffers` thread would be mutually exclusive. The `fillbuffers` thread would have to wait while the initial

---

[1]   Printed with Permission of UNIX Systems Laboratories, Inc. All Rights Reserved.

thread emptied the contents of the current buffer. The initial thread would then have to wait for the `fillbuffers` thread to refill the buffer.

To synchronize the thread executions, each buffer is given an associated status denoting the state of the buffer. A REFRESH status implies that `fillbuffers` must refresh the contents of the buffer before the initial thread can use it. The BUSY status value denotes that the buffer is currently being emptied by the initial thread. The END_OF_FILE status signifies that there is no more input for either buffer.

The `fillbuffers` thread remains in a while loop on the condition that the END_OF_FILE has not been reached. Inside this loop, `fillbuffers` is waiting for its current buffer's status to REFRESH. When the status is set to REFRESH, then `fillbuffers` reads in the next block from the input file into the current buffer. If any data was read, then the buffer's status is changed to BUSY, otherwise to END_OF_FILE.

But what should be done when the `fillbuffers` current buffer has a BUSY status value? If the `fillbuffers` thread executes more frequently than the initial thread, both buffers could have a BUSY status, waiting for the initial thread to empty them. In this instance any CPU time given to `fillbuffers` is effectively wasted until the current buffer is emptied.
One option would be for the `fillbuffers` thread to suspend itself and wait for the initial thread to resume its execution. This, however, forces the initial thread to schedule the execution of the `fillbuffers` thread. Instead, the `fillbuffers` thread will simply yield the processor.

Compile dbio program:
```
cc -D_REENTRANT -o dbio dbio.c -lthread
```
Compile streamio program:
```
cc -o streamio streamio.c
```
Compile rawio program:
```
cc -o rawio rawio.c
```

Listing 3.7   *dbio.c -- A double-buffered I/O copy program.*

```
1   #include    <stdio.h>
2   #include    <synch.h>
3   #include    <thread.h>
4
5   typedef struct    _dbio  {
6        char         buffer[BUFSIZ];
7        int          status;
8        int          size;
9        char         *cp;
10       struct _dbio        *nextdbio;
11  } dbio_t;
```

Listing 3.7   *continued.*

```
12   #define      REFRESH               1
13   #define      BUSY                  2
14   #define      END_OF_FILE           3
15
16   dbio_t       dbio[] = {
17        { { "\0" }, REFRESH, 0, NULL, &dbio[1] },
18        { { "\0" }, REFRESH, 0, NULL, &dbio[0] }
19   };
20
21
22   void *
23   fillbuffers( void * arg )
24   {
25        int          fd;
26        int          size;
27        dbio_t  *current;
28        dbio_t  *next;
29
30        fd      = (int) arg;
31        current = &dbio[0];
32
33        while( current->status != END_OF_FILE )
34             if( current->status == REFRESH ) {
35                  current->cp      = current->buffer;
36                  if( current->size=read(fd,current->buffer,BUFSIZ))
37                  {
38                       current->status = BUSY;
39                       current =  current->nextdbio;
40                  }
41                  else
42                       current->status = END_OF_FILE;
43             }
44             else
45                  thr_yield();
46        thr_exit((void *)0);
47   }
48
49   int
50   nextc(void)
51   {
52        register int          c;
53        static       dbio_t  *currentdbio = &dbio[0];
54
55        while( currentdbio->status == REFRESH )
56             thr_yield();
```

Listing 3.7   *continued.*

```
57          if (currentdbio->status == END_OF_FILE )
58                  return(0);
59          c = *currentdbio->cp;
60          ++currentdbio->cp;
61
62          if( ! --currentdbio->size ) {
63                  currentdbio->status = REFRESH;
64                  currentdbio = currentdbio->nextdbio;
65          }
66          return(c);
67  }
68
69  void *
70  main(void)
71  {
72          register int      fd;
73          register int      c;
74
75          if( (fd = open("testFile", 0 )) == -1 ) {
76                  fprintf(stderr,"can't open testFile for input\n");
77                  thr_exit((void *)1);
78          }
79
80          if(thr_create(NULL,0,fillbuffers,(void *)fd,0,NULL) != 0 ) {
81                  fprintf(stderr,"can't create fillbuffers thread\n");
82                  thr_exit((void *)1);
83          }
84          while( (c = nextc()) )
85                  putchar(c);
86          thr_exit((void *)0);
87  }
```

Listing 3.8   *streamio.c* -- A simple stream I/O copy program.

```
1  #include <unistd.h>
2  #include <stdio.h>
3
4  void
5  main(void)
6  {
7          FILE   *fp;
8          int    c;
9
10         fp = fopen("testFile","r");
```

Listing 3.8   *continued.*

```
11          if( fp == NULL ) {
12                  fprintf(stderr,"streamio: can't open testFile\n");
13                  exit(1);
14          }
15          while( (c = fgetc(fp)) != EOF )
16                  putchar(c);
17          fclose(fp);
18          return(0);
19  }
```

Listing 3.9   rawio.c -- A raw I/O copy program.

```
1   #include      <stdio.h>
2
3   typedef struct      _bio   {
4          char          buffer[BUFSIZ];
5          int           status;
6          int           size;
7          char          *cp;
8   } bio_t;
9
10  #define      REFRESH            1
11  #define      BUSY               2
12  #define      END_OF_FILE        3
13  int
14  nextc(fd)
15  {
16          bio_t bio = { {   "\0"   }, REFRESH,   0,   NULL };
17          int   c;
18
19          if( bio.status == REFRESH ) {
20                  bio.size   = read(fd,bio.buffer,BUFSIZ);
21                  bio.cp     = bio.buffer;
22                  bio.status = (bio.size) ? BUSY : END_OF_FILE;
23          }
24          if (bio.status == END_OF_FILE )
25                  return(0);
26          c = *bio.cp;
27          ++bio.cp;
28          if( ! --bio.size ) {
29                  bio.status = REFRESH;
30          }
31          return(c);
32  }
```

Listing 3.9   *continued.*

```
33  void
34  main(void)
35  {
36          int     errorCondition;
37          int     fd;
38          int     c;
39
40          fd = open("testFile", 0 );
41
42          if( fd == -1 ) {
43                  fprintf(stderr,"can't open testFile for input\n");
44                  exit(1);
45          }
46          while( (c = nextc(fd)) )
47                  putchar(c);
48          close(fd);
49          return(0);
50  }
```

3.7 Thread-Specific Data

3.7.1   Creating a Thread-Specific Data Key

The UNIX Threads Interface supports thread-specific data through a key-value pair mechanism. The thr_keycreate function (*Figure 3.11*) creates a key that is visible to all the sibling threads in the UNIX process. Each sibling thread can bind its own representation of a value to the generated key. The value is maintained on a per-thread basis and persists for the life of the calling thread, or until explicitly replaced.

NAME:
      thr_keycreate - Create a thread-specific key.

SYNOPSIS:
```
        #include <thread.h>

        int
        thr_keycreate(thread_key_t *key,void(*destructor)
                      (void *value))
```

Figure 3.11   thr_keycreate() synopsis. [¶]

The generated key is stored in the location pointed to by the `key` parameter. When the `key` is created, the `thr_keycreate` function will set the initial value of the `key` in all active and subsequently created threads to `NULL`.

Assuming that the storage for `key` is allocated as a global variable within the application, any thread can use the `key` to bind a per-thread-specific value. The `key` must be protected by a synchronization primitive to prevent a conflict of its use. (*Synchronization primitives are covered in detail in the next several chapters*).

Using the `key-value` mechanism, multithreaded applications will typically assign a pointer to a datum as the value component.   The storage for this datum may be statically or dynamically allocated. When the datum is dynamically allocated, a destructor function should be specified to release this storage upon thread termination.

PROGRAMMER'S NOTE:

Terminating a thread will take longer when numerous key-value pairs are used within an application, as the destructor functions must be called. This can have an adverse impact on the performance of your application.

As part of the thread termination process, the `thr_exit` function will examine the list of generated keys for the UNIX process. If the terminating thread has a bound value for a key, and the key has a destructor function associated with it, the `thr_exit` function will call the destructor function with the bound value as an argument.

PROGRAMMER'S NOTE:

An application should avoid having the destructor function calling `thr_setspecific` or `thr_getspecific`. It may not be possible to destroy all thread-specific values. The order of calling the destructor functions is undefined.

3.7.2   Setting Thread-Specific Data

The `thr_setspecifc` function associates a thread-specific value with a previously created key (*see Figure 3.12*). The value is maintained by the UNIX threads library on a per-thread basis, and thus different threads may bind different values to the same key. Once a thread has bound a value to the key, the value will remain throughout the life of the thread.

The parameter `key` is a key obtained with a previous call to `thr_keycreate`. The effect of calling `thr_setspecific` with a key value not obtained from `thr_keycreate`, or after the key has been deleted is undefined.

```
NAME:
      thr_setspecific - Associate thread-specific value with key.

SYNOPSIS:
      #include <thread.h>

      int
      thr_setspecific(thread_key_t key, void *value)
```

Figure 3.12   `thr_setspecific()` synopsis. [1]

From an application design perspective, the `value` parameter can be specified as a pointer to an aggregate datum, or could be a typecast of some simple datum. In the former case, a complex data structure could be associated with the key, thus having one or more members as thread-specific data. The latter case is useful only when a single datum needs to be maintained.

Changing the key's value to point to a new memory address will not result in the destructor function being called. The storage associated with the old value must be released prior to binding a new value.

3.7.3   Retrieving Thread-Specific Data

The `thr_getspecific` function (*Figure 3.13*) returns the value currently bound to a particular key. The parameter `key` is a key obtained with a previous call to `thr_keycreate`. The current value associated with the `key` is stored at the location pointed to by the `value` parameter. The effect of calling the `thr_getspecific` function with a `key` value not obtained with the `thr_keycreate` function or after the key has been deleted is undefined.

```
NAME:
      thr_getspecific - Return the thread-specific value of key.

SYNOPSIS:
      #include <thread.h>

      int
      thr_getspecific(thread_key_t key, void **value)
```

Figure 3.13   `thr_getspecific()` synopsis. [1]

---

[1] Printed with Permission of UNIX Systems Laboratories, Inc. All Rights Reserved.

3.7.4   Deleting a Thread-Specific Data Key

The `thr_keydelete` function (*Figure 3.14*) deletes a key previously created with a call to `thr_keycreate`. The key to be deleted cannot be in use. An application should synchronize threads referencing the key and the thread calling `thr_keydelete` to prevent a resource conflict.

NAME:
        `thr_keydelete` - Delete thread-specific key.

SYNOPSIS:
        `#include <thread.h>`

        `int`
        `thr_keydelete(thread_key_t key)`

Figure 3.14   `thr_keydelete()` synopsis. [¶]

EXAMPLE:

Program `cshell` (*Listing 3.10 through Listing 3.14*) is a shell command server. The arguments to `shell` are the shell commands to execute. The output from the shell commands is written to the standard output of the shell server.

In a traditional UNIX process model shell server (*Figure 3.15*), the requests are processed sequentially. For each request, the shell server calls the `popen`[30] function. The shell server reads from the output pipe of `popen` and writes the data to standard output.

A multithreaded shell server (*Figure 3.16*) can execute one `popen` function per shell request as separate threads. Each thread thus represents an instance of a client shell server. The only challenge is in processing the output from the `popen` calls. To process the output from `popen`, the client shell server thread must read the file stream returned by `popen`, and write the data to standard output. When multiple client shell servers attempt to write their data concurrently, the output would be unintelligible. The client shell servers must therefore copy

---

[30] The Solaris 2.4 manual pages indicate that `popen()` is not MT-safe. A future release may support a multithreaded safe version of `popen`. As an alternative, use the lower-level `pipe`, `fork`, and `exec` calls.

[¶] Printed with Permission of UNIX Systems Laboratories, Inc. All Rights Reserved.

the output into a buffer. When the client shell server thread completes, it returns a pointer to this buffer. The output can then be processed by the main shell server.

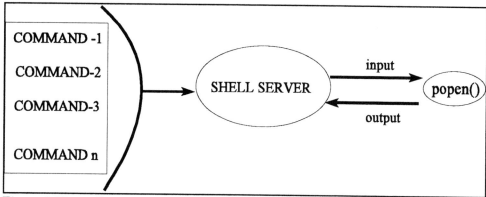

Figure 3.15   Single-threaded shell server.

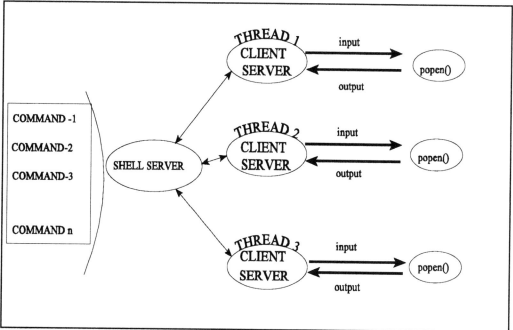

Figure 3.16   Multithreaded shell server.

The next issue to address is a method for the client shell servers to process error conditions. With the output buffers being dynamically allocated, and readjusted by the `copybuffer` function, we must handle out-of-memory error conditions. If too many `popen` functions are called simultaneously, we could also exhaust the available file descriptors. To address the various error conditions, each client shell server must have a thread-specific application error variable.

The main function accepts one or more quoted arguments as client shell requests. For each command-line request, the initial thread will create a multiplexed `clientshell` thread. The thread identifiers are saved. If the thread cannot be created, the `perror` function is called to process the error condition.

After creating the `clientshell` threads, the initial (*main*) thread enters a loop to join with their execution stream. The inner loop will locate the terminated thread in the list of valid `clientshell` threads. When all threads have terminated, the `thr_join` function call will fail with an `EINVAL` error condition. The initial thread then terminates by calling `thr_exit(0)`, which terminates the UNIX process.

Compile shell program:

```
cc -c -D_REENTRANT cshell.c
cc -c -D_REENTRANT clientshell.c
cc -c -D_REENTRANT threadLog.c
cc -o cshell cshell.o clientshell.o threadLog.o -lthread
```

Listing 3.10   *cshell.c* -- The `cshell` main function.

```
1   #include <thread.h>
2   #include <stdio.h>
3   #include <unistd.h>
4   #include <stdlib.h>
5   #include <errno.h>
6   #include <sys/types.h>
7   #include "clientshell.h"
8
9   void *
10  main(int argc, char **argv)
11  {
12          clientList_t    clientList;
13          client_t        **clientPtr;
14          int             index;
15          int             errorCondition;
16          thread_t        departedTid;
17          char            *cp;
18          void            *status;
```

Listing 3.10 *continued.*

```
19        clientPtr  = &(clientList.head);
20        for( index=0; index < (argc -1 ); ++index ) {
21             *clientPtr = malloc(sizeof(client_t));
22             (*clientPtr)->command = argv[index+1];
23             errorCondition=thr_create(NULL,0,clientshell,;
24                          *clientPtr,0, &(*clientPtr)->tid);
25             if( errorCondition )  {
26                   perror("cshell");
27                   break;
28             }
29             clientPtr  = &(*clientPtr)->next;
30        }
31
32        while((errorCondition=thr_join(0,&departedTid,&status))==0) {
33             clientPtr  = &(clientList.head);
34
35             while( *clientPtr && (*clientPtr)->tid != departedTid )
36                   clientPtr = &(*clientPtr)->next;
37
38             if( *clientPtr && status != NULL ) {
39                   cp = (char *) status;
40                   fprintf(stdout,"%s\n",cp);
41             }
42
43
44             else
45                   fprintf(stderr,"Invalid thread [%ld] \n",
46                                        departedTid);
47        }
48        if( errorCondition != EINVAL )
49             perror("cshell");
50        thr_exit((void *)0);
51 }
```

A clientshell thread is represented in the shell process through a client_t type data structure. The member tid will contain the thread identifier of the clientshell thread. The member command is a pointer to the requested shell command, while the arguments member points to the shell command arguments. To avoid hard-coded limits on the number of clients, the client_t type structures are dynamically allocated. The shell process uses a single linked list to represent the clients. The clientList_t type structure contains a pointer to the first and last members in the list.

Listing 3.11   *clientshell.h* -- The client shell header file.

```
1   typedef struct     _client      {
2          thread_t    tid;
3          char        *command;
4          char        **arguments;
5          struct      _client      *next;
6   } client_t;
7
8   typedef struct     _clientList {
9          struct      _client      *head;
10         struct      _client      *tail;
11  } clientList_t;
12
13  void * clientshell( void * );
14  char * copybuffer( char *, char *, int, int);
```

Listing 3.12   *clientshell.c* --The client shell functions.

```
1   #include <unistd.h>
2   #include <malloc.h>
3   #include <thread.h>
4   #include <errno.h>
5   #include <memory.h>
6   #include <synch.h>
7   #include "clientshell.h"
8   #include "threadLog.h"
9
10  mutex_t        cmutex = {0 };
11  /*****************************************************************
12   *   FUNCTION:   copybuffer
13   *
14   *   This function appends the input (cptr) onto the output buffer
15   *   given by bufferPtr.  The buffer pointed to by bufferPtr is
16   *   replaced by a new character buffer whose size is (count * size).
17   ****************************************************************/
18  char *
19  copybuffer( char *bufferPtr, char *cptr, int count, int size)
20  {
21         char    *newbuffer;
22
23         newbuffer = (char *)malloc( (count +1) * size);
24         if( newbuffer == NULL)   {
25                 threadLogError( ENOMEM);
26                 return(NULL);
27         }
```

Listing 3.12   *continued.*

```
28          if( count )
29               memcpy(newbuffer, bufferPtr, (count +1) * size);
30          memcpy(newbuffer + ( count * size), cptr, size);
31          if( bufferPtr )
32               free(bufferPtr);
33          memset(cptr, '\0', size);
34          return(newbuffer);
35  }
36
37  /*******************************************************************
38   *   THREAD:  clientshell
39   *
40   *   This thread will open a pipe to the UNIX command given by arg.
41   *   The output of command execution is returned as the exit status
42   *   of this thread.
43   *******************************************************************/
44  void *
45  clientshell( void *arg )
46  {
47          client_t     *client            = NULL;
48          FILE         *fileStream = NULL;
49          char         *input             = NULL;
50          char         *output       = NULL;
51          int           errorCondition= 0;
52          int           iterations = 0;
53
54          client = (client_t *) arg;
55          if( client->command == NULL ) {
56               threadLogMessage("clientShell: No command specified");
57               thr_exit(NULL);
58          }
59
60          fileStream = popen( client->command, "r");
61          if( fileStream == NULL ) {
62               threadLogMessage("clientShell: Cannot create subshell");
63               thr_exit(NULL);
64          }
65
66          input = malloc( BUFSIZ );
67          if( input == NULL ) {
68               pclose(fileStream);
69               threadLogMessage("clientshell: out of memory");
70               thr_exit(NULL);
71          }
```

Listing 3.12   *continued.*

```
72              iterations = 0;
73              while(fread(input,BUFSIZ,1,fileStream)!=0 && errorCondition==
74  0){
75                      output=copybuffer(output,input,iterations,BUFSIZ);
76                      if( output == NULL )
77                              errorCondition = threadError();
78                      ++iterations;
79              }
80              if( ! errorCondition && feof(fileStream) ) {
81                      output = copybuffer(output,input,iterations,BUFSIZ);
82                      if( output == NULL )
83                              errorCondition = threadError();
84              }
85
86              pclose(fileStream);
87              threadLogError( errorCondition );
88              free( input);
89
90              if( output == NULL || threadHasError() )
91                      threadLogMessage(stderr,"[%s] failed",client->command);
92              thr_exit(output);
93  }
```

The thread error logging utility threadLog (*Listing 3.13 and Listing 3.14*) establishes the thread-specific key threadErrorKey for use as an application-specific error variable. To log an application error code, the thread calls the threadLogError function. If the threadErrorKey has not been previously set, the thrLogInitialize function will be called to initialize the key. Once initialized, the specified error condition is recorded for the thread.

The threadError function returns the current error code of the calling thread, or zero if there is no error value. A thread will typically call the threadError function to determine if there is a current error value, and if so, will call the threadLogMessage to display the error condition to the specified stream.

Listing 3.13   *threadLog.h* -- The thread error logging header file.

```
1  int  threadHasError(void);
2  void threadLogError(int );
3  void threadLogMessage(FILE *, char *, ...);
4  int  threadLogInitialize(void);
```

Listing 3.14   *threadLog.c* -- The thread logging functions.

```
1   #include <thread.h>
2   #include <stdarg.h>
3   #include <malloc.h>
4   #include "threadLog.h"
5
6   static thread_key_t      *threadErrorKey      = NULL;
7
8   int
9   thrLogInitialize(void)
10  {
11          int    *errorCode;
12
13          if( threadErrorKey == NULL ) {
14                  threadErrorKey = malloc(sizeof(thread_key_t));
15                  if( threadErrorKey == NULL )
16                          return(-1);
17                  memset(threadErrorKey,'\0',sizeof(thread_key_t));
18                  if( thr_keycreate(threadErrorKey, free) != 0 ) {
19                          free(threadErrorKey);
20                          threadErrorKey = NULL;
21                          return(-1);
22                  }
23          }
24          errorCode = malloc(sizeof(int));
25          if( errorCode ) {
26                  free(errorCode);
27                  return(-1);
28          }
29          *errorCode= 0;
30          return( thr_setspecific( *threadErrorKey, errorCode));
31  }
32
33  int
34  threadError(void)
35  {
36          int    *errorCode = NULL;
37
38          if( threadErrorKey != NULL )
39                  errorCode = (int *) thr_getspecific( *threadErrorKey);
40          return( errorCode ? *errorCode : 0 );
41  }
42  int
43  threadHasError(void)
44  {
45          int    *errorCode = NULL;
46
47
```

Listing 3.14   *continued.*

```
48            if( threadErrorKey != NULL )
49                    errorCode = (int *) thr_getspecific( *threadErrorKey);
50
51            return( errorCode ?( *errorCode ? 1 : 0) : 0 );
52    }
53
54    int
55    threadClearError(void)
56    {
57            int     *errorCode = NULL;
58
59            if( threadErrorKey != NULL )
60                    errorCode = (int *) thr_getspecific( *threadErrorKey );
61            if( errorCode )
62                    *errorCode = 0;
63            return(0);
64    }
65
66    void
67    threadLogError( int code )
68    {
69            int     *errorCode;
70
71            if( threadErrorKey == NULL && thrLogInitialize() != 0 )
72                    return;
73
74            errorCode = thr_getspecific( *threadErrorKey);
75            if( ! errorCode && thrLogInitialize()  != 0 )
76                    return;
77            errorCode  = thr_getspecific( *threadErrorKey );
78            *errorCode = code;
79            return;
80    }
81
82    void
83    threadLogMessage(FILE *fp, char *format, ...)
84    {
85            va_list       args;
86            int           *errorCode = NULL;
87
88            if( fp == NULL || format == NULL )
89                    return;
90            if( threadErrorKey == NULL )
91                    if( thrLogInitialize() != 0 )
92                            return;
93            va_start(args, format);
```

Listing 3.14   *continued.*

```
94          fprintf(fp,"Thread [%d]: ", thr_self());
95          vfprintf(fp, format, args);
96          va_end(args);
97          if( threadErrorKey ) {
98              errorCode =(int *) thr_getspecific(*threadErrorKey);
99              if( errorCode != NULL && *errorCode != 0)
100                 fprintf(fp, "\nError [%u].", *errorCode);
101         }
102         fprintf(fp, "\n");
103         return;
104 }
```

4

User-Level Synchronization

A challenging aspect of multithreaded application development is planning for the interactions between sibling threads. With the sibling threads executing in the same address space, two or more siblings can collide if they attempt to use a common resource concurrently. Application developers must now consider the issues of synchronization, serialization, and mutual exclusion. What was once the forte of kernel developers has now moved to the domain of the application developer [Litt92].

One thread, for example, can be deleting a resource while another thread is still using it, thus resulting in a fatal error. Concurrent updates can affect more than application data. UNIX-specific process values can cause problems as well, such as the current working directory or a stream position pointer [McSw89]. We therefore need to apply a synchronization primitive to control the use of a shared resource.

This chapter provides a high-level discussion of the synchronization primitives available with the UNIX Threads Interface. The primitives can be used between sibling threads, or between cooperating processes. The UNIX Threads Interface provides the following synchronization primitives:

- · Mutual exclusion locks
- · Condition variables
- · Semaphores
- · Recursive mutual exclusion locks
- · Reader-Writer locks
- · Barriers

4.1 Mutual Exclusion Locks

A mutual exclusion lock (a *mutex*) denotes that the use of a shared resource is mutually exclusive between competing threads. To use the resource, a thread must first LOCK the mutex guarding the resource. The requesting thread will wait for the mutex to become available if it is currently locked by another thread. When the use of the resource is complete, the thread must UNLOCK the mutex, thereby permitting other threads to use the resource. The integrity of the shared resource will be ensured only if all threads requiring the resource follow the LOCK-UNLOCK convention.

4.2 Condition Variables

A condition variable provides a convenient mechanism to notify interested threads of an event, or condition. With this primitive, a thread can suspend its execution until the condition is satisfied. When the thread resumes execution, it validates the condition. If the condition is satisfied, the thread can resume normal execution. A typical example would be for a thread to suspend its execution until a message is received from another thread. In this example, the "message is present" condition must be satisfied for the requesting thread to resume execution.

4.3 Semaphores

A semaphore primitive protects a limited set of shared resources. The semaphore has a count associated with it, defining the number of resources in the set. Before using the shared resource, a thread must first acquire the semaphore, which reduces the number of available resources in the set. When the semaphore count reaches zero, a requesting thread's execution will be suspended until a semaphore is released.

4.4 Recursive Mutual Exclusion Locks

A recursive mutual exclusion lock (*rmutex*) is similar to a mutex, with the exception that a thread can recursively LOCK the rmutex. The implementation maintains an owner relationship for the thread holding the LOCK on the rmutex. The owner of the rmutex can lock the rmutex again. In this sense, the owner holds multiple locks on the rmutex. Each lock must be released before the rmutex can be made available to competing threads.

4.5 Reader-Writer Locks

Reader-Writer locks, also known as Concurrent Read-Exclusive Write (CREW) locks, permit multiple threads to have read-only access to a shared resource. When a thread must modify the resource, it must first acquire the exclusive write lock. The implementation will not permit the exclusive write lock until all reader locks have been released. Reader-Writer locks are useful for shared resources that are searched more often than modified.

4.6 Barriers

A barrier synchronization primitive provides a rendezvous point for threads cooperating in the barrier. The barrier is initialized with a count denoting the number of participating threads. When a thread reaches a barrier, its execution will be suspended until all of the participating threads arrive at the barrier. At that point, all threads are permitted to resume execution.

4.7 Synchronization Implementation Issues

In providing these synchronization primitives, two methods were considered for their low-level implementation. When a thread attempts to acquire the rights to use a resource and finds the resource busy, the synchronization primitive can busy `wait`, or it can `sleep wait`.

In a `busy wait` implementation, a thread will enter a tight loop and continuously attempt to acquire the synchronization rights. Once acquired, the thread will exit the tight loop and continue with normal processing. This algorithm has the advantage that if the synchronization rights will become available in a short time, the overhead is less than the `sleep wait` implementation.

The disadvantage, however, is that when the synchronization primitive is unavailable for lengthy durations, the cost of the `busy wait` can become prohibitive. Another disadvantage of a `busy wait` implementation is that the processor spends its time continuously attempting to acquire the rights. Thus, the processor cannot perform any other useful work. This also implies that the processor cannot be executing the thread currently holding the synchronization primitive.

The use of a `busy wait` algorithm is inappropriate for a uniprocessor computer system. With only one processor, it would not make sense to ever `busy wait` on a synchronization primitive. The thread holding the synchronization primitive will not execute until the requesting thread relinquishes the CPU. The `busy wait` algorithm should be reserved for multiprocessor computer systems.

In the `sleep wait` algorithm, the requesting thread is placed on a sleep queue when the synchronization primitive is unavailable. This implementation requires the operating system to provide some mechanism for determining the availability of the synchronization primitive, and a means for selecting the one, of possibly many, waiting threads to acquire the synchronization rights.

The advantage of the `sleep wait` algorithm is that the requesting thread sleeps until it can obtain the synchronization rights. With the thread in a `sleep wait`, the processor becomes available to execute other threads. Another advantage of this implementation is that it works equally well on uniprocessor and multiprocessor computer systems, as opposed to the `busy wait` implementation.

The disadvantage in using the `sleep wait` algorithm lies in the overhead associated with its implementation. In using a `sleep wait` algorithm on a multiprocessor, the cost in terms of CPU cycles to put the requesting thread to sleep, and the subsequent wake up, could be greater than the cost of busy waiting. The other disadvantage is that the overhead also increases the size of the kernel.

In an attempt to capitalize on both cases, [CBBC91] suggests the use of an Advisory-Processor-Lock (APL). With the APL, the owner of the lock registers an approximate time for which it will keep the lock. A requesting thread can use this information to determine if a `busy wait`, or a `sleep wait` would be more advantageous.

The disadvantage of the APL implementation, however, is that it does not address the restriction of using the `busy wait` algorithm on a uniprocessor. The APL implementation also retains the advisory information with the appropriate synchronization primitive, resulting in additional overhead associated with maintaining and administering the state. This adds to the complexity of the synchronization primitives. While useful within the operating system code itself, Advisory Processor Locks are not necessarily advantageous at the application programming level.

PROGRAMMER'S NOTE:

The UNIX Threads Interface does not define the implementation of the basic synchronization primitives. The implementation can use a `sleep wait` algorithm, or a `busy wait` algorithm.   To address the concerns of those applications requiring finer control, the `UnixWare 2.0` UNIX Threads Interface offers a `spin lock` primitive. An alternative `spin lock` type `barrier` primitive is also provided.

4.8 Using Synchronization Primitives

The synchronization primitives are available for use between sibling threads of a single UNIX process, or between multiple UNIX processes executing in disjoint address spaces. In both cases the synchronization primitives provide a formalism to avoid conflicts while using a shared resource. If a thread attempts to use the resources outside the synchronization primitive API paradigm, however, the behavior of the program is nondeterministic.

Reducing the number of shared resources allows the use of a larger number of threads, thus leading to a higher level of parallelism in the application program. Increasing the number of threads in the application will not lead to a higher level of parallelism if the threads remain blocked waiting for a shared resource.

A simple approach to designing multithreaded applications is to divide the application into subsystems and use a synchronization primitive, such as a mutual exclusion lock, for each subsystem. A thread can enter the subsystem only by acquiring the mutual exclusion lock protecting the subsystem's resources. The disadvantage to this approach, however, is that the level of parallelism will again be limited if the threads must quickly enter and exit any subsystem. A solution would be to partition the subsystem's resources into two or more resource sets. When a thread enters a subsystem, it acquires the subsystem lock, and then acquires a resource set lock. This solution will increase the level of parallelism available, but will add overhead in administering the locks [Nude91].

The use of the synchronization primitives requires careful consideration of the interactions between the threads using the resource. The synchronization primitives provide the necessary protection to ensure a consistent view of the resources. Yet, in using the synchronization primitives, caution must be exercised to avoid introducing a problem known as deadlock.

A deadlock occurs when a thread has acquired the synchronization rights and then requests to acquire these rights again. [HaCo88] describes two methods for creating a deadlock situation. In the first method, a thread acquires the lock and subsequently attempts to acquire the same lock. The second method results from direct thread interaction. Consider, for example, the situation arising from thread-1 acquiring lock A, and then requesting lock B at the same time thread-2 acquires lock B and then requests lock A. In the second situation, a deadlock between thread-1 and thread-2 results, since neither will make any progress. Each will wait indefinitely for the other to release its lock. The use of an *ordered resources* helps to avoid deadlock situations. In a lock-hierarchy, lock A must be acquired before lock B.

4.9 Examples

The primitives provided through the UNIX synchronization library adequately address the rudimentary operations for statically declared primitives. Administration of dynamically allocated primitives, however, is less than sufficient. Many of the examples in this section form the basis for a library of auxiliary functions to address this need.

Each example is presented as an object module consisting of static functions with scope limited to the module. The module includes a data structure with function pointers to those operations available to the application program. These operations provide the public interface. The remainder of the module's functions are considered private to the module.

This programming style does have the disadvantage of an additional level of indirection to call a module's public function. This performance penalty, however, is less than one might anticipate. Applications requiring a higher degree of performance can simply rename the functions and remove the static definition.

5

Mutex Locks

This chapter introduces the mutual exclusion (mutex) synchronization primitive. Mutual exclusion is the most common form of synchronization. Many of the other primitives provided through the synchronization library are built upon the mutex. This chapter provides a description of the mutex and the basic operations.

An application can apply a mutex to protect a shared resource whose use is mutually exclusive between competing threads. The section of code manipulating the shared resource is often referred to as a *critical section*. To use the resource, a thread must first LOCK the mutex. The requesting thread will wait for the mutex to become available if it is currently locked by another thread. When the use of the resource is complete, the thread must UNLOCK the mutex, thereby permitting other threads to use the resource. The integrity of the shared resource will be ensured only if all threads requiring the resource follow the LOCK-UNLOCK convention.

5.1 Mutual Exclusion: An Overview

A mutual exclusion lock protects a resource whose use is mutually exclusive between competing users, referred to as *consumers*. Mutual exclusion is the most common form of synchronization and applies to many everyday resources. Consider, for example, an office chair (*the resource*). Only one person (*consumer*) may sit in the chair at a time. The first person to sit in the chair is considered the owner of the resource. Another consumer wishing to use the same resource must then wait for the resource to become available.

Mutual exclusion applies to any resource in which there can be only one active consumer. To synchronize the use of the resource a mutual exclusion lock is applied, referred to simply as a mutex. The state of the mutex denotes whether the resource is available for a consumer, or if it is already in use. Prior to using the mutex, we must therefore initialize it to a known state by calling the mutex_init function.

The scope of the mutex lock is determined by specifying its type in the mutex_init function call. A mutex type of USYNC_PROCESS denotes the mutex is for use between two or more UNIX processes. Alternatively, a mutex type of USYNC_THREAD specifies that the mutex will be used between sibling threads of a single UNIX process.

A consumer wishing to use the resource must first request the mutex by calling the mutex_lock function. If the mutex is in the UNLOCKED state, then this function will transition the mutex to the LOCKED state. Once locked, the consumer becomes the owner of the mutex and thus the implied owner of the resource. When the resource is no longer required, the owner must call the mutex_unlock function, thus making it available for another consumer.

In requesting a mutex lock, a consumer may find it is already locked by another consumer. In this instance, the requesting consumer must wait for the mutex to be unlocked. The implication is that in waiting, the requesting consumer is blocked and cannot perform any other useful tasks. The mutex operations are not recursive. A deadlock will occur when a thread has a mutex already locked and calls the mutex_lock function again for the same mutex.

An application can be designed to request the mutex lock, and immediately return with an error indication if the mutex is currently locked by another consumer. To support this, the UNIX Threads Interface provides the mutex_trylock function. If the mutex is in use by another consumer, then the request will fail and the function returns immediately. The requesting thread may then perform other tasks unrelated to the protected resource. The operations available to manipulate a mutex appear in Table 5.1.

Table 5.1   The Mutex Synchronization API

mutex_init()	Initialize a mutex to a known state
mutex_lock()	Request to lock the mutex
mutex_trywait()	Try only one time to lock the mutex
mutex_unlock()	Unlock the mutex
mutex_destroy()	Disable the use of this mutex

5.2 Establishing the Mutex

A mutex lock is represented with a mutex_t type data structure, as defined in the <synch.h> include file. The storage for the mutex lock can be defined statically, or dynamically allocated through a memory allocation function such as malloc. The mutex_init function (*Figure 5.1*) will initialize a mutex to the UNLOCKED state.

The `mutex` parameter is the address of the mutex to initialize. The second parameter defines the `type` of mutex, which must be `USYNC_THREAD` or `USYNC_PROCESS`. The third parameter, `arg`, is reserved for future use and should be specified as `NULL`.

NAME:

  `mutex_init` - Initialize a mutex lock.

SYNOPSIS:

  `#include <synch.h>`

  `int`
  `mutex_init( mutex_t *mutex, int type, void *arg)`

Figure 5.1 `mutex_init()` synopsis. [1]

A type parameter value of `USYNC_PROCESS` will initialize the mutex for use between `UNIX` processes executing in disjoint address spaces. The mutex data structure itself must reside in a memory segment shared between the `UNIX` processes. Alternatively, a type parameter value of `USYNC_THREAD` will initialize the mutex for use between sibling threads of a single `UNIX` process. The scope of the mutex data structure, however, must be visible to all the sibling threads that reference it.

PROGRAMMER'S NOTE:

The `mutex_init` function will overwrite the current state of the mutex. It is the application program's responsibility to ensure a mutex, currently in use, is not reinitialized.

In using a `USYNC_THREAD` type mutex, any sibling thread having access to the mutex data structure can request the lock. Similarly, any sibling thread can unlock the mutex. Thus, the `mutex_init` function does not maintain a relationship between the thread locking the mutex and the mutex itself. The mutex is simply noted as being in the `UNLOCKED` or `LOCKED` state. The same is true for a `USYNC_PROCESS` type mutex.

For multithreaded applications, the `USYNC_THREAD` type mutex will be frequently used. To avoid the overhead of initializing the mutex, the `UNIX` Threads Interface provides that a zero filled `mutex_t` type data structure is treated as a `USYNC_THREAD` type mutex in the `UNLOCKED` state.

[1] Printed with Permission of UNIX Systems Laboratories, Inc. All Rights Reserved.

5.3 Locking the Mutex

The mutex_lock function (*Figure 5.2*) locks the mutex found at the address pointed to by the mutex parameter. If the specified mutex is currently locked (*the mutex has state* LOCKED), then the calling thread will wait until it is able to obtain the mutex. A successful call to the mutex_lock function transitions the mutex to the LOCKED state, and returns zero to the calling thread. If an error condition occurs, then the appropriate error indication value is returned and the mutex remains unchanged.

NAME:

        mutex_lock - Lock a mutex.

SYNOPSIS:

        #include <synch.h>

        int
        mutex_lock(mutex_t *mutex)

Figure 5.2   mutex_lock() synopsis. [1]

From the point of view of the calling thread, the mutex_lock function is atomic. If the mutex_lock function is interrupted by a signal, or a forkall system call, the function will not return until it holds the locked mutex. Thus, if mutex_lock is interrupted, an error indication, such as EINTR, will not be returned to the calling thread.

PROGRAMMER'S NOTE:

The process of locking a mutex is not recursive. If the mutex is currently locked by a thread, and the thread calls the mutex_lock function, then the thread will become deadlocked.

When a thread exits while holding a USYNC_THREAD mutex, the mutex will never be unlocked. Any other thread waiting for the mutex will wait indefinitely. Similarly, if a process exits while holding a USYNC_PROCESS mutex, the mutex will not be unlocked, and other UNIX processes or threads waiting for the mutex will wait indefinitely.

---

[1] Printed with Permission of UNIX Systems Laboratories, Inc. All Rights Reserved.

PROGRAMMER'S NOTE:

A thread calling the `mutex_lock` function cannot be interrupted. It is strongly advisable to test new application algorithms with a program stub and to execute the process as a background process. This will prevent your terminal session from locking in the event of a deadlock.

When calling the `mutex_lock` function, the requesting thread will always wait until the mutex can be locked. If the mutex is held by another thread, the requesting thread could wait for an unbounded time. Meanwhile, the thread cannot perform any other useful work. In certain applications, such as in a client-server modeling, it is not always desirable to wait for the mutex. The requesting thread may want to acknowledge the failure and perform other useful work.

NAME:

       `mutex_trylock` - Try to acquire a mutex.

SYNOPSIS:

```
#include <synch.h>

int
mutex_trylock( mutex_t *mutex )
```

Figure 5.3   `mutex_trylock()` synopsis. [1]

The `mutex_trylock` function (*Figure 5.3*) makes a single attempt to lock the mutex. If the mutex is available, then the `mutex_trylock` function transitions the mutex to the LOCKED state and returns a zero status to the requesting thread. When the requesting thread has completed its use of the resource, it must then call the `mutex_unlock` function to unlock the mutex. If the mutex could not be locked by the `mutex_trylock` function, an error indication value of EBUSY is immediately returned to the requesting thread.

5.4 Unlocking the Mutex

After locking the mutex, a thread can use the protected resource. When the processing has completed, the thread must unlock the mutex by calling the `mutex_unlock` function (*Figure 5.4*). The `mutex_unlock` function will unlock the mutex found at the address pointed to by the `mutex` parameter.

---

[1] Printed with Permission of UNIX Systems Laboratories, Inc. All Rights Reserved.

NAME:

      `mutex_unlock` - Unlock a mutex.

SYNOPSIS:

```
#include <synch.h>

int
mutex_unlock( mutex_t *mutex )
```

Figure 5.4   `mutex_unlock()` synopsis. [1]

When the `mutex_unlock` function successfully transitions the mutex to the UNLOCKED state, it will determine if there are any threads currently waiting on this mutex (i.e., a thread called the `mutex_lock()` function while the current thread already had the mutex in the LOCKED state). If so, at least one of these waiting threads will attempt the acquisition of the mutex.

PROGRAMMER'S NOTE:

The UNIX Threads Interface states that a waiting bound thread has precedence over a waiting multiplexed thread. If a bound thread that was blocked on the mutex cannot be awakened, or if there were no bound threads waiting for this mutex, then the `mutex_unlock` function looks for a multiplexed thread. If there is more then one bound thread waiting on this mutex, the order in which the threads are permitted to attempt acquisition is not specified by the UNIX Threads Interface. Thus, certain implementations may follow a First-In-First-Out order, while others may use a Last-In-First-Out order.

5.5 Invalidating the Mutex

`mutex_destroy` (*Figure 5.5*) disables a mutex to prevent its further use. This disabling is achieved by setting the mutex type field to a value not recognized by the mutex operations. If the mutex has been successfully destroyed, then a zero status value is returned to the requesting thread.

The `mutex_destroy` function will examine the mutex's queue to determine if there are any threads waiting for the mutex to become available. It is possible for the mutex to become unlocked, and a thread to remain blocked, waiting on the mutex. Consider, for example, three threads in an application. The first thread locks the mutex and begins processing using the

---

[1] Printed with Permission of UNIX Systems Laboratories, Inc. All Rights Reserved.

mutually exclusive resource protected by this mutex. A second thread then attempts to lock the same mutex, and blocks, waiting for the mutex to become available. The first thread then unlocks the mutex. The third thread then attempts to destroy the mutex before the second thread has a chance to execute. In this scenario the `mutex_destroy` function must not destroy the mutex, since thread-2 is currently blocked, waiting for the mutex to become available. If the mutex was invalidated, then thread-2 would deadlock and remain blocked indefinitely. The same principle applies to a USYNC_PROCESS-type mutex.

NAME:
      `mutex_destroy` - Disable a mutex.

SYNOPSIS:
```
#include <synch.h>

int
mutex_destroy( mutex_t *mutex)
```

Figure 5.5   `mutex_destroy()` synopsis. [1]

The `mutex_destroy` function must determine if the mutex is currently in the LOCKED state. A mutex may currently be locked, in which case we cannot invalidate the mutex. In any of these cases, an error indication value of EBUSY will be returned to the calling thread, and the mutex will remain unchanged.

5.6 Using the Mutex

This section will discuss two examples for using the mutex. Each example provides auxiliary functions not available through the basic synchronization operations. The `threadMutex` example provides auxiliary functions for administering dynamically allocated USYNC_THREAD type mutexes. The `mthreadLog` example provides auxiliary functions for logging per-thread generated messages. Both examples are presented as modules.

The threadMutex Module

The `threadMutex` module (*Listings 5.1 and 5.2*) provides auxiliary functions for administering dynamically allocated USYNC_THREAD type mutexes. This module is reused throughout examples in this book, and should be added as the first module of our `libtsync.a` thread auxiliary library. Additional modules will be added to this library in subsequent chapters.

---

[1] Printed with Permission of UNIX Systems Laboratories, Inc. All Rights Reserved.

Compile threadMutex Module
```
        lint -D_REENTRANT -c -I${INSTALLROOT}/hdr threadMutex.c
        cc -D_REENTRANT -c -I${INSTALLROOT}/hdr threadMutex.c
        ar rv ${INSTALLROOT}/lib/libtsync.a threadMutex.o
```

Listing 5.1 shows the `threadMutex.h` header file from the `$(INSTALLROOT)/hdr` directory. The `threadMutex_t` type definition provides the `create`, `createLocked`, and `destroy` members as function pointers. The last line of this header file denotes the `threadMutex_f` variable as being of type `threadMutex_t`.

Listing 5.1   *threadMutex.h* -- The `threadMutex` module header file.

```
1   typedef struct _threadMutex_f {
2           mutex_t *(*create)(void);
3           mutex_t *(*createLocked)(void);
4           int       (*destroy)(mutex_t *);
5   } threadMutex_t;
6   extern threadMutex_t threadMutex_f;
```

The `Create` function allocates and initializes a `USYNC_THREAD` type mutex. Upon success, a pointer to the initialized mutex is returned to the calling thread. If an error condition occurs, the `threadLog_f` module (described at the end of this chapter) is called and a `NULL` value is returned to the requesting thread.

The `create` member of the `threadMutex_f` data structure is set to the address of the `Create` function. The function is called by specifying `threadMutex_f.create()`. To use this module, an application must include the `threadMutex.h` header file, and be linked with the `libtsync.a` library.

The `CreateLocked` function will call the `Create` function to dynamically allocate a mutex. The allocated mutex is then locked by calling `mutex_lock`. Upon success, a pointer to the locked mutex is returned to the calling thread. If an error condition occurs, the `threadLog` module is used to record the type of error encountered, and a `NULL` value is returned to the requesting thread. This function by specifying `threadMutex_f.createLocked`.

The final function for the `threadMutex` module is the `Destroy` function. It will call the `mutex_destroy` function to invalidate the mutex, and upon success will free the storage space associated with the specified mutex. The remainder of this source module shows the definition of the `threadMutex_f` data structure. The members of this structure are defined as the addresses of the various functions available in the `threadMutex` module.

Listing 5.2   *threadMutex.c* -- The `threadMutex` module.

```
1   #include <stdlib.h>
2   #include <memory.h>
3   #include <synch.h>
4   #include <thread.h>
5   #include <errno.h>
6   #include "mthreadLog.h"
7   #include "threadMutex.h"
8
9   static mutex_t      *Create(void);
10  static mutex_t      *CreateLocked(void);
11  static int           Destroy(mutex_t *);
12
13  static mutex_t *
14  Create(void)
15  {
16          mutex_t       *mutexPtr           = NULL;
17          int            errorCondition    = 0;
18
19          mutexPtr = (mutex_t *) malloc(sizeof(mutex_t));
20
21          if( mutexPtr == NULL )
22                  threadLog_f.setError(ENOMEM);
23          else {
24                  memset((void *)mutexPtr,'\0', sizeof(mutex_t));
25                  errorCondition = mutex_init( mutexPtr, USYNC_THREAD,
26                              NULL);
27
28                  if ( errorCondition ) {
29                          threadLog_f.setError( errorCondition );
30                          free((void *) mutexPtr );
31                          mutexPtr = NULL;
32                  }
33          }
34          return(mutexPtr);
35  }
36
37  static mutex_t *
38  CreateLocked(void)
39  {
40          mutex_t       *mutexPtr           = NULL;
41          int            errorCondition    = 0;
42
43          mutexPtr = Create();
44
45          if ( mutexPtr ) {
46                  errorCondition   = mutex_lock( mutexPtr );
```

Listing 5.2 *continued.*

```
47                    if( errorCondition ) {
48                            threadLog_f.setError( errorCondition );
49                            free( (void *)mutexPtr );
50                            mutexPtr = NULL;
51                    }
52            }
53
54            return(mutexPtr);
55    }
56
57    static int
58    Destroy( mutex_t *mutexPtr)
59    {
60            int     errorCondition = 0;
61
62            errorCondition = mutex_destroy(mutexPtr);
63            if( errorCondition )
64                    threadLog_f.setError( errorCondition );
65            else
66                    free((void *)mutexPtr);
67            return( errorCondition );
68    }
69
70    threadMutex_t        threadMutex_f = {
71            Create,
72            CreateLocked,
73            Destroy,
74    };
```

Thread Logging Module

The thread logging facility, provided in Chapter 3, can suffer a contention of its resources. Consider, for example, the thrLogInitialize function. This function determines if the logging facility is currently active, and will allocate the thread-specific value for the thread's error code. If two threads were to call the thrLogInitialize function simultaneously, both could find the threadErrorKey variable as having a NULL value, and then call malloc to allocate the memory for it. This can be a subtle bug that would show up only when both threads call this function at the same time. The mthreadLog module (*Listings 5.3 and 5.4*) corrects this problem by applying mutex synchronization primitives to control the access to critical resources. This module can be added to our libtsync.a thread auxiliary library.

The mthreadLog module provides several new features. The default output stream, stderr, can be changed to a named file by calling the threadLog_f.open function. The size of the log file is minimized by calling the threadLog_f.setWaterMarks function.

Listing 5.4 shows the modified thread logging source file. The `Initialize` function uses a mutex to protect the `threadKey` data structure. Locking the mutex prevents multiple threads from concurrently testing the `threadKey.isSet` member. The `GetError`, `HasError`, `ClearError`, and `SetError` functions remain unchanged. The `Message` function will use the stream member of the `threadLog` data structure as the current stream.

Compile `mthreadLog` Module:

```
lint -D_REENTRANT -c -I${INSTALLROOT}/hdr mthreadLog.c
cc -D_REENTRANT -c -I${INSTALLROOT}/hdr mthreadLog.c
ar rv ${INSTALLROOT}/lib/libtsync.a mthreadLog.o
```

Listing 5.3   *mthreadLog.h* -- The thread logging module header file.

```
 1 #if ! defined(MTHREADLOG_H)
 2 #      define MTHREADLOG_H
 3
 4 typedef struct    {
 5       thread_key_t        appErrno;
 6       int           isSet;
 7       mutex_t            mutex;
 8 } threadKey_t;
 9
10 typedef struct    {
11       char    fileName[BUFSIZ];
12       FILE    *stream;
13       int     calls;
14       mutex_t        mutex;
15       long    head;
16       long    tail;
17 } threadLog_t;
18
19 /*******************************************************************
20  *      Define the default values for the low and high water marks of
21  *      the thread log stream.
22  *******************************************************************/
23 #      define HIGHWATERMARK    200
24 #      define LOWWATERMARK     100
25 /*******************************************************************
26  *      Define the threadLog module function pointers.  To use the
27  *      threadLog module, an application must reference the functions
28  *      given in this data structure.  Using threadlog_f.setError()
29  *      for example, will call the threadLog module's setError
30  *      function.
31  *******************************************************************/
```

Listing 5.3   *continued.*

```
 1 typedef struct _threadlog_t    {
 2        int    (*getError)(void);
 3        int    (*hasError)(void);
 4        int    (*clearError)(void);
 5        void   (*setError)(int);
 6        void   (*message)(char *, ...);
 7        int    (*open)( char *);
 8        int    (*close)(void);
 9        int    (*setWaterMarks)(int, int);
10 } threadLog_t;
11 extern threadlog_t        threadLog_f;
12 #endif
```

The Open function accepts a single parameter as the name of the log file. The named log file is opened and the file stream is recorded for subsequent calls to the threadLog_f.message function. A NULL log file name will result in the current stream defaulting to stderr. The low watermark and high watermark values are set for this stream. The SetWaterMarks function will adjust the low and high watermarks. Finally, the threadLog_f data structure is initialized to the appropriate functions found in the mthreadLog.c source module.

Listing 5.4   *mthreadLog.c -- The thread logging module.*

```
 1 #include <stdio.h>
 2 #include <stdarg.h>
 3 #include <stdlib.h>
 4 #include <thread.h>
 5 #include <synch.h>
 6 #include <errno.h>
 7 #include <string.h>
 8 #include <unistd.h>
 9 #include "mthreadLog.h"
10
11 static threadKey_t        threadKey    = { 0 , 0 };
12 static threadLog_t        threadLog    = {"",stderr,0,{0},0L,0L};
13 static int    HighWaterMark = HIGHWATERMARK;
14 static int    LowWaterMark  = LOWWATERMARK;
15 static int    ClearError(void);
16 static int    Close(void);
17 static int    GetError(void);
18 static int    HasError(void);
19 static void   Message(char *, ...);
20 static int    Open(char *);
21 static void   SetError(int);
```

Listing 5.4 *continued.*

```
22 static int  SetWaterMarks(int, int);
23 static int  initialize(void);
24 static void minimize(void);
25 /******************************************************************
26  *      Function GetError()
27  *
28  *      Returns the last recorded mthreadLog application-specific
29  *      error code, or zero if no error.
30  ******************************************************************/
31 static int
32 GetError(void)
33 {
34        int    *errorCode = NULL;
35        if( threadKey.isSet )
36              errorCode=(int *) thr_getspecific( threadKey.appErrno);
37        return( errorCode ? *errorCode : 0 );
38 }
39
40 /******************************************************************
41  *      Function HasError()
42  *
43  *      This function returns one if the thread has a nonzero recorded
44  *      application error value; otherwise it returns zero.
45  ******************************************************************/
46 static int
47 HasError(void)
48 {
49        int    *errorCode = NULL;
50
51        if( threadKey.isSet )
52              errorCode=(int *) thr_getspecific( threadKey.appErrno);
53        return( errorCode ? ( *errorCode ? 1 : 0) : 0 );
54 }
55
56 /******************************************************************
57  *      Function ClearError()
58  *
59  *      This function resets the application-specific appErrno value
60  *      to zero.
61  ******************************************************************/
62 static int
63 ClearError(void)
64 {
65        int    *errorCode = NULL;
66
67        if( threadKey.isSet )
68              errorCode=(int *)thr_getspecific( threadKey.appErrno );
```

Listing 5.4 *continued.*

```
69         if( errorCode != NULL )
70              *errorCode = 0;
71         return(0);
72 }
73
74 /*****************************************************************
75  *      Function SetError()
76  *
77  *      This function records the application-specific error code as
78  *      a thread-specific value for the calling thread.
79  *****************************************************************/
80 static void
81 SetError(int code)
82 {
83         int    *errorCode = NULL;
84
85              /*****************************************************
86               *  this first test will ensure that the appErrno key
87               *  has been created.
88               *****************************************************/
89         if( threadKey.isSet && initialize() != 0 )
90              return;
91
92         errorCode = thr_getspecific( threadKey.appErrno );
93         if( errorCode == NULL ) {
94              if( initialize()  != 0 )
95                   return;
96              errorCode  = thr_getspecific( threadKey.appErrno );
97         }
98         *errorCode = code;
99         return;
100 }
101
102 /*****************************************************************
103  *      Function Message()
104  *
105  *      This function records the specified message in the threadLog.
106  *      If there is a recorded appErrno thread-specific value for the
107  *      calling thread, then its value is also recorded in the
108  *      threadLog.
109  *****************************************************************/
110 static void
111 Message(char *format, ...)
112 {
113         va_list        args;
114         int           *errorCode = NULL;
```

Listing 5.4 *continued.*

```
115        if( format == NULL )
116             return;
117
118             /*******************************************************
119              *        CRITICAL SECTION
120              *
121              *        We cannot have two or more threads updating
122              *        thread threadLog.calls value, since the
123              *        operation is not guaranteed to be atomic.  We
124              *        also may call the minimize function to limit
125              *        the size of the threadLog.
126              *******************************************************/
127        mutex_lock( &threadLog.mutex );
128        if( threadLog.stream != stderr ) {
129             ++threadLog.calls;
130
131             if( threadLog.calls == LowWaterMark )
132                  threadLog.head = ftell( threadLog.stream);
133
134             /*******************************************************
135              *   If we have reached the high watermark, then we
136              *   need to minimize the threadLog.stream.
137              *******************************************************/
138             if( threadLog.calls == HighWaterMark ) {
139                  threadLog.tail = ftell(threadLog.stream) -1L;
140                  minimize();
141             }
142        }
143
144             /*******************************************************
145              *   Now output the message to the threadLog.stream.
146              *******************************************************/
147        va_start(args, format);
148        fprintf(threadLog.stream,"Thread [%d]: ", thr_self());
149        vfprintf(threadLog.stream, format, args);
150        va_end(args);
151             /*******************************************************
152              *   If the thread has an appErrno thread-specific value,
153              *   and the value is nonzero, then record the current
154              *   error value to the threadLog.stream.
155              *******************************************************/
156        if( threadKey.isSet ) {
157             errorCode =(int *) thr_getspecific(threadKey.appErrno);
158             if( errorCode != NULL && *errorCode != 0)
159                  fprintf(threadLog.stream,
160                                  "Error [%u].",*errorCode);
161        }
```

Listing 5.4   *continued.*

```
162           fprintf(threadLog.stream, "\n");
163           mutex_unlock( &threadLog.mutex );
164                   /************************************************
165                    *      END OF CRITICAL SECTION
166                    ************************************************/
167           return;
168  }
169
170  /********************************************************************
171   *      Function Open()
172   *
173   *      This function opens a file as the new threadLog.stream.
174   ********************************************************************/
175  static int
176  Open( char *fileName)
177  {
178           int    errorCondition = 0;
179
180                   /*********************************************************
181                    *    CRITICAL SECTION
182                    *
183                    *    This is a critical section, since we don't want
184                    *    another thread using the stream while we are
185                    *    changing the stream value.
186                    *********************************************************/
187           mutex_lock( &threadLog.mutex );
188
189                   /*********************************************************
190                    *    If the current stream is not stderr, then we
191                    *    already have a stream open and we must explicitly
192                    *    close that stream before opening a new one.
193                    *********************************************************/
194           if( threadLog.stream != stderr   )
195               errorCondition = EAGAIN;
196
197                   /*********************************************************
198                    *    If we can open the new threadLog stream for write,
199                    *    then set the default low and high watermarks. Also
200                    *    reset the defaults for the number of calls.
201                    *********************************************************/
202           else if( fileName != NULL ) {
203               threadLog.stream = fopen(fileName,"w+");
204               if( threadLog.stream != NULL ) {
205
206                   /*********************************************************
207                    *    NOTE: we do not call the threadLog_f.setWaterMarks
208                    *          function to reset the default values.   That
```

Listing 5.4 *continued.*

```
209                  *           would cause a deadlock, since we already have
210                  *           the threadLog.mutex locked!  Instead, we can
211                  *           reset them right here.
212               ****************************************************/
213              LowWaterMark  = LOWWATERMARK;
214              HighWaterMark = HIGHWATERMARK;
215              strcpy(threadLog.fileName, fileName);
216              threadLog.calls = 0;
217              threadLog.head  = 0;
218              threadLog.tail  = 0;
219          }
220          else
221              errorCondition = -1;
222      }
223      else
224          errorCondition = EINVAL;
225      mutex_unlock( &threadLog.mutex );
226          /*****************************************************
227           *   END OF CRITICAL SECTION
228           *****************************************************/
229      if( errorCondition )
230          SetError(errorCondition);
231      return(errorCondition);
232 }
233
234 /**********************************************************************
235  *      Function Close()
236  *
237  *      This function closes the current threadLog stream and resets
238  *      the stream to stderr.
239  **********************************************************************/
240 static int
241 Close(void)
242 {
243      int    errorCondition = 0;
244          /*****************************************************
245           *   CRITICAL SECTION
246           *****************************************************/
247      mutex_lock( &threadLog.mutex);
248      if( threadLog.stream != stderr) {
249          errorCondition  = fclose(threadLog.stream);
250          threadLog.stream = stderr;
251      }
252      mutex_unlock( &threadLog.mutex);
253          /*****************************************************
254           *   END OF CRITICAL SECTION
255           *****************************************************/
```

Listing 5.4 *continued.*

```
256        if ( errorCondition )
257             SetError(errorCondition);
258        return(errorCondition);
259 }
260
261 /****************************************************************
262 *     Function SetWaterMarks()
263 *     This function sets the application-specific values of the low
264 *     and high watermarks for the thread log.
265 ****************************************************************/
266 static int
267 SetWaterMarks(int lowWaterMark, int highWaterMark )
268 {
269        if(  lowWaterMark > highWaterMark )
270             return(EINVAL);
271
272             /****************************************************
273              *   CRITICAL SECTION
274              ****************************************************/
275        mutex_lock( &threadLog.mutex );
276        LowWaterMark  = lowWaterMark;
277        HighWaterMark = highWaterMark;
278        mutex_unlock( &threadLog.mutex );
279             /****************************************************
280              *   END OF CRITICAL SECTION
281              ****************************************************/
282        return(0);
283 }
284
285 /****************************************************************
286 *     THE FOLLOWING FUNCTIONS ARE LOCAL TO THE MTHREADLOG MODULE.
287 *     THEY ARE NOT DIRECTLY ACCESSIBLE BY THE APPLICATION.
288 ****************************************************************/
289
290 /****************************************************************
291 *     Function initialize()
292 *
293 *     This function is called by the SetError() function.  Although
294 *     it is a local function, it will enter a critical section.  The
295 *     threadKey.mutex must not be locked prior to calling this
296 *     function or a deadlock will result.
297 ****************************************************************/
298 static int
299 initialize(void)
300 {
301        int    *errorCode  = NULL;
302        int     errorCondition = 0;
```

Listing 5.4 *continued.*

```
303                 /*****************************************************
304                 *    CRITICAL SECTION
305                 *
306                 *    The test of the isSet member is a critical section.
307                 *    We must prevent concurrent access here, so we apply
308                 *    a mutex.
309                 *****************************************************/
310       mutex_lock( &threadKey.mutex );
311
312                 /*****************************************************
313                 * If we have not performed the initialization already,
314                 *
315                 * then create the thread-specific appErrno key.
316                 * Thread-specific errors will then be recorded using
317                 * this key.
318                 *****************************************************/
319       if( ! threadKey.isSet ) {
320           errorCondition=thr_keycreate(&threadKey.appErrno, free);
321           if( ! errorCondition )
322                 threadKey.isSet = 1;
323       }
324
325                 /*****************************************************
326                 *    END OF CRITICAL SECTION
327                 *****************************************************/
328
329       mutex_unlock( &threadKey.mutex );
330
331                 /*****************************************************
332                 *    We now allocate an integer to use as the thread-
333                 *    specific errorCode that we tie to the appErrno key.
334                 *****************************************************/
335       if( ! errorCondition ) {
336           errorCode = malloc(sizeof(int));
337
338           if( errorCode == NULL )
339                 errorCondition = ENOMEM;
340           else {
341                 *errorCode= 0;
342                 errorCondition=thr_setspecific(
343                             threadKey.appErrno, errorCode);
344                 if( errorCondition )
345                       free(errorCode);
346           }
347       }
348       return( errorCondition );
349 }
```

Listing 5.4 *continued.*

```
350 /******************************************************************
351  *      Function minimize()
352  *
353  *      This function is local to the threadLog module.  It is not
354  *      directly accessible by the application. This function will
355  *      reset the current head and tail for the threadLog stream to
356  *      minimize the size of the output file to at most HighWaterMark
357  *      entries.
358  ******************************************************************/
359 static void
360 minimize(void)
361 {
362         int     fdr;
363         int     fdw;
364         int     count;
365         char    buffer[1024];
366
367         fseek( threadLog.stream, threadLog.head, SEEK_SET);
368         fdr = fileno(threadLog.stream);
369         unlink( threadLog.fileName);
370         threadLog.stream = fopen(threadLog.fileName,"w+");
371         fdw = fileno(threadLog.stream);
372         while( (count = read(fdr,buffer,1024)) > 0 )
373                 write(fdw, buffer, count);
374         close(fdr);
375         threadLog.head   = 0;
376         threadLog.calls  = 0;
377         threadLog.tail   = 0;
378 }
379
380 /******************************************************************
381  *      The mthreadLog module is defined here.  The application uses
382  *      the function pointers in this data structure to access the
383  *      threadLog functions.
384  ******************************************************************/
385 threadlog_t threadLog_f = {
386         GetError,
387         HasError,
388         ClearError,
389         SetError,
390         Message,
391         Open,
392         Close,
393         SetWaterMarks
394 };
```

Listing 5.5 presents a simple example of using the thread logging feature. The source module `mthreadmain.c` must be compiled and linked with our auxiliary thread library `libtsync` and the system `libthread` library.

Compile mthreadmain program:
```
        cc -D_REENTRANT -c -I ${INSTALLROOT}/hdr mthreadmain.c
        cc mthreadmain.o ${INSTALLROOT}/lib/libtsync.a -lthread -o \
            mhreadmain
```

Listing 5.5   *mthreadmain.c* -- An example program using the thread loggging module.

```
 1 #include <stdio.h>
 2 #include <unistd.h>
 3 #include <synch.h>
 4 #include <thread.h>
 5 #include "mthreadLog.h"
 6
 7 void *
 8 main(void)
 9 {
10         threadLog_f.open("logfile");
11         threadLog_f.setError( 10 );
12         threadLog_f.message("logfile: error code should be 10\n");
13         threadLog_f.clearError();
14         threadLog_f.message("all done");
15         threadLog_f.close();
16         thr_exit((void *)0);
17 }
```

The lineCount Program

The `lineCount` program accepts one or more file names as parameters, and displays the cumulative number of new line characters found in the files. The output is similar to the last line of a `wc -1` command. The program will create one thread per file name specified to determine the number of new line characters in the file. The thread will then update the global variable lineCount. After all threads have completed, the total line count is then displayed.

There are several design alternatives for this program. The main function could serially process each command line argument similar to the wc(1) program. For our purposes, however, we wish to use multiple threads to overlap computation and I/O requests. With this in mind, it seems appropriate to create one `lineCount` thread per command-line argument to count the number of new line characters in the specified file. The number of open files permitted per process is determined by the configuration of the system. We therefore cannot create too many `lineCount` threads.

Another challenge is that each `lineCount` thread will make various requests for kernel services, such as `open()`, `fstat()`, and `mmap()`. While the kernel is servicing these requests, the thread and its associated LWP (if provided by the implementation) will remain blocked. We therefore need to ensure an appropriate number of LWPs are available for the multiplexed threads to provide a reasonable level of concurrency. The `lineCount` program will set the maximum currency by calling `thr_setconcurrency()` to a value no greater than 20. If the number of active threads reaches this limit, the main function will call a `rendezvous` function to wait for the current threads to complete. The `main` function will then create additional threads as needed for the remainder of the command-line arguments.

The `lineCount` program has one critical section that requires a mutex to ensure appropriate behavior. Each `lineCount` thread will call `incrLineCount` to update the total number of lines. If two or more threads attempt to update the `LineCount` variable concurrently, then the integrity of the value cannot be ensured. The `incrLineCount` function uses a mutex to ensure appropriate behavior.

Listing 5.6   *lineCount.c* -- A simple line-counting program.

```
 1 #include <sys/types.h>
 2 #include <sys/stat.h>
 3 #include <sys/mman.h>
 4 #include <stdio.h>
 5 #include <fcntl.h>
 6 #include <thread.h>
 7 #include <synch.h>
 8 int LineCount = 0;        /* Total number of lines in files.   */
 9 /***********************************************************************
10 *      incrLineCount       FUNCTION
11 *      This function increments the total number of lines found.
12 *      Each thread will call this function to increment the count.
13 ***********************************************************************/
14 void
15 incrLineCount(int c)
16 {
17         static mutex_t    mutex = { 0 };
18         /**********************************************************
19         *        CRITICAL SECTION START
20         *        We must prevent multiple threads from concurrently
21         *        increasing the counter.
22         **********************************************************/
23         mutex_lock( &mutex );
24         LineCount += c;
25         /**********************************************************
26          *        CRITICAL SECTION END
27         **********************************************************/
28         mutex_unlock( &mutex );
29 }
```

Listing 5.6 *continued.*

```
30 /****************************************************************
31  *      countLines    THREAD
32  *
33  *      This thread will mmap the file specified as arg and count the
34  *      number of new-line characters found.  When complete, it calls
35  *      incrLineCount() function to increment global new-line count.
36  ****************************************************************/
37 void *
38 countLines(void *arg)
39 {
40         char         *cp;
41         int          fd;
42         caddr_t      address;
43         struct stat  statusBuffer;
44         int          newLineCount = 0;
45         /****************************************************************
46          *      Open the specified file in read-only mode.  On error,
47          *      exit the thread.  Note that arg is used as the exit
48          *      status value.
49          ****************************************************************/
50         fd=open((char *)arg,O_RDONLY);
51         if( fd == -1 )
52                 thr_exit(arg);
53         /****************************************************************
54          *      We now fstat() the file to determine the size.  We
55          *      use this information to memory-map the file into the
56          *      address space.
57          ****************************************************************/
58         fstat(fd, &statusBuffer);
59         address=mmap(NULL, statusBuffer.st_size, PROT_READ,
60                                                 MAP_PRIVATE, fd,0);
61         if( ! address )
62                 thr_exit(arg);
63         /***************************************************************
64          *      We can now scan through the specified address space
65          *      and count the number of new-line characters.
66          ***************************************************************/
67     for(cp=address;cp<(char *)(address+statusBuffer.st_size+1);++cp
68                 if( *cp == '\n' )
69                         ++newLineCount;
70                 /**************************************************
71                  *      We are now ready for cleanup.  This includes
72                  *      closing the file descriptor and releasing the
73                  *      memory-mapped area.  Finally, we call the
74                  *      incrLineCount() to increment the total number of
75                  *      lines found.  This thread can then exit.
76                  **************************************************/
```

Listing 5.6 *continued.*

```
77        close(fd);
78        munmap(address, statusBuffer.st_size);
79        incrLineCount( newLineCount);
80        thr_exit( NULL );
81 }
82
83 /********************************************************************
84  *      Rendezvous   FUNCTION
85  *
86  *      This function is called to synchronize the execution of the
87  *      main with the multiplexed threads.  When the maxConcurrent
88  *      threads are running, main() calls this function to wait for
89  *      some to complete.
90  ********************************************************************/
91 int
92 rendezvous(int *count)
93 {
94        void   *status      = NULL;
95
96        while( thr_join(0,NULL,&status) ==0 ) {
97               if(status)   {
98                      fprintf(stderr,"Error. cannot open %s\n", status);
99                      break;
100              }
101              --(*count);
102        }
103        return( *count );
104 }
105
106 /********************************************************************
107  *      main   PROGRAM
108  *
109  *      The lineCount program will create a multiplexed thread for
110  *      each command-line arg.  The thread will count the number of
111  *      lines found in the file specified by arg.  The global line
112  *      count is then updated accordingly.  Finally, the program will
113  *      display the global line count.
114  ********************************************************************/
115 int
116 main(int argc, char *argv[])
117 {
118        int    index;
119        int    threadCount    = 0;
120        int    errorCondition = 0;
121        int    maxConcurrency = 0;
122        void   *status        = NULL;
```

Listing 5.6 *continued.*

```
123                  /*****************************************************
124                   *      We need to determine the maximum concurrency level
125                   *      to use.  We permit up to 20 LWPs in the pool, but
126                   *      if the argument count is under 20, we set
127                   *      concurrency to that number.
128                   *****************************************************/
129          maxConcurrency = (argc - 1) < 20 ? (argc - 1 ) : 20;
130          thr_setconcurrency( maxConcurrency );
131                  /*****************************************************
132                   *      For each of the command-line arguments, we create
133                   *      a thread.  If the number of active threads is
134                   *      greater than maxConcurrency, we call rendezvous()
135                   *      to wait for the completion of the threads.
136                   *****************************************************/
137          for(index=0; index < argc; ++index ) {
138              errorCondition=thr_create(NULL,0,countLines,
139                                         argv[index+1], 0,NULL);
140              if( errorCondition )
141                  break;
142              ++threadCount;
143              if( threadCount > maxConcurrency )  {
144                  errorCondition = rendezvous( &threadCount );
145                  if( errorCondition )
146                      break;
147              }
148          }
149                  /*****************************************************
150                   *      If there are any threads still running, then we
151                   *      need to call rendezvous to wait on them.
152                   *****************************************************/
153          if( ! errorCondition && threadCount )
154              errorCondition = rendezvous( &threadCount );
155          if( errorCondition != -1 )
156              fprintf(stdout,"totals lines: %d\n", LineCount);
157          thr_exit(0);
158 }
```

6
Condition Variables

6.1 Condition Variables: An Overview

Condition variables are used to communicate information between cooperating threads, making it possible for a thread to suspend its execution while waiting for a condition to be satisfied before proceeding. The UNIX Threads Interface provides condition variables for use between sibling threads of a single UNIX process, or for use between two or more UNIX processes executing in disjoint address spaces.

Unlike the other synchronization primitives, a condition variable is stateless. Instead, the condition variable is associated with one or more shared variables protected by a mutex, and a predicate (*conditional expression*) based on those shared variables. A thread acquires the mutex and evaluates the predicate. If the predicate evaluates to TRUE, then the thread continues its execution. When the predicate evaluates to FALSE, however, the requesting thread must unlock the mutex and suspend itself waiting for another thread to signal that the condition has changed. Once signaled, the first thread will awaken with the mutex in the LOCKED state. The thread returns from its wait on condition and continues processing.

When a thread is to modify the condition, it must first acquire the mutex protecting the condition. After locking the mutex, the thread can *set* the condition by changing the shared variables to satisfy the predicate. The thread must then awaken any threads waiting on the *condition* to change. After signaling these threads, it must release the mutex. This permits one of the awakened threads to acquire the mutex and return from its wait on condition.

There are two basic methods to awaken threads waiting on a condition. The first method is to awaken one out of possibly many threads. This method is referred to as *signaling* a condition. The other method is to awaken all threads waiting on the condition. This technique is known as a *broadcast*. With the broadcast method, the awakened threads are set to a RUNNABLE state simultaneously. Each thread has an equal chance to acquire the mutex, assuming equal thread priorities.

When a waiting thread receives a signal that the condition has changed, the thread reacquires the mutex and returns from the `wait on condition`. There are two important points to remember here. First, a change in the condition does not guarantee the predicate will evaluate to TRUE. The thread must therefore reevaluate the predicate and be prepared to possibly enter the `wait on condition` again. The second point is that the thread now holds the mutex in a LOCKED state. The thread must unlock the mutex at some point to permit other threads waiting on this mutex to proceed.

Condition variables are useful in producer-consumer multithreaded applications. Suppose, for example, that a multithreaded application has one thread to manage a queue. When a new data structure is added to the queue, the manager must be activated to remove the data structure from the queue, process it, and then resume waiting for the next request to enter the queue. There are many different implementations of this algorithm possible. Using a condition variable to represent the state of queue, however, provides an eloquent implementation while minimizing the interthread communication overhead.

Table 6.1   The Condition Variable API

cond_init()	Initialize a condition variable
cond_wait()	Wait on a condition
cond_signal()	Signal a change in the condition
cond_broadcast()	Broadcast a change in the condition
cond_destroy()	Invalidate a condition variable

6.2 Initializing a Condition Variable

To use a condition variable the application must define a `cond_t` type data structure, a separate mutual exclusion lock (*a mutex*), and a predicate. These three components are required for each condition variable in use by the application. The `cond_init()` function (*Figure 6.1*) initializes the condition variable.

The first parameter `cond` is the address of the condition variable data structure. The type parameter determines if the `cond` data structure is to be initialized as a USYNC_THREAD or a USYNC_PROCESS type condition variable. A USYNC_THREAD type condition variable is for use between sibling threads of a single UNIX process, while a USYNC_PROCESS type condition variable is for use between two or more UNIX processes executing in disjoint address spaces. The UNIX Threads Interface will treat a zero filled condition variable as an initialized USYNC_THREAD type condition variable. The `arg` parameter is currently unused and should be specified as NULL. This parameter is reserved for future use.

NAME:
>   cond_init - Initialize a condition variable.

SYNOPSIS:
>   int
>   cond_init(cond_t *cond, int type, void *arg)

Figure 6.1   `cond_init()` synopsis. [1]

A successful call to `cond_init` will initialize the condition variable and return a zero status value to the calling thread. Otherwise, the condition variable will remain unchanged and an appropriate error indication value will be returned.

PROGRAMMER'S NOTE:

Caution must be exercised not to reinitialize a condition variable while one or more threads (or UNIX processes) are currently waiting on it. The `cond_init` function does not examine the `cond` argument prior to initialization and will simply overwrite its state if called more than once for the same condition.

6.3 Waiting for a Condition Variable

The condition variable's predicate is a critical resource. We must therefore apply a mutual exclusion lock to prevent multiple threads from concurrently updating the condition variable. When a thread is to access the predicate, it must first lock the mutex. If the predicate is FALSE, the thread must call the `cond_wait` function and wait for a thread to signal that the predicate's condition has changed. In calling the `cond_wait` function, the requesting thread continues to hold the mutex associated with the condition. The `cond_wait` function will unlock the mutex specified by the second parameter `mutex` and wait for the condition variable specified as the first argument to change. After the thread completes its use of the resource, it must unlock the mutex. The mutex plays an integral role in the use of a condition variable.

When the condition is signaled or broadcasted, or if the wait is interrupted, the `cond_wait` function will acquire the mutex and return to the calling thread. In servicing the interrupt, the mutex is reacquired by the `cond_wait` function before a signal handler or any other user-level code can be executed.

---

[1] Printed with Permission of UNIX Systems Laboratories, Inc. All Rights Reserved.

NAME:

> `cond_wait` - Wait for the condition specified by argument.

SYNOPSIS:

> ```
> #include <synch.h>
>
> int
> cond_wait( cond_t *cond, mutex_t *mutex)
> ```

Figure 6.2   `cond_wait()` synopsis. [1]

PROGRAMMER'S NOTE:

There is the potential for a race condition between the time the condition variable changes and the mutex is acquired by the `cond_wait` function prior to returning control to the calling thread. The calling thread must therefore always check the predicate upon return from this function call.

Upon a successful call to `cond_wait`, the mutex will be reacquired and a zero status value will be returned to the calling thread. Even though a zero status value may be returned, the calling thread should reevaluate the predicate before proceeding. If the predicate evaluates to FALSE, then the thread should call `cond_wait` again.

PROGRAMMER'S NOTE:

Condition variables are not asynchronous-safe and should not be used to communicate between signal handlers and base-level user code. Semaphores provide asynchronous-safe communications for such cases.

There are three important points to remember in using the `cond_wait` function call. First, a change in the condition variable does not guarantee that the predicate will be satisfied. It simply means the condition has changed. The second is that the calling thread has the mutex in the LOCKED state. This thread must remember to subsequently unlock the mutex. The third and final point is that the `cond_wait` function can be interrupted and thus the return value from this function call must be examined.

The `cond_wait` function will cause the requesting thread to block until the condition variable changes. Once blocked, the requesting thread remains in a WAIT state until awakened by a thread

---

[1] Printed with Permission of UNIX Systems Laboratories, Inc. All Rights Reserved.

issuing the `cond_signal` or `cond_broadcast` functions. Often, however, a thread may wish to wait only a specified time for the condition variable to change.

NAME:

       `cond_timedwait -`   Wait at most `timestruct_t` seconds for a condition variable to change.

SYNOPSIS:

```
#include <synch.h>
#include <sys/time.h>

int
cond_timedwait(cond_t *cond, mutex_t *mutex,
               timestruc_t *abstime)
```

Figure 6.3   `cond_timedwait()` synopsis. [1]

As with the `cond_wait` function, the requesting thread must lock the mutex prior to calling the `cond_timedwait` function (*Figure 6.3*). The parameter `mutex` is the mutual exclusion lock protecting the predicate associated with the condition.

The `cond_timedwait` function applies the specified time constraint to determine how long to wait for the condition to change. The `cond_timedwait` function will unlock the mutex specified as the second parameter. A wake-up alarm for `abstime` seconds will then be set. The requesting thread will block, waiting for the condition variable specified as the first parameter to be signaled. If the condition is signaled, or broadcast, the `cond_timedwait` function will reacquire the mutex and return a zero status value to the calling thread. Alternatively, if a wake-up alarm is signaled, the `cond_timedwait` function reacquires the mutex and will return an `ETIME` error indication value to the calling thread.

PROGRAMMER'S NOTE:

There is a potential race condition that exists in the `cond_timedwait` function between the time the condition is signaled and the time the mutex is relocked. It is therefore possible that the condition signaled could be changed by another thread during the race condition. The requesting thread should always check that the indicated condition remains valid upon return from this function.

---

[1] Printed with Permission of UNIX Systems Laboratories, Inc. All Rights Reserved.

The parameter abstime represents the time at which cond_timedwait should time out. The time is expressed in elapsed seconds and nanoseconds since Universal Coordinated Time, January 1, 1970. To construct the value for abstime, convert the current time to timestruct_t and add to the desired waiting time. The gettimeofday function will return the current time.

The cond_timedwait function can be interrupted by an EINTR signal. If the function is interrupted while blocking, the cond_timedwait function will reacquire the mutex and return an EINTR signal to the calling thread.

6.4 Signaling the Condition

When a thread is to modify a condition variable's predicate, it must first acquire the associated mutex lock. Once locked, the thread can set the condition to evaluate to TRUE. After modifying the condition, the thread must notify all waiting threads that the condition has changed. Finally, the calling thread must release the mutex.

There are two methods available to notify threads blocked on a condition variable. The thread changing the condition can signal the change to a specific blocked thread, or can broadcast the change to all the blocked threads. The UNIX Threads Interface provides the cond_signal function to signal a single thread that the condition has changed. The cond_broadcast function will signal all waiting threads that the condition has changed.

The cond_signal Function

The cond_signal function (*Figure 6.4*) will awaken a single thread currently waiting on the condition variable specified as parameter cond. The only validity checking performed by cond_signal is to ensure that the cond_t type data structure, cond, is either of type USYNC_THREAD or USYNC_PROCESS. If the type is neither, then no further action is taken and an EINVAL error indication is returned to the calling thread.

NAME:
        cond_signal - Wake up a single thread waiting on the specified condition variable.

SYNOPSIS:
```
        #include <synch.h>

        int
        cond_signal (cond_t *cond)
```

Figure 6.4   cond_signal() synopsis. [1]

When signaling a change to a `USYNC_THREAD` type condition variable, the `cond_signal` function gives precedence to bound threads waiting on the condition. If there are no bound threads the `cond_signal` function will signal a blocked multiplexed thread.

PROGRAMMER'S NOTE:

A `cond_signal` will typically be more efficient if the associated mutex used by waiters is held across the call.

The cond_broadcast Function

The `cond_broadcast` function (*Figure 6.5*) will broadcast a condition variable change to all threads currently waiting on the condition variable specified as parameter `cond`. The condition variable must be of type `USYNC_THREAD` or `USYNC_PROCESS`; otherwise an `EINVAL` error indication value is returned to the calling thread.

NAME:
    `cond_broadcast` - Wake up all threads waiting for the specified condition
variable.

SYNOPSIS:
```
int
cond_broadcast(cond_t *cond)
```

Figure 6.5   `cond_broadcast()` synopsis. [¶]

Broadcasting a change to a `USYNC_THREAD` type condition variable will awaken both bound and multiplexed threads waiting on this condition. For multiplexed threads, the `cond_broadcast` function must first lock the condition variable's wait queue, move the wait queue to a temporary queue, and then unlock the wait queue. This prevents new threads from being added to the wait queue while the multiplexed threads are being dequeued and made runnable. For each multiplexed thread dequeued, the `cond_broadcast` function will attempt to activate an LWP from the pool. If an LWP cannot be activated, the `cond_broadcast()` function will continue without generating an error message.

[¶] Printed with Permission of UNIX Systems Laboratories, Inc. All Rights Reserved.

PROGRAMMER'S NOTE:

Considerable time could be spent awakening all of the threads waiting on the condition variable, only to find that most of these threads will just go back to sleep waiting for the same condition [CAMP91]. This phenomenon is known as the Thundering Herd.

6.5 Invalidating the Condition Variable

When the application no longer requires the use of a condition variable, the condition variable should be invalidated by calling the cond_destroy() function (*Figure 6.6*). This function invalidates the condition variable and releases any associated implementation-allocated dynamic resources. The cond_destroy() function will return an EBUSY error indication if a thread is currently referencing the condition variable.

NAME:
        cond_destroy - Destroy a condition variable.

SYNOPSIS:
        #include <synch.h>

        int
        cond_destroy(cond_t *cond)

Figure 6.6   cond_destroy() synopsis. [1]

6.6 Using the Condition Variable

The threadCondv Module

The threadCondv module (*Listings 6.1 and 6.2*) provides the auxiliary functions to administer dynamically allocated USYNC_THREAD type condition variables. The threadCondv.h header file (*Listing 6.1*) uses a data structure to provide the references to these functions. To use the threadCondv module, include this header file and reference the members of the threadCondv_f data structure, as in threadCondv_f.create().

The `threadCondv_f.create` function (*Listing 6.2*) will allocate the appropriate storage for a condition variable using the `malloc` function. On success, the condition variable is initialized for use between sibling threads. If an error occurs, the `threadLog_f.setError` function is called to log the appropriate error type. The `threadCondv_f.destroy` function accepts as a single parameter the address of the condition variable to be invalidated. Upon success, the function will call `free` to release the memory storage for this condition variable.

Compile threadCondv module:

```
cc -D_REENTRANT -c -I${INSTALLROOT}/hdr threadCondv.c
ar rv ${INSTALLROOT}/lib/libtsync.a threadCondv.o
```

Listing 6.1   *threadCondv.h* -- The `threadCondv` module header file.

```
1  typedef struct _threadCondv_f {
2        cond_t *(*create)(void);
3        int    (*destroy)(cond_t *);
4  } threadCondv_t;
5
6  extern threadCondv_t threadCondv_f;
```

Listing 6.2   *threadCondv.c* -- The `threadCondv` module.

```
1  #include <stdlib.h>
2  #include <memory.h>
3  #include <synch.h>
4  #include <thread.h>
5  #include <errno.h>
6  #include "mthreadLog.h"
7  #include "threadCondv.h"
8
8  static      cond_t      *Create(void);
9  static      int         Destroy(cond_t *);
10
11 /*****************************************************************
12  *     CREATE FUNCTION
13  *
14  *     Allocates and initializes a condition variable cond_t.
15  *****************************************************************/
16 static cond_t *
17 Create(void)
18 {
19       cond_t *condvPtr      = NULL;
20       int    errorCondition = 0;
```

Listing 6.2 *continued.*

```
21          condvPtr = (cond_t *) malloc(sizeof(cond_t));
22          if( condvPtr == NULL )
23                  threadLog_f.setError(ENOMEM);
24          else {
25                  memset((void *)condvPtr,'\0', sizeof(cond_t));
26                  errorCondition=cond_init(condvPtr,USYNC_THREAD,NULL);
27                  if ( errorCondition ) {
28                          free((void *) condvPtr );
29                          condvPtr = NULL;
30                          threadLog_f.setError( errorCondition );
31                  }
32          }
33          return(condvPtr);
34  }
35
36  /*****************************************************************
37   *      DESTROY        FUNCTION
38   *
39   *      Deallocates a dynamically allocated condition variable.
40   *****************************************************************/
41  static int
42  Destroy( cond_t *condvPtr)
43  {
44          int     errorCondition = 0;
45
46          errorCondition = cond_destroy(condvPtr);
47
48          if( errorCondition )
49                  threadLog_f.setError( errorCondition );
50          else
51                  free((void *)condvPtr);
52          return( errorCondition );
53  }
54
55  threadCondv_t        threadCondv_f = {
56          Create,
57          Destroy,
58  };
```

Protecting Queues with Condition Variables

A standard approach to passing information between sibling threads is to create a queue with one thread, the producer, pushing messages on to the queue while another thread, the consumer, pops the messages from the queue. Using a condition variable, the producer and consumer thread can synchronize their access to the queue. The implementation of such a queue appears in Figure 6.7.

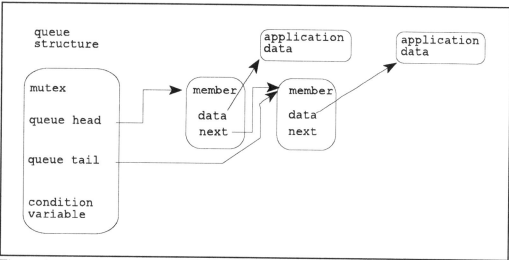

Figure 6.7   A sibling thread communication queue.

The threadQcond auxiliary functions (*Listings 6.3 and 6.4*) provide a generic implementation of a queue for use between sibling threads. The qmember_t type definition (*Listing 6.3*) includes a pointer to the data (*the message*) and a pointer to the next member in the queue. The queue itself is described by the qcond_t type definition. The mutex and condition members will be used by the producer and consumer to synchronize their use of the queue. The queueHead and queueTail members point respectively to the first and last members in the queue.

Compile threadQcond module:

```
cc -D_REENTRANT -c -I${INSTALLROOT}/hdr threadQcond.c
ar rv ${INSTALLROOT}/lib/libtsync.a threadQcond.o
```

Listing 6.3   *threadQcond.h* -- The threadQcond header file.

```
1   /*****************************************************************
2    *      Each member of the queue consists of a pointer to the message,
3    *      and a pointer to the next member in the queue.
4    *****************************************************************/
5   typedef struct _qmember {
6          void            *data;
7          struct _qmember *next;
8   }qmember_t;
```

Listing 6.3 *continued.*

```
9   /*********************************************************
10   *     When the condition of the queue changes, i.e., messages are
11   *     pushed, then condition must be signaled to consumer.
12   *********************************************************/
13   typedef struct _qcond_t {
14          mutex_t      *mutex;
15          cond_t       *condition;
16          qmember_t    *queueHead;
17          qmember_t    *queueTail;
18   }qcond_t;
19
20   /*********************************************************
21   *     The operations available for the threadQcond module include
22   *     the create, destroy, qpop, and qpush functions.
23   *********************************************************/
24   typedef struct _threadQcond_t {
25          qcond_t      *(*create)(void);
26          int          (*destroy)( qcond_t *);
27          void         *(*qpop)(qcond_t *);
28          int          (*qpush)(qcond_t *, void *);
29   } threadQcond_t;
30
31   extern threadQcond_t      threadQcond_f;
```

The functions available through the threadQcond module include the Create, Destroy, Qpop, and Qpush functions. The Create function (*Listing 6.3*) will dynamically allocate a condition queue and perform the appropriate initialization. The mutex member is allocated through the threadMutex module by calling the threadMutex_f.create() function. Similarly, the condition member is allocated through the threadCondv module by calling the threadCondv_f.create() function. When the condition queue is no longer required, it is deallocated by the Destroy function.

Once the condition queue has been created, the Qpush function will push a message onto the queue. The Qpush function accepts the two parameters qcond and data. The qcond parameter is a pointer to a condition queue allocated by the Create function. The data parameter is a pointer to some data representing the information to be added to the queue. Before the Qpush function can add a message to the queue, it must first lock the mutex protecting the queue. The Qpush function then allocates a qmember_t data structure and sets the data member to the address specified by the data parameter (*a pointer to a message*). After the queue's head and tail are adjusted, the Qpush function calls the cond_signal function to signal that a new message has been added to the queue. Finally, it must unlock the mutex protecting the queue.

The Qpop function locks the condition queue's mutex, and then enters a loop checking to see if there are any messages in the queue. If there are no messages, then the Qpop function will call the `cond_wait` function specifying the queue's condition variable and mutex. If there were no errors, then the message is removed from the queue, and the queue's mutex is subsequently unlocked.

After the message structure has been allocated and the message queue's head and tail adjust, the `Qpush` function calls the `cond_signal` function to signal that a message has been added to the queue.

Listing 6.4   *threadQcond.c* -- The `threadQcond` module.

```
 1  #include <synch.h>
 2  #include <stdlib.h>
 3  #include <memory.h>
 4  #include <errno.h>
 5  #include "threadCondv.h"
 6  #include "threadMutex.h"
 7  #include "threadQcond.h"
 8  #include "mthreadLog.h"
 9
10  static       int          Destroy(qcond_t *);
11  static       int          Qpush(qcond_t *, void *);
12  static       void         *Qpop(qcond_t *);
13  static       qcond_t      *Create(void);
14
15  /*******************************************************************
16   *     CREATE         FUNCTION
17   *
18   *     Allocate and initialize a qcond_t type structure.  The
19   *     structure provides the mechanisms for a queue with an
20   *     associated condition variable.
21   *******************************************************************/
22  static qcond_t *
23  Create(void)
24  {
25          qcond_t       *qcond;
26
27          qcond   = (qcond_t *) malloc(sizeof(qcond_t));
28          if ( qcond == NULL ) {
29                  threadLog_f.setError(ENOMEM);
30                  return(NULL);
31          }
32
33          memset(qcond, '\0', sizeof(qcond_t));
34          qcond->mutex       = threadMutex_f.create();
35          qcond->condition = threadCondv_f.create();
36          if ( qcond->mutex == NULL || qcond->condition == NULL) {
```

Listing 6.4 *continued.*

```
37                  if( qcond->condition )
38                          threadCondv_f.destroy(qcond->condition);
39                  if( qcond->mutex )
40                          threadMutex_f.destroy(qcond->mutex);
41                  free( (void *) qcond );
42                  qcond = NULL;
43          }
44          return(qcond);
45  }
46
47  /*****************************************************************
48   *      DESTROY      FUNCTION
49   *
50   *    Destroy a previously allocated qcond_t type structure.
51   *****************************************************************/
52  static int
53  Destroy(qcond_t *qcond)
54  {
55          int    errorCondition = 0;
56
57          if( qcond == NULL )
58                  return(EINVAL);
59          errorCondition = threadMutex_f.destroy( qcond->mutex );
60          if( errorCondition )
61                  return(errorCondition);
62          errorCondition = threadCondv_f.destroy(qcond->condition);
63          if( ! errorCondition ) {
64                  free((void *)qcond->condition);
65                  free((void *)qcond->mutex);
66                  free((void *)qcond);
67          }
68          return( errorCondition );
69  }
70
71  /*****************************************************************
72   *      Qpop    FUNCTION
73   *
74   *    Pop a message off of the specified queue.
75   *****************************************************************/
76  static void *
77  Qpop( qcond_t *qcond )
78  {
79          void            *data                = NULL;
80          qmember_t       *qmember= NULL;
81          int              errorCondition = 0;
```

Listing 6.4 *continued.*

```
 82              if( qcond == NULL ) {
 83                    threadLog_f.setError(EINVAL);
 84                    return(NULL);
 85              }
 86
 87              errorCondition = mutex_lock( qcond->mutex );
 88              if( ! errorCondition ) {
 89                    while( qcond->queueHead == NULL ) {
 90                          errorCondition  =  cond_wait(  qcond->condition,
 91                                                          qcond->mutex);
 92                          if( errorCondition )
 93                                break;
 94                    }
 95                    if( ! errorCondition ) {
 96                          qmember = qcond->queueHead;
 97                          data    = qmember->data;
 98                          if( qcond->queueHead == qcond->queueTail )
 99                                qcond->queueTail = NULL;
100                          qcond->queueHead = qmember->next;
101                          free( qmember );
102                    }
103                    mutex_unlock( qcond->mutex);
104              }
105
106              if( errorCondition )
107                    threadLog_f.setError(errorCondition);
108              return( data );
109      }
110
111      /******************************************************************
112       *      Qpush FUNCTION
113       *
114       *      Push a message onto the specified queue.
115       ******************************************************************/
116      static int
117      Qpush( qcond_t *qcond, void *data)
118      {
119              int            errorCondition = 0;
120              qmember_t    *qmember;
121
122              if(  qcond == NULL || data == NULL)
123                    return(EINVAL);
124
125              errorCondition = mutex_lock( qcond->mutex );
126              if( ! errorCondition ) {
127                    qmember = (qmember_t *)malloc(sizeof(qmember_t));
```

Listing 6.4 *continued.*

```
128                    if( ! qmember ) {
129                            mutex_unlock(qcond->mutex);
130                            return(ENOMEM);
131                    }
132
133                    memset(qmember,'\0',sizeof(qmember_t));
134                    qmember->data = data;
135                    qmember->next = NULL;
136                    if( ! qcond->queueHead ) {
137                            qcond->queueHead = qmember;
138                            qcond->queueTail = qmember;
139                    }
140                    else {
141                            qcond->queueTail->next = qmember;
142
143                            qcond->queueTail        = qmember;
144                    }
145                    cond_signal(qcond->condition);
146                    mutex_unlock(qcond->mutex);
147            }
148        return(errorCondition);
149 }
150
151 /******************************************************************
152  *      The threadQcond module's public interface is defined here.
153  *      The application uses the function pointers in this data
154  *      structure to access the threadQcond functions.
155  ******************************************************************/
156 threadQcond_t        threadQcond_f = {
157        Create,
158        Destroy,
159        Qpop,
160        Qpush
161 };
```

A Sibling Thread Communication Link

With the condition queue in place we can now develop basic communication link functions for use between sibling threads. The premise of the communication link functions is that the multithreaded application will have a producer and a consumer thread to be created.

Before describing the details of these functions, certain terminology must be agreed upon. Each thread connected with a communication link (comlink_t) is referred to as a communication thread (comthread_t). The execution of the comthread can be described by its communication point data structure member (compoint_t). A comthread is either a producer or a consumer, as determined by its `type` member. A producer will push information into the `comlink`, while a consumer will pop information from the `comlink` (*see Figure 6.8*).

The application must call the `comlink_f.allocate()` function and initialize the data structure with the appropriate information for the producer and consumer `comthreads`. Next, the application calls the `comlink_f.initialize()` function. This function will create the producer and consumer `comthreads`.

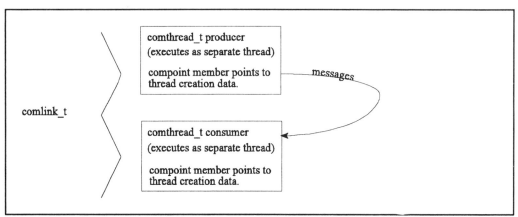

Figure 6.8   Diagram of a communication link with a producer and a consumer thread.

Compile comthread module:

```
cc -D_REENTRANT -c -I${INSTALLROOT}/hdr comlink.c
cc -D_REENTRANT -c -I${INSTALLROOT}/hdr compoint.c
cc -D_REENTRANT -c -I${INSTALLROOT}/hdr comqueue.c
cc -D_REENTRANT -c -I${INSTALLROOT}/hdr comtest.c
cc -D_REENTRANT -c -I${INSTALLROOT}/hdr comthread.c
ar rv ${INSTALLROOT}/lib/libcomlink.a comlink.o compoint.o \
        comqueue.o comthread.o
```

Listing 6.5   *comlink.h* -- The `comlink` module header file.

```
1  typedef unsigned int comstatus_t;
2
3  /************************************************************
4   *      Define the values representing the status of the communication
5   *      link
6   ************************************************************/
7  #define IS_INITIALIZED  0x0001   /* Comlink is initialized.  */
```

Listing 6.5 *continued.*

```
 8   #define IS_ACTIVE        0x0002   /* Producer and consumer
 9                                      * points of the comlink are
10                                      * running.
11                                      */
12
13   #define IS_SUSPENDED     0x0004   /* The comlink is currently
14                                      * in the suspended state.
15                                      */
16
17   #define IS_BUSY          0x0008   /* Comlink is busy.          */
18
19   #define IS_DEACTIVE      0x0010   /* Comlink producer and
20                                      * consumer are no longer active.
21                                      */
22
23   #define PRODUCER         0x0020   /* Producer comthread type. */
24
25   #define CONSUMER         0x0040   /* Consumer comthread type. */
26   /****************************************************************
27    *     A compoint_t type structure contains the parameters for the
28    *     comthread thread creation.
29    ****************************************************************/
30   typedef struct _compoint_t  {
31        void                *stackAddress;
32        size_t               stackSize;
33        void                *(*startRoutine)(void *);
34        unsigned long        flags;
35   } compoint_t;
36
37   /****************************************************************
38    *     Each comlink has two comthread structures, one for the
39    *     producer and one for the consumer.
40    *           compoint    Points to the thread creation parameters
41    *           identifier  Is the tid of the communication thread
42    *           comstatus   A bitwise OR of the constants defined above
43    *           type        Is either PRODUCER or CONSUMER
44    *           mutex       Points to a dynamically allocated mutex for
45    *                       synchonizing access to this structure
46    ****************************************************************/
47   typedef struct _comthread_t  {
48        compoint_t          *compoint;
49        thread_t             identifier;
50        comstatus_t          comstatus;
51        int                  type;
52        mutex_t             *mutex;
53   } comthread_t;
```

Listing 6.5 *continued.*

```
54  /***************************************************************
55   *      The conqueue_t structure represents the queue used for message
56   *      passing between the consumer and the producer.  The "type"
57   *      member is currently unused.  It can be set to represent the
58   *      type of message data being shared.
59   ***************************************************************/
60
61  typedef struct _comqueue_t    {
62        int                    type;
63        qcond_t               *queue;
64  } comqueue_t;
65
66  /***************************************************************
67   *      The communication link structure represents an active link
68   *      between a producer and consumer thread.
69   *             producer     Points to the producer side of the link
70   *             consumer     Points to the consumer side of the link
71   *             conqueue     Points to the queue used for message passing
72   *             comstatus    Represents the current status of the link
73   *             mutex        Points to a dynamically allocated mutex for
74   *                          synchronizing access to this structure
75   ***************************************************************/
76  typedef struct    _comlink_t    {
77        comthread_t           *producer;
78        comthread_t           *consumer;
79        comqueue_t            *comqueue;
80        comstatus_t            comstatus;
81        mutex_t               *mutex;
82  } comlink_t;
83
84  /***************************************************************
85   *      There are a series of modules available for each of the type
86   *      definitions required for the comlink.  The interface for using
87   *      these types are described below.
88   ***************************************************************/
89  struct _compoint_f {
90        compoint_t  *(*allocate)(void);
91        int          (*deallocate)(compoint_t *);
92  };
93
94  struct _comthread_f {
95        comthread_t *(*allocate)(const int);
96        int          (*deallocate)(comthread_t *);
97  };
```

Listing 6.5   *continued.*

```
98   struct _comlink_f {
99          comlink_t    *(*allocate)(const int);
100         int           (*deallocate)(comlink_t *);
101         int           (*initialize)(comlink_t *);
102         int           (*drop)( comlink_t *);
103  };
104
105  struct _comqueue_f        {
106         comqueue_t   *(*allocate)(const int);
107         int           (*deallocate)(comqueue_t *);
108  };
109
110
111  extern struct _compoint_f   compoint_f;
112  extern struct _comthread_f  comthread_f;
113  extern struct _comlink_f    comlink_f;
114  extern struct _comqueue_f   comqueue_f;
```

Listing 6.6   *comlink.c* -- The `comlink` module.

```
1    #include <stdio.h>
2    #include <synch.h>
3    #include <stdlib.h>
4    #include <thread.h>
5    #include <synch.h>
6    #include <string.h>
7    #include <errno.h>
8    #include "threadQcond.h"
9    #include "threadMutex.h"
10   #include "mthreadLog.h"
11   #include "comlink.h"
12
13   static        mutex_t       comlinkMutex = {0 };
14   static        comlink_t    *Allocate(int);
15   static        int           Deallocate(comlink_t *);
16   static        int           Drop(comlink_t *);
17   static        int           Initialize(comlink_t *);
18   /*****************************************************************
19    *      Allocate      FUNCTION
20    *
21    *      Allocate and initialize a comlink_t type data structure.
22    *****************************************************************/
23   static comlink_t *
24   Allocate(int type)
25   {
```

Listing 6.6 *continued.*

```
26       comlink_t    *comlink    = NULL;
27       comthread_t  *producer   = NULL;
28
29       comthread_t  *consumer   = NULL;
30       comqueue_t   *comqueue   = NULL;
31       mutex_t      *mutex      = NULL;
32
33       /*********************************************************
34        *     Allocate the memory for the comlink, including memory
35        *     for the various components of the structure.
36        *********************************************************/
37       comlink  = (comlink_t *)malloc(sizeof(comlink_t));
38       producer = comthread_f.allocate(PRODUCER);
39       consumer = comthread_f.allocate(CONSUMER);
40       comqueue = comqueue_f.allocate(type);
41       mutex    = threadMutex_f.create();
42
43       /*********************************************************
44        *     If we failed to allocate the memory for any component
45        *     of the comlink, then deallocate all components and
46        *     return a NULL pointer.
47        *********************************************************/
48       if(!comlink || !producer || !consumer || !comqueue || !mutex)
49       {
50            if( comlink  )   free(comlink);
51            if( producer )   comthread_f.deallocate(producer);
52            if( consumer )   comthread_f.deallocate(consumer);
53            if( comqueue )   comqueue_f.deallocate(comqueue);
54            if( mutex )         threadMutex_f.destroy(mutex);
55            return(NULL);
56       }
57
58       /*********************************************************
59        *     All of the memory has been allocated, so initialize
60        *     the structure members.
61        *********************************************************/
62       memset(comlink,'\0',sizeof(comlink_t));
63       comlink->producer = producer;
64       comlink->consumer = consumer;
65       comlink->comqueue = comqueue;
66       comlink->comstatus= IS_INITIALIZED;
67       comlink->mutex    = mutex;
68       return( comlink );
69  }
```

Listing 6.6 *continued.*

```
70   /****************************************************************
71    *      Deallocate  FUNCTION
72    *
73    *      Deallocate the members of the comlink_t type structure, and
74    *      then release the memory associated with the comlink_t
75    *      structure itself.
76    ****************************************************************/
77   static int
78   Deallocate( comlink_t *comlink)
79   {
80          if( ! comlink )
81                  return(EINVAL);
82
83                  /****************************************************
84                   *      CRITICAL SECTION START
85                   *      We have to avoid multiple threads calling this
86                   *      function concurrently.  This is a critical
87                   (      section.
88                   ****************************************************/
89          mutex_lock( &comlinkMutex );
90          if(  mutex_lock( comlink->mutex) == 0 ) {
91              comlink->comstatus = IS_DEACTIVE;
92              comthread_f.deallocate(comlink->producer);
93              comthread_f.deallocate(comlink->consumer);
94              comqueue_f.deallocate(comlink->comqueue);
95              mutex_unlock(comlink->mutex);
96              threadMutex_f.destroy( comlink->mutex );
97              free(comlink);
98          }
99
100                 /****************************************************
101                  *      CRITICAL SECTION END
102                  ****************************************************/
103         mutex_unlock( &comlinkMutex );
104         return(0);
105  }
106
107  /****************************************************************
108   *      Initialize  FUNCTION
109   *
110   *      This function initializes the communications in the comlink.
111   *      Two threads will be created here.  One for the producer side
112   *      of the comlink, and one for the consumer side of the comlink.
113   *      Each thread will be created and given the address of the
114   *      communication queue as its only argument.
115   ****************************************************************/
```

Listing 6.6   *continued.*

```
116   static int
117   Initialize(comlink_t *comlink)
118   {
119         int          producerError   = 0;
120         int          consumerError   = 0;
121         int          comlinkError    = 0;
122
123               /**********************************************
124               *       CRITICAL SECTION   START
125               *       We have to prevent a sibling from deallocating the
126               *       comlink while we are validating the parameters.
127               *       We are in a critical section until we lock the
128               *       comlink's mutex.
129               ***********************************************/
130         mutex_lock( &comlinkMutex );
131
132         if( ! comlink ||(! comlink->producer && ! comlink->consumer ))
133               comlinkError = EINVAL;
134
135         if(comlink->producer)
136               if( ! (comlink->producer->comstatus & IS_INITIALIZED) ||
137                   (comlink->producer->comstatus & IS_ACTIVE) )
138                   comlinkError = EINVAL;
139
140         if(comlink->consumer)
141               if( ! (comlink->consumer->comstatus & IS_INITIALIZED) ||
142                   (comlink->consumer->comstatus & IS_ACTIVE) )
143                   comlinkError = EINVAL;
144
145         if( ! comlinkError )
146               comlinkError = mutex_lock( comlink->mutex );
147
148         mutex_unlock( &comlinkMutex );
149               /**********************************************
150               *       CRITICAL SECTION   END
151               ***********************************************/
152
153               /**********************************************
154               *       Lock the producer's mutex and the consumer's
155               *       mutex.
156               ***********************************************/
157         if( comlink->producer != NULL )
158               producerError= mutex_lock( comlink->producer->mutex);
159
160         if( comlink->consumer != NULL )
161               consumerError= mutex_lock( comlink->consumer->mutex);
```

Listing 6.6 *continued.*

```
162                /****************************************************
163                 *     Now clean up if there are any errors,
164                 ****************************************************/
165        if( comlinkError | producerError | consumerError ) {
166            threadLog_f.message("comlink.init mutex lock failed\n");
167            if( ! comlinkError   )
168                    mutex_unlock(comlink->mutex);
169
170            if( ! producerError && comlink->producer )
171                    mutex_unlock(comlink->producer->mutex);
172
173            if( ! consumerError && comlink->consumer )
174                    mutex_unlock(comlink->consumer->mutex);
175            return( EINVAL );
176        }
177                /****************************************************
178                 *     If there is a producer component of this comlink,
179                 *     then create its producer thread in the suspended
180                 *     state.  The only argument to this producer thread
181                 *     is the address of the communication queue.
182                 ****************************************************/
183        if( comlink->producer )
184            producerError =
185            thr_create(comlink->producer->compoint->stackAddress,
186                        comlink->producer->compoint->stackSize,
187                        comlink->producer->compoint->startRoutine,
188                        comlink->comqueue,
189                        comlink->producer->compoint->flags |
190                             THR_SUSPENDED,
191                             &(comlink->producer->identifier));
192                /****************************************************
193                 *     If there is a consumer component of this comlink,
194                 *     then create its consumer thread in the suspended
195                 *     state. The only argument to this consumer thread
196                 *     is the address of the communication queue.
197                 ****************************************************/
198        if( comlink->consumer )
199            consumerError =
200            thr_create(comlink->consumer->compoint->stackAddress,
201                        comlink->consumer->compoint->stackSize,
202                        comlink->consumer->compoint->startRoutine,
203                        comlink->comqueue,
204                        comlink->consumer->compoint->flags |
205                             THR_SUSPENDED,
206                             &(comlink->consumer->identifier));
```

Listing 6.6 *continued.*

```
207                 /********************************************
208            *      If there were no errors, then mark the consumer
209            *      and the producer threads as being ACTIVE, and
210            *      resume the execution of the producer and the
211            *      consumer.
212            ********************************************/
213         if( ! (producerError | consumerError) ) {
214             if( comlink->producer ) {
215                 comlink->producer->comstatus |= IS_ACTIVE;
216                 thr_continue( comlink->producer->identifier );
217             }
218             if( comlink->consumer ) {
219                 comlink->consumer->comstatus |= IS_ACTIVE;
220                 thr_continue( comlink->consumer->identifier );
221             }
222         }

223
224                 /********************************************
225            *      We are now done with the comlink, so we can UNLOCK
226            *      the comlink's mutex, the producer's mutex, and the
227            *      consumer's mutex.
228            ********************************************/
229         mutex_unlock( comlink->mutex );

230
231         if( comlink->producer )
232             mutex_unlock( comlink->producer->mutex);

233
234
235         if( comlink->consumer )
236             mutex_unlock( comlink->consumer->mutex);

237
238         return( producerError | consumerError | comlinkError );
239 }

240
241 /****************************************************************
242  *     Drop   FUNCTION
243  *
244  *     This function will terminate the communications.
245  ****************************************************************/
246 static int
247 Drop( comlink_t *comlink )
248 {
249         int     errorCondition = 0;
250         int     producerError  = 0;
251         int     consumerError  = 0;
```

Listing 6.6   *continued.*

```
252              /***********************************************
253              *     CRITICAL SECTION  START
254              *     We enter a critical section while we validate the
255              *     comlink parameter.  This prevents another thread
256              *     from deallocating the comlink while we are using
257              *     it.
258              ***********************************************/
259         mutex_lock( &comlinkMutex );
260         if( ! comlink || comlink->comstatus & IS_ACTIVE)
261              errorCondition = EINVAL;
262         else
263              errorCondition = mutex_lock(comlink->mutex);
264
265              /***********************************************
266              *     Lock the producer's mutex and the consumer's
267              *     mutex.
268              ***********************************************/
269         if( comlink->producer != NULL )
270              producerError= mutex_lock( comlink->producer->mutex);
271
272         if( comlink->consumer != NULL )
273              consumerError= mutex_lock( comlink->consumer->mutex);
274
275         mutex_unlock( &comlinkMutex );
276              /***********************************************
277              *     CRITICAL SECTION  END
278              ***********************************************/
279         if( ! (errorCondition || consumerError || producerError) ) {
280              /*******************************************
281              *  At this point, we must terminate the producer thread
282              *  if it is running.  To do this properly, we need to
283              *  send the thread a signal or a message that it
284              *  should terminate.  These topics are covered in
285              *  the advanced topics section of this book.
286              *  For now, we will simply suspend its execution.
287              *******************************************/
288              if( comlink->producer &&
289                (comlink->producer->comstatus & IS_ACTIVE)){
290                        thr_suspend(comlink->producer->identifier);
291                        comlink->producer->comstatus &= ~IS_ACTIVE;
292              }
293
294              /*******************************************
295              *  We must also terminate the consumer thread if it is
296              *  running.  For now, we will simply suspend its
297              *  execution.
298              *******************************************/
```

Listing 6.6 *continued.*

```
299                     if( comlink->consumer &&
300                         (comlink->consumer->comstatus & IS_ACTIVE)){
301                                 thr_suspend(comlink->consumer->identifier);
302                                 comlink->consumer->comstatus &= ~IS_ACTIVE;
303                     }
304                 comlink->comstatus &= IS_ACTIVE;
305                 mutex_unlock( comlink->consumer->mutex );
306                 mutex_unlock( comlink->producer->mutex );
307                 mutex_unlock( comlink->mutex );
308             }
309         return(0);
310 }
311
312 /*******************************************************************
313  *     The comlink module is defined here.  The application uses the
314  *     function pointer members to access the functions available
315  *     in this module.
316  *******************************************************************/
317 struct _comlink_f comlink_f = {
318             Allocate,
319             Deallocate,
320             Initialize,
321             Drop
322 };
```

A call to the comlink_f.initialize() function will initialize the communication link. In initializing the link, a producer and a consumer comthread_t must be specified. The initialization function will then start the producer and the consumer as separate threads. The threads are created with the THR_SUSPEND flag specified to prevent the threads from executing. This flag is required to ensure that both the producer and the consumer threads are created without any error conditions. Upon success, the comlink_f.initialize() function will thr_continue() both the producer and the consumer threads. Otherwise, the threads are terminated and an error condition is returned.

Every producer and consumer are represented by comthread_t type data structures. The compoint member of this data structure holds the information used in creating the corresponding thread. The compoint module appears in Listing 6.7.

Listing 6.7   *compoint.c* -- The compoint module.

```
1 #include <stdio.h>
2 #include <synch.h>
3 #include <stdlib.h>
4 #include <thread.h>
5 #include <synch.h>
6 #include <string.h>
```

Listing 6.7 *continued.*

```
7   #include <errno.h>
8   #include "threadQcond.h"
9   #include "comlink.h"
10
11  static        compoint_t  *Allocate(void);
12  static        int          Deallocate(compoint_t *);
13
14  /****************************************************************
15   *      Allocate     FUNCTION
16   *
17   *      This function will allocate and initialize a communication
18   *      point type structure.
19   ****************************************************************/
20  static compoint_t *
21  Allocate(void)
22  {
23          compoint_t  *compoint;
24
25          compoint = malloc(sizeof(compoint_t));
26          if(compoint != NULL)
27                  memset(compoint,'\0',sizeof(compoint_t));
28          return(compoint);
29  }
30
31  /****************************************************************
32   *      Deallocate   FUNCTION
33   *
34   *      This function will deallocate the memory of a communication
35   *      point previously allocated.
36   ****************************************************************/
37  static int
38  Deallocate(compoint_t *compoint)
39  {
40          if( compoint == NULL )
41                  return(EINVAL);
42          free(compoint);
43          return(0);
44  }
45  /****************************************************************
46   *      The compoint module is defined here.  The members of the data
47   *      structure are the public functions available for the compoint
48   *      module.
49   ****************************************************************/
50  struct _compoint_f compoint_f = {
51                      Allocate,
52                      Deallocate
53  };
```

The message queue used in the communication between the producer and consumer is represented as a comqueue_t type data structure. The comqueue module, Listing 6.8, provides an allocate() and deallocate() function for this data structure type.

Listing 6.8   *comqueue.c* -- The comqueue module.

```
1   #include <stdio.h>
2   #include <synch.h>
3   #include <stdlib.h>
4   #include <thread.h>
5   #include <synch.h>
6   #include <string.h>
7   #include <errno.h>
8   #include "threadQcond.h"
9   #include "comlink.h"
10
11  static        comqueue_t   *Allocate(int);
12  static        int           Deallocate(comqueue_t *);
13
14  /*****************************************************************
15   *    Allocate     FUNCTION
16   *
17   *    This function will allocate and initialize a communication
18   *    queue type structure.
19   *****************************************************************/
20  static comqueue_t *
21  Allocate( int type )
22  {
23          comqueue_t   *comqueue;
24          qcond_t      *qcond;
25
26          qcond  = threadQcond_f.create();
27          comqueue = malloc(sizeof(comqueue_t));
28
29          if( ! comqueue || ! qcond ) {
30                  if( comqueue )    free(comqueue);
31                  if( qcond    )    threadQcond_f.destroy(qcond);
32                  return(NULL);
33          }
34
35          memset(comqueue,'\0',sizeof(comqueue_t));
36          comqueue->type  = type;
37          comqueue->queue = qcond;
38          return( comqueue );
39  }
```

Listing 6.8   *continued.*

```
40   /*****************************************************************
41    *      Deallocate   FUNCTION
42    *
43    *      This function will deallocate the resources associated with
44    *      the specified communication queue.
45    *****************************************************************/
46   static int
47   Deallocate( comqueue_t *comqueue)
48   {
49          if( ! comqueue )
50                  return(EINVAL);
51          threadQcond_f.destroy( comqueue->queue );
52          free( comqueue);
53          return(0);
54   }
55
56   struct _comqueue_f comqueue_f = {
57                  Allocate,
58                  Deallocate
59   };
```

The comthread module, Listing 6.9, also provides an allocate() and deallocate() function. This module also uses the threadMutex module from Chapter 5.

Listing 6.9   *comthread.c -- The* comthread *module.*

```
 1   #include <stdio.h>
 2   #include <synch.h>
 3   #include <stdlib.h>
 4   #include <thread.h>
 5   #include <synch.h>
 6   #include <string.h>
 7   #include <errno.h>
 8   #include "threadQcond.h"
 9   #include "threadMutex.h"
10   #include "comlink.h"
11
12   static       mutex_t       comthreadMutex = { 0 };
13   static       comthread_t *Allocate(const int);
14   static       int          Deallocate(comthread_t *);
15   /*****************************************************************
16    *      Allocate   FUNCTION
17    *
18    *      This function allocates the storage for a comthread_t type
19    *      data structure and initializes the structure's components.
20    *****************************************************************/
```

Listing 6.9   *continued*.

```
21   static comthread_t *
22   Allocate(const int type )
23   {
24          comthread_t  *comthread  = NULL;
25          compoint_t   *compoint   = NULL;
26          mutex_t       *mutex     = NULL;
27
28          if( type != PRODUCER && type != CONSUMER )
29                  return(NULL);
30
31          comthread    = malloc(sizeof(comthread_t));
32          compoint     = compoint_f.allocate();
33          mutex        = threadMutex_f.create();
34
35          if( ! comthread  || ! compoint || ! mutex ) {
36                  if( comthread )   free(comthread);
37                  if( compoint  ) compoint_f.deallocate(compoint);
38                  if( mutex     ) threadMutex_f.destroy(mutex);
39                  return(NULL);
40          }
41
42          memset(comthread,'\0',sizeof(comthread_t));
43          comthread->comstatus = IS_INITIALIZED;
44          comthread->type      = type;
45          comthread->compoint  = compoint;
46          comthread->mutex     = mutex;
47          return(comthread);
48   }
49
50   /*****************************************************************
51    *     Deallocate   FUNCTION
52    *
53    *     This function deallocates the storage for the specified
54    *     comthread_t type data structure.
55    *****************************************************************/
56
57
58   static int
59   Deallocate(comthread_t *comthread)
60   {
61          int errorCondition = 0;
62                  /***************************************************
63                   *     CRITICAL SECTION   START
64                   *
65                   *     We need to prevent multiple threads from calling
66                   *     this function concurrently with the same argument.
67                   ***************************************************/
```

Listing 6.9   *continued*.

```
68          mutex_lock( &comthreadMutex );
69          if( comthread == NULL || mutex_lock(comthread->mutex) )
70                  errorCondition = EINVAL;
71          mutex_unlock( &comthreadMutex );
72                  /*********************************************************
73                   *      CRITICAL SECTION   END
74                   *********************************************************/
75
76          if( ! errorCondition ) {
77                  if( comthread->comstatus & IS_BUSY ) {
78                          errorCondition = IS_BUSY;
79                          mutex_unlock( comthread->mutex );
80                  }
81                  else {
82                          comthread->comstatus = IS_DEACTIVE;
83                          compoint_f.deallocate( comthread->compoint );
84                          mutex_unlock(comthread->mutex);
85                          threadMutex_f.destroy(comthread->mutex);
86                          free(comthread);
87                  }
88          }
89          return(errorCondition);
90  }
91
92  struct _comthread_f comthread_f = {
93                  Allocate,
94                  Deallocate
95  };
```

Listing 6.10 provides an example of using the comlink. A writerThread (*producer*) and a readerThread (*consumer*) represent the communication link points. The main function allocates the comlink, and subsequently allocates a separate comthread for the producer and the consumer. It then calls the comlink_f.initialize() function to establish the communications link between the producer and consumer.

Compile comtest program:

```
cc -D_REENTRANT comlink.o compoint.o comqueue.o comtest.o \
        comthread.o ${INSTALLROOT} /lib/libtsync.a -lthread -ldl
        -o comtest
```

Listing 6.10   *comtest.c* -- A sample code fragment using the `comlink` module.

```
 1   #include <stdio.h>
 2   #include <synch.h>
 3   #include <stdlib.h>
 4   #include <thread.h>
 5   #include <synch.h>
 6   #include <string.h>
 7   #include <errno.h>
 8   #include "threadQcond.h"
 9   #include "comlink.h"
10
11   static char *HelloMessage = "Hello, World";
12   static char *FromMessage  = "From Writer";
13
14   /****************************************************************
15    *      writerThread        THREAD
16    *
17    *      This thread is the writer side of a communication queue.  The
18    *      thread will push several messages onto the queue, and will
19    *      then terminate.
20    ****************************************************************/
21   void *
22   writerThread(void *arg)
23   {
24           comqueue_t   *comqueue;
25           int           index=0;
26
27           comqueue = arg;
28           threadQcond_f.qpush( comqueue->queue, HelloMessage);
29           threadQcond_f.qpush( comqueue->queue, FromMessage);
30           thr_exit((void *)0);
31   }
32
33   /****************************************************************
34    *      readerThread        THREAD
35    *
36    *      This thread will read two messages from the specified
37    *      communication queue and then write these messages to standard
38    *      output.
39    ****************************************************************/
40   void *
41   readerThread(void *arg)
42   {
43           comqueue_t   *comqueue   = NULL;
44           char         *cp         = NULL;
45           comqueue = arg;
46           cp = threadQcond_f.qpop( comqueue->queue);
```

Listing 6.10 *continued.*

```
47            if( cp )
48                    fprintf(stdout,"Reader: POPPED: %s\n", cp);
49            cp = threadQcond_f.qpop( comqueue->queue);
50            if( cp )
51                    fprintf(stdout,"Reader: POPPED: %s\n", cp);
52            thr_exit((void *)0);
53    }
54
55    /****************************************************************
56     *    MAIN   FUNCTION
57     *
58     *    This is an example main() program using the thread
59     *    communication link module for connecting a reader and a writer
60     *    thread.
61     ****************************************************************/
62    void *
63    main(void)
64    {
65            comlink_t    *comlink = NULL;
66            comlink = comlink_f.allocate( 1 );
67            if( comlink == NULL ) {
68                    fprintf(stderr,"Error. can't allocate a comlink\n");
69                    thr_exit((void *)1);
70            }
71
72            comlink->consumer->compoint->stackAddress = NULL;
73            comlink->consumer->compoint->stackSize     = 0;
74            comlink->consumer->compoint->startRoutine= readerThread;
75            comlink->consumer->compoint->flags    = 0;
76            comlink->producer->compoint->stackAddress= NULL;
77            comlink->producer->compoint->stackSize     = 0;
78            comlink->producer->compoint->startRoutine = writerThread;
79            comlink->producer->compoint->flags    = 0;
80            comlink_f.initialize( comlink );
81            thr_exit((void *)0);
82    }
83
```

7

Semaphores

7.1 Semaphores: An Overview

A semaphore, originally described by [Dijk65], is a general-purpose synchronization primitive that has been widely used in application programming for some time. A semaphore protects one or more resources shared between UNIX processes executing in disjoint address spaces, or between sibling threads of a single UNIX process. This primitive provides additional flexibility over the mutex primitive, which permits only one thread to use a resource at a time.

In its simplest form, there are two atomic operations applied to semaphores: lock [*generically called the* semaphore P() *operation*] and unlock [*known as the* semaphore V() *operation*]. These operations are considered atomic in that if the semaphore is currently unavailable, the requesting thread will wait until the operation completes.

A semaphore protecting a single resource is called a *binary* semaphore. The use of a binary semaphore provides the same functionality as the mutex synchronization primitive, but is more expensive in terms of overhead. It is therefore better to use the mutex primitive instead of the binary semaphore to protect a single resource.

A *counting* semaphore protects more than one resource. The number of protected resources must be established prior to using the semaphore. A thread requesting a resource will block when the semaphore count is zero.

The use of a counting semaphore is similar to how a rental company with a predefined number of widgets rents them. In this example, the widget is considered the resource. A consumer can rent the widget provided that there is at least one in the current inventory. Otherwise, the consumer must wait for one to be made available. The consumer would therefore block (*sleep*) until a resource is available.

As with the other synchronization primitives, it is possible for a multithreaded application to deadlock when using semaphores inappropriately. Consider, for example, a binary semaphore that is currently locked by a thread. When the thread attempts to acquire the semaphore again, a deadlock results, since it cannot acquire a binary semaphore that it already has locked. Similar problems can occur when using semaphores between two or more UNIX processes executing in disjoint address spaces.

Table 7.1   The Semaphore API

sema_init()	Initialize a semaphore
sema_wait()	Block until semaphore acquired
sema_trywait()	Try one time to acquire a semaphore
sema_post()	Release a semaphore
sema_destroy()	Invalidate a semaphore

7.2 Initializing the Semaphore

The storage for a sema_t type data structure can be statically or dynamically allocated. The sema_init function initializes the specified semaphore to a known state. The number of resources to be protected by the semaphore must be specified. The number of resources must be a value greater than or equal to zero.

A binary semaphore has a resource count of one, while a general counting semaphore has a larger resource count. The sema_init function (*Figure 7.1*) also requires the application to specify the semaphore type, which must be either USYNC_PROCESS or USYNC_THREAD. A USYNC_PROCESS type semaphore cannot protect resources shared between sibling threads of a single UNIX process. Similarly, a USYNC_THREAD type semaphore cannot protect resources shared between two UNIX processes executing in disjoint address spaces.

The sema_init function will return an EBUSY error indication value if one or more threads are currently referencing the semaphore being initialized. If the application program zero fills the sema_t type data structure while it is currently in use, then its state is overwritten. This action may result in a deadlock or other unpredictable side effects.

A statically initialized semaphore is interpreted as a USYNC_THREAD type semaphore and can be used only between sibling threads of a single UNIX process. The sema_count is set to zero and there are no available resources for this semaphore.

```
NAME:
        sema_init() - Initialize semaphore.

SYNOPSIS:
        #include <synch.h>

        int
        sema_init( sema_t *sema, int sema_count, int type,
                void *arg)
```

Figure 7.1   `sema_init()` synopsis. [1]

The semaphore functions are not reentrant. If a thread currently has the semaphore locked and calls the `sema_wait` function, it will remain blocked indefinitely. The `deadlock` will continue until the thread or the application terminates.

7.3 Acquiring the Semaphore

The `sema_wait` function (*Figure 7.2*) performs the semaphore lock operation, regardless of whether the semaphore is to protect resources shared between UNIX processes executing in disjoint address spaces, or to protect resources shared between sibling threads of a single UNIX process.

```
NAME:
        sema_wait - Acquire a semaphore.

SYNOPSIS:
        #include <synch.h>

        int sema_wait(sema_t *sema)
```

Figure 7.2   `sema_wait()` synopsis. [1]

The `sema_wait` function is implemented as a blocking semaphore acquisition function. When an application attempts to acquire a semaphore through the `sema_wait` function, the requesting thread or UNIX process will remain blocked until it can successfully lock the semaphore. An alternative method for acquiring the semaphore is provided through the `sema_trywait` function. The `sema_trywait` function (*Figure 7.3*) will return an EBUSY error indication value if the semaphore is unavailable.

NAME:

       `sema_trywait` -Try once to acquire a semaphore.

SYNOPSIS:

```
#include <synch.h>

int sema_trywait(sema_t *sema)
```

Figure 7.3   `sema_trywait()` synopsis. [1]

7.4 Unlocking the Semaphore

When an application requires the use of a resource protected by a semaphore, the application must first lock the semaphore by calling the `sema_wait` function. Once locked, the application can use the resource in a controlled, synchronized fashion. After the processing of the resource has completed, the application must unlock the semaphore by calling the `sema_post` function (*Figure 7.4*).

NAME:

       `sema_post` - Unlock a semaphore.

SYNOPSIS:

```
#include <synch.h>

int sema_post( sema_t *sema )
```

Figure 7.4   `sema_post()` synopsis. [1]

PROGRAMMER'S NOTE:

In selecting a thread to release from the synchronization object, bound threads are given priority over multiplexed threads.

7.5 Invalidating the Semaphore

The `sema_destroy` function (*Figure 7.5*) will invalidate a semaphore no longer required by the application. The function will validate the semaphore as either a `USYNC_PROCESS` or `USYNC_THREAD` type semaphore. Otherwise, the `sema_destroy` function will return an `EINVAL` error indication value.

NAME:
        `sema_destroy` - Invalidate a semaphore.

SYNOPSIS:
```
#include <synch.h>

int
sema_destroy( sema_t *sema )
```

Figure 7.5   `sema_destroy()` synopsis. [1]

The `sema_destroy` function will lock the semaphore's mutex and invalidate the semaphore's condition variable. If this condition variable cannot be invalidated, the `sema_destroy` function will return an `EBUSY` error indication value to the calling thread.

After invalidating the condition variable, the `sema_destroy` function invalidates the semaphore's type field. It then enters a loop, attempting to invalidate the mutex lock used to implement the semaphore. The `sema_destroy` function will not return until the mutex has been invalidated.

The `sema_destroy` function does not release the memory allocated for the `sema_t` type data structure. It will invalidate only the existing data structure. The memory for a dynamically allocated `sema_t` type data structure must be released by the application after the `sema_destroy` has successfully returned.

7.6 Using Semaphores

The threadSema Module

The `threadSema` module (*Listings 7.1 and 7.2*) provides the necessary functionality to administer dynamically allocated `USYNC_THREAD` type semaphores. The `threadSema_t` type definition (*Listing 7.1*) describes the functions available through this module. The `threadSema.c` source file (*Listing 7.2*) shows the `Create` function. This function accepts as a parameter the number

---

[1] Printed with Permission of UNIX Systems Laboratories, Inc. All Rights Reserved.

of resources to be protected with the dynamically allocated semaphore. The semaphore storage is allocated and initialized, and the address of this storage is returned to the calling thread. If an error condition occurs, the error will be recorded with the `threadLog` module.

Listing 7.1   *threadSema.h* -- The `threadSema` module header file.

```
1   typedef struct _threadSema_f     {
2           sema_t  *(*create)(int);
3           int      (*destory)(sema_t *);
4   } threadSema_t;
5
6   extern threadSema_t threadSema_f;
```

Compile threadSema module:
```
        cc -D_REENTRANT -c -I${INSTALLROOT}hdr threadSema.c
        ar rv ${INSTALLROOT}lib/libtsync.a threadSema.o
```

Listing 7.2   *threadSema.c* -- The `threadSema` module.

```
1   #include <malloc.h>
2   #include <memory.h>
3   #include <synch.h>
4   #include <thread.h>
5   #include <errno.h>
6   #include "mthreadLog.h"
7   #include "threadSema.h"
8
9   /***************************************************************
10   *     Function Prototypes
11   ***************************************************************/
12  static      int           Destroy(sema_t *);
13  static      sema_t        *Create(const int);
14
15  /***************************************************************
16   *     Create        FUNCTION
17   *
18   *     The create function will allocate a semaphore and initialize
19   *     the semaphore with the specified resource count.
20   ***************************************************************/
```

Listing 7.2 *continued.*

```
21   static sema_t *
22   Create(const int resources)
23   {
24              sema_t *semaPtr          = NULL;
25       int     errorCondition  = 0;
26
27       semaPtr = (sema_t *) malloc(sizeof(sema_t));
28       if( semaPtr == NULL )
29            threadLog_f.setError(ENOMEM);
30       else {
31            memset((void *)semaPtr,'\0',sizeof(semaPtr));
32            errorCondition = sema_init( semaPtr, resources,
33                            USYNC_THREAD, NULL);
34            if ( errorCondition ) {
35                free((void *) semaPtr );
36                semaPtr = NULL;
37                threadLog_f.setError( errorCondition );
38            }
39       }
40       .return(semaPtr);
41   }
42
43   /**************************************************************
44    *    Destroy              FUNCTION
45    *
46    *    The destroy function deallocates a Semaphore.
47    **************************************************************/
48   static int
49   Destroy( sema_t *semaPtr)
50   {
51       int     errorCondition = 0;
52
53       errorCondition = sema_destroy(semaPtr);
54       if( errorCondition )
55            threadLog_f.setError( errorCondition );
56       else
57            free((void *)semaPtr);
58       return( errorCondition );
59   }
60
61   /**************************************************************
62    *    Define the threadSema module interface
63    **************************************************************/
64   threadSema_t  threadSema_f = {
65       Create,
66       Destroy,
67   };
```

The processSema Module

The processSema module (*Listings 7.3 and 7.4*) is a general utility to allocate and initialize sema_t type structures for use between UNIX processes executing in disjoint address spaces. The processSema_t type definition describes the functions available through this module.

The processSema_t type definition in the processSema header file describes the functions available through this module. The psema_t type definition describes the memory mapped area, currently including only the type sema_t member. The size of the memory mapped region is represented by the SEMA_MAP_SIZE macro. The processSema_f variable is set in the processSema module.

Listing 7.3   *processSema.h* -- The processSema module header file.

```
1   typedef struct _processSema_t {
2          int              (*setMax)(const int);
3          sema_t         *(*create)(const int, const int);
4          int              (*destroy)(const int);
5          sema_t         *(*locate)(const int);
6   } processSema_t;
7
8   typedef struct _psema_t {
9          sema_t              sema;
10  } psema_t;
11
12  #define SEMA_MAP_SIZE    (sizeof(psema_t) * maxProcSemas)
13  #define TRUE             1
14  #define FALSE            0
15  #define MAX_PROCESS_SEMAS      100
16
17  extern processSema_t      processSema_f;
```

The processSema.c source file (*Listing 7.4*) provides the functions available through this module. These functions are declared as static and thus their scope is limited to the source file. To use these functions, the application must include the processSema.h header file and access the members of the processSema_f data structure. These members are pointers to the appropriate functions.

The processSema_f.setMax function permits the application to change the maximum number of semaphores available in the memory mapped area from the default of MAX_PROCESS_SEMAS. If the memory mapped area is currently in use by the application, then the size of the map cannot be changed and an EAGAIN error condition is returned.

The processSema_f.create function accepts two parameters: the count describing the number of resources protected by this semaphore, and an index into the memory mapped area. An invalid index will result in an EINVAL error indication being returned to the calling thread. The threadLog_f.setError function is called to record the error condition.

The `processSema_f.destroy` function will destroy a semaphore no longer required by the application. The function returns a zero status upon success, or an appropriate error indication value.

The `processSema_f.locate` function is used to locate an indexed semaphore in the memory mapped area. Only one `UNIX` process should create the semaphores while subsequent processes simply access the appropriate semaphores.

Listing 7.4   *processSema.c* -- The `processSema` module.

```
 1  #include <fcntl.h>
 2  #include <synch.h>
 3  #include <thread.h>
 4  #include <errno.h>
 5  #include <memory.h>
 6  #include <unistd.h>
 7  #include <stdlib.h>
 8  #include <sys/ipc.h>
 9  #include <sys/shm.h>
10  #include <sys/mman.h>
11  #include "processSema.h"
12  #include "mthreadLog.h"
13
14  static   int       maxProcSemas      = MAX_PROCESS_SEMAS;
15  static   mutex_t    processMutex     = {0 };
16  static   psema_t   *procSemas        = NULL;
17  static   int        semafd           = -1;
18
19  /*****************************************************************
20   *     Function Prototypes
21   *****************************************************************/
22  static       int           Destroy(const int);
23  static       int           SetMax(const int);
24  static       sema_t       *Create(const int, const int);
25  static       sema_t       *Locate(const int);
26  static       int           accessMap(const char *,const int);
27
28  /*****************************************************************
29   *     SetMax      FUNCTION
30   *
31   *     This function sets the maximum number of USYNC_PROCESS type
32   *     semaphores that will be used by the cooperating processes.
33   *     We must prevent concurrent access to the semafd and
34   *     maxProcSemas variables to prevent two threads from modifying
35   *     their values.
36   *****************************************************************/
```

Listing 7.4 *continued.*

```
37   static int
38   SetMax(const int number )
39   {
40          int    errorCondition = 0;
41          mutex_lock( &processMutex );
42
43          if( semafd == -1 )
44                  maxProcSemas = number;
45          else
46                  errorCondition = EAGAIN;
47
48          mutex_unlock( &processMutex );
49          return(errorCondition);
50   }
51
52   /****************************************************************
53    *     Create       FUNCTION
54    *
55    *     The create function will initialize a process type semaphore
56    *     with the resources count specified.  The semaphore to
57    *     initialize is located at the specified index.
58    ***************************************************************/
59   static sema_t *
60   Create( const int resources, const int index )
61   {
62          sema_t *semaPtr         = NULL;
63          int     errorCondition  = FALSE;
64
65                         /***************************************
66                          *   CRITICAL SECTION START
67                          *
68                          *   We must prevent concurrent access here
69                          *   or multiple threads will call the
70                          *   accessMap function concurrently.  The
71                          *   integrity of the access map would not
72                          *   be ensured.
73                          ***************************************/
74          mutex_lock( &processMutex );
75
76          if( index > maxProcSemas)
77                  errorCondition = EINVAL;
78
79          else   {
80                  if( semafd == -1 )
81                  errorCondition=accessMap("sema.map",O_CREAT|O_RDWR|
82                                                        O_TRUNC);
83
```

Listing 7.4   *continued*.

```
84                  if( ! errorCondition ) {
85                      semaPtr=&(procSemas[index].sema);
86                      errorCondition=sema_init(semaPtr,resources,
87                                           USYNC_PROCESS, NULL);
88                  }
89              }
90                      /****************************************
91                       *  CRITICAL SECTION END
92                       ****************************************/
93          mutex_unlock( &processMutex );
94
95          if ( errorCondition ) {
96              semaPtr = NULL;
97              threadLog_f.setError( errorCondition );
98          }
99          return(semaPtr);
100     }
101     /******************************************************************
102      *    Destroy      FUNCTION
103      *
104      *    The destroy function will invalidate the semaphore located
105      *    at the specified index.
106      ******************************************************************/
107     static int
108     Destroy( const int index )
109     {
110          int     errorCondition  = 0;
111          sema_t *semaPtr         = NULL;
112                      /****************************************
113                       * If two threads attempt to destroy the same
114                       * semaphore concurrently, the sema_destroy
115                       * function will permit one to succeed, and the
116                       * other will get an error condition. Therefore,
117                       * this is not a critical section.
118                       ****************************************/
119          if( index > maxProcSemas )
120              errorCondition = EINVAL;
121          else  {
122              semaPtr = &(procSemas[index].sema);
123              errorCondition = sema_destroy(semaPtr);
124          }
125          if( errorCondition )
126              threadLog_f.setError( errorCondition );
127          return( errorCondition );
128     }
```

Listing 7.4 *continued*.

```
129   /*****************************************************************
130    *      Locate        FUNCTION
131    *
132    *    One process will create the map, the other process will use
133    *    locate.  The locate function will access the semaphore map,
134    *    and locate the semaphore at the specified index.
135    *****************************************************************/
136   static sema_t *
137   Locate( const int index )
138   {
139         sema_t        *semaPtr      = NULL;
140         int     errorCondition = FALSE;
141                        /***************************************
142                         *   CRITICAL SECTION       START
143                         *
144                         *   we must prevent concurrent calls to
145                         *   accessMap to ensure the integrity of
146                         *   the map.
147                         ***************************************/
148         mutex_lock( &processMutex );
149
150         if( index > maxProcSemas )
151               errorCondition = EINVAL;
152         else  {
153               if( semafd == -1 )
154                   errorCondition=accessMap("sema.map",O_CREAT|O_RDWR);
155
156               if( ! errorCondition )
157                     semaPtr = &(procSemas[index].sema);
158         }
159                        /***************************************
160                         *   CRITICAL SECTION       END
161                         ***************************************/
162         mutex_unlock( &processMutex );
163         if( errorCondition ) {
164               threadLog_f.setError(errorCondition);
165               semaPtr = NULL;
166         }
167         return(semaPtr);
168   }
169
170   /*****************************************************************
171    *    Define the processSema_f interface.
172    *****************************************************************/
173   processSema_t       processSema_f = {
174               SetMax,
175               Create,
176               Destroy,
177               Locate
178   };
```

Listing 7.4 *continued.*

```
179     /***********************************************************************
180      *      accessMap    FUNCTION
181      *
182      *      This function is local to the processSema module.
183      *      The accessMap function will access the specified file and
184      *      memory map its content.  If the mode parameter includes the
185      *      O_TRUNC bit, then the file will be created and initialized
186      *      to zero values.  Otherwise, the file is simply opened.
187      ***********************************************************************/
188     static int
189     accessMap(const char *fname,const int mode)
190     {
191             int    errorCondition = 0;
192             char   *cp;
193
194             if( mode & O_TRUNC ) {
195                     semafd = creat(fname,S_IRUSR|S_IWUSR);
196
197                     if(semafd != -1 ) {
198                             close(semafd);
199                             semafd = open(fname,mode);
200                             if(( cp = malloc(SEMA_MAP_SIZE)) == NULL )
201                                     errorCondition = ENOMEM;
202                             else  {
203                                     memset(cp,'\0',SEMA_MAP_SIZE);
204                                     write(semafd,cp,SEMA_MAP_SIZE);
205                                     free(cp);
206                                     lseek(semafd,0L,0);
207                             }
208                     }
209                     else
210                             errorCondition = errno;
211             }
212             else if( (semafd = open(fname,mode))  == -1 )
213                     errorCondition = errno;
214             if( ! errorCondition ) {
215                     procSemas = (psema_t *)mmap(0,SEMA_MAP_SIZE,
216                         PROT_READ|PROT_WRITE,MAP_SHARED,semafd,0);
217                     if( (char *)procSemas == (caddr_t)-1)
218                             errorCondition = errno;
219             }
220             close(semafd);
221             semafd = 0;
222             return(errorCondition);
223     }
```

The `psleeper` and `pwaiter` programs in Listings 7.5 and 7.6 provide an example of using the `processSema` module. The `psleeper` program initializes a semaphore at index number 5 for use between the two processes. It acquires the semaphore and then calls `sleep` to wait for 30 seconds. After the 30 expires, `psleeper` will call the `sema_post` function to release the semaphore.

When the `psleeper` program enters the sleep state, execute the `pwaiter` program. The `pwaiter`program calls the `processSema_f.locate` function, which returns a pointer to the semaphore at index number 5. It can then call the `sema_wait` function to wait for the semaphore to become available.

Listing 7.5   *psleeper.c* -- Example program creating `processSema` semaphores.

```
1    #include <synch.h>
2    #include <thread.h>
3    #include "processSema.h"
4
5    /****************************************************************
6     *      Psleeper      PROGRAM
7     *
8     *      This example creates a set of process type semaphores.  It
9     *      will acquire the semaphore at index 5, and then go to sleep
10    *      for 30 seconds.  While this program is executing the sleep,
11    *      you  should  execute  program  pwaiter  to  see  the  behavior.
12    ****************************************************************/
13   int
14   main(void)
15   {
16           int      errorCondition = 0;
17           sema_t        *semaPtr     = NULL;
18                         /***************************************
19                          * We first identify the maximum number
20                          * of USYNC_PROCESS type semaphores.
21                          ***************************************/
22           processSema_f.setMax(10);
23                         /***************************************
24                          *  We need to establish the semaphore at
25                          *  index 5 to have one resource.
26                          ***************************************/
27           semaPtr = processSema_f.create(1, 5 );
28           if( semaPtr == NULL ) {
29                   fprintf(stderr,"psemaTest failed to create sema[5]\n");
30                   thr_exit(0);
31           }
32                         /***************************************
33                          *  We can now acquire the semaphore.
34                          ***************************************/
```

Listing 7.5   *continued.*

```
35          fprintf(stderr,"psemaTest is now acquiring the sema\n");
36          errorCondition = sema_wait( semaPtr );
37          if( errorCondition )
38                  fprintf(stderr,"psemaTest could not lock sema [5]\n");
39          else  {
40                      /******************************************
41                       *  Now that we have the semaphore, we will go
42                       *  to sleep for 30 seconds. This delay permits
43                       *  us to run the pwaiter example.
44                       ******************************************/
45                  fprintf(stderr,"semaphore has been acquired\n");
46                  fprintf(stderr,"now going to sleep for 30 seconds\n");
47                  sleep(30);
48                      /******************************************
49                       *  We are now awake and can release the
50                       *  semaphore. This will permit the pwaiter
51                       *  example to acquire the semaphore.
52                       ******************************************/
53
54                      fprintf(stderr,"now releasing the semaphore\n");
55                  sema_post( semaPtr );
56                  fprintf(stderr,"semaphore has been released\n");
57          }
58          thr_exit(0);
59  }
```

Listing 7.6   *pwaiter.c -- Example program using* processSema *semaphores.*

```
1   #include <synch.h>
2   #include <thread.h>
3   #include "processSema.h"
4
5   /*********************************************************************
6    *      Pwaiter      PROGRAM
7    *
8    *      This example will locate the process type semaphore at index
9    *      5 and will wait to acquire the semaphore.  See Psleeper
10   *      program for semaphore creation.
11   *********************************************************************/
12  int
13  main(void)
14  {
15          int             errorCondition = 0;
16          sema_t          *semaPtr       = NULL;
```

Listing 7.6 *continued.*

```
17                        /******************************************
18                         *   we begin by locating the semaphore at index 5.
19
20                         *   The semaphore was created by psleeper example.
21                         ******************************************/
22        semaPtr = processSema_f.locate(5 );
23        if( semaPtr == NULL ) {
24              fprintf(stderr,"pSema failed to locate semaphore\n");
25              thr_exit(0);
26        }
27                        /******************************************
28                         *   now that we have located the semaphore we can
29                         *   request the lock.
30                         ******************************************/
31        fprintf(stderr,"psemaTest is now acquiring the sema\n");
32        errorCondition = sema_wait( semaPtr );
33
34        if( errorCondition )
35              fprintf(stderr,"psemaTest could not lock sema [5]\n");
36        else   {
37              fprintf(stderr,"semaphore has been acquired\n");
38              sema_post( semaPtr );
39              fprintf(stderr,"semaphore has been released\n");
40        }
41        thr_exit(0);
42  }
```

Protecting Client Shells with Semaphores

Multithreading is especially useful for client-server programs. An application program can create separate threads to service each client's request. Program sclient in Listings 7.7 through 7.9 provides an example of this technique. The program executes the command-line arguments as child processes using the popen[31] function call.

The popen function will create a pipe to a shell executing as a child process. The arguments to the popen function are the command string to execute in the child shell process, and a flag indicating if the returned file pointer is connected to the standard input of the child shell process, or the standard output. For our purposes, the popen will use the r flag to indicate that the sclient will read the standard output of the client shell process (*see Figure 7.6*).

---

[31] The Solaris 2.4 manual pages indicate that popen() is not MT-Safe. A future release may support a multithreaded safe version of the popen call.

The `sclient` program uses the semaphore synchronization primitive to control the number of concurrent child shell processes that will be created with the `popen` call. This will prevent the `sclient` program from exceeding the system-imposed limit on the number of open file pointers per process.

Another challenge in designing the `sclient` program is that all sibling threads will share the same file descriptors. The `clientshell` thread will read the output of its client shell process. Sibling threads could write this data to the standard output of the `sclient` program. The problem is then to synchronize the use of the standard output descriptor. Otherwise, the data from one thread would be interspersed with data from a sibling. Applying a mutex would not be efficient for those cases where the child shell process produces more than one buffer of output. The `clientshell` thread would need to lock the `mutex`, read all of the child shell process output from the file pointer, and write this data to standard output prior to unlocking the `mutex`. A simpler method to solve this problem is to use the `copybuffers` function (*see Listing 7.9, lines 117—148*).

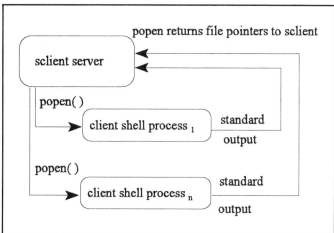

Figure 7.6   The `sclient` program creates child shell
                   processes to execute the command strings.

For each command-line argument, the `main` function will allocate a `client_t` structure (*see Listing 7.8*) and will point the `command` member to the current command-line argument. A thread is then created with a pointer to the `client_t` structure, and will begin execution at the `clientshell` function. The allocated `client_t` structure is added to a linked list of `client_t` structures.

The `clientshell` thread validates the `client_t` argument and will call the `sema_wait` function to wait for an available semaphore. When the semaphore is acquired, the `clientshell` will call the `popen` function to execute the specified command. The `clientshell` thread will buffer the output of the child shell process. When the child process terminates, the `clientshell` thread will call the `thr_exit` function with a pointer to the buffered output.

After the main program creates all of the necessary `clientshell` threads, it will enter a loop to wait on their termination status. When a sibling thread terminates, the `main` function will find its associated `client_t` structure and will examine the exit status for the thread. If a `non-NULL` value is returned, then the main function will write the contents of the status to the standard output.

```
Compile sclient program:
        cc -c -I${INSTALLROOT}hdr cshell.c
        cc -c -I${INSTALLROOT}hdr sclientshell.c
        cc cshell.o sclientshell.o ${INSTALLROOT}lib/libtsync.a \
            -lthread -o sclient
```

Listing 7.7   *sclientshell.h* -- The client shell header file.

```
1  typedef struct     _client     {
2        thread_t     tid;
3        char         *command;
4        struct       _client     *next;
5  } client_t;
6
7  typedef struct     _clientList {
8        struct       _client     *head;
9        struct       _client     *tail;
10 } clientList_t;
11
12 void * clientshell(void * );
13 char * copybuffer(char *,char *,int, int);
14 int    clientshellinit(int);
```

Listing 7.8   *cshell.c* -- The client shell utility.

```
1  #include <thread.h>
2  #include <stdio.h>
3  #include <unistd.h>
4  #include <malloc.h>
5  #include <errno.h>
6  #include <sys/types.h>
7  #include "clientshell.h"
```

Listing 7.8   *continued.*

```
8    /*****************************************************************
9    *      main    PROGRAM
10   *
11   *      sclient program accepts zero or more command line arguments
12   *      and will execute each arguments as a client subshell thread.
13   *      The output of each subshell is buffered to ensure all output
14   *      from the subshell is printed together.
15   ****************************************************************/
16   void *
17   main(int argc, char **argv)
18   {
19          clientList_t       clientList;
20          client_t           **clientPtr;
21          int                index;
22          int                errorCondition;
23          thread_t           departedTid;
24
25          void               *status;
26
27          clientPtr  = &(clientList.head);
28                  /******************************************************
29                  *   We start by initializing the clientshell semaphore
30                  *   to permit only 3 concurrent subshell threads.
31                  ******************************************************/
32          if( clientshellinit(3) != 0 ) {
33              perror("cshell: can't initialize subshell\n");
34              exit(0);
35          }
36                  /******************************************************
37                  *   For each command-line argument, we create a
38                  *   client_t type structure and initialize it to
39                  *   the command-line arg.  The client_t structure
40                  *   is added to our clientList structure.
41                  ******************************************************/
42          for( index=0; index < (argc -1 ); ++index ) {
43              *clientPtr              = malloc(sizeof(client_t));
44              (*clientPtr)->command = argv[index+1];
45              errorCondition=thr_create(NULL, 0, clientshell,
46                          *clientPtr,0, &(*clientPtr)->tid);
47
48              if( errorCondition )  {
49                  perror("cshell");
50                  exit(0);
51              }
52              clientPtr  = &(*clientPtr)->next;
53          }
```

Listing 7.8 *continued.*

```
54                    /*******************************************************
55                     *   Now that all of the threads have been created,
56                     *   we call thr_join to synchronize with them.  The
57                     *   status value returned by thr_join will point to
58                     *   the buffered output of the client shell.
59                     *******************************************************/
60          while((errorCondition=thr_join(0,&departedTid,&status))==0) {
61               clientPtr  = &(clientList.head);
62
63               while( *clientPtr && (*clientPtr)->tid != departedTid )
64                    clientPtr = &(*clientPtr)->next;
65               if( *clientPtr && status != NULL ) {
66                    fprintf(stdout,"%s\n", (char *) status);
67                    free(status);
68               }
69          }
70
71          if( errorCondition != EINVAL )
72               perror("sclient");
73
74          thr_exit((void *)0);
75     }
```

Listing 7.9 *sclientshell.c -- The client shell auxiliary functions.*

```
1   #include <unistd.h>
2   #include <stdlib.h>
3   #include <thread.h>
4   #include <errno.h>
5   #include <memory.h>
6   #include <synch.h>
7   #include "threadSema.h"
8   #include "clientshell.h"
9   #include "mthreadLog.h"
10
11  static sema_t       *clientSemaphore = NULL;
12
13  /*********************************************************************
14   *      clientshell THREAD
15   *
16   *      The clienthsell() function is called as a thread from the
17   *      initial application thread.  The parameter arg points to a
18   *      client_t type data structure.
19   *********************************************************************/
```

Listing 7.9 *continued.*

```
20   void *
21   clientshell( void *arg )
22   {
23        client_t      *client              = NULL;
24        FILE          *fileStream          = NULL;
25        char          *input               = NULL;
26        char          *output              = NULL;
27        int            errorCondition      = 0;
28        int            iterations          = 0;
29
30        client = (client_t *) arg;
31                      /*********************************************
32                       *   If there is no command to execute, then
33                       *   complain and exit this thread.
34                       *********************************************/
35        if( client->command == NULL ) {
36             threadLog_f.message("clientShell: command is NULL");
37             thr_exit(NULL);
38        }
39                      /*************************************************
40                       *   If the clientshellinit() function was not
41                       *   called, then complain and exit this thread.
42                       *************************************************/
43        if( clientSemaphore == NULL ) {
44             threadLog_f.message("subshells not initialized.");
45             thr_exit(NULL);
46        }
47                      /*************************************************
48                       *   We create a buffer for the shell output.  If
49                       *   this fails, then we complain and exit the
50                       *   thread.
51                       *************************************************/
52        input = malloc( BUFSIZ );
53        if( input == NULL ) {
54             errorCondition = ENOMEM;
55             threadLog_f.message("clientshell: out of memory");
56             thr_exit(NULL);
57        }
58        memset(input,'\0',BUFSIZ);
59                      /*************************************************
60                       *   Wait for an available subshell.  The maximum
61                       *   number of subshells is determined by the
62                       *   clientSemaphore value.
63                       *************************************************/
64        if( sema_wait( clientSemaphore ) != 0 ) {
65             threadLog_f.message("can't get a subshell");
66             thr_exit(NULL);
```

Listing 7.9 *continued.*

```
67              }
68
69                         /***************************************************
70                          *   Now that we hold a semaphore, we can create
71                          *   the client subshell through a popen call.
72                          ***************************************************/
73          fileStream = popen( client->command, "r");
74          if( fileStream == NULL ) {
75              threadLog_f.message("Cannot create subshell");
76              sema_post(clientSemaphore);
77
78              thr_exit(NULL);
79          }
80                         /***************************************************
81                          *   Every time we read BUFSIZ bytes from the input
82                          *   filestream, we call copybuffer to readjust the
83                          *   size of the buffer holding the output.
84                          ***************************************************/
85          iterations = 0;
86          while(fread(input,BUFSIZ,1,fileStream)!=0 && errorCondition==
87      0){
88              output=copybuffer(output,input,iterations,BUFSIZ);
89              if( output == NULL ) {
90                  errorCondition = threadLog_f.getError();
91                  break;
92              }
93              ++iterations;
94          }
95
96                         /***************************************************
97                          *   the last fread will return a nonzero error
98                          *   code on end of file.  We need to check the
99                          *   fileStream to ensure we get the last output
100                         *   buffer.
101                         ***************************************************/
102         if( ! errorCondition && feof(fileStream) ) {
103             output = copybuffer(output,input,iterations,BUFSIZ);
104             if( output == NULL )
105                 errorCondition = threadLog_f.getError();
106         }
107                        /***************************************************
108                         *   We can now close the filestream and perform
109                         *   other cleanup operations.
110                         ***************************************************/
111         pclose(fileStream);
112         if( input )
113             free(input);
```

Listing 7.9 *continued.*

```
114
115            if( output == NULL || threadLog_f.hasError() )
116                    threadLog_f.message("[%s] failed",client->command);
117            sema_post( clientSemaphore );
118            thr_exit(output);
119    }
120
121    /*******************************************************************
122     *      copybuffer   FUNCTION
123     *
124     *      This function accumulates the buffered output from the client
125     *      shell into a single buffer.  If a client shell produces more
126     *      than BUFSIZ output, we need to accumulate the total output
127     *      into a single buffer.
128     *              bufferPtr   points to the accumulated output
129     *              cptr        points to the new output to append
130     *              count       is the number of BUFSIZ buffers currently
131     *                          accumulated in bufferPtr
132     *              size        is the size of the output to be append
133     *******************************************************************/
134    char *
135    copybuffer( char *bufferPtr, char *cptr, int count, int size)
136    {
137            char   *newbuffer;
138            newbuffer = (char *)malloc( (count +1) * size);
139            if( newbuffer == NULL)   {
140                    threadLog_f.setError( ENOMEM);
141                    return(NULL);
142            }
143            memset(newbuffer,'\0',(count+1)*size);
144            if( count )
145                    memcpy(newbuffer, bufferPtr, (count +1) * size);
146            memcpy(newbuffer + ( count * size), cptr, size);
147            if( bufferPtr )
148                    free(bufferPtr);
149            memset(cptr, '\0', size);
150            return(newbuffer);
151    }
152
153    /*******************************************************************
154     *      clientshellinit   FUNCTION
155     *
156     *      This function calls threadSema_f.create to establish the
157     *      semaphore count for the number of permissable client shells.
158
159    *******************************************************************/
```

Listing 7.9 *continued.*

```
160  int
161  clientshellinit(int count )
162  {
163          clientSemaphore = threadSema_f.create( count );
164          if( clientSemaphore )
165                  return(0);
166          return(1);
167  }
```

8

Recursive Mutex Locks

8.1 Recursive Mutex Locks: An Overview

Recursive mutual exclusion locks are similar to the general mutex locks. With recursive mutex locks, however, the owner can reacquire the mutex without blocking indefinitely. The owner must eventually release the recursive mutex lock once for each lock request granted.

Similar to the general mutex, a recursive mutex appears in everyday situations. Consider a telephone, for example, with a call-waiting feature. Only one person can acquire the resource (*the phone*) at a time. The current owner of the phone therefore holds a mutex lock protecting the phone. While in the middle of a conversation, the current owner hears the call-waiting tone. By depressing the receiver, the person can begin the second conversation. The resource now has two locks associated with it, one for each conversation. The resource cannot be used by another consumer until the second lock is released.

The UNIX threads implementation provides the recursive mutex synchronization primitive for use between the sibling threads of a single UNIX process, or for use between UNIX processes executing in disjoint address spaces. When creating a recursive mutex, the application can specify a mutex type of USYNC_THREAD or USYNC_PROCESS.

Table 8.1   The Recursive Mutex API

rmutex_init()	Initialize a recursive mutex
rmutex_lock()	Lock a recursive mutex
rmutex_trylock()	Attempt to lock a recursive mutex
rmutex_unlock()	Unlock a recursive mutex
rmutex_delete()	Invalidate a recursive mutex

8.2 Creating the Recursive Mutex

The `rmutex_init` function (*Figure 8.1*) initializes a recursive mutex to the unlocked state. The `rmutex` parameter must point to a valid recursive mutex data structure. The second parameter `type` determines the use of the rmutex. A `USYNC_THREAD` type denotes that the rmutex will be used between sibling threads, while a `USYNC_PROCESS` type identifies the rmutex as being used between processes executing in disjoint address spaces. The third parameter `arg` is reserved for future use and should be specified as `NULL`.

NAME:
>   `rmutex_init` - Initialize a recursive mutex lock.

SYNOPSIS:
>   `#include <synch.h>`
>
>   `int`
>   `rmutex_init(rmutex_t *rmutex, int type, void *arg)`

Figure 8.1   `rmutex_init()` synopsis. [1]

8.3 Locking the Recursive Mutex

The `rmutex_lock` function (*Figure 8.2*) will lock a recursive mutex lock for the calling thread. The `rmutex_lock` function examines the specified recursive mutex to determine its state. If the mutex is currently in the `UNLOCKED` state, the `rmutex_lock` function will lock the recursive mutex on behalf of the calling thread. In doing so, the function records the calling thread's identifier as the current owner of the recursive mutex. The mutex's recursion value is set to one.

Alternatively, if the recursive mutex is currently in the `LOCKED` state, the `rmutex_lock` function must determine if the requesting thread is the current owner. If so, the `rmutex_lock` function will increment the recursion count and immediately return as if the calling thread had successfully acquired a new lock on the mutex. When the recursive mutex is in the `LOCKED` state with another thread as the current owner, the requesting thread enters a block-wait state until the mutex becomes available.

From the point of view of the calling thread, the `rmutex_lock` function is atomic. If the function call is interrupted by the receipt of a signal, or a `forkall` system call, the function will not return until it holds the locked recursive mutex. Thus, an error indication such as `EINTR` is not returned to the calling thread.

---

[1] Printed with Permission of UNIX Systems Laboratories., Inc. All Rights Reserved.

```
NAME:
        rmutex_lock - Lock a recursive mutex.

SYNOPSIS:

        int
        rmutex_lock( rmutex_t *rmutex)
```

Figure 8.2   `rmutex_lock()` synopsis. [1]

The `rmutex_trylock` function (*Figure 8.3*) will conditionally lock a recursive mutex on behalf of the calling thread. This function behaves similarly to the `rmutex_lock` function, with the exception that the calling thread receives an error indication if the lock request fails.

The `rmutex_trylock` function will make a single attempt to lock the recursive mutex. If the lock request succeeds, then the recursion count is incremented and control is returned to the requesting thread. When the recursive mutex is currently locked by another thread, the `rmutex_trylock` function will return an `EBUSY` error indication value to the calling thread.

```
NAME:
        rmutex_trylock - Try to acquire a recursive mutex.

SYNOPSIS:

        int
        rmutex_trylock( rmutex_t *rmutex )
```

Figure 8.3   `rmutex_trylock()` synopsis. [1]

8.4 Unlocking the Recursive Mutex

To unlock a recursive mutex, the owner must call the `rmutex_unlock` function once for each lock request granted. The `rmutex_unlock` function will decrement the recursion count associated with the recursive mutex. When the recursion count reaches zero, the owner releases the recursive mutex.

The `rmutex_unlock` function examines the identity of the caller and will then decrement the recursion count if the caller is the current owner of the specified recursive mutex. If the count is

[1] Printed with Permission of UNIX Systems Laboratories., Inc. All Rights Reserved.

still greater then zero, then control returns to the calling thread without releasing the recursive mutex. Once released, at least one waiting thread can attempt to acquire the recursive mutex.

NAME:
        `rmutex_unlock` - Unlock a recursive mutex.

SYNOPSIS:
```
int
rmutex_unlock( rmutex_t *rmutex )
```

Figure 8.4   `rmutex_unlock()` synopsis. [1]

In releasing the recursive mutex, the `rmutex_unlock` function will select a waiting thread to acquire the mutex. When unlocking a `USYNC_THREAD` type mutex, the `rmutex_unlock` function will give precedence to a bound thread waiting for the mutex.

8.5 Invalidating the Recursive Mutex

The `rmutex_destroy` function invalidates the recursive mutex. The parameter rmutex is the address of the recursive mutex to invalidate. Once invalidated, a thread cannot use the recursive mutex unless it is first reinitialized. The `rmutex_destroy` function returns an `EBUSY` error indication value if the recursive mutex is in the `LOCKED` state.

NAME:
        `rmutex_destroy` - Destroy a recursive mutex.

SYNOPSIS:
```
int
rmutex_destroy(rmutex_t *rmutex)
```

Figure 8.5   `rmutex_destroy()` synopsis. [1]

8.6 Using the Recursive Mutex

The threadRmutex Module

The `threadRmutex` module (*Listings 8.1 and 8.2*) provides the functionality to administer dynamically allocated `USYNC_THREAD` type recursive mutexes. The `threadRmutex.h` header file (*Listing 8.1*) includes the type definition for the `threadRmutex` module's functions. To use

---

[1] Printed with Permission of UNIX Systems Laboratories, Inc. All Rights Reserved.

this module, an application must include this header file and reference the functions through the `threadRmutex_f` data structure. As with previous examples, the `threadRmutex` module uses the `threadLog` module to record error conditions. The three functions provided with this module are the `Create()`, `CreateLocked()`, and `Destroy()` functions.

Listing 8.1   *threadRmutex.h* -- The `threadRmutex` module header file.

```
1  typedef  struct _threadRmutex_f      {
2       rmutex_t    *(*create)(void);
3       rmutex_t    *(*createLocked)(void);
4       int             (*destroy)(rmutex_t *);
5  } threadRmutex_t;
6
7  extern threadRmutex_t threadRmutex_f;
8
```

```
Compile threadRmutex module:
       cc -D_REENTRANT -c -I${INSTALLROOT}hdr threadRmutex.c
       ar rv ${INSTALLROOT}lib/libtsync.a threadRmutex.o
```

The `Create` function allocates and initializes a recursive mutex. The `CreateLocked` function calls the `Create` function to allocate the rmutex, and upon success will issue the `rmutex_lock` call to lock the recursive mutex. A pointer to the locked recursive mutex is returned to the calling thread.

The `Destroy` function will invalidate the recursive mutex and deallocate the memory. Upon success, a zero value is returned to the calling thread. If an error condition occurs, the `threadLog_f` module is called to record the error and the storage for the recursive mutex is left unchanged.

Listing 8.2   *threadRmutex.c* -- The `threadRmutex` module.

```
1  #include <stdlib.h>
2  #include <synch.h>
3  #include <thread.h>
4  #include <string.h>
5  #include <errno.h>
6  #include "mthreadLog.h"
7  #include "threadRmutex.h"
```

Listing 8.2 *continued.*

```
8    /*******************************************************************
9     *      Function Prototypes
10    *******************************************************************/
11   static int          Destroy(rmutex_t *);
12   static rmutex_t     *Create(void);
13   static rmutex_t     *CreateLocked(void);
14   /*******************************************************************
15    *      Create        FUNCTION
16    *
17    *      The create function will allocate and initialize an rmutex
18    *      synchronization primitive for use between sibling threads.
19    *******************************************************************/
20   static rmutex_t    *
21   Create(void)
22   {
23          rmutex_t *rmutexPtr      = NULL;
24          int      errorCondition  = 0;
25          rmutexPtr = (rmutex_t *) malloc(sizeof(rmutex_t));
26          if( rmutexPtr == NULL )
27                 threadLog_f.setError(ENOMEM);
28          else {
29                 memset((void *) rmutexPtr,'\0',sizeof(rmutex_t));
30                 errorCondition=rmutex_init(rmutexPtr,USYNC_THREAD,
31                                                            NULL);
32                 if ( errorCondition ) {
33                        free((void *) rmutexPtr );
34                        rmutexPtr = NULL;
35                        threadLog_f.setError( errorCondition );
36                 }
37          }
38          return(rmutexPtr);
39   }
40
41   /*******************************************************************
42    *      CreateLocked       FUNCTION
43    *
44    *      The createdLocked function returns a locked rmutex to the
45    *      calling thread.  This function will call the create function
46    *      to allocate and initialize the rmutex.
47    *******************************************************************/
48   static rmutex_t *
49   CreateLocked(void)
50   {
51          rmutex_t *rmutexPtr      = NULL;
52          int      errorCondition  = 0;
53
54          rmutexPtr = Create();
```

Listing 8.2   *continued.*

```
55          if ( rmutexPtr ) {
56                  errorCondition   = rmutex_lock( rmutexPtr );
57                  if( errorCondition ) {
58                          free( (void *)rmutexPtr);
59                          rmutexPtr = NULL;
60                          threadLog_f.setError( errorCondition );
61                  }
62          }
63          return(rmutexPtr);
64  }
65
66  /*****************************************************************
67   *     Destroy       FUNCTION
68   *
69   *     The destroy function will invalidate the specified rmutex and
70   *     upon success, will free the storage space of the rmutex.
71   *****************************************************************/
72  static int
73  Destroy( rmutex_t *rmutexPtr)
74  {
75          int    errorCondition = 0;
76          errorCondition = rmutex_destroy(rmutexPtr);
77          if( errorCondition )
78                  threadLog_f.setError( errorCondition );
79          else
80                  free((void *)rmutexPtr);
81          return( errorCondition );
82  }
83
84  /*****************************************************************
85   *     Define the threadRmutex interface.
86   *****************************************************************/
87  threadRmutex_t     threadRmutex_f = {
88       Create,
89       CreateLocked,
90       Destroy,
91  };
```

The processRmutex Module

The processRmutex module (*Listings 8.3 and 8.4*) provides the functionality to administer dynamically allocated recursive mutexes for use between UNIX processes executing in disjoint address spaces. The processRmutex_t type definition describes the functions available through this module. The prmutex_t type definition describes the members of the memory mapped area.

Compile processRmutex module:
```
cc -D_REENTRANT -c -I${INSTALLROOT}hdr processRmutex.c
ar rv ${INSTALLROOT}lib/libpsync.a processRmutex.o
```

Listing 8.3   *processRmutex.h* -- The processRmutex module header file.

```
1   typedef struct _processRmutex_f      {
2        int        (*setMax)(const int);
3        rmutex_t *(*create)(const int);
4        rmutex_t *(*createLocked)(const int);
5        int        (*destroy)(const int);
6        rmutex_t *(*locate)(const int);
7   } processRmutex_t;
8
9   typedef struct _prmutex_t {
10       rmutex_t    rmutex;
11  } prmutex_t;
12  #define RMUTEX_MAP_SIZE (sizeof(prmutex_t) * maxProcRmutexes)
13  #define TRUE           1
14  #define FALSE          0
15
16  /*    defined constants to use as default values         */
17  #define MAX_PROCESS_RMUTEXES  100
18  extern processRmutex_t processRmutex_f;
```

The processRmutex.c source file (*Listing 8.4*) provides the functions available through this module. These functions are declared as static, and thus their scope is limited to the processRmutex.c source file. To use these functions, the application must include the processRmutex.h header file and access the members of the processRmutex_f data structure. These members are pointers to the appropriate functions. The Create, Destroy, and Locate functions all start by locking the processMutex. This action ensures that two threads cannot access these functions concurrently.

Listing 8.4   *processRmutex.c* -- The processRmutex module.

```
1   #include <fcntl.h>
2   #include <synch.h>
3   #include <thread.h>
4   #include <stdlib.h>
5   #include <errno.h>
6   #include <memory.h>
7   #include <unistd.h>
8   #include <sys/mman.h>
```

Listing 8.4 *continued.*

```
 9   #include <sys/ipc.h>
10   #include <sys/shm.h>
11   #include "processRmutex.h"
12   #include "mthreadLog.h"
13
14   static   int              maxProcRmutexes= MAX_PROCESS_RMUTEXES;
15   static   mutex_t          processMutex   = { 0 };
16   static   prmutex_t       *procRmutexes   = NULL;
17   static   int              rmutexfd       = -1;
18   /******************************************************************
19    *      Function Prototypes
20    ******************************************************************/
21   static rmutex_t    *Create(const int);
22   static rmutex_t    *CreateLocked(const int);
23   static int          Destroy(const int);
24   static int          SetMax(const int);
25   static rmutex_t    *Locate(const int);
26   static int          accessMap(const char *,const int);
27
28   /******************************************************************
29    *      SetMax      FUNCTION
30    *
31    *      The SetMax function will initialize the number of
32    *      USYNC_PROCESS type recursive mutex primitives.
33    ******************************************************************/
34   static int
35   SetMax(const int number)
36   {
37           int    errorCondition = 0;
38                       /**********************************************
39                        *      CRITICAL SECTION START
40                        *      We must prevent concurrent updates to the
41                        *      maxProcRmutex variable.  The assignment will
42                        *      succeed only if we have not yet accessed the
43                        *      rmutex map.
44                        **********************************************/
45           mutex_lock( &processMutex );
46           if( rmutexfd == -1 )
47                   maxProcRmutexes = number;
48           else
49                   errorCondition = EAGAIN;
50           mutex_unlock( &processMutex );
51                       /**********************************************
52                        *      CRITICAL SECTION END
53                        **********************************************/
54           return(errorCondition);
55   }
```

Listing 8.4   *continued.*

```
56   /*********************************************************************
57    *      Create       FUNCTION
58    *
59    *      This function will initialize the rmutex found at the
60    *      specified index.  If this is the first call to Create, then
61    *      the rmutex map must be accessed.  A pointer to the specified
62    *      rmutex is returned to the calling thread.
63    *********************************************************************/
64   static rmutex_t *
65   Create(const int index)
66   {
67           rmutex_t *rmutexPtr      = NULL;
68           int       errorCondition= FALSE;
69
70                           /***********************************************
71                            *      CRITICAL SECTION  START
72                            *      We must prevent concurrent calls to
73                            *      accessMap to ensure the integrity of the
74                            *      memory-mapped area.
75                            ***********************************************/
76           mutex_lock( &processMutex );
77           if( index > maxProcRmutexes )
78                   errorCondition = EINVAL;
79           else if( rmutexfd == -1 )
80               errorCondition=accessMap("rmutex.map",
81                                           O_CREAT|O_RDWR|O_TRUNC);
82           mutex_unlock( &processMutex );
83                           /***********************************************
84                            *      CRITICAL SECTION END
85                            ***********************************************/
86
87                           /***********************************************
88                            *      The initialization of the rmutex itself is
89                            *      not part of the critical section.
90                            ***********************************************/
91           if( ! errorCondition ) {
92               rmutexPtr = &(procRmutexes[index].rmutex);
93               errorCondition=rmutex_init(rmutexPtr,USYNC_PROCESS,
94                                           NULL);
95           }
96           if(errorCondition) {
97                   threadLog_f.setError(errorCondition);
98                   rmutexPtr=NULL;
99           }
100          return(rmutexPtr);
101  }
```

Listing 8.4 *continued.*

```
102    /**********************************************************************
103     *       CreatedLocked       FUNCTION
104     *
105     *       The createdLocked function will return a pointer to a locked
106     *       recursive mutex found at the specified index.  This function
107     *       calls the Create function to initialize the mutex.
108
109     **********************************************************************/
110    static rmutex_t *
111    CreateLocked(const int index)
112    {
113            rmutex_t      *rmutexPtr          = NULL;
114            int            errorCondition    = 0;
115
116            rmutexPtr = Create(index);
117
118            if ( rmutexPtr ) {
119                    errorCondition   = rmutex_lock( rmutexPtr );
120            if( errorCondition ) {
121                            rmutexPtr = NULL;
122
123                            threadLog_f.setError(errorCondition);
124                    }
125            }
126            return(rmutexPtr);
127    }
128
129
130    /**********************************************************************
131     *       Destroy       FUNCTION
132     *
133     *       The destroy function invalidates the rmutex found at the
134     *       specified index.
135     **********************************************************************/
136    static int
137    Destroy(const int index)
138    {
139            int            errorCondition    = 0;
140            rmutex_t      *rmutexPtr          = NULL;
141
142            if( index > maxProcRmutexes )
143                    errorCondition = EINVAL;
144
145            else   {
146                    rmutexPtr = &(procRmutexes[index].rmutex);
147                    errorCondition = rmutex_destroy(rmutexPtr);
148            }
```

Listing 8.4   *continued.*

```
149              if( errorCondition )
150                    threadLog_f.setError(errorCondition);
151              return( errorCondition );
152      }
153
154      /********************************************************************
155       *      Locate        FUNCTION
156       *
157       *      The locate function returns a pointer to the rmutex found
158       *      at the specified location.
159
160       ********************************************************************/
161      static rmutex_t *
162      Locate(const int index)
163      {
164              rmutex_t *rmutexPtr      = NULL;
165              int       errorCondition= FALSE;
166                       /***********************************************
167                        *      CRITICAL SECTION   START
168                        *      We must prevent concurrent threads from
169                        *      attempting to access the rmutex memory-mapped
170                        *      region.
171                        ***********************************************/
172              mutex_lock( &processMutex );
173              if( index > maxProcRmutexes )
174                    errorCondition = EINVAL;
175              else if( rmutexfd == -1 )
176                    errorCondition=accessMap("rmutex.map",O_CREAT|O_RDWR);
177              mutex_unlock( &processMutex );
178                       /***********************************************
179                        *      CRITICAL SECTION   END
180                        ***********************************************/
181              if( ! errorCondition )
182                    rmutexPtr = &(procRmutexes[index].rmutex);
183              else {
184                    threadLog_f.setError(errorCondition);
185                    rmutexPtr = NULL;
186              }
187              return(rmutexPtr);
188      }
189
190      /********************************************************************
191       *      Define the processRmutex interface
192
193       ********************************************************************/
194
```

Listing 8.4 *continued.*

```
195  processRmutex_t    processRmutex_f = {
196              SetMax,
197              Create,
198              CreateLocked,
199              Destroy,
200              Locate
201  };
202
203  /*******************************************************************
204   *      accessMap    FUNCTION
205   *
206   *      This function is local to the processRmutex module.  The
207   *      function will access the specified file and memory-map its
208   *      contents. If the mode includes the O_TRUNC flag, then the file
209   *      is created and initialized with zero values.  Otherwise, the
210   *      file is simply opened.
211   *******************************************************************/
212  static int
213  accessMap(const char *fname,const int mode)
214  {
215          int    errorCondition = 0;
216          char   *cp;
217
218          if( mode & O_TRUNC ) {
219                  rmutexfd = creat(fname,S_IRUSR|S_IWUSR);
220
221                  if( rmutexfd != -1 ) {
222                          close(rmutexfd);
223                          rmutexfd = open(fname,mode);
224                          if(( cp = malloc(RMUTEX_MAP_SIZE)) == NULL )
225                                  errorCondition = ENOMEM;
226                          else   {
227                                  memset(cp,'\0',RMUTEX_MAP_SIZE);
228                                  write(rmutexfd,cp,RMUTEX_MAP_SIZE);
229                                  free(cp);
230                                  lseek(rmutexfd,0L,0);
231                          }
232                  }
233                  else
234                          errorCondition = errno;
235          }
236          else if( (rmutexfd = open(fname,mode)) == -1 )
237                  errorCondition = errno;
238          if( ! errorCondition ) {
239                  procRmutexes = (prmutex_t *)mmap(0,RMUTEX_MAP_SIZE,
240                      PROT_READ|PROT_WRITE,MAP_SHARED,rmutexfd,0);
241
```

Listing 8.4   *continued.*

```
242
243                     if( (char *)procRmutexes == (caddr_t)-1)
244                             errorCondition = errno;
245             }
246             close(rmutexfd);
247             rmutexfd = 0;
248             return(errorCondition);
249     }
```

Working with Trees

In application programming it is very useful to depict certain related data structures using a tree diagram. There are several functions that must be implemented to provide an appropriate representation of the tree. We must first agree on the terminology as used in this description.

The `threadTree.h` header file (*Listing 8.5*) provides a type definition for a basic tree implementation. The tree has a root, a recursive mutex to protect access to the tree, and a reference count. Table 8.2 summarizes the functions available to access the tree. The `threadTree_f` data structure will be used to hold pointers to these functions.

Table 8.2   Tree Operations

create	Create a tree structure
attach	Attach a node to the tree
delete	Delete a tree structure
operator	A generic function to apply the specified operator to each node of the tree
traverse	A generic function to traverse the various nodes of the tree

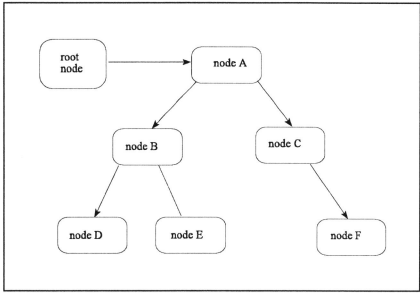

Figure 8.6   A threadTree module tree layout.

In discussions of trees, we would normally distinguish between a leaf and a node. For this description, however, we simply say that a node is added to the tree. The node has a parent, potentially a left child and potentially a right child (*see Figure 8.6*).

Each node in the tree is given a unique key identifier. The ordering of the nodes within the tree guarantees that a node with a lower key value is always to the left, while a node with a higher key value is always to the right. Thus if node-A has key value 100, then node-B's key value cannot be greater than 100. We are also guaranteed that no two nodes will have the same key value. Each node can also have a pointer to some data representing the node.

```
Compile threadTree module:
     cc -D_REENTRANT -c -I${INSTALLROOT}hdr node.c
     cc -D_REENTRANT -c -I${INSTALLROOT}hdr tree.c
     ar rv ${INSTALLROOT}lib/libtsync.a node.o tree.o
```

Listing 8.5   *threadTree.h* -- The `threadTree` module header file.

```
1   typedef struct      _tree {
2         struct _node        *root;
3         rmutex_t            *rmutex;
4         long                 referenceCount;
5   } tree_t;
6
7   typedef struct _tree_t  {
8         tree_t *(*create)(void);
9         int     (*attach)(tree_t *, struct _node *, struct _node *);
10        int     (*delete)(tree_t *);
11        int     (*operator)(struct _node *,int (*function)(),rmutex_t
12  *);
13        int     (*traverse)(tree_t *, int (*function)() );
14  } tree_f_t;
15  extern tree_f_t threadTree_f;
```

The `threadTree.c` source file (*Listing 8.6*) provides the details for the tree functions. The `threadTree_f.create()` function simply allocates the tree structure and the tree's recursive mutex by calling the `threadRmutex` module.

Listing 8.6   *threadTree.c* -- The `threadTree` module.

```
1   #include <synch.h>
2   #include <synch.h>
3   #include <errno.h>
4   #include <stdlib.h>
5   #include <memory.h>
6   #include <synch.h>
7   #include "mthreadLog.h"
8   #include "threadRmutex.h"
9   #include "tree.h"
10  #include "node.h"
11
12  /*****************************************************************
13   *      Function Prototypes
14   *****************************************************************/
15  static int          Attach(tree_t *,node_t *,node_t *);
16  static int          Delete(tree_t *);
17  static int          Operator(node_t *,int (*function)(),rmutex_t *);
18  static int          Traverse(tree_t *,int (*function)());
19  static tree_t       *Create(void);
```

Listing 8.6   *continued.*

```
20   /*********************************************************************
21    *      Create        FUNCTION
22    *
23    *      This function will return a pointer to an allocated and
24    *      initialized tree_t type structure.
25    *********************************************************************/
26   static tree_t *
27   Create(void)
28   {
29          tree_t        *tree  = NULL;
30
31          tree = malloc( sizeof(tree_t));
32          if( tree == NULL )
33                  threadLog_f.setError(ENOMEM);
34          else {
35                  memset((void *)tree, '\0', sizeof(tree_t));
36                  tree->rmutex = threadRmutex_f.create();
37                  if( tree->rmutex == NULL ) {
38                          free(tree);
39                          tree = NULL;
40                  }
41          }
42          return( tree );
43   }
44
45   /*********************************************************************
46    *      Delete        FUNCTION
47    *
48    *      This function will deallocate the specified tree_t type
49    *      structure.  If the tree is currently in use, the function
50    *      will return an EBUSY error indication.
51    *********************************************************************/
52   static int
53   Delete(tree_t *tree)
54   {
55          int    error = 0;
56
57          if( tree != NULL && tree->rmutex != NULL )
58                  error = rmutex_lock( tree->rmutex);
59          else
60                  error = EINVAL;
61          if( error )
62                  return(error);
63          if( ! tree->referenceCount ) {
64                  rmutex_unlock(tree->rmutex);
65                  error = threadRmutex_f.destroy(tree->rmutex);
```

Listing 8.6 *continued.*

```
66
67                      if( ! error )
68                              free( tree);
69              }
70              else {
71                      error = EBUSY;
72                      rmutex_unlock(tree->rmutex);
73              }
74              return( error );
75  }
76
77  /*******************************************************************
78   *      attach      FUNCTION
79   *
80   *      The attach function will attach the given subtree to the
81   *      specified tree.  The function will recursively call itself to
82   *      find the appropriate location within tree to attach the
83   *      subtree.
84   *******************************************************************/
85  static int
86  Attach( tree_t *tree, node_t *subtree, node_t *currentNode)
87  {
88          int    errorCondition = 0;
89
90          if( tree == NULL || subtree == NULL || currentNode == NULL)
91                  errorCondition = EINVAL;
92          else
93                  errorCondition = rmutex_lock(tree->rmutex);
94          if( errorCondition )
95                  return(errorCondition);
96                          /*************************************************
97                           *      If the current node's key is less then the
98                           *      subtree's key, we need to determine if there
99                           *      is a right-hand child.  If so, we will call
100                          *      attach() again at this location.  Otherwise,
101                          *      we attach the subtree to the right of the
102                          *      current node.
103                          *************************************************/
104         if( currentNode->key < subtree->key  )
105               if( currentNode->cr )
106                     errorCondition=Attach(tree,subtree,
107                                             currentNode->cr );
108               else {
109                     currentNode->cr = subtree;
110                     subtree->parent = currentNode;
111               }
112
```

Listing 8.6 *continued.*

```
113                         /**************************************************
114                          *      If the current node's key is greater than
115                          *      the subtree's key, we need to decide if
116                          *      there is a left-hand child.  If so, call
117                          *      attach at this left-hand child.  Otherwise,
118                          *      make the current node's left child point to
119                          *      the subtree.
120                          ******************************************/
121         else if (currentNode->key > subtree->key )
122               if( currentNode->cl )
123                     errorCondition=Attach(tree,subtree,
124                                            currentNode->cl );
125               else {
126                     currentNode->cl = subtree;
127                     subtree->parent = currentNode;
128               }
129         else
130               errorCondition = EINVAL;
131         rmutex_unlock(tree->rmutex);
132         return(errorCondition);
133 }
134
135 /**********************************************************************
136  *      Traverse      FUNCTION
137  *
138  *      Traverse will apply the specified function to each node of the
139  *      given tree.  This function will lock the tree's recursive
140  *      mutex, and then call the operator function.
141  **********************************************************************/
142 static int
143 Traverse( tree_t *tree, int (*function)())
144 {
145         node_t *node = NULL;
146         int    error = 0;
147
148         if( tree == NULL || function == NULL )
149               return(EINVAL);
150
151         error = rmutex_lock( tree->rmutex);
152
153         if( ! error ) {
154               node = tree->root;
155               error= Operator(node, function, tree->rmutex );
156               rmutex_unlock(tree->rmutex);
157         }
158         return(error);
159 }
```

Listing 8.6   *continued.*

```
160  /*******************************************************************
161  *      Operator     FUNCTION
162  *
163  *      The operator function locks the specified rmutex and applies
164  *      the given function to the node.  The function will recursively
165  *      call itself for each left child.  If the current node does not
166  *      have a left child, then function is applied to the current
167  *      node.  Next, the operator function will recursively call
168  *      itself for each right child.
169  *******************************************************************/
170  static int
171  Operator( node_t *node, int (*function)(), rmutex_t *rmutex)
172  {
173          int    error = 0;
174
175          if( node == NULL )
176                  return(-1);
177          rmutex_lock( rmutex );
178
179                          /***********************************************
180                          *      We recursively call the operator function
181                          *      for each left-hand child of the current
182                          *      node.
183                          ***********************************************/
184          if( node->cl )
185                  error = Operator(node->cl, function, rmutex );
186
187                          /***********************************************
188                          *      We now apply the function to the current
189                          *      node.
190                          ***********************************************/
191          if( ! error )
192                  error = function(node);
193                          /***********************************************
194                          *      We will recursively call the operator
195                          *      function for the right-hand side of the
196                          *      current node.
197                          ***********************************************/
198          if( node->cr && ! error )
199                  error = Operator(node->cr, function, rmutex );
200          rmutex_unlock( rmutex );
201          return(error);
202  }
203  /*******************************************************************
204  *      Define the threadTree module interface.
205
206  *******************************************************************/
```

Listing 8.6 *continued.*

```
207  tree_f_t threadTree_f = {
208       Create,
209       Attach,
210       Delete,
211       Operator,
212       Traverse
213  };
```

The `threadTree_f.attach()` function permits a subtree to be attached to an existing tree. That is to say, suppose node-B, from above, was detached from the tree. This branch can subsequently be attached using the `threadTree_f.attach()` function. In calling the `threadTree_f.attach()` function, the application must specify the `currentNode` parameter as the root node of the tree.

The `threadTree_f.attach()` function must first lock the tree's recursive mutex prior to doing any work. The tree's recursive mutex protects against concurrent updates to the tree. The `threadTree_f.attach()` function determines if the current node's key value is less than the root node of the branch being attached. If so, then we need to traverse to the right; otherwise we traverse to the left. The `threadTree_f.attach()` function is recursive and thus will call itself again to find the appropriate position in the tree at which to attach the subtree.

The `threadTree_f.traverse()` accepts as parameters a pointer to the tree, and a function to apply to each node of the tree. This function performs certain validations and will call the `threadTree_f.operator()` function passing the root node of the tree.

The `threadTree_f.operator()` function examines if there is a left child, and if so, calls itself passing the left child as the current node. The specified function is applied to the current node. Finally, if the current node has a right child, the `threadTree_f.operator()` function is called again, passing the right child as the current node. In this manner, the specified function can be applied to all nodes of the tree.

The `threadNode.h` header file (*Listing 8.7*) provides the details of a thread node. The `node_t` type data structures show a node as having a `key`, a `referenceCount`, a pointer to its `data`, and references for its parent and children. The `threadNode_f` data structure contains the pointers to the functions available through this module.

Listing 8.7 *threadNode.h* -- The `threadNode` module header file.

```
1   typedef struct      _node {
2        int                  key;
3        int                  referenceCount;
4        void                 *data;
5        struct _node         *parent;
6        struct _node         *cr;
7        struct _node         *cl;
8   } node_t;
9
10  typedef struct _node_t   {
11       node_t *(*create)(unsigned long, void *);
12       int     (*add)(tree_t *, unsigned long, void *);
13       node_t *(*find)(tree_t *,unsigned long, node_t *);
14       void   *(*delete)(tree_t *, unsigned long);
15       void   *(*reference)(tree_t *, unsigned long);
16       int     (*unreference)(tree_t *, unsigned long);
17  } node_f_t;
18  extern node_f_t     threadNode_f;
```

The `threadNode.c` source file (*Listing 8.8*) provides the functionality of the `threadNode` module. The `threadNode_f.create()` function is used to allocate a node for the tree. The `threadNode_f.add()` function is called to add a node to the tree. The distinction here is that the application can simply call the `threadNode_f.add()` function, which will in turn call the `threadNode_f.create()` function to allocate the node.

Listing 8.8 *threadNode.c* -- The `threadNode` module.

```
1   #include <errno.h>
2   #include <stdlib>
3   #include <memory.h>
4   #include <synch.h>
5   #include "mthreadLog.h"
6   #include "tree.h"
7   #include "node.h"
8
9   /*****************************************************************
10  *      Function Prototypes
11  *****************************************************************/
12  static     int     Add(tree_t *,const unsigned long,void *);
13  static     int     Unreference(tree_t *,const unsigned long);
14  static     node_t *Create(const unsigned long,void *);
```

Listing 8.8 *continued.*

```
15  static        node_t  *Find(tree_t *,const unsigned long,node_t *);
16  static        void    *Delete(tree_t *, const unsigned long);
17  static        void    *Reference(tree_t *,const unsigned long);
18
19  /*********************************************************************
20   *      Create       FUNCTION
21   *
22   *      The create function will allocate and initialize a node_t
23   *      type structure.  The node's key is set to the value of the
24   *      key parameter.  The node's data is set to the value of the
25   *      data parameter.
26   *********************************************************************/
27  static node_t *
28  Create(const unsigned long key, void *data)
29  {
30          node_t          *node;
31          node = malloc( sizeof(node_t));
32          if( node == NULL )
33                  threadLog_f.setError(ENOMEM);
34          else {
35                  (void) memset((void *)node, '\0', sizeof(node_t));
36                  node->key   = key;
37                  node->data  = data;
38          }
39          return( node );
40  }
41
42  /*********************************************************************
43   *      Add     FUNCTION
44   *
45   *      This function will add a new node to the given tree.  The node
46   *      is initialized with the specified key and data parameters.
47   *      This function calls the Create function to initialize the
48   *      node.
49   *********************************************************************/
50  static int
51  Add(tree_t *tree,const unsigned long key,void *data)
52  {
53          int     errorCondition = 0;
54          if( tree == NULL )
55                  errorCondition = EINVAL;
56          else
57                  errorCondition = rmutex_lock( tree->rmutex );
58          if( errorCondition )
59                  return(errorCondition);
60          if( tree->root == NULL )
61                  tree->root = Create( key, data );
```

Listing 8.8   *continued.*

```
62          else
63                  errorCondition=threadTree_f.attach(tree,
64                                  Create(key,data),tree->root);
65          rmutex_unlock( tree->rmutex );
66          return( errorCondition );
67  }
68
69  /*********************************************************************
70   *    Find   FUNCTION
71   *
72   *    This function returns a pointer to the node in the specified
73   *    tree whose key matches the value of parameter key.
74   *********************************************************************/
75  static node_t *
76  Find( tree_t *tree,const unsigned long key,node_t *node)
77  {
78          node_t *currentNode    = NULL;
79          int    errorCondition  = 0;
80
81          if( tree == NULL || node == NULL )
82                  errorCondition = EINVAL;
83          else
84                  errorCondition = rmutex_lock( tree->rmutex );
85          if( errorCondition ) {
86                  threadLog_f.setError(errorCondition);
87                  return(NULL);
88          }
89
90          if( node->key == key )
91                  currentNode = node;
92          else if( (node->key < key) && (node->cr != NULL ) )
93                  currentNode = Find(tree, key, node->cr);
94          else if( (node->key > key) && (node->cl != NULL) )
95                  currentNode = Find(tree, key, node->cl);
96          rmutex_unlock( tree->rmutex);
97          return( currentNode );
98  }
99
100 /*********************************************************************
101  *    Delete      FUNCTION
102  *
103  *    This function will delete the node whose key matches the value
104  *    of parameter key, from the specified tree.  This function will
105  *    call the Find function to locate the node.  This function will
106  *    call the attach function to attach the left-hand child and
107  *    right-hand child of the deleted node to the tree.
108  *********************************************************************/
```

Listing 8.8 *continued.*

```
109   static void *
110   Delete(tree_t *tree, const unsigned long key)
111   {
112         int       errorCondition  = 0;
113         void    *data             = NULL;
114         node_t *node              = NULL;
115
116         if( tree == NULL )
117               errorCondition = EINVAL;
118         else
119               errorCondition = rmutex_lock(tree->rmutex);
120         if( errorCondition ) {
121               threadLog_f.setError(errorCondition);
122               return(NULL);
123         }
124         node = Find(tree, key, tree->root);
125         if( node != NULL ) {
126               if( node->referenceCount )
127                     errorCondition = EBUSY;
128               else if( node->parent == NULL ) {
129                     if( node->cl ) {
130                           tree->root = node->cl;
131                           node->cl->parent = NULL;
132                           if( node->cr ) {
133                                 node->cr->parent = NULL;
134                                 threadTree_f.attach(tree,node->cr,
135                                                       tree->root);
136                           }
137                     }
138                     else {
139                           tree->root = node->cr;
140                           if( node->cr )
141                                 node->cr->parent = NULL;
142                     }
143               }
144               else {
145                     if( node == node->parent->cl ) {
146                           node->parent->cl = node->cl;
147                           if( node->cl )
148                                 node->cl->parent = node->parent;
149                           if( node->cr )
150                                 node->cr->parent = NULL;
151                           threadTree_f.attach(tree,node->cr,
152                                                 tree->root);
153                     }
154                     else {
155                           node->parent->cr = node->cl;
```

Listing 8.8   *continued.*

```
156                         if( node->cl )
157                               node->cl->parent = node->parent;
158                         if( node->cr )
159                               node->cr->parent = NULL;
160                         threadTree_f.attach(tree,node->cr,
161                                              tree->root);
162                    }
163               }
164          if( ! errorCondition && node != NULL ) {
165               data = node->data;
166               free( node );
167          }
168     }
169     if( errorCondition )
170          threadLog_f.setError(errorCondition);
171     rmutex_unlock( tree->rmutex );
172
173     return( data );
174 }
175
176 /********************************************************************
177  *     Reference    FUNCTION
178  *
179  *     The reference function will locate the node whose value
180  *     matches the specified key, and will increment the reference
181  *     count to that node.
182  ********************************************************************/
183 static void *
184 Reference( tree_t *tree,const unsigned long key)
185 {
186     node_t *node            = NULL;
187     void    *data            = NULL;
188     int      errorCondition  = 0;
189     if( tree == NULL )
190          errorCondition = EINVAL;
191     else
192          errorCondition= rmutex_lock( tree->rmutex );
193     if( ! errorCondition ) {
194          node = Find( tree, key, tree->root);
195          if( node )
196               if( node->referenceCount)
197                    errorCondition = EBUSY;
198               else {
199                    ++tree->referenceCount;
200                    ++node->referenceCount;
201                    data = node->data;
202                    }
```

Listing 8.8   *continued.*

```
203                     rmutex_unlock(tree->rmutex);
204             }
205             return(data);
206 }
207
208 /*****************************************************************
209  *      Unreference FUNCTION
210  *
211  *      This function will decrement the reference count of the node
212  *      whose value matches the specified key.
213  *****************************************************************/
214 static int
215 Unreference( tree_t *tree,const unsigned long key)
216 {
217         int     errorCondition  = 0;
218         node_t *node            = NULL;
219
220         if( tree == NULL )
221                 errorCondition = EINVAL;
222         else
223                 errorCondition = rmutex_lock( tree->rmutex) ;
224         if( ! errorCondition ) {
225                 node = Find( tree, key, NULL);
226                 if( node != NULL ) {
227                         if( node->referenceCount) {
228                                 --node->referenceCount;
229                                 --tree->referenceCount;
230                         }
231                         else
232                                 errorCondition = EINVAL;
233                 }
234                 rmutex_unlock(tree->rmutex);
235         }
236         return(errorCondition);
237 }
238
239 /*****************************************************************
240  *      Define the threadNode module interface.
241  *****************************************************************/
242 node_f_t        threadNode_f = {
243     Create,
244     Add,
245     Find,
246     Delete,
247     Reference,
248     Unreference,
249 };
```

The threadNode_f.find() function will locate a particular node in the tree based on its key. The function is similar to the threadTree_f.traverse() function. The difference here is that the threadNode_f.find() function will locate the particular node and return a pointer to it.

The threadNode_f.delete() function is used to remove a node from a tree based on its corresponding key value. The function will call the threadNode_f.find() function to locate the node, and will then adjust the parent and child pointers.

The threadNode_f.reference() and threadNode_f.unreference() functions reference a particular node in the tree. By referencing the node, the application may then alter its data without fear of another thread deleting the node.

9

Reader-Writer Locks

9.1 Reader-Writer Locks: An Overview

Although the most common form of synchronization is mutex, it is not necessarily the best synchronization primitive for all cases. The primary disadvantage to using the mutex primitive is that only one thread can be using the protected resource. Other threads requesting to use the resource must `block wait` until the resource becomes available. While this approach is desirable for certain resources, there are many instances where the mutex primitive does not offer the maximum performance.

The UNIX Threads Interface offers a `Reader-Writer` primitive to permit concurrent reads, and exclusive writes to a protected resource.[32] The Reader-Writer lock is a single entity that can be locked in READ mode or WRITE mode.

There are many cases where the Reader-Writer lock provides additional flexibility and performance. Database accesses, for example, can be synchronized with a Reader-Writer lock. The database program can support concurrent reads of the database records, since they are guaranteed not to change while the read operations are taking place. When the database is to be updated, however, the write operation must have exclusive access.

When a thread requires the use of a protected resource, it must first acquire the Reader-Writer lock. If the request is for a READ mode lock and the lock is currently held in WRITE mode, then the requesting thread will `block-wait` until the resource becomes available. Alternatively, if the request is for a READ mode lock and the resource is already locked in READ mode, then the count of threads using the READ mode lock is incremented.

In requesting a WRITE mode lock, the Reader-Writer lock must not be held by any other thread. When the thread requesting the WRITE mode lock can gain exclusive use of the resource, then the lock will be granted and the operation will continue. Otherwise, the requesting thread will

---

[32] This primitive is sometimes referred to as a Concurrent Read-Exclusive Write (CREW) lock.

`block-wait`. While the lock is held in WRITE mode, no other thread can gain access to the resource, even for another WRITE operation.

The UNIX Threads Interface provides the Reader-Writer locks with a predisposition to WRITE lock requests. This avoids starving the WRITE operations. Therefore, if a lock is currently held in READ mode and a request is made for a WRITE mode lock, further READ mode lock requests will block until the WRITE mode lock has been granted and subsequently released.

Table 9.1   The Reader-Writer Lock API

`rwlock_init()`	Initialize a Reader-Writer lock
`rw_rdlock()`	Lock a Reader-Writer lock for Read
`rw_tryrdlock()`	Try to lock a Reader-Writer lock for Read
`rw_wrlock()`	Lock a Reader-Writer lock for Write
`rw_trywrlock()`	Try to lock a Reader-Writer lock for Write
`rw_unlock()`	Unlock a Reader-Writer lock
`rwlock_destroy()`	Attempt to destroy a Reader-Writer lock

9.2 Creating the Reader-Writer Lock

The `rwlock_init` function will initialize the Reader-Writer lock to an UNLOCKED state (*see Figure 9.1*). The first parameter to the `rwlock_init` function is the address of the `rwlock_t` type data structure. The second parameter, `type`, defines the use of the Reader-Writer lock. In specifying the type as USYNC_THREAD, the Reader-Writer lock will be marked for use between sibling threads of a single UNIX process. A USYNC_PROCESS type is for use between UNIX processes executing in disjoint address spaces. The third parameter to the `rwlock_init` function call is reserved for future use, and consequently should be specified as a NULL argument.

Caution must be exercised to avoid reinitializing a Reader-Writer lock while threads are waiting at the Reader-Writer lock. The `rwlock_init` function overwrites the current state of the Reader-Writer lock. If one or more threads are waiting for the Reader-Writer lock to become available, and another thread initializes the lock, then the waiting threads will block indefinitely.

A successful call to the `rwlock_init` function will return a zero status value to the calling thread, and the `rwlock` will be initialized to the UNLOCKED stated. Otherwise, an appropriate error indication value will be returned and the `rwlock` will remain unchanged.

```
NAME:
        rwlock_init - Initialize a Reader-Writer lock.

SYNOPSIS:
        #include <synch.h>

        int
        rwlock_init(rwlock_t *rwlock, int type, void *arg)
```

Figure 9.1   `rwlock_init()` synopsis. [1]

The Reader-Writer lock operations provided by the UNIX Threads Interface are not recursive. If a thread has been granted a WRITE mode lock for a USYNC_THREAD type Reader-Writer lock, and subsequently requests the WRITE mode lock again without having unlocked the Reader-Writer lock, then the thread will become deadlocked. Similarly, if a thread is granted a READ mode lock and subsequently requests a WRITE mode lock without having first unlocked the Reader-Writer lock, then the thread will become deadlocked.

There are no relationships maintained between the requesting thread and the Reader-Writer lock data structure. Thus, a sibling may unlock a Reader-Writer lock held by another thread or a UNIX process.

9.3 Read Mode Reader-Writer Locks

A thread can request a READ mode lock for a Reader-Writer lock by calling the `rw_rdlock` function (*see Figure 9.2*). The parameter `rwlock` is the address of the Reader-Writer lock to transition to the LOCKED state. On success, the `rw_rdlock` function will increment the reference count describing the number of active READ operations, and will return a zero status value to the calling thread.

```
NAME:
        rw_rdlock - Acquire a Reader-Writer lock in read mode.

SYNOPSIS:
        #include <synch.h>

        int
        rw_rdlock(rwlock_t *rwlock)
```

Figure 9.2   `rw_rdlock()` synopsis. [1]

[1] Printed with Permission of UNIX System Laboratories, Inc. All Rights Reserved.

The Reader-Writer lock synchronization primitive gives precedence to WRITE mode requests. If there is a current WRITE mode lock on the Reader-Writer lock, or if there are pending WRITE mode lock requests, the rw_rdlock function will wait until those requests are satisfied.

From the point of view of the application, the rw_rdlock function is atomic. The rw_rdlock function will call appropriate signal handlers as necessary, and resume its wait for the READ mode lock request. Thus, the rw_rdlock function will not return an EINTR error indication.

The rw_tryrdlock function (*Figure 9.3*) will make a single attempt to acquire a READ mode lock. Upon success, the rw_tryrdlock function will return a zero status value to the calling thread. If there is a current WRITE mode lock on the Reader-Writer lock, or if there are pending WRITE mode lock requests, the rw_tryrdlock function will return an EBUSY error indication value.

```
NAME:
        rw_tryrdlock - Attempt to acquire a Reader-Writer lock in read mode.

SYNOPSIS:
        #include <synch.h>

        int
        rw_tryrdlock(rwlock_t *rwlock)
```

Figure 9.3   rw_tryrdlock() synopsis. [1]

9.4 Write Mode Reader-Writer Locks

The rw_wrlock function will acquire an exclusive WRITE mode lock on the Reader-Writer lock (*see Figure 9.4*). Before calling this function, however, the Reader-Writer lock must have been initialized to a known state. The rw_wrlock function will block if there is a current READ mode or WRITE mode lock on the Reader-Writer lock. A successful call to the rw_wrlock function will lock the Reader-Writer lock for an exclusive WRITE operation, and return a zero status value to the calling thread. Otherwise, the rw_wrlock function will return an appropriate error indication value.

From the point of view of the application, the rw_wrlock function is atomic. The rw_wrlock function will call appropriate signal handlers as necessary, and then resume its wait for the WRITE mode lock request. Consequently, if the rw_wrlock function is interrupted, an error indicationsuch as EINTR is never returned to the calling thread.

```
NAME:
        rw_wrlock - Acquire a Reader-Writer lock in write mode.

SYNOPSIS:
        #include <synch.h>

        int
        rw_wrlock(rwlock_t *rwlock)
```

Figure 9.4   rw_wrlock() synopsis. [1]

The rw_trywrlock function (*Figure 9.5*) will make a single attempt to acquire a WRITE mode lock. A successful call to the rw_trywrlock function will lock the Reader-Writer lock in WRITE mode, and return a zero status value to the calling thread. If the lock is currently held by either a Reader or a Writer, then the rw_trywrlock function will return an EBUSY error indication value to the calling thread.

```
NAME:
        rw_trywrlock - Attempt once to acquire a Reader-Writer lock in write mode.

SYNOPSIS:
        #include <synch.h>

        int
        rw_trywrlock( rwlock_t *rwlock )
```

Figure 9.5   rw_trywrlock() synopsis.

9.5 Unlocking the Reader-Writer Lock

The rw_unlock function will unlock the Reader-Writer lock found at the location pointed to by parameter rwlock (*see Figure 9.6*). The rw_unlock function determines the type of lock being removed by examining the rwlock_t type data structure. A successful call to rw_unlock will unlock the Reader-Writer lock and return a zero status value to the calling thread. Otherwise, thelock remains unchanged and an appropriate error indication value is returned.

[1] Printed with Permission of UNIX System Laboratories, Inc. All Rights Reserved.

NAME:
>   rw_unlock - Releases a Reader-Writer lock.

SYNOPSIS:
>   #include <synch.h>
>
>   int
>   rw_unlock(rwlock_t *rwlock)

Figure 9.6   rw_unlock() synopsis. [1]

If the reader reference count is greater then zero, the rw_unlock assumes the operation applies to a READ mode lock, and will decrement the count by one. Otherwise, the rw_unlock function will release a WRITE mode lock and transition the Reader-Writer lock to the UNLOCKED state.

When the rw_unlock function applies to a READ mode lock, and the resulting reader reference count remains greater than zero, the rw_unlock function will return a zero status value to thecalling thread. The remaining READ mode locks stay active. If, however, the resulting reader reference count is zero, the rw_unlock function will transition the Reader-Writer lock to the UNLOCKED state.

The rw_unlock function must determine if there is a pending READ mode or WRITE mode request for the UNLOCKED Reader-Writer lock. The rw_unlock function will activate the first request. If the first request is for a READ mode lock, than the Reader is activated along with all subsequent readers (*up to the next Writer*). Alternatively, if the first request is for a WRITE mode lock, then only this request will become active.

9.6 Invalidating the Reader-Writer Lock

The rwlock_destroy function disables the use of the reader-writer lock found at the location pointed to by the rwlock parameter (*see Figure 9.7*). A successful call to the rwlock_destroy function invalidates the Reader-Writer lock and returns a zero status value to the calling thread. This function does not, however, free the memory associated with the lock.

The rwlock_destroy function will return an EINVAL error indication if the rwlock is not a USYNC_THREAD or a USYNC_PROCESS type lock. If there is a current READ mode or WRITE mode lock on the Reader-Writer lock, the rwlock_destroy function will return an EBUSY error indication value to the calling thread. In either case, the Reader-Writer lock is not modified. The rwlock_destroy will also release all dynamically allocated buffers used by the implementation for statistic and performance data collection in the DEBUG mode.

---

[1] Printed with Permission of UNIX System Laboratories, Inc. All Rights Reserved.

NAME:

       `rwlock_destroy` - Attempt to invalidate a Reader-Writer lock.

SYNOPSIS:

       `#include <synch.h>`

       `int`
       `rwlock_destroy( rwlock_t *rwlock )`

Figure 9.7   `rwlock_destroy()` synopsis. ¶

9.7 Using Reader-Writer Locks

The threadrw Module

The threadrw module (*Listings 9.1 and 9.2*) provides a dynamic allocation and deallocation of `USYNC_THREAD` type Reader-Writer locks. The `threadrw_t` type definition describes the types of functions available through this module. The macros `READER` and `WRITER` are used to distinguish between the modes of the lock.

Listing 9.1   *threadrw.h* -- threadrw module header file.

```
1  #define READER 1     /* Create read mode rwlocks   */
2  #define WRITER 2     /* Create write mode rwlocks  */
3
4  typedef struct _threadrw_t    {
5       rwlock_t  *(*create)(void);
6       rwlock_t  *(*createLocked)(const int);
7       int        (*destroy)(rwlock_t *);
8  } threadrw_t;
9  extern threadrw_t threadrw_f;
```

Compile threadrw module:

    cc -D_REENTRANT -c -I${INSTALLROOT}hdr threadrw.c

    ar rv ${INSTALLROOT}lib/libtsync.a threadrw.o

¶ Printed with Permission of UNIX System Laboratories, Inc. All Rights Reserved.

The `threadrw.c` source file provides the functions associated with the module. The `Create` function does not require the mode to be specified, since the Reader-Writer lock is initialized in the same manner for either mode.

The `threadrw_f.createLocked()` function accepts a parameter type describing the mode of the Reader-Writer lock. Specifying a type value of `WRITER` will cause a `rw_wrlock()` call to request the lock. Conversely, a `READER` type will cause a `rw_rdlock()` call to request the lock.

The function `Destroy` will make a single attempt to invalidate the specified Reader-Writer lock. On success, the `Destroy` function will release the memory space allocated for the Reader-Writer lock. Otherwise, the function will return an appropriate error indication value to the calling thread.

Listing 9.2   *threadrw.c* -- threadrw source module.

```
1    #include <errno.h>
2    #include <stdlib.h>
3    #include <memory.h>
4    #include <synch.h>
5    #include "mthreadLog.h"
6    #include "threadrw.h"
7
8    /*************************************************************
9     *    Function Prototypes
10    *************************************************************/
11   static      int          Destroy(rwlock_t *);
12   static      rwlock_t   *Create(void);
13   static      rwlock_t   *CreateLocked(const int);
14
15   /*************************************************************
16    *    Create            Function
17    *
18    *    The create function allocates and initializes a rwlock_t type
19    *    data structure.  A pointer to this allocated structure is
20    *    returned, or NULL on failure.
21    *************************************************************/
22   static rwlock_t *
23   Create(void)
24   {
25        rwlock_t *rwlockPtr       = NULL;
26        int       errorCondition = 0;
27
28        rwlockPtr = (rwlock_t *) malloc(sizeof(rwlock_t));
29        if( rwlockPtr == NULL )
30             errorCondition = ENOMEM;
31
32        else {
```

Listing 9.2 *continued.*

```
33              memset((void *)rwlockPtr,'\0',sizeof(rwlock_t));
34              errorCondition= rwlock_init(rwlockPtr, USYNC_THREAD,
35                                          NULL);
36          if( errorCondition ) {
37                  free( (void *)rwlockPtr);
38                  rwlockPtr = NULL;
39              }
40          }
41          if( errorCondition )
42              threadLog_f.setError(ENOMEM);
43          return(rwlockPtr);
44  }
45
46  /*******************************************************************
47   *    CreatedLocked   FUNCTION
48   *
49   *    The createdLocked function returns a pointer to an rwlock_t
50   *    type structure already locked in read mode if type is READER,
51   *    or write mode if type is WRITER.
52   *******************************************************************/
53  static rwlock_t *
54  CreateLocked( const int type)
55  {
56      rwlock_t *rwlockPtr       = NULL;
57      int       errorCondition = 0;
58
59      if ( type != READER && type != WRITER ) {
60              threadLog_f.setError(EINVAL);
61              return(NULL);
62      }
63      rwlockPtr = Create();
64      if( rwlockPtr ) {
65          if( type == WRITER )
66              errorCondition = rw_wrlock( rwlockPtr );
67          else
68              errorCondition = rw_rdlock( rwlockPtr );
69
70          if( errorCondition ) {
71              free( (void *)rwlockPtr );
72              rwlockPtr = NULL;
73              threadLog_f.setError(errorCondition);
74          }
75      }
76      return(rwlockPtr);
77  }
```

Listing 9.2   *continued.*

```
 78   /*****************************************************************
 79    *    Destroy          FUNCTION
 80    *
 81    *    The destroy function will invalidate the rwlock_t type
 82    *    structure and will release the storage associated with it.
 83    *****************************************************************/
 84   static int
 85   Destroy(rwlock_t *rwlockPtr )
 86   {
 87        int   errorCondition = 0;
 88        errorCondition = rwlock_destroy(rwlockPtr);
 89        if( ! errorCondition )
 90             free( (char *)rwlockPtr);
 91        return(errorCondition);
 92   }
 93
 94   /*****************************************************************
 95    *    Define the threadrw module interface.
 96    *****************************************************************/
 97   threadrw_t threadrw_f = {
 98        Create,
 99        CreateLocked,
100        Destroy
101   };
```

The threadLinks Module

In developing a generic linked list multithreaded module, we must consider that the list will be read more frequently than updated. This situation is an example of where to use a Reader-Writer lock. The threadLinks module (*Listings 9.3 and 9.4*) provides the basic operations for manipulation of a linked list.

A linked list is represented by a linkbase_t type data structure. This data structure has a pointer to the head of the list, and to the tail. There is also a Reader/ Writer lock associated with the list. Prior to adding entries to the linkbase, we must first allocate the linkbase type structure. Each link in the linkbase maintains a pointer to the next link, a pointer to the previous link, a pointer to the representative data, and finally, a reference count. Thus we are actually working with a doubly linked list in this instance.

The threadLinks.h header file (*Listing 9.3*) contains the basic definitions for our linked list. The link_t type data structure defines the members of the individual links. The linkbase_t type data structure defines the linkbase. For the threadLink module, we define various functions available through the threadLink_f data structure.

Listing 9.3   *threadLinks.h* -- threadLinks module header file.

```
1   #if ! defined(THREADLINKS_H)
2   #define THREADLINKS_H
3   /*******************************************************************
4    *    A link_t structure has a forward and backward pointer.  The
5    *    data member is for application-specific data.  The
6    *    referenceCount member is for maintaining a record of the
7    *    number of threads currently using the link.
8    *******************************************************************/
9   typedef struct _link {
10      struct _link    *forward;
11      struct _link    *backward;
12      void            *data;
13      unsigned long    referenceCount;
14  } link_t;
15  /*******************************************************************
16   *    a linkbase_t structure has a pointer to the first and last
17   *    links in the linkbase.  The rwlock is used for synchronizing
18   *    access to the linkbase.
19   *******************************************************************/
20  typedef struct _linkbase {
21      struct    _link    *head;
22      struct    _link    *tail;
23      rwlock_t  *rwlock;
24  } linkbase_t;
25  /*******************************************************************
26   *    the threadLink module provides the following functions.
27   *******************************************************************/
28  typedef struct _threadLink_t   {
29      linkbase_t   *(*create)(void );
30      int           (*destroy)(linkbase_t *);
31      int           (*add)(linkbase_t *,void *);
32      int           (*delete)(linkbase_t *,void *,
33                          int (*destructor)(void *));
34      void         *(*removeFirst)(linkbase_t *);
35      int           (*operation)(linkbase_t *,
36                          void *(*function)(void *));
37      int           (*apply)(linkbase_t *,
38                          int (*function)(void *,void *),
39                          void *);
40      void         *(*applySuccess)(linkbase_t *,
41                          int (*function)(void *,void *),
42                          void *);
43      void         *(*reference)( linkbase_t *,void *);
44      int           (*unreference)( linkbase_t *,void *);
45  } threadlink_t;
46  extern threadlink_t threadLink_f;
47  #endif
```

Compile threadLink module:

    cc -D_REENTRANT -c -I${INSTALLROOT}hdr threadLinks.c
    ar rv ${INSTALLROOT}lib/libtsync.a threadLinks.o

The `threadLinks.c` source file (*Listing 9.4*) provides the desired functionality for the `threadLinks` module. The `threadLink_f.create()` function creates a new `linkbase`. If a `linkbase` cannot be allocated, the `threadLog` module is called to record the error condition. On success, a pointer to the `linkbase` is returned.

The `threadLink_f.destroy()` function will invalidate the `linkbase`'s Reader-Writer lock and free the memory associated with the `linkbase`. The individual `links` are not released by this function. Caution must be exercised not to call this function unless the `linkbase` is empty.

The `threadLink_f.add()` function is used to add a new member to the `linkbase`. This function will allocate a new `link` pointer, initialize the pointer, and add it to the `linkbase`. In adding the `link`, the `threadLink_f.add()` function will first issue a `rw_wrlock()` call to lock the `linkbase` in `write` mode. This will prevent concurrent updates to the `linkbase`. The parameter `data` is a pointer to the application data for this link.

The `threadLink_f.delete()` function is used to remove a `link` from the `linkbase`. The second parameter, `data`, is a pointer to the application data associated with the `link`. The third parameter, `destructor`, is a pointer to the function to call to release the memory associated with the data. This function must lock the Reader-Writer lock in `write` mode to updating the `linkbase`.

The function `threadLink_f.apply()` function is used to traverse the `linkbase`. The first parameter is a pointer to the `linkbase`. The second parameter is a pointer to the function to call for each `link` in the `linkbase`. The function will lock the Reader-Writer lock in `read` mode. This is possible since the `linkbase` itself is not modified, assuming the specified function does not release the memory associated with the `link`.

The `threadLink_f.applySuccess()` function is also used to traverse the `linkbase`, sequentially applying the specified function to the `links` until the function returns a zero value. A pointer to the application data associated with the `link` is returned to the requesting thread.

The `threadLink_f.deleteFirst()` function will remove the first `link` from the `linkbase`. A pointer to the application `data` associated with this first `link` is returned to the calling thread. If the `linkbase` is empty, or if the first link's reference count is nonzero, then a `NULL` value is returned. The `threadLog` module is called to record any error conditions.

The `threadLink_f.reference()` and `threadLink_f.unreference()` functions are used to increment and subsequently decrement the reference count associated with a `link`. The parameter `data` is a pointer to the application data of the `link`.

The `threadLink_f.operation()` function creates a multiplexed thread with an application-defined `start` function for each `link` in the `linkbase`.

Listing 9.4   *threadLinks.c* -- the threadLinks source module.

```
1   #include <thread.h>
2   #include <synch.h>
3   #include <stdlib.h>
4   #include <errno.h>
5   #include <memory.h>
6   #include "threadLinks.h"
7   #include "threadrw.h"
8   #include "mthreadLog.h"
9
10  /*******************************************************************
11   *    Function Prototypes
12   *******************************************************************/
13  static int          Add(linkbase_t *,void *);
14  static int          Apply(linkbase_t *,
15                          int (function)(void *, void*), void *arg);
16  static int          Delete(linkbase_t *,void *,
17                          int (destructor)(void *));
18  static int          Destroy(linkbase_t *);
19  static void         *RemoveFirst(linkbase_t *);
20  static int          Operation(linkbase_t *,void *(function)(void *));
21  static int          Unreference(linkbase_t *,void *);
22  static linkbase_t   *Create(void);
23  static void         *ApplySuccess(linkbase_t *,
24                          int (function)(void *,void *),void *arg );
25  static void         *Reference(linkbase_t *,void *);
26
27  /*******************************************************************
28   *    Create          Function
29   *
30   *    The create function allocates and initializes a linkbase_t
31   *    type structure.  A pointer to the allocated structure is
32   *    returned.
33   *******************************************************************/
34  static linkbase_t *
35  Create( void )
36  {
37      linkbase_t * linkbasePtr = NULL;
38
39      threadLog_f.setError(0);
40      linkbasePtr = (linkbase_t *) malloc(sizeof(linkbase_t));
41      if( linkbasePtr == NULL )
42          threadLog_f.setError(ENOMEM);
43
44
```

Listing 9.4 *continued.*

```
45        else {
46              memset(linkbasePtr,'\0',sizeof(linkbase_t));
47              linkbasePtr->rwlock   = threadrw_f.create();
48              if( linkbasePtr->rwlock == NULL ) {
49                    free(linkbasePtr);
50                    linkbasePtr = NULL;
51              }
52        }
53        return( linkbasePtr);
54 }
55
56 /*******************************************************************
57  *    Destroy         FUNCTION
58  *
59  *    The destroy function will invalidate and release the storage
60  *    associated with the linkbase.
61  *******************************************************************/
62 static int
63 Destroy( linkbase_t *linkbasePtr )
64 {
65        int   errorCondition = 0;
66
67        threadLog_f.setError(0);
68
69        if( ! linkbasePtr )
70              errorCondition = EINVAL;
71        else if ( linkbasePtr->head )
72              errorCondition = EBUSY;
73        else
74              errorCondition=threadrw_f.destroy( linkbasePtr->rwlock);
75
76        if( ! errorCondition )
77              free(linkbasePtr);
78        else
79              threadLog_f.setError(errorCondition);
80        return(errorCondition);
81 }
82
83 /*******************************************************************
84  *    Add  FUNCTION
85  *
86  *    The add function will add a new link to the specified
87  *    linkbase. The link will be initialized with a pointer to the
88  *    specified data.
89  *******************************************************************/
```

Listing 9.4   *continued.*

```
90    static int
91    Add(linkbase_t *linkbasePtr, void *data )
92    {
93        int     errorCondition = 0;
94        link_t *linkPtr        = NULL;
95
96        if( linkbasePtr == NULL  ||  data == NULL )
97            return(EINVAL);
98        linkPtr = (link_t *) malloc( sizeof(link_t));
99        if( linkPtr == NULL )
100           return(ENOMEM);
101       memset(linkPtr,'\0', sizeof(link_t));
102       linkPtr->data = data;
103       errorCondition = rw_wrlock( linkbasePtr->rwlock );
104       if( errorCondition )
105           free(linkPtr);
106       else if( linkbasePtr->head == NULL ) {
107           linkbasePtr->head = linkPtr;
108           linkbasePtr->tail = linkPtr;
109       }
110       else {
111           linkbasePtr->tail->forward = linkPtr;
112           linkPtr->backward          = linkbasePtr->tail;
113           linkbasePtr->tail      = linkPtr;
114       }
115       rw_unlock( linkbasePtr->rwlock);
116       return(errorCondition);
117   }
118
119   /********************************************************************
120    *    Delete          FUNCTION
121    *
122    *    The delete function will remove from the linkbase that link
123    *    with a pointer to the specified application data.  If the
124    *    link can be found, and the destructor is non NULL, then the
125    *    destructor function will be called with a pointer to the
126    *    application data.
127    ********************************************************************/
128   static int
129   Delete(linkbase_t *linkbasePtr,void *data,int (destructor)(void *))
130   {
131       link_t    *linkPtr        = NULL;
132       int    errorCondition    = 0;
```

Listing 9.4   *continued.*

```
133          threadLog_f.setError(0);
134
135      if( linkbasePtr == NULL  ||  data == NULL )
136          errorCondition = EINVAL;
137      else
138          errorCondition = rw_wrlock( linkbasePtr->rwlock );
139
140      if( errorCondition ) {
141          threadLog_f.setError(errorCondition);
142          return(errorCondition);
143      }
144
145      linkPtr = linkbasePtr->head;
146
147      while( linkPtr ) {
148          if( linkPtr->data == data )
149              break;
150          linkPtr = linkPtr->forward;
151      }
152
153      if( linkPtr ) {
154          if( linkPtr->referenceCount != 0 )
155              errorCondition = EBUSY;
156          else {
157              if( linkPtr->backward )
158                  linkPtr->backward->forward= linkPtr->forward;
159
160              if( linkPtr->forward )
161                  linkPtr->forward->backward= linkPtr->backward;
162
163              if( linkbasePtr->tail == linkPtr )
164                  linkbasePtr->tail = linkPtr->backward;
165
166              if( linkbasePtr->head == linkPtr )
167                  linkbasePtr->head = linkPtr->forward;
168          }
169      }
170      else
171          errorCondition = ESRCH;
172      rw_unlock( linkbasePtr->rwlock);
173      if( errorCondition )
174          threadLog_f.setError(errorCondition);
175      if( !errorCondition && linkPtr ) {
176          if( destructor ) {
177              errorCondition = destructor(linkPtr->data);
```

Listing 9.4 *continued.*

```
178                    if( ! errorCondition )
179                        free( (void *) linkPtr );
180              }
181          else free((void *)linkPtr);
182      }
183      return(errorCondition);
184 }
185 /*******************************************************************
186  *    RemoveFirst    FUNCTION
187  *
188  *    The RemoveFirst function will remove the first link in the
189  *    linkbase.  A pointer to the application-specific data is
190  *    returned.  If the first link has a nonzero reference count,
191  *    then the link is unchanged and NULL is returned to the calling
192  *    thread.  The threadLog module will set the errorCondition to
193  *    EBUSY.
194  *******************************************************************/
195 static void *
196 RemoveFirst(linkbase_t *linkbasePtr )
197 {
198      link_t *linkPtr    = NULL;
199      void  *data      = NULL;
200      int    errorCondition = 0;
201      if( linkbasePtr != NULL )  {
202          errorCondition = rw_wrlock(linkbasePtr->rwlock);
203          if( ! errorCondition )  {
204              linkPtr =linkbasePtr->head;
205              if( linkPtr ) {
206                  if( linkPtr->referenceCount == 0 )  {
207                      if(linkbasePtr->tail==linkbasePtr->head)
208                              linkbasePtr->tail = NULL;
209                      linkbasePtr->head = linkPtr->forward;
210                      data = linkPtr->data;
211                      free(linkPtr);
212                  }
213                  else
214                          errorCondition = EBUSY;
215              }
216              rw_unlock( linkbasePtr->rwlock);
217          }
218      }
219      else
220          errorCondition = EINVAL;
221      if( errorCondition )
222          threadLog_f.setError(errorCondition);
223       return(data);
224 }
```

Listing 9.4 *continued.*

```
225   /*********************************************************************
226    *    Operation FUNCTION
227    *
228    *    For each link of linkbase, the operation function will create
229    *    a multiplexed thread starting with the specified function.
230    *    The function is given the application data pointer of the link
231    *    as an argument.
232    *********************************************************************/
233   static int
234   Operation( linkbase_t *linkbasePtr,void *(function)(void *) )
235   {
236           int      errorCondition    = 0;
237           link_t *linkPtr            = NULL;
238
239           if( linkbasePtr == NULL  ||  function == NULL )
240                return(EINVAL);
241
242           errorCondition = rw_rdlock( linkbasePtr->rwlock );
243
244           if( errorCondition )
245                return(errorCondition);
246
247           linkPtr = linkbasePtr->head;
248
249           if( ! linkPtr ) {
250                rw_unlock(linkbasePtr->rwlock);
251                return(ESRCH);
252           }
253
254           while( linkPtr ) {
255                errorCondition=thr_create(NULL,0,function,
256                                    linkPtr->data,0,NULL);
257                if( errorCondition )
258                    break;
259                linkPtr = linkPtr->forward;
260           }
261           rw_unlock( linkbasePtr->rwlock);
262           return( errorCondition );
263   }
264
265   /*********************************************************************
266    *    Apply          FUNCTION
267    *
268    *    The specified function is synchronously called for  each
269    *    link in the linkbase.
270    *********************************************************************/
271
```

Listing 9.4 *continued.*

```
272  static int
273  Apply(linkbase_t *linkbasePtr, int (function)(void *,void*),
274        void *arg)
275  {
276        int   errorCondition    = 0;
277        link_t   *linkPtr   = NULL;
278
279        if( linkbasePtr == NULL  ||   function == NULL)
280              return(EINVAL);
281        errorCondition = rw_rdlock( linkbasePtr->rwlock );
282        if( errorCondition )
283              return(errorCondition);
284        linkPtr = linkbasePtr->head;
285        while( linkPtr ) {
286              function(linkPtr->data, arg);
287              linkPtr = linkPtr->forward;
288        }
289        rw_unlock( linkbasePtr->rwlock);
290        return( 0 );
291  }
292
293
294  /*******************************************************************
295   *    Reference FUNCTION
296   *
297   *    Increment the reference count of the link with a pointer to
298   *    the specified application data.
299   *******************************************************************/
300  static void *
301  Reference( linkbase_t *linkbasePtr, void *data )
302  {
303        int    errorCondition  = 0;
304        link_t *linkPtr            = NULL;
305
306        if( linkbasePtr == NULL  ||   data == NULL ) {
307              threadLog_f.setError(EINVAL);
308              return(NULL);
309        }
310        errorCondition = rw_rdlock( linkbasePtr->rwlock );
311        if( errorCondition ) {
312              threadLog_f.setError(errorCondition);
313              return(NULL);
314        }
315
316        linkPtr = linkbasePtr->head;
317
```

Listing 9.4 *continued.*

```
318        while( linkPtr ) {
319            if( linkPtr->data == data )  {
320                    linkPtr->referenceCount++;
321                    break;
322                }
323
324            linkPtr = linkPtr->forward;
325        }
326
327        rw_unlock( linkbasePtr->rwlock);
328        if( ! linkPtr ) {
329            threadLog_f.setError(ESRCH);
330            data = NULL;
331        }
332
333        return( linkPtr->data );
334    }
335
336
337    /******************************************************************
338     *    Unreference    FUNCTION
339     *
340     *    Decrement the reference count of the link with a pointer
341     *    to the specified application data.
342     ******************************************************************/
343    static int
344    Unreference( linkbase_t *linkbasePtr, void *data )
345    {
346        int     errorCondition  = 0;
347        link_t *linkPtr            = NULL;
348
349        if( linkbasePtr == NULL || data == NULL )
350            return(EINVAL);
351        errorCondition = rw_rdlock( linkbasePtr->rwlock );
352        if( errorCondition )
353            return( errorCondition );
354        linkPtr = linkbasePtr->head;
355        while( linkPtr ) {
356            if( linkPtr->data == data )  {
357                    linkPtr->referenceCount--;
358                    break;
359                }
360            linkPtr = linkPtr->forward;
361        }
362        rw_unlock( linkbasePtr->rwlock);
363
```

Listing 9.4 *continued.*

```
364       if( ! linkPtr )
365            errorCondition = ESRCH;
366       return( errorCondition );
367 }
368
369 /*****************************************************************
370  *    ApplySuccess    FUNCTION
371  *
372  *    Synchronously call the specified function for each link in the
373  *    linkbase.  The function is called with a pointer to the
374  *    application data of the link and arg.  If the function returns
375  *    a zero value, then the ApplySuccess function terminates and
376  *    returns a pointer to the application data associated with the
377  *    link.
378  *****************************************************************/
379 static void *
380 ApplySuccess(linkbase_t *linkbasePtr,int (function)(void *,void *),
381            void *arg )
382 {
383       int    errorCondition    = 0;
384       link_t *linkPtr          = NULL;
385
386       if( linkbasePtr == NULL  || function == NULL ) {
387            threadLog_f.setError(EINVAL);
388            return(NULL);
389       }
390       errorCondition = rw_rdlock( linkbasePtr->rwlock );
391       if( errorCondition ) {
392            threadLog_f.setError(errorCondition);
393            return(NULL);
394       }
395       linkPtr = linkbasePtr->head;
396       if( ! linkPtr ) {
397            rw_unlock(linkbasePtr->rwlock);
398            threadLog_f.setError(ESRCH);
399            return(NULL);
400       }
401       while( linkPtr ) {
402            if( function(linkPtr->data, arg ) == 0 )
403                 break;
404            linkPtr = linkPtr->forward;
405       }
406       rw_unlock( linkbasePtr->rwlock);
407       if( linkPtr != NULL )
408            return( linkPtr->data );
409       return(NULL);
410 }
```

Listing 9.4   *continued.*

```
411   /**************************************************************
412    *    Define the threadLink module interface
413    **************************************************************/
414   threadlink_t threadLink_f = {
415        Create,
416        Destroy,
417        Add,
418        Delete,
419        RemoveFirst,
420        Operation,
421        Apply,
422        ApplySuccess,
423        Reference,
424        Unreference,
425   };
```

10

Synchronization with Barrier Locks

10.1   Barrier Locks: An Overview

An application uses a barrier synchronization primitive to ensure that all parallel processes have completed execution of a code block before permitting the processes to continue to the next block. When a participating parallel process arrives at a barrier it will wait until all the participating processes arrive. The processes can proceed after the last participating process arrives. Barriers have been available in some earlier releases of various UNIX implementations, such as the DYNIX operating system [BeOi87].

The initialization of the barrier synchronization primitive records the number of threads participating in the synchronization. The participating threads can execute until they arrive at the barrier. The threads will resume execution after the last participating thread arrives at the barrier.

In using a barrier synchronization primitive, caution must be exercised to ensure all participating threads will ultimately reach the barrier. Otherwise, the participating threads will not have the chance to execute past the barrier. Thus if a participating thread issues a thr_exit call prior to reaching the barrier, or becomes blocked waiting for another synchronization primitive that cannot be satisfied, then all participating threads will remain blocked. The UNIX Threads Interface provides the barrier synchronization primitive for use between the sibling threads of a single UNIX process, or for use between UNIX processes executing in disjoint address spaces.

Table 10.1   The Barrier API

barrier_init()	Initialize a barrier
barrier_wait()	Wait at a barrier
barrier_destroy()	Invalidate a barrier

10.2   Initializing Barrier Locks

A barrier is represented in an application as a `barrier_t` type data structure. As with the other synchronization primitives, the barrier must be initialized to a known state. The `barrier_init` function (*see Figure 10.1*) will initialize the barrier as a `block-wait` type barrier.

The `barrier` parameter is the address of the barrier to initialize. The second parameter, `count`, identifies the number of threads participating in the barrier. The `type` parameter must be either `USYNC_PROCESS` or `USYNC_THREAD`. The `arg` parameter is reserved for future enhancements and should always be specified as `NULL`.

NAME:
        `barrier_init` - Initialize a blocking type barrier.

SYNOPSIS:
```
int
barrier_init(barrier_t *barrier,int count,int type,
             void *arg)
```

Figure 10.1   `barrier_init()` synopsis. [1]

10.3   Blocking at the Barrier

The `barrier_wait` function (*Figure 10.2*) provides a simple rendezvous mechanism for the threads participating in the barrier. When a thread reaches the barrier, it will block-wait until the remaining participating threads have reached the barrier. When the last thread reaches the barrier, all of the participating threads, including the last thread, will be released from the barrier and resume execution. The barrier is reinitialized after the participating threads have been released.

PROGRAMMER'S NOTE:

From the point of view of the application, these functions are atomic. If interrupted by a signal, the functions will call the appropriate signal handling function, if necessary, and subsequently resume their wait. If the `barrier_wait` function blocks, it will not return until the barrier is removed.

The order in which the participating threads are released from the barrier is scheduling policy-specific for bound threads and may be dependent on scheduling parameters for multiplexed threads. The operation will keep statistics and performance data under the DEBUG option.

NAME:
> `barrier_wait` - Blocks the calling thread at barrier.

SYNOPSIS:
```
int
barrier_wait(barrier_t * barrier)
```

Figure 10.2   `barrier_wait()` synopsis. [1]

10.4   Invalidating the Barrier

The `barrier_destroy()` function (*Figure 10.3*) will invalidate the specified barrier. In destroying the barrier, the functions will release all dynamically allocated resources associated with the barrier.

NAME:
> `barrier_destroy` - Invalidate a barrier structure.

SYNOPSIS:
```
int
barrier_destroy(barrier_t * barrier)
```

Figure 10.3   `barrier_destroy()` synopsis. [1]

10.5   Using a Barrier

The threadBarrier Module

The `threadBarrier` (*Listings 10.1 and 10.2*) provides the `create` and `destroy` functions for administering dynamically allocated `USYNC_THREAD` barriers. The `threadBarrier.h` header file (*Listing 10.1*), details the `threadBarrier_f_t` data structure containing pointers to the `threadBarrier` module functions.

---

[1] Printed with Permission of UNIX Systems Laboratories, Inc. All Rights Reserved.

Listing 10.1   *threadBarrier.h* -- The `threadBarrier` module header file.

```
1   typedef struct _threadBarrier_f      {
2        barrier_t  *(*create)(const int);
3        int         (*destroy)(barrier_t *);
4   } threadBarrier_f_t;
5
6   extern threadBarrier_f_t threadBarrier_f;
```

Compile threadBarrier module:

```
cc -D_REENTRANT -c -I${INSTALLROOT}hdr threadBarrier.c
ar rv ${INSTALLROOT}lib/libtsync.a threadBarrier.o
```

The `threadBarrier_f.create` function accepts as a single argument the number of threads participating in the barrier. If the `barrier_t` type structure cannot be allocated, the `threadLog` module is called to record the error condition. On success, the `threadBarrier_f.create` function will return a pointer to the allocated barrier. The `threadBarrier_f.destroy` function invalidates the specified barrier and releases its associated resources. If the function call fails, the `threadLog` module is called to record the error condition. The function returns zero on success, or the appropriate error indication value.

Listing 10.2   *threadBarrier.c* -- The `threadBarrier` module source file.

```
1   #include <stdlib.h>
2   #include <memory.h>
3   #include <synch.h>
4   #include <thread.h>
5   #include <errno.h>
6   #include "mthreadLog.h"
7   #include "threadBarrier.h"
8
9   /************************************************************
10  *      FUNCTION PROTOTYPES
11  ************************************************************/
12  static barrier_t  *Create(const int);
13  static int         Destroy(barrier_t *);
14
15  /************************************************************
16  *      Create               FUNCTION
17  *
18  *      The create function allocates and initializes a barrier_t
19  *      type structure.  A pointer to the allocated barrier is
20  *      returned to the calling thread.  On error, a NULL pointer is
21  *      returned and the threadLog module is called to record the
22  *      error condition.
23  ************************************************************/
```

Listing 10.2 *continued.*

```
24   static barrier_t *
25   Create(const int resources)
26   {
27           barrier_t   *barrierPtr         = NULL;
28           int          errorCondition    = 0;
29
30           threadLog_f.setError(0);
31           barrierPtr = (barrier_t *) malloc(sizeof(barrier_t));
32
33           if( barrierPtr == NULL )
34                   threadLog_f.setError(ENOMEM);
35
36           else {
37                   memset((void *)barrierPtr,'\0',sizeof(barrierPtr));
38                   errorCondition = barrier_init( barrierPtr, resources,
39                       USYNC_THREAD, NULL);
40
41                   if ( errorCondition ) {
42                           free((void *)barrierPtr );
43                           barrierPtr = NULL;
44                           threadLog_f.setError( errorCondition );
45                   }
46           }
47           return(barrierPtr);
48   }
49
50
51   /****************************************************************
52    *     Destroy             FUNCTION
53    *
54    *     The destroy function invalidates and releases the resources
55    *     associated with the specified barrier.  This function returns
56    *     the status value of the barrier_destroy call.
57    ****************************************************************/
58   static int
59   Destroy( barrier_t *barrierPtr)
60   {
61           int   errorCondition = 0;
62
63           errorCondition = barrier_destroy(barrierPtr);
64
65           if( ! errorCondition )
66                   free((void *)barrierPtr);
67
68           return( errorCondition );
69   }
```

Listing 10.2 *continued.*

```
70   /**************************************************************
71    *      Define the threadBarrier module interface.
72    **************************************************************/
73   threadBarrier_f_t threadBarrier_f = {
74        Create,
75        Destroy,
76   };
```

Synchronizing Compilations

The process of constructing an executable program is often studied in parallel processing. The software construction process can execute compilations in parallel but must synchronize the loader to trigger after the compilations are complete.[33]   A performance gain can be achieved in this model by overlapping computation with I/O requests.

There are several design considerations that must be addressed in this model. The operating system configuration will determine the number of file descriptors per process, and the number of bound threads per user. We must therefore synchronize the number of concurrent compilations to avoid exceeding the system-imposed limits of these resources. Another design consideration is how to handle the output of the parallel compilations. Consider that when one or more of the parallel compilations encounters syntax errors in the source files, the compiler will generate appropriate messages. If the child processes executing the compilations share the same standard output and standard error file descriptors, then the error messages from one compilation will be interspersed with error messages from the other. We therefore need to buffer the output to address this problem.

The `bcompile.c` source module (*Listings 10.3 through 10.5*) is similar to the `cc(1)` command[34] and provides good discussion related to synchronization issues.   The program accepts the `-D` and `-I` compilation options, the `-o` load option, along with source, object and library names. The `main` function is responsible for processing command-line arguments, creating the concurrent compilations threads, and executing the `load` function. Several linked lists are used to appropriately group the command-line arguments (see Table 10.2 for a description of the linked

---

[33] The standard `make` utility offered with the Software Development Toolkit does not provide this capability. The nmake software construction tool, available at `www.research.att.com/ssr/orgs`, does offer parallel computations. This tool is described in [Kris95].

[34] The `bcompile` program, as presented here, is not meant as a replacement for the C compiler. The example is meant only for discussions related to synchronization.

lists). The -D and -I command-line options, for example, are added to the ccoptList. These options will be applied to all subsequent compilations.

Table 10.2   The bcompile Program Linked Lists

ccoptList	The list of cc(1) compilation options common for all source files
compileList	The list of source file names to be compiled
objectList	The list of object files to use with the load command
libList	The list of command-line libraries to use with the load command

The main function calls the initCompilation function to initialize the compilation options common to all compiles. The pointer to each option is added to the Ccargs array of character pointers. We maintain a reference to the last entry used in this array. The Ccargs array will be used when we exec the standard C compiler.

A barrier is then created to synchronize the execution of function main with the execution of the compilation threads. Note that the number of threads participating in the barrier is the number of compilation threads plus the main (initial) thread. A call to threadLink_f.apply is then made for the compileList linkbase, resulting in the creation of one multiplexed thread per link in the list. Each thread will start execution at the compile function.

The compile function allocates a client_t type structure for use with a modified sclientshell module.[35] We then enter a critical section as we add the source file name to the next available entry in the Ccargs array, and copy the array to the allocated client_t structure's argument member. If multiple threads executed this code in parallel, we could end up with several threads compiling the same source file. The compile function will then create another thread starting execution at the clientshell function.

The clientshell function will use a semaphore to synchronize the number of concurrent child processes. This is necessary to minimize the use of limited system-imposed resources, such as the number of open file descriptors.

---

[35] An earlier version of sclientshell was presented in Chapter 3. That version used the popen function to execute the client process. The modified sclientshell uses pipe, fork, and exec calls for similar functionality.

The `compile` thread and its associated `clientshell` thread will then join execution streams. The ouput from the `clientshell` thread is displayed, and the `compile` thread enters the barrier established by the `main` function. The multiplexed `compile` threads and the initial thread will resume execution after all threads have entered the barrier.   The `main` function then calls the `load` function to execute the final phase of the compilation.

Compile bcompile program:
```
cc -c -D_REENTRANT -I. -I${INSTALLROOT}hdr bcompile.c
cc -c -D_REENTRANT -I. -I${INSTALLROOT}hdr sclientshell.c
cc -O -D_REENTRANT -I. -I${INSTALLROOT}hdr bcompile.o \
        sclientshell.o  ${INSTALLROOT}/lib/libtsync.a -lthread
        -o bcompile
```

Listing 10.3   *bcompile.c* -- A parallel compilation program with a barrier synchronization.

```
1   #include <thread.h>
2   #include <synch.h>
3   #include <stdio.h>
4   #include <stdlib.h>
5   #include <string.h>
6   #include <errno.h>
7   #include "threadBarrier.h"
8   #include "threadLinks.h"
9   #include "clientshell.h"
10
11  /*****************************************************************
12   *      Function Prototypes
13   *****************************************************************/
14  static void *compile(void *);
15  static void  usage(void);
16  static int   load(void);
17  static int   addLinkopts(void *, void *);
18  static int   addCCopts(void *, void *);
19  static void  initCompilation(void);
20  static void  initLink(void);
21
22  /*****************************************************************
23   *     Global Static Variables
24   *****************************************************************/
25  static barrier_t   *compileBarrier; /* a barrier to synchronize   */
26                                      * the load after compilation */
27  static int         compileCount=0;  /* the number of compilations */
28                                      * we will do.                 */
```

Listing 10.3 *continued.*

```
29
30   static linkbase_t   *compileList;       /* the list of source files   */
31                                           /* to compile                 */
32
33   static linkbase_t   *ccoptList;         /* the list of cc compilation */
34                                           /* options.                   */
35
36   static linkbase_t   *objectList;        /* the list of object files   */
37                                           /* to given to the linker     */
38
39   static linkbase_t *linkoptList;         /* the list of cc link        */
40                                           /* options                    */
41
42   static linkbase_t *libList;             /* the list of cc link options*/
43
44   static char            *output= NULL;   /* the output file given on    */
45                                           /* the command line.           */
46
47   static char *Umsg="bcompile -I dir -D define -l lib source -o
48   output";
49
50   #define     MAX_OPTIONS 512
51
52
53   static char *CompileCommand   = "cc";
54   static char *LinkOption       = "-o";
55   static char *CompileOption    = "-c";
56   static char *IncludeOption    = "-I";
57   static char *DefineOption     = "-D";
58   static char *LibOption        = "-l";
59   static char *CCargs[MAX_OPTIONS]   = { 0 };
60   static char **ccargv = &(CCargs[1]);
61   static char *Linkargs[MAX_OPTIONS]   = { 0 };
62   static char **linkargv=&(Linkargs[1]);
63   static mutex_t copyMutex    = { 0 };
64   static mutex_t writeMutex   = { 0 };
65
66   void *
67   main(int argc, char **argv)
68   {
69         char   *argEnd;
70         int    c;
71         int    errorCondition = 0;
```

Listing 10.3   *continued.*

```
72                        /***********************************************
73                         *   We start by initializing the clientshell
74                         *   semaphore to permit only 10 concurrent subshell
75                         *   threads.
76                         ***********************************************/
77      if( clientshellinit(10) != 0 ) {
78          perror("cshell: can't initialize subshell\n");
79          exit(0);
80      }
81                        /***********************************************
82                         * Create the linkbases for the common compilation
83                         * options, the list of source files, the list of
84                         * object files, and the link options.
85                         ***********************************************/
86      ccoptList    = threadLink_f.create();
87      compileList  = threadLink_f.create();
88      objectList   = threadLink_f.create();
89      linkoptList  = threadLink_f.create();
90      libList      = threadLink_f.create();
91
92                        /***********************************************
93                         * Initialize the compilation option list.
94                         ***********************************************/
95      threadLink_f.add(ccoptList,CompileOption);
96
97                        /***********************************************
98
99                         * Process the command-line arguments.
100                        ***********************************************/
101     while((c=getopt(argc, argv, "o:l:D:I:")) != EOF) {
102         switch(c) {
103
104         case 'o' :
105                        /***********************************************
106                         *    -o file was found.  Add the "-o" option to
107                         *    the link option list, then the name of the
108                         *    output file.
109                         ***********************************************/
110             threadLink_f.add(linkoptList,LinkOption);
111             threadLink_f.add(linkoptList,optarg);
112             output = optarg;
113             break;
114
```

Listing 10.3 *continued.*

```
115                    case 'l' :
116                        /************************************************
117                         *      -l lib was found.  Add the "-l" option to
118                         *      the link option list, then the name of the
119                         *      library.
120                         ************************************************/
121                        threadLink_f.add(libList,LibOption);
122                        threadLink_f.add(libList,optarg);
123                        break;
124                    case 'D' :
125                        /************************************************
126                         *      -D define was found.  Add the "-D" option to
127                         *      the cc options list and then add the macro
128                         *      itself.
129                         ************************************************/
130                        threadLink_f.add(ccoptList,DefineOption);
131                        threadLink_f.add(ccoptList,optarg);
132                        break;
133                    case 'I' :
134                        /************************************************
135                         *      -I includeDir was found.
136                         ************************************************/
137                        threadLink_f.add(ccoptList,IncludeOption);
138                        threadLink_f.add(ccoptList,optarg);
139                        break;
140                    case '?' :
141                        fprintf(stderr,"invalid option: %c\n", c);
142                        usage();
143                }
144        }
145        /****************************************************
146         *   Anything else should be either a
147         *           file.c              source file
148         *           file.o              object file
149         *           library.a    library
150         ****************************************************/
151    while( optind < argc ) {
152        argEnd=(char *)(argv[optind]+strlen(argv[optind]) - 1);
153        if( argEnd <= argv[optind] ) {
154            fprintf(stderr,"invalid arg %s\n", argv[optind]);
155            usage();
156        }
```

Listing 10.3   *continued.*

```
157                 if( *((char *) argEnd - 1) == '.' ) {
158                     switch ( *argEnd) {
159                     case 'c' :
160                         threadLink_f.add(compileList, argv[optind]);
161                         ++compileCount;
162                         break;
163                     case 'o' :
164                         threadLink_f.add(objectList, argv[optind]);
165                         break;
166                     case 'a':
167                         threadLink_f.add(libList, argv[optind]);
168                         break;
169                     default :
170                         fprintf(stderr,"unknown argument %s\n",
171                                                 argv[optind]);
172                         usage();
173                     }
174                 }
175                 else {
176                     fprintf(stderr,"invalid file\n", argv[optind]);
177                     usage();
178                 }
179                 ++optind;
180         }
181         /*****************************************************
182          *   If we have compiles to do, create a barrier
183          *   for each compile thread plus one for this initial
184          *   thread.  Then use the threadLink_f.operation to
185          *   create the compile threads for each link in the
186          *   compileList.
187          *****************************************************/
188     if( compileCount ) {
189         initCompilation();
190         compileBarrier = threadBarrier_f.create(compileCount+1);
191         threadLink_f.operation(compileList, compile);
192         barrier_wait(compileBarrier);
193     }
194         /*****************************************************
195          *   If we have output to create, then call the load
196          *   function to perform the link edit.
197          *****************************************************/
198     if( output && ! errorCondition )  {
199         initLink();
200         errorCondition = load();
```

Listing 10.3 *continued.*

```
201                 if( errorCondition )
202                     fprintf(stderr,"load failed\n");
203         }
204         thr_exit(0);
205 }
206
207 /*****************************************************************
208  *      Usage           FUNCTION
209  *
210  *      Display the usage message.
211  *****************************************************************/
212 static void
213 usage(void)
214 {
215         fprintf(stderr,"%s\n", Umsg);
216         exit(1);
217 }
218
219 /*****************************************************************
220  *      initCompilation          FUNCTION
221  *
222  *      Prepare the common options for the cc command line.
223  *****************************************************************/
224 void
225 initCompilation(void)
226 {
227         CCargs[0] = CompileCommand;
228                     /*************************************************
229                      *      Call threadLink_f.apply to sequentially
230                      *      apply the addCCopts function to each element
231                      *      in the linked list.  Note that we pass
232                      *      ccargv as the argument portion to this
233                      *      command.
234                      *************************************************/
235         threadLink_f.apply( ccoptList, addCCopts, &ccargv);
236 }
237
238 /*****************************************************************
239  *      addCCopts     FUNCTION
240  *
241  *      This function is called by the threadLink_f.apply() to add
242  *      each element of the ccoptList to the cc argument vector.  Note
243  *      that each call increments the argument vector position.
244  *****************************************************************/
```

Listing 10.3 *continued.*

```
245 static int
246 addCCopts(void *data, void *arg)
247 {
248         char      **argList;
249         void      ***argv = (void ***)arg;
250
251         argList = (char **) *(argv);
252         *argList=data;
253         ++(*argv);
254 }
255
256 /*****************************************************************
257  *      Compile              THREAD
258  *
259  *      This thread is responsible for constructing the compilation
260  *      command.  It then creates a thread starting at the clientshell
261  *      function to perform the actual fork/exec.  This thread will
262  *      then join with the clientshell thread and will display any
263  *      error messages resulting from the compilation.
264  *****************************************************************/
265 void *
266 compile(void *data)
267 {
268         client_t    *clientPtr;
269         void        *status          = NULL;
270         int          errorCondition  = 0;
271
272                     /*********************************************
273                      *   Allocate and initialize a client structure.
274                      *********************************************/
275         clientPtr = (client_t *) malloc(sizeof(client_t));
276         clientPtr->command       = CompileCommand;
277         clientPtr->argument      = malloc(sizeof(char *) *MAX_OPTIONS);
278
279                     /*********************************************
280                      *    CRITICAL SECTION   START
281                      *
282                      *    Each compilation uses the common command-
283                      *    line argument found in the character pointer
284                      *    array CCargs.  The last entry to be added
285                      *    to the array is a pointer to the filename
286                      *    to be compiled.  This is the only entry
287                      *    that cannot be shared between the threads.
288                      *    We therefore use a mutex to synchronize the
```

Listing 10.3   *continued.*

```
289                          *       access.
290                          **********************************************/
291       mutex_lock( &CopyMutex );
292       *ccargv = data;
293       memcpy(clientPtr->argument,CCargs,
294                          sizeof(char *) *MAX_OPTIONS);
295       mutex_unlock( &CopyMutex );
296                  /***********************************************
297                   *      CRITICAL SECTION    END
298                   **********************************************/
299
300                  /***********************************************
301                   *   Use clientshell to do the actual work for us.
302                   **********************************************/
303       errorCondition=thr_create(NULL,0,clientshell,
304                          (void *) clientPtr, THR_NEW_LWP,
305                          &(clientPtr->tid));
306
307                  /***********************************************
308                   *   Wait for the thread to terminate, and display
309                   *   any output returned.  Then change the name
310                   *   of the file to have a ".o" suffix and add the
311                   *   file to the objectList.
312                   **********************************************/
313       if( ! errorCondition )  {
314           errorCondition = thr_join(clientPtr->tid,NULL,&status);
315           if( ! errorCondition ) {
316               if( status )  {
317                  /***********************************************
318                   *      CRITICAL SECTION            START
319                   *
320                   * We must prevent multiple threads from
321                   * writing to standard output concurrently.
322                   **********************************************/
323                  mutex_lock( &WriteMutex );
324                  fprintf(stdout,"%s", status);
325                  mutex_unlock( &WriteMutex );
326                  /***********************************************
327                   *      CRITICAL SECTION            END
328                   **********************************************/
329                  free(status);
330               }
331               *((char *)data+strlen(data) -1) = 'o';
332               threadLink_f.add(objectList,data);
```

Listing 10.3 *continued.*

```
333
334                   }
335           }
336                   /***********************************************
337           *    Finally, we will wait at this barrier for the
338           *    rest of the threads.
339                   ***********************************************/
340         free(clientPtr->argument);
341         free(clientPtr);
342         barrier_wait(compileBarrier);
343         thr_exit((void *)errorCondition);
344 }
345
346 /*****************************************************************************
347  *     load   FUNCTION
348  *
349  *     Generate the link command string and call shellclient to do
350  *     the work for us.
351  *****************************************************************************/
352 static int
353 load(void)
354 {
355         client_t     *clientPtr;
356         int           errorCondition = 0;
357         void         *status = NULL;
358
359                   /***********************************************
360           *    Allocate a clientPtr and initialize the
361           *    command to the compile command.
362                   ***********************************************/
363         clientPtr            = malloc(sizeof(client_t));
364         clientPtr->command   = CompileCommand;
365         clientPtr->argument  = malloc(sizeof(char *) *MAX_OPTIONS);
366                   /***********************************************
367           *    We need to add the objects from the objectList
368           *    to the link command argument vector.
369                   ***********************************************/
370         memcpy(clientPtr->argument,Linkargs,
371                         sizeof(char *) *MAX_OPTIONS);
372                   /***********************************************
373           *    We create a clientshell thread to do the
374           *    actual work for us.
375                   ***********************************************/
```

Listing 10.3   *continued.*

```
376          errorCondition = thr_create(NULL,0,clientshell,clientPtr,
377                                       0,&(clientPtr->tid));
378                      /***********************************************
379                       *  Display any output we get from clientshell.
380                       ***********************************************/
381      if( ! errorCondition ) {
382              thr_join(clientPtr->tid,NULL, &status);
383              if( status ) {
384                      fprintf(stderr,"%s", status);
385                      free(status);
386              }
387      }
388      free(clientPtr->argument);
389      free(clientPtr);
390      return(errorCondition);
391 }
392
393 /*********************************************************************
394  *     initLink            FUNCTION
395  *
396  *     Prepare the link options.
397  *********************************************************************/
398 void
399 initLink(void)
400 {
401      int    errorCondition = 0;
402      Linkargs[0] = CompileCommand;
403                      /***********************************************
404                       *     Call threadLink_f.apply to sequentially
405                       *     apply the link options, the object files,
406                       *     and the libraries.
407                       ***********************************************/
408      threadLink_f.apply(linkoptList,addLinkopts,&linkargv);
409      threadLink_f.apply(objectList,addLinkopts,&linkargv);
410      threadLink_f.apply(libList,addLinkopts,&linkargv);
411 }
412
413 /*********************************************************************
414  *     addLinkopts FUNCTION
415  *
416  *     This function is called by the threadLink_f.apply() to add
417  *     each element of the ccoptList to the cc argument vector.  Note
418  *     that each call increments the argument vector position.
419  *********************************************************************/
```

Listing 10.3   *continued.*

```
420 static int
421 addLinkopts(void *data, void *arg)
422 {
423        char   **argList;
424        void   ***argv = (void ***) arg;
425
426        argList = (char **) *(argv);
427        *argList=data;
428        ++(*argv);
429 }
```

Listing 10.4   *clientshell.h* -- The modified client shell process module header file.

```
 1 typedef struct    _client       {
 2        thread_t    tid;
 3        char      *command;
 4        char       **argument;
 5        struct    _client     *next;
 6 } client_t;
 7
 8 typedef struct    _clientList {
 9        struct    _client     *head;
10        struct    _client     *tail;
11 } clientList_t;
12
13 void * clientshell(void * );
14 char * copybuffer(char *,char *,int, int);
15 int    clientshellinit(int);
```

Listing 10.5   *sclientshell.c* -- The modified client shell module.

```
 1 #include <unistd.h>
 2 #include <stdlib.h>
 3 #include <thread.h>
 4 #include <errno.h>
 5 #include <memory.h>
 6 #include <synch.h>
 7 #include "threadSema.h"
 8 #include "clientshell.h"
 9 #include "mthreadLog.h"
10
```

Listing 10.5 *continued.*

```
11 static sema_t      *clientSemaphore = NULL;
12
13 /****************************************************************
14  *     clientshell THREAD
15  *
16  *     The clientshell() function is called as a thread from the
17  *     initial application thread.  The parameter arg points to a
18  *     client_t type data structure.
19  ****************************************************************/
20 void *
21 clientshell( void *arg )
22 {
23       client_t    *client     = NULL;
24       char        *input      = NULL;
25       char        *output     = NULL;
26       pid_t        pid;
27       int          errorCondition = 0;
28       int          iterations  = 0;
29       int          outputPipe[2];
30
31       client = (client_t *) arg;
32                   /***********************************************
33                    *   If there is no command to execute, then
34                    *   complain and exit this thread.
35                    ***********************************************/
36       if( client->command == NULL ) {
37           threadLog_f.message("No command specified");
38           thr_exit(NULL);
39       }
40                   /***********************************************
41                    *   If the clientshellinit() function was not
42                    *   called, then complain and exit this thread.
43                    ***********************************************/
44       if( clientSemaphore == NULL ) {
45           threadLog_f.message("No subshells specified");
46           thr_exit(NULL);
47       }
48                   /***********************************************
49                    *   Wait for available subshell.  The maximum
50                    *   number of subshells is determined by the
51                    *   clientSemaphore value.
52                    ***********************************************/
53       if( sema_wait( clientSemaphore ) != 0 ) {
54           threadLog_f.message("clientShell: no subshell");
```

Listing 10.5 *continued.*

```
55                   free(input);
56                   thr_exit(NULL);
57           }
58                           /************************************************
59                            * Create a pipe so that we can redirect the
60                            * output of the child process.  The parent
61                            * process will read the output into an allocated
62                            * buffer and will return the address of the
63                            * buffer to the calling thread.
64                            ************************************************/
65           if( pipe(outputPipe) != 0 ) {
66                   threadLog_f.message("clientShell: can't create pipe\n");
67                   free(input);
68                   close(outputPipe[0]);
69                   close(outputPipe[1]);
70                   sema_post(clientSemaphore);
71                   thr_exit(NULL);
72           }
73
74                   /************************************************
75                    *   Create the child process.
76                    ************************************************/
77           pid = fork1();
78                           /************************************************
79                            *  If pid < 0, then we have an error condition.
80                            ************************************************/
81           if( pid < 0 ) {
82                   threadLog_f.message("clientShell: cannot fork\n");
83                   free(input);
84                   close(outputPipe[0]);
85                   close(outputPipe[1]);
86                   sema_post(clientSemaphore);
87                   thr_exit(NULL);
88           }
89           if( pid > 0 ) {
90                           /************************************************
91                            *  We are the parent, so prepare for child input.
92                            ************************************************/
93                   input = malloc( BUFSIZ );
94                   memset(input,'\0',BUFSIZ);
95                           /************************************************
96                            *  The parent closes the pipe's write end.
97                            ************************************************/
```

Listing 10.5 *continued.*

```
98                  close(outputPipe[1]);
99                      /************************************************
100                     *   Every time we read BUFSIZ bytes from the input
101                     *   filestream, we call copybuffer to readjust the
102                     *   size of the buffer holding the output.
103                     ************************************************/
104             iterations = 0;
105             while((errorCondition=read(outputPipe[0],input,BUFSIZ))>
106 0)
107             {
108                     output=copybuffer(output,input,iterations,BUFSIZ);
109                     if( output == NULL ) {
110                         errorCondition = threadLog_f.getError();
111                     break;
112                     }
113                     ++iterations;
114             }
115             close(outputPipe[0]);
116         }
117
118     else  {
119                     /************************************************
120                     *   We must be the child process, so close the
121                     *   write end of the pipe.
122                     ************************************************/
123             close(outputPipe[0]);
124                     /************************************************
125                     * Duplicate the pipe descriptor as the standard
126                     * output and the standard error.  This will
127                     * permit us to buffer all output from the child.
128                     ************************************************/
129             if(dup2(outputPipe[1],STDOUT_FILENO)!=STDOUT_FILENO) {
130                     fprintf(stderr,"dup2() call failed on stdout\n");
131                     exit(0);
132             }
133             if(dup2(outputPipe[1],STDERR_FILENO)!=STDERR_FILENO) {
134                     fprintf(stderr,"dup2() call failed on stderr\n");
135                     exit(0);
136             }
137                     /************************************************
138                     *   Now execute the client command.
139                     ************************************************/
140             errorCondition =
141                         execvp(client->command,client->argument);
```

Listing 10.5 *continued.*

```
142
143                 if( errorCondition < 0 ) {
144                     fprintf(stderr,"exec(%s) failed [%d] errno %d \n",
145                             client->command, errorCondition,
146                             errno);
147                     exit(0);
148                 }
149         }
150                     /***********************************************
151                      *   Only the parent can reach here.  Take care of
152                      *   the garbage collection and then release the
153                      *   semaphore.
154                      ***********************************************/
155         if( input )
156             free( input);
157
158         if( threadLog_f.hasError() )
159             threadLog_f.message("[%s] failed",client->command);
160         sema_post( clientSemaphore );
161         thr_exit(output);
162 }
163
164 /*****************************************************************
165  *     copybuffer   FUNCTION
166  *
167  *     This function accumulates the buffered output from the client
168  *     shell into a single buffer.  If a client shell produces more
169  *     than BUFSIZ output, we need to accumulate the total output
170  *     into a single buffer.
171  *         bufferPtr    Points to the accumulated output
172  *         cptr         Points to the new output to append
173  *         count        Is the number of BUFSIZ buffers currently
174  *                      accumulated in bufferPtr
175  *         size         Is the size of the output to be appended
176  *****************************************************************/
177 char *
178 copybuffer( char *bufferPtr, char *cptr, int count, int size)
179 {
180         char   *newbuffer;
181
182         newbuffer = (char *)malloc( (count +1) * size);
183         if( newbuffer == NULL)  {
184             threadLog_f.setError( ENOMEM);
185             return(NULL);
```

Listing 10.5   *continued.*

```
186        }
187
188        memset(newbuffer,'\0',(count+1)*size);
189        if( count )
190                memcpy(newbuffer, bufferPtr, (count +1) * size);
191        memcpy(newbuffer + ( count * size), cptr, size);
192        if( bufferPtr )
193                free(bufferPtr);
194        memset(cptr, '\0', size);
195        return(newbuffer);
196 }
197
198 /********************************************************************
199  *      clientshellinit    FUNCTION
200  *
201  *      This function calls threadSema_f.create to establish the
202  *      semaphore count for the number of permissable client shells.
203  ********************************************************************/
204 int
205 clientshellinit(int count )
206 {
207        clientSemaphore = threadSema_f.create( count );
208        if( clientSemaphore )
209                return(0);
210        return(1);
211 }
```

Using the bcompile program:

```
time cc -D_REENTRANT -I. -I${INSTALLROOT}hdr -o bc      \
        -l thread compile.c sclientshell.c              \
        ${INSTALLROOT}lib/libtsync.a
time ./bcompile -D _REENTRANT -I. -I${INSTALLROOT}hdr \
        -o bc                                           \
        -l thread compile.c sclientshell.c              \
        ${INSTALLROOT}lib/libtsync.a
```

Sample output from compilation script:

```
+ timex cc -D _REENTRANT -I. -I/home/cjn/src.d/hdr -o bc -l thread
compile2.c sclientshell.c /home/cjn/src.d/lib/libtsync.a
compile.c:
sclientshell.c:
```

Sample output from compilation script: *continued.*

```
real   2.91
user   1.75
sys    0.47

+ timex ./bcompile -D _REENTRANT -I. -I/home/cjn/src.d/hdr -o bc -l
thread compile.c sclientshell.c /home/cjn/src.d/lib/libtsync.a
real   2.71
user   0.02
sys    0.05
```

11
Signal Management

11.1   The Signal Handling Model

Software signals provide a convenient mechanism to notify a currently executing process of an asynchronous event or condition. A common example of using signals is in terminating a process. A *kill -9* command, for example, will send a SIGKILL signal to a process.

When an event occurs, the corresponding signal is said to be *generated* and is subsequently *delivered* to a process. The signal is considered to have been *delivered* when the process has acted upon the receipt of the signal. Between the time when the signal is generated but not yet delivered, the process is said to have a *pending* signal.

The software signals defined in the <signal.h> header file can be asynchronously generated, or in some cases synchronously generated. A signal generated by an event independent of a UNIX process, such as a hardware failure, is considered asynchronously generated. A signal is said to be synchronously generated when the signal is caused by a direct action of a UNIX process. This includes signals generated by alarm, abort, and others. The SIGUSR1 and SIGUSR2 signals can be generated only asynchronously.

The delivery of a signal to an application process will result in a predefined (*default*) action associated with the signal received. This default action may ignore the signal, abnormally terminate the process, or execute a *signal handling* function. Simple application programs will typically use the default action associated with the signal.

A UNIX process can specify the signal handling function to be executed when a particular signal is received. The normal flow of control through the process will be interrupted upon receipt of the signal to call this function. When the signal handling function completes its execution, control can be passed back to the point where the process was interrupted. An application process can specify that a signal is to be ignored, or that the process is to terminate abnormally. In establishing the action associated with the signal, the application process is said to have registered the signal's *disposition*.

In earlier releases of the UNIX operating system, a process had the opportunity to block the receipt of a signal, deferring when the signal would be delivered. This behavior is different from ignoring a signal.

When delivering a signal to a process, the UNIX operating system determines if the process is currently blocking the receipt of the signal. If the signal can be delivered to the process, the result is either the default action, a signal handling function, or the signal must be ignored. A blocked signal remains pending until the process unblocks the receipt of the signal.

The signal handling and management capabilities have been extended for the UNIX Threads Interface. For consistency and backward compatibility, we can send a signal to a UNIX process as a single entity. This permits the use of a SIGKILL signal to terminate a UNIX process.

With UNIX threads provided as an *in-the-process* concept [Cox92], we can conclude that a UNIX process cannot send a signal to a specific thread of another UNIX process. That is to say, a UNIX process does not know how many threads are associated with a different UNIX process executing in a disjoint address space. In some cases, however, sending a signal to a sibling thread is desirable, and this is allowed.

We therefore have two different abstractions to consider: one is the signal handling between UNIX processes, and the other is the signal handling between the sibling threads of a single UNIX process [Issa91]. In Figure 11.1, for example, $PROCESS_m$ can send a signal to $PROCESS_n$. This action shows the UNIX process level abstraction. $PROCESS_n$ has two user-level threads, labeled $THREAD_a$ and $THREAD_b$. The threads abstraction for signal handling occurs when $THREAD_a$ sends a signal to its sibling $THREAD_b$.

PROGRAMMER'S NOTE:

Multithreaded applications should avoid using the setjmp and longjmp functions. These functions can leave the UNIX threads library in an inconsistent state. [1]

For a signal to affect the UNIX process as a single entity, the sibling threads must share the same signal disposition. One thread cannot ignore a particular signal while another thread permits the default action to occur. Thus, the last thread to register a particular signal as ignored, caught, or defaulted, imposes its disposition of the signal on all of the sibling threads. System functions establishing a signal disposition, such as the sigaction, signal, sigset, and sigignore functions, will affect the UNIX process level registration of the signal.

[1] Printed with Permission of UNIX Systems Laboratories, Inc. All Rights Reserved.

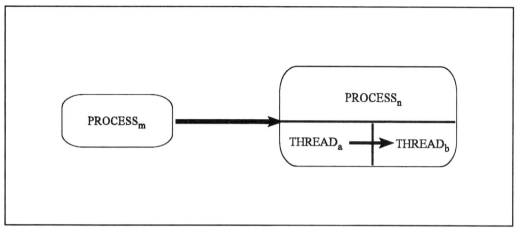

Figure 11.1   Signal handling and management.

In prior releases of the UNIX operating system each process had its own signal mask. When a process required that certain signals should be deferred, it would call the sigprocmask function, specifying which signals to block. This feature worked extremely well when the process was viewed as a single entity. Yet with the extended process model, this feature may have a negative affect on the performance of the application.

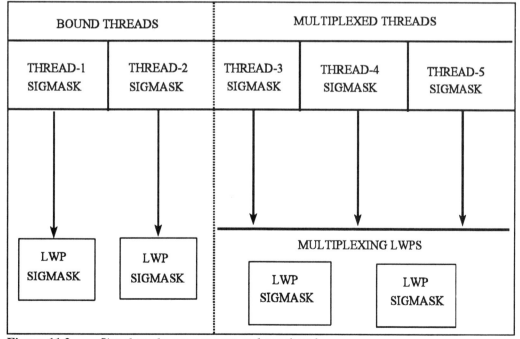

Figure 11.2   Signal masks are per LWP and per thread.

In the extended process model, each thread can have a different signal mask. UNIX thread implementations supporting lightweight processes also have a different signal mask per LWP (*see Figure 11.2*).

Depending on the implementation, the sigset, signal, and sigignore system calls will modify the calling LWP's signal mask. If the implementation does not use lightweight processes, then the calling thread's signal mask will be modified. The UNIX Threads Interface provides two additional functions, thr_kill and thr_sigsetmask, for signal handling between the sibling threads of a UNIX process.

11.2   Implications of Using Signals

To gain a better understanding of the implications in using signals, let us discuss several design issues related to the UNIX threads library providing user-level threads. With multiple execution streams within a UNIX process, the standard library (libc, libthread, *etc.*) functions had to be designed to minimize the chance for a deadlock situation, with respect to the synchronization primitives [Harp82].

Consider what would happen, for example, if a thread calls the thr_create function and is then interrupted by a signal during a critical section. The thr_create function will lock the mutex guarding updates to the linked list of threads associated with the UNIX process. If a signal is delivered after the thread has locked the mutex, and the corresponding signal handler function causes the thread to terminate, then the mutex remains in the LOCKED state! Subsequent calls to thr_create will block indefinitely, waiting for the mutex to become available.

To prevent this problem, the UNIX threads library establishes a common signal handler function for use within critical sections of the library. The common signal handler executes with all signals masked. When a signal is delivered, the common signal handler will determine if signals are enabled. The common signal handler will then execute the defined signal handling function. If the thread is in a critical section, however, the signal handlers are disabled and the signal will remain pending.

When the signal handlers are enabled, the common signal handler will adjust the lightweight process's signal mask to match the mask defined for the specified signal handler. If however, signal handlers are disabled, the common signal handler saves the signal and the signal state, and returns to the interrupt point blocking all signals to the lightweight process.

The use of the common signal handler is transparent to the application programmer and is used only by the UNIX threads library. The common signal handler is installed by the UNIX threads library for a particular signal only when the application calls the sigaction or signal function. Otherwise, when this signal arrives, its default action will take place.

During process initialization, the UNIX threads library will call the sigaction function to install the common handler for the SIGLWP signal. This is a special signal designed for, and used by, the UNIX threads library. Application programs cannot alter the behavior of the SIGLWP signal. The UNIX threads library will silently ignore attempts to change the behavior of this signal.

As mentioned, a thread can send a signal to a sibling thread. The thr_kill function adds the signal to the target thread's pending signals. If the thread is currently bound and doesn't block the signal, the thr_kill function will also send the signal to the target thread's LWP via the _lwp_kill function. In such cases, the common signal handler will process the thread's pending signal.

When the thread is not currently bound, the thr_kill function will post the signal to the target thread and will transition the thread to the RUNNABLE state. When the thread transitions to the ON PROCESSOR state, the thread library code performing the thread context switch will recognize that the thread has a pending signal and will send the pending signal to the LWP on which the thread is running.

While the new signal handling and management functionality provides additional features, there is the potential for a noticeable performance penalty. This will occur when many multiplexed threads are in use and each thread has a different signal mask. When the multiplexed thread is bound to a multiplexing LWP, a sigprocmask function call may be required to ensure that the underlying LWP's signal mask is the same as the multiplexed thread. For most implementations the sigprocmask function call will be made only when the signal mask is different. Thus, this design will impact the performance of a multithreaded application only when the multiplexing threads use different signal masks.

The UNIX threads library provides libc signal system interface wrappers so that the wrapper will affect both the thread and the LWP signal masks. The system interfaces for which a wrapper is provided appear in Table 11.1.

PROGRAMMER'S NOTE:

When an application creates one or more multiplexing DAEMON threads with a different signal mask than the multiplexing threads, their impact on the application performance will be proportional to the frequency with which they run. Applications creating DAEMON threads with a signal mask different from the multiplexing threads should consider bound rather than multiplexed threads to minimize the impact on performance. [1]

---

[1] Printed with Permission of UNIX Systems Laboratories, Inc. All Rights Reserved.

Table 11.1   UNIX Threads Library `libc` Signal System Interface Wrappers [1]

`sigaction`	Examines and/or specifies the action to be taken on delivery of a specific signal. The motivation to provide this wrapper is to set the common signal handler, and to prohibit the user from changing signal handlers to `SIGLWP` and `SIGWAITING`.
`sigprocmask`	Sets the thread's and `LWP`'s signal masks.
`setcontext`	Sets the calling thread context.
`sighold`	Adds a signal to the calling thread's signal mask.
`sigrelse`	Removes a signal from the calling thread's signal mask.
`signal`	Modifies the signal dispositions.
`sigset`	Modifies the signal dispositions.
`sigignore`	Sets the dispositions of a signal to `SIG_IGN`.
`sigsuspend`	Replaces the thread's signal mask with the signal mask provided, and suspends the calling thread until a signal is delivered whose action is either to execute a signal-catching function or to terminate the process.
`sigpause`	Replaces the thread's signal mask with the signal mask provided and suspends the calling thread until a signal is delivered whose action is either to execute a signal catching function or to terminate the process.
`sigpause`	Removes a signal from the calling thread's signal mask and suspends the thread until a signal is received.
`sigpending`	Examines the signals that are blocked and pending.
`sigwait`	Waits for the delivery of a signal to the calling thread.

11.3　　Base Signals and Signal Sets

The base signals are defined in the `<signal.h>` header file. Three new signals, `SIGWAITING`, `SIGLWP`, and `SIGAIO`, have been added in support of the UNIX threads abstraction. The `SIGWAITING` signal will not be generated by the kernel unless the process has called the `sigaction` function with the `SA_WAITSIG` flag set.[36]

The `SIGWAITING` signal is generated by the kernel when all LWPs in a process are blocked for an indeterminate time. The generation of the `SIGWAITING` signal permits a threads library to increase the concurrency level when all LWPs are blocked but there are threads that can proceed. The `SIGWAITING` signal may also be generated under other circumstances, where equivalent action in a threads library would be appropriate. The `SIGWAITING` signal is ignored by default.

PROGRAMMER'S NOTE:

The `SIGWAITING` signal needs to be explicitly enabled since some existing applications blindly establish handlers for all signals, and then do not know what to do with `SIGWAITING`. [1]

Most implementations of the UNIX threads library will ignore attempts to mask, send, or modify the disposition of the `SIGLWP` and `SIGWAITING` signals. From a generalized application perspective, these signals should not be used or relied upon. They should be viewed as exclusively for use by the UNIX threads implementation.

The valid signals, their corresponding signal number, and the default action for the signal are described in Table 11.2. Note that the term *action* is not the same as the term *disposition*. The disposition is one of: `SIG_DFL` (*use a default action*), or `SIG_IGN` (*ignore the signal*), or it is the *function_address* of the signal handler (*see Figure 11.3*).

---

[36] The `SA_WAITSIG` has the same bit pattern as `SA_NOCLDWAIT` to avoid taking up more of the available flag bits; this works because the `sigaction` is signal-specific and there is no ambiguity. [1]

[1] Printed with Permission of UNIX Systems Laboratories, Inc. All Rights Reserved.

Table 11.2   Signal Definitions [1]

SIGNAL	NUMBER	DEFAULT	DESCRIPTION
SIGHUP	1	Exit	Hangup
SIGINT	2	Exit	Interrupt
SIGQUIT	3	Core	Quit
SIGILL	4	Core	Illegal Instruction
SIGTRAP	5	Core	Trace/breakpoint trap
SIGABRT	6	Core	Abort
SIGEMT	7	Core	Emulation trap
SIGFPE	8	Core	Arithmetic exception
SIGKILL	9	Exit	Killed
SIGBUS	10	Core	Bus error
SIGSEGV	11	Core	Segmentation fault
SIGSYS	12	Core	Bad system call
SIGPIPE	13	Exit	Broken pipe
SIGALRM	14	Exit	Alarm clock
SIGTERM	15	Exit	Terminated
SIGUSR1	16	Exit	User signal 1
SIGUSR2	17	Exit	User signal 2
SIGCHLD	18	Ignore	Child status changed
SIGPWR	19	Ignore	Power fail restart
SIGWINCH	20	Ignore	Window size change
SIGURG	21	Ignore	Urgent socket condition
SIGPOLL	22	Exit	Pollable event

[1] Printed with Permission of UNIX Systems Laboratories, Inc. All Rights Reserved.

Table 11.3   Signal Definitions (cont.) ¶

SIGNAL	NUMBER	DEFAULT	DESCRIPTION
SIGSTOP	23	Stop	Stopped signal
SIGTSTP	24	Stop	Stopped user
SIGCONT	25	Ignore	Continued
SIGTTIN	26	Stop	Stopped tty input
SIGTTOU	27	Stop	Stopped tty output
SIGVTALRM	28	Exit	Virtual timer expired
SIGPROF	29	Exit	Profiling timer expired
SIGXCPU	30	Core	CPU time limit exceeded
SIGXFSZ	31	Core	File size limit exceeded
SIGWAITING	32	Ignore	All LWPs are blocked interruptibly
SIGLWP	33	Ignore	Signal reserved (thread library implementation)
SIGAIO	34	Ignore	Asynchronous I/O signal

A signal's disposition affects the UNIX process level registration of the signal, and thus the disposition is shared between all sibling threads. Signal handling occurs only when the servicing thread is scheduled to run. Thus, if a multiplexed thread is to service the signal, there may be a delay in the delivery of the signal if the thread is not currently in the ON PROCESSOR state. This latency can be reduced by having signals caught by bound threads. Depending on certain criteria, explained in the following, caught signals are handled either by a specific thread of the UNIX process, or an arbitrary thread.

Synchronously generated signals are initiated by a specific thread (*i.e., a division by zero; a request for a SIGALRM signal; a reference to an invalid address*), and are delivered to and handled by that thread. The thread will use the common handler function currently defined for the UNIX process.

Asynchronously generated signals are not initiated by a specific thread (*i.e., a* SIGINT *signal from the terminal, a signal from another process via* kill), and are handled by an arbitrary thread of the UNIX process that meets either of the following conditions:

    1.   The thread is blocked in a sigwait system call whose argument includes the type of signal caught,

    2.   The thread has a signal mask that does not include the type of signal caught.

A signal will be delivered to only one thread of a UNIX process. It is impossible for the application to predict which of several eligible threads will receive the signal. An alternative is for the application to create one eligible thread per signal type. Synchronously generated signals, however, will be delivered only to the thread whose actions caused the signal to be generated.

SIG_DFL
    A disposition of SIG_DFL specifies that the default action is to be taken upon receipt of the signal. The default action is one of:

    Exit   When it gets the signal, the receiving process is to be terminated with all the consequences outlined in exit().

    Core   When it gets the signal, the receiving process is to be terminated with all of the consequences outlined in exit(). In addition, a core image of the process is constructed in the current working directory.

    Stop   When it gets the signal, the receiving process is stopped.

    Ignore   When it gets the signal, the receiving process is to ignore it. This is identical to setting the disposition to SIG_IGN.

SIG_IGN
    A signal disposition of SIG_IGN specifies that the signal is to be ignored.

function_address
    A signal disposition of *function_address* specifies that upon receipt of the signal, the receiving process is to execute the signal handler function at the specified address.

Figure 11.3   Signal dispositions. [¶]

Signal Sets

A *signal set* provides a simple method to represent multiple signals in a single data structure. A signal set is represented in an application by the `sigset_t` type data structure. Signal sets are used by the `sigaction`, `sigpending`, `sigprocmask`, `sigsuspend`, and `sigwait` functions.

A `sigset_t` type data structure can be statically defined, or dynamically allocated using a memory allocation function, such as `malloc`. There are five functions available to manipulate a signal set (*see Figure 11.4*). The `sigemptyset` function will initialize the set to exclude all signals defined by the system. The `sigfillset` function initializes the set to include all signals defined by the system.

NAME:

        `signal sets` - Signal set administration functions.

SYNOPSIS:

```
#include <signal.h>

int sigaddset(sigset_t *set, int signo)

int sigfillset(sigset_t *set)

int sigemptyset(sigset_t *set)

int sigismember(sigset_t *set, int signo)

int sigdelset(sigset_t *set, int signo)
```

Figure 11.4   The signal set functions. [1]

Specific signals can be added to the signal set by calling the `sigaddset` function and specifying the particular signal to add. The `sigismember` function will return an integer value of 1 if the specified signal belongs to the signal set. The `sigdelset` function will delete a specific signal from a signal set.

11.4   The Signal Mask

A UNIX process's signal mask identifies zero or more signals whose delivery is to be deferred. Thus, if the signal is generated for the process, it will remain pending. With the extended UNIX process model, signal masks are now maintained per UNIX thread. A thread inherits the signal

---

[1] Printed with Permission of UNIX Systems Laboratories, Inc. All Rights Reserved.

mask from its creator thread. The thread can call the `thr_sigsetmask` function (*see Figure 11.5*) to modify its mask.[37]

The functionality of the `thr_sigsetmask` call is determined by the value of the parameter `how`, which must be `SIG_SETMASK`, `SIG_BLOCK`, or `SIG_UNBLOCK`. If the value is `SIG_SETMASK`, the thread's current signal mask is replaced by the signal set pointed to by argument `set`. When the value is `SIG_BLOCK`, the signal set pointed to by the argument `set` is added to the thread's current signal mask. A value of `SIG_UNBLOCK` denotes that the signal set pointed to by argument `set` is to be removed from the thread's current signal mask. If the argument `set` is specified as `NULL`, the value of `how` is not significant and the thread's signal mask remains unchanged.

NAME:

       `thr_sigsetmask` - Change or examine the thread's signal mask.

SYNOPSIS:

```
#include <signal.h>
#include <thread.h>

int
thr_sigsetmask(int how, const sigset_t *set, sigset_t
*oset)
```

Figure 11.5   `thr_sigsetmask()` synopsis. [¶]

Argument `oset`, if specified, points to a `sigset_t` type structure. The thread's previous signal mask is stored at this location. The `thr_sigsetmask` call is useful to query the thread's current signal mask.

Certain signals, such as `SIGKILL` and `SIGSTOP`, cannot be blocked by an application. This restriction is silently enforced by the system. The `SIGLWP` and `SIGWAITING` signals may also be blocked by the implementation.

The `sigpending` function (*see Figure 11.6*) retrieves those signals that have been sent to the calling `UNIX` process but are being blocked from delivery by the process's signal mask. The list of pending signals is stored in the signal set pointed to by the argument `set`. This function does not alter the `UNIX` process's signal mask and thus any pending signals remain pending.

---

[37] In certain implementations, the `thr_sigsetmask` function is mapped to the `sigprocmask` function, while others may have different behavior. For portability, always use the `thr_sigsetmask` function.

[¶] Printed with Permission of UNIX Systems Laboratories, Inc. All Rights Reserved.

NAME:
> `sigpending` - Examine signals that are blocked and pending.

SYNOPSIS:
> `#include <signal.h>`
>
> `int`
> `sigpending(sigset_t *set)`

Figure 11.6   `sigpending()` synopsis. [1]

The set returned by the `sigpending` call is the union of all signals pending to the calling thread but blocked by the threads signal mask, and the signals pending to the process but blocked by every currently running thread in the process.

PROGRAMMER'S NOTE:

The set of pending signals returned from the call to `sigpending` is only advisory. A pending signal might be delivered to a sibling thread (if any become eligible) after the return of this system call.

11.5   Signal Delivery

There are two methods for handling the delivery of a signal in a multithreaded application. The first method is to specify a signal handler function to execute when the signal is received by the UNIX process. In the second method, a thread is created to handle the receipt of the signal.

The `sigaction` function will identify a signal handler function to be called upon receipt of a particular signal. This function can be used for both asynchronously generated signals and synchronously generated signals. In either case, a thread's execution path will be temporarily interrupted to service the receipt of the signal.

The `sigwait` function is used to `block-wait` for the receipt of a signal from a specified set of signals. With this function, a thread can `block-wait` for the receipt of a signal. When the signal is caught, the thread will resume execution. In this manner, the functionality of a signal handler would follow the call to `sigwait`, and thus the executing thread can be thought of as the signal handler. This will only work for asynchronously generated signals, as synchronously generated signals are sent to the thread that caused the event.

---

[1] Printed with Permission of UNIX Systems Laboratories, Inc. All Rights Reserved.

The sigaction Function

The sigaction function (*see Figure 11.7*) modifies the disposition of a signal for a UNIX process. This function can also be used to examine the current disposition. Modifying the disposition of a signal affects the UNIX process-level registration of that signal.

Through the sigaction function, the application can specify a signal handling function to be called whenever a particular signal is received by the UNIX process. When the signal is delivered to a thread, the thread's execution stream is interrupted to execute the signal handling function. Upon return from the signal handling function, the thread's execution stream is restored.

The parameter sig is a signal number from Table 11.3, and denotes the signal for which the action is to be applied. The parameter act, if non NULL, is a pointer to a sigaction structure describing the new disposition for the signal. The parameter oact, if non NULL, is a pointer to a sigact structure that will be set to the signal's disposition prior to calling sigaction.

NAME:

      sigaction - Examine or modify a signal's disposition.

SYNOPSIS:

```
#include <signal.h>

int
sigaction(int sig, const struct sigaction *act,
          struct sigaction *oact)
```

Figure 11.7   sigaction() synopsis. [1]

The sigaction structure is defined in the <signal.h> header file, and includes members for setting the specified signals disposition. Members include:

```
void        (*sa_handler)
sigset_t    sa_mask
int         sa_flags;
```

The sa_handler member must be specified as one of the dispositions listed in Figure 11.3. The sa_mask member is a signal set specifying the signals to be blocked while the signal handler is active. The sa_mask member can be modified using the sigsetops functions described in the previous section. The sa_flags member specifies a set of flags to modify the delivery of the signal. The sa_flags member can be specified as a bitwise-OR of one or more of the flags listed in Table 11.4.

---

[1] Printed with Permission of UNIX Systems Laboratories, Inc. All Rights Reserved.

Table 11.4   The sigaction sa_flag Definitions [¶]

SA_ONSTACK	This flag is used to specify alternate signal stacks. If set and the signal is caught and an alternate signal stack has been declared by the receiving LWP, the signal is delivered on that stack. Otherwise, the signal should be delivered on the current stack of the receiving LWP. Note, however, that alternate signal stacks are supported only per-LWP, not per thread.
SA_RESETHAND	If set and the signal is caught, the disposition is reset to SIG_DFL and the signal will not be blocked on entry to the signal handler.
SA_NODEFER	If set and the signal is caught, the signal will not be automatically blocked by the kernel while it is being caught.
SA_RESTART	If set and the signal is caught, a system call that is interrupted by the execution of this signal's handler is transparently restarted by the system. Otherwise, that system call returns an EINTR error. Note, however, that not all system calls can be restarted [i.e. sleep(2) and pause(2)].
SA_SIGINFO	If cleared and the signal is caught, sig is passed as the only argument to the signal catching function. If set and the signal is caught, two additional arguments are passed to the signal-catching function. If the second argument is not equal to NULL, it points to a siginfo_t structure containing the reason why the signal was generated [see siginfo(5)]. The third parameter points to a ucontext_t structure containing the receiving process's context when the signal was delivered [see ucontext(5)].
SA_NOCLDWAIT	If set and sig equals SIGCHLD, the system will not create zombie processes when children of the calling process exit. If the calling process subsequently issues a wait(2), it blocks until all of the calling process's child processes terminate, and then returns a value of -1, with errno set to ECHLD.
SA_NOCLDSTOP	If set and signal equals SIGCHLD, sig will not be sent to the calling process when its child processes stop or continue.
SA_WAITSIG	When sig is SIGWAITING, this flag request the generation of the SIGWAITING signal type when all LWPs of the process are blocked at an interruptible priority.

The handler established by `sigaction` for an LWP is common to all LWPs in a process. The SA_ONSTACK flag enables alternate signal stacks for the specified signal for the process as a whole; for alternate stack handling to take place for an LWP, that LWP must have declared the alternate stack with `sigaltstack`.

The SA_WAITING flag enables the generation of the SIGWAITING signal, which is sent to the process when all LWPs are blocked for an indeterminate time, and possibly at other times when equivalent action would be appropriate.

Thread libraries will generally use SIGLWP and SIGWAITING and will likely prevent the use of these signals. The threads library will silently ignore attempts to send, mask, or change disposition of those signals.

As an example of using `sigaction`, consider the `sigactExample` program (*Listing 11.1*). The `signalSet` data structure is used to establish the signal mask for the initial thread. Using the `sigfillset` and `sigdelset` functions, the initial thread will mask off all signals except for the SIGINT and SIGFPE signals. The initial thread's signal mask is then set using the `thr_sigsetmask`.

The `action` data structure is used to set the `sigint` function as the signal handler for SIGINT signals, and the `sigfpe` function as the signal handler for the SIGFPE signal. The main thread creates three additional threads. The new threads will inherit the signal mask from the creator thread (*in this example, the initial thread*).

The `threadOne` thread will cause a SIGFPE signal to be generated when it performs the division statement. This behavior provides an example of a synchronously generated signal. The SIGFPE signal will therefore be sent only to `threadOne`. Upon receipt of the signal, the `sigfpe` signal handler will be called.

The `threadTwo` and `threadThree` threads both unblock the SIGALRM signal and then enter a loop sleeping for one second during each iteration. The SIGALRM signal is unblocked such that by performing a sleep operation, the SIGALRM signal will be delivered to the appropriate thread.

While the program is executing, try pressing the interrupt key to asynchronously generate a SIGINT signal. The signal will be delivered to either the initial thread, `threadOne`, `threadTwo`, or `threadThree`. Upon delivery of the signal, the thread that caught the signal will execute the `sigint` signal handling function.

Listing 11.1   *sigactExample.c* -- An example program using `sigact`.

```
 1 #include <thread.h>
 2 #include <stdio.h>
 3 #include <unistd.h>
 4 #include <signal.h>
 5 #include <synch.h>
 6 #include "mthreadLog.h"
 7
 8 static        void    sigfpe(int);
 9 static        void    sigint(int);
10 static        void   *threadOne(void *);
11 static        void   *threadThree(void *);
12 static        void   *threadTwo(void *);
13
14 typedef struct sigaction sigaction_t;
15
16 void *
17 main(void)
18 {
19        sigset_t    signalSet   = { 0 };
20        sigaction_t action      = { 0 };
21
22                    /* Fill the signal set with all available */
23                    /* signals.                               */
24        sigfillset( &signalSet );
25
26                    /* Remove SIGINT from set.                */
27        sigdelset(  &signalSet, SIGINT);
28
29                    /* Remove SIGFPE from set.                */
30        sigdelset(  &signalSet, SIGFPE);
31
32                    /* Now set the signal mask (initial       */
33                    /* thread).                               */
34        thr_sigsetmask(SIG_SETMASK,&signalSet,NULL);
35
36                    /* Fill the action sa_mask with all       */
37                    /* signals.                               */
38        sigfillset( &action.sa_mask );
39
40                    /* Set the handler to function sigfpe.    */
41        action.sa_handler = sigfpe;
```

Listing 11.1   *continued.*

```
42
43                       /* Establish SIGFPE signal handler.          */
44         sigaction(SIGFPE,&action,NULL);
45
46                       /* Now set handler to function sigint.      */
47         action.sa_handler = sigint;
48                       /* Establish SIGINT signal handler.          */
49         sigaction(SIGINT,&action,NULL);
50         printf("creating threads\n");
51         thr_create( NULL, 0, threadOne,    NULL, THR_NEW_LWP, NULL);
52         thr_create( NULL, 0, threadTwo,    NULL, THR_NEW_LWP, NULL);
53         thr_create( NULL, 0, threadThree, NULL, THR_NEW_LWP, NULL);
54         thr_exit((void *)0);
55 }
56
57 static void *
58 threadOne(void *arg)
59 {
60         int    a, b;
61         float c;
62         a = 100;
63         b = 0;
64         printf("hello, world from threadOne [tid: %d]\n", thr_self());
65         c = a / b;
66         printf("%f\n", c);
67         printf("thread one is now complete and exiting\n");
68         thr_exit((void *)0);
69 }
70
71 static void *
72 threadTwo(void *arg)
73 {
74         sigset_t    signalSet    = { 0 };
75         int          counter      = 0;
76                       /* Set signalSet to empty.              */
77         sigemptyset( &signalSet );
78                       /* Add SIGALRM to signalSet.           */
79         sigaddset(   &signalSet, SIGALRM);
80                       /* Set threadTwo's signal mask        */
81         thr_sigsetmask(SIG_UNBLOCK,&signalSet,NULL);
82         printf("hello, world from threadTwo [tid: %d]\n", thr_self());
```

Listing 11.1 *continued.*

```
83        for(counter=0; counter < 10; ++ counter ) {
84                sleep(1);
85        }
86        printf("thread two is now complete and exiting\n");
87        thr_exit((void *)0);
88 }
89
90
91 static void *
92 threadThree(void *arg)
93 {
94        sigset_t    signalSet   = { 0 };
95        int         counter     = 0;
96
97                        /* Set signalSet to empty.          */
98        sigemptyset( &signalSet );
99
100                       /* Add SIGALRM to signalSet.        */
101        sigaddset(  &signalSet, SIGALRM);
102
103                       /* Set threadThree's signal mask    */
104        thr_sigsetmask(SIG_UNBLOCK,&signalSet,NULL);
105        printf("hello, world from threadThree [tid: %d]\n",
106                                              thr_self());
107
108        for(counter=0; counter < 10; ++counter) {
109                sleep(1);
110        }
111        printf("thread three is now complete and exiting\n");
112        thr_exit((void *)0);
113 }
114
115 void
116 sigfpe(int signum)
117 {
118        printf("divide by zero exception caught by thread [%d]\n",
119                    thr_self() );
120        thr_exit((void *)0);
121 }
122
```

Listing 11.1 *continued.*

```
83 void
84 sigint(int signum)
85 {
86        printf("interrupt exception caught by thread [%d]\n",
87                    thr_self() );
88 }
```

Sample output from executing the sigactExample **program:**

```
creating threads
hello, world from threadOne [tid: 2]
divide by zero exception caught by thread [2]
hello, world from threadTwo [tid: 3]
hello, world from threadThree [tid: 4]
interrupt exception caught by thread [4]
interrupt exception caught by thread [4]
interrupt exception caught by thread [4]
thread three is now complete and exiting
thread two is now complete and exiting
```

When the initial thread creates the sibling threads, it specifies the THR_NEW_LWP flag to the thr_create function call. This flag is desirable for a UNIX threads implementation using underlying lightweight processes. All of the threads in this example are multiplexed, and thus, if the size of the LWP pool was not increased, the sleep function call would block at the LWP level, and the sibling threads would make little progress.

The sigsuspend Function

The sigsuspend function (*Figure 11.8*) replaces the UNIX process's signal mask with the set of signals pointed to by the argument set. The UNIX process is then suspended until the delivery of a signal whose action is to execute a signal handling function, or to terminate the UNIX process.

NAME:

        `sigsuspend` - Install a signal mask and suspend process until signal.

SYNOPSIS:

```
#include <signal.h>

int
sigsuspend(const sigset_t *set)
```

Figure 11.8   `sigsuspend()` synopsis. [¶]

If the action is to terminate the process, then `sigsuspend` does not return. Alternatively, if the action is to execute a signal-catching function, then `sigsuspend` returns after the signal-catching function returns. Upon return, the UNIX process's signal mask is restored to the set that existed before the call to `sigsuspend`.

The sigwait Function

The `sigwait` function (*Figure 11.9*) automatically chooses and clears a pending signal from `set` and returns the number of the signal chosen. If no signal in *set* is pending at the time of the call, the function is suspended until one or more signals become pending. This suspension is indefinite in extent.

If more than one active entity in a process is using `sigwait` for a signal, or is catching the signal, the signal is delivered to exactly one of those by either returning from the `sigwait` function or invoking the signal handler. In effect, all LWPs or threads are competing to consume the pending signal, and exactly one wins.

NAME:

        `sigwait` - Block until a signal in the requested set is posted.

SYNOPSIS:

```
#include <signal.h>

int
sigwait(sigset_t *set)
```

Figure 11.9   `sigwait()` synopsis. [¶]

The semantics of `sigwait` make it ideal to design the application with a thread dedicated to handling certain signal types. The functionality that might have been placed in a separate signal handler function could be placed after the return from `sigwait` to be executed when a signal

[¶] Printed with Permission of UNIX Systems Laboratories, Inc. All Rights Reserved.

arrives. Once handling is complete, the thread could call `sigwait` again to block itself until the arrival of the next signal.

PROGRAMMER'S NOTE:

A thread which iteratively calls `sigwait` should be created with the THR_DAEMON flag set. Otherwise, the thread will continue to exist and the initial thread's `thr_exit` will never succeed, since it waits for all sibling threads to terminate. [1]

With the `sigwait` function selecting and clearing a pending signal, there is a subtle implication here that the signal has not yet been delivered to the UNIX process. That is to say, all threads in the UNIX process (*including the thread*) using `sigwait` should mask the relevant signal types. Otherwise, the signal will be delivered to one of the threads that has not masked the signal. The application should not define a signal handler for this signal prior to calling `sigwait`. The implication is that if a signal handler is installed, then the receipt of the signal will be delivered to that signal handler.

The code to handle a signal type on return from `sigwait` is not considered a handler for the UNIX process disposition of that signal type. It is important that signal types handled by a thread using `sigwait` be included in the signal mask of every thread; otherwise, the default response for the process will be triggered. Even the thread calling `sigwait` should mask that signal type, because a signal of that type may arrive while the thread is between calls to `sigwait`.

PROGRAMMER'S NOTE:

Do not mix the use of `sigwait` and `sigaction` for a given signal number because the results may be unpredictable (*and are likely not to be portable in any event*). [1]

The `sigwaitExample.c` program (*Listing 11.2*) provides an example of using the `sigwait` function. The initial thread will mask off all signals except the SIGALRM signal. Next, the initial thread creates three sibling threads. Each of the three sibling threads inherits the thread signal mask from its creator (*in this case the initial*) thread.

Listing 11.2   *sigwaitExample.c* -- An example program using `sigwait`.

```
1 #include <thread.h>
2 #include <stdio.h>
3 #include <unistd.h>
4 #include <signal.h>
5 #include <synch.h>
6 static void    *threadTwo(void *);
```

[1] Printed with Permission of UNIX Systems Laboratories, Inc. All Rights Reserved.

Listing 11.2 *continued.*

```
 7 static void     *threadThree(void *);
 8 static void     *sigint(void *);
 9 void *
10 main(void)
11 {
12        sigset_t     signalSet   = { 0 };
13        sigfillset( &signalSet );
14        sigdelset(  &signalSet, SIGALRM);
15        thr_sigsetmask(SIG_SETMASK,&signalSet,NULL);
16        printf("creating threads\n");
17        thr_create( NULL, 0, sigint, NULL,
18                      (THR_DAEMON|THR_BOUND|THR_DETACHED), NULL);
19        thr_create( NULL, 0, threadTwo,   NULL, THR_NEW_LWP, NULL);
20        thr_create( NULL, 0, threadThree, NULL, 0, NULL);
21        thr_exit((void *)0);
22 }
23 static void *
24 threadTwo(void *arg)
25 {
26        sigset_t     signalSet = { 0 };
27        int          counter   = 0;
28
29        printf("hello, world from threadTwo [tid: %d]\n", thr_self());
30        sleep(10);
31        printf("thread two is now complete and exiting\n");
32        thr_exit((void *)0);
33 }
34
35 static void *
36 threadThree(void *arg)
37 {
38        sigset_t     signalSet = { 0 };
39        int          counter   = 0;
40        printf("hello, world from threadThree [tid: %d]\n",
41                                                    thr_self());
42        sleep(10);
43        printf("thread three is now complete and exiting\n");
44        thr_exit((void *)0);
45 }
```

Listing 11.2 *continued.*

```
46 void *
47 sigint(void *arg)
48 {
49        sigset_t      signalSet;
50
51        sigemptyset( &signalSet);
52        sigaddset(   &signalSet, SIGINT);
53        while(1) {
54              printf("thread sigint [tid: %d] awaiting SIGINT\n",
55                                            thr_self());
56              sigwait(&signalSet);
57              printf("interrupt exception caught by thread [%d]\n",
58                                            thr_self() );
59              thr_yield();
60        }
61        thr_exit((void *)0);
62 }
```

The `sigint` thread will be used to handle the delivery of SIGINT signals. Since this thread's only purpose is to service the interrupt signal, the thread is created with the THR_DAEMON and the THR_DETACHED flags set. Thus, when all nondaemon threads complete, or the initial thread calls exit, then the daemon thread will silently be terminated. The sibling threads `threadTwo` and `threadThree` are created as multiplexed threads.

While running this program, try pressing the interrupt key. Note that in every case the interrupt is handled by the `sigint` thread although the order of the messages may vary depending on scheduling and other factors. An example of the output is given in the following:

Sample output from executing the `sigwaitExample` program:
```
creating threads
hello, world from threadTwo [tid: 3]
thread sigint [tid: 2] awaiting SIGINT
hello, world from threadThree [tid: 4]
interrupt exception caught by thread [2]
thread sigint [tid: 2] awaiting SIGINT
interrupt exception caught by thread [2]
thread sigint [tid: 2] awaiting SIGINT
thread two is now complete and exiting
thread three is now complete and exiting
```

The signal Functions

The `signal` functions (*Figure 11.10*) are shown here for completeness. In multithreaded application design, however, it is advisable to use the newer signal functions described in this chapter.

```
NAME:
        signal, sigset, sigrelse, sigignore, sigpause - Simplified signal
        management.

SYNOPSIS:
        #include <signal.h>

        void (*signal(int sig, void (*disp)(int)))(int)
        void (*sigset(int sig, void (*disp)(int)))(int)
        int sighold(int sig)
        int sigrelse(int sig)
        int sigignore(int sig)
        int sigpause(int sig)
```

Figure 11.10   The `signal` functions. [1]

11.6   Signals between UNIX Processes

The extended process model supports the notion of signals between UNIX processes, and signals between sibling threads. The `sigsend` and `kill` functions send signals between UNIX processes. The `thr_kill` function will send signals between sibling threads.

The sigsend and sigsendset Functions

The `sigsend` function (*Figure 11.11*) sends a signal to the process or group of processes specified by the arguments `idtype` and `id`. The signal to be sent is given by the argument `sig`. The argument `idtype` must be one of the valid values listed in Table 11.5. The value of argument `id` is interpreted based on the `idtype`. Collectively, these two arguments will be interpreted to represent zero or more target processes.

The value of argument `sig` must be a valid UNIX signal number, or the value zero. When given as zero, the `sigsend` function will perform error checking, but the signal is not actually sent. This behavior is useful for checking the integrity of the processes specified by `idtype` and `id`.

The sending process must have permission to send a signal to the target process. To do so, the real or effective user ID of the sending process must match the real or saved user ID of the receiving

---

[1] Printed with Permission of UNIX Systems Laboratories, Inc. All Rights Reserved.

process, unless the sending process has the P_OWNER privilege, or sig is SIGCONT and the sending process has the same session ID as the receiving process.

NAME:

      sigsend, sigsendset - Send a signal to a process of group of processes.

SYNOPSIS:

```
#include <sys/types.h>
#include <signal.h>
     #include <sys/procset.h>

int
sigsend(idtype_t idtype, id_t id, int sig)

int
sigsendset(const procset_t *psp, int sig)
```

Figure 11.11   sigsend() synopsis. [1]

Table 11.5   The idtype_t Values [1]

P_PID	sig is sent to the process with process ID id
P_PGID	sig is sent to any process with process group ID id
P_SID	sig is sent to any process with session ID id
P_UID	sig is sent to any process with effective user ID id
P_GID	sig is sent to any process with effective group ID id
P_CID	sig is sent to any process with scheduler class ID id
P_ALL	sig is sent to all processes and id is ignored

The sigsendset function provides an alternate interface for sending signals to sets of processes. This function sends signals to the set of processes specified by the procset_t type data structure given as argument psp. The procset_t type structure is defined in the <sys/procset.h> header file and includes the following members: [1]

```
idop_t        p_op
idtype_t      p_lidtype
id_t          p_lid
idtype_t      p_ridtype
id_t          p_rd
```

The members p_lidtype and p_lid specify the ID type and ID of one set of processes, generically referred to as the left set. Similarly, the members p_ridtype and p_rid specify the ID type and ID of a second set of processes known as the right set. The ID types and IDs are specified just as for the idtype and id arguments of the sigsend function.

The member p_op specifies the operation to be performed on the two sets of processes to get the set of processes to which the system call is to apply. The valid values for p_op and the processes they specify are given in Table 11.6.

Table 11.6   The procset_t Type p_op Member Values [1]

POP_DIFF	Set difference; processes in left set and not in right set
POP_AND	Set intersection; processes in both left and right sets
POP_OR	Set union; process in either the left or right sets or both
POP_XOR	Set exclusive-or; process in left or right set, but not in both

The kill Function

The kill function (*Figure 11.2*) will send a specified signal to a UNIX process, or to a group of UNIX processes. The signal is considered to be asynchronously generated. The process or group of processes to which the signal is to be sent is specified by the value of argument pid. The signal that is to be sent is specified by sig and is either one from the list given in signal(5) or the value zero. If sig is zero, then error checking is performed but no signal is actually sent. This feature can be used to check the validity of pid.

```
NAME:
        kill - Send a signal to a process or a group of processes.

SYNOPSIS:
        #include <sys/types.h>
        #include <signal.h>

        int
        kill( pid_t pid, int sig)
```

Figure 11.12   kill() synopsis(). [1]

The real or effective user ID of the sending process must match the real or saved user ID of the receiving process unless the effective user ID of the sending process is superuser, or sig is SIGCONT and the sending process has the same session ID as the receiving process.

[1] Printed with Permission of UNIX Systems Laboratories, Inc. All Rights Reserved.

When the value of pid is greater than the value zero, the signal specified as sig will be sent to the process whose process ID is equal to that of pid. Specifying a negative value for pid is interpreted as a process group identifier, and sig will be sent to all processes whose process group ID is equal to the absolute value of pid, and for which the process has permission to send a signal. Certain values for pid have special interpretation (*see Table 11.7*).

Table 11.7   Special Interpretations of PID for the kill System Call [1]

Value	Interpretation
0	The signal will be sent to all processes, excluding proc0 and proc1, whose process group ID is equal to the process group ID of the sender. Permission is needed to send a signal to process groups.
-1	If the effective user ID of the sender is not superuser, then sig will be sent to all of the processes, excluding proc0 and proc1, whose real user ID is equal to that of the effective user ID of the sender.
-1	If the effective user ID of the sender is superuser, then sig will be sent to all processes, excluding proc0 and proc1.

The thr_kill Function

Sibling threads can send signals to each other using the thr_kill function (*Figure 11.13*) call. In this sense, the signal is considered to be asynchronously generated. The parameter tid is the identifier of the thread to receive the signal. The scope of tid is limited to the current UNIX process, as the thr_kill function cannot be used to send signals between UNIX processes executing in disjoint address spaces.

The signal to be sent is given as parameter sig. If sig is specified as zero, then error checking is performed but no signal is actually sent. A zero signal is useful to ensure the integrity of the specified thread.

NAME:

       `thr_kill()` - Send a signal to a sibling thread.

SYNOPSIS:

```
#include <thread.h>
#include <sys/types.h>
#include <signal.h>

int
thr_kill(thread_t tid, int sig)
```

Figure 11.13   `thr_kill()` synopsis. [1]

It is important to understand that the disposition of the signal is registered at the UNIX process level. Therefore, sending a SIGKILL signal to a particular sibling will terminate the entire UNIX process.

The `thr_kill` function is useful to send explicit signals to particular threads. It can also be used to verify a thread's existence. The one disadvantage to the UNIX Threads Interface is that it does not provide a method to poll for the existence of a thread. Instead, the application program must resort to using `thr_kill` with a signal number of zero.

PROGRAMMER'S NOTE:

The `thr_kill` will return success for a target thread in the ZOMBIE state.

Example:

The `thrkillExample.c` source file (*Listing 11.3*) provides an example of using the `thr_kill` function to asynchronously generate a signal. The initial thread begins by establishing the thread's signal mask. All signals are blocked except for the SIGINT, SIGFPE, and SIGALRM signals. The initial thread creates `threadOne`, `threadTwo`, and `threadThree`, which inherit the initial thread's signal mask.

Any thread may execute the signal handler for the SIGINT signal. The SIGFPE and SIGALRM signals, however, when synchronously generated, will be directed to the thread causing their event. When asynchronously generated, any thread will be able to service the signal.

[1] Printed with Permission of UNIX Systems Laboratories, Inc. All Rights Reserved.

Listing 11.3   *thrkillExample.c* - An example program using the `thr_kill` function.

```
 1 #include <thread.h>
 2 #include <stdio.h>
 3 #include <unistd.h>
 4 #include <signal.h>
 5 #include <synch.h>
 6
 7 static void *threadOne(void *);
 8 static void *threadTwo(void *);
 9 static void *threadThree(void *);
10 static void  sigfpe(int);
11 static void  sigint(int);
12 static thread_t   tid2;
13 typedef struct sigaction sigaction_t;
14 void *
15 main(void)
16 {
17         sigset_t   signalSet   = { 0 };
18         sigaction_t action      = { 0 };
19
20         sigfillset( &signalSet );
21         sigdelset( &signalSet, SIGINT);
22         sigdelset( &signalSet, SIGFPE);
23         sigdelset( &signalSet, SIGALRM);
24         thr_sigsetmask(SIG_SETMASK,&signalSet,NULL);
25         sigfillset( &action.sa_mask );
26         action.sa_handler = sigfpe;
27         sigaction(SIGFPE,&action,NULL);
28         action.sa_handler = sigint;
29         sigaction(SIGINT,&action,NULL);
30         printf("creating threads\n");
31         thr_create( NULL, 0, threadOne,   NULL, THR_NEW_LWP, NULL);
32         thr_create( NULL, 0, threadTwo,   NULL, 0, &tid2);
33         thr_create( NULL, 0, threadThree, NULL, 0, NULL);
34         thr_exit((void *)0);
35 }
36
37 static void *
38 threadOne(void *arg)
39 {
40         int   a, b;
41         float c;
```

Listing 11.3 *continued.*

```
42          a = 100;
43          b = 0;
44          printf("hello, world from threadOne [tid: %d]\n", thr_self());
45          c = a / b;
46          printf("thread one is now complete and exiting\n");
47          thr_exit((void *)0);
48 }
49
50 static void *
51 threadTwo(void *arg)
52 {
53          sigset_t    signalSet   = { 0 };
54          printf("hello, world from threadTwo [tid: %d]\n", thr_self());
55          sleep(10);
56          printf("thread two is now complete and exiting\n");
57          thr_exit((void *)0);
58 }
59
60 static void *
61 threadThree(void *arg)
62 {
63          sigset_t    signalSet   = { 0 };
64          printf("hello, world from threadThree [tid: %d]\n",
65                  thr_self());
66          thr_kill( tid2, SIGINT);
67          sleep(5);
68          printf("thread three is now complete and exiting\n");
69          thr_exit((void *)0);
70 }
71
72 void
73 sigfpe(int signum)
74 {
75          printf("divide by zero exception caught by thread [%d]\n",
76                  thr_self() );
77          thr_exit((void *)0);
78 }
```

Listing 11.3 *continued.*

```
79 void
80 sigint(int signum)
81 {
82         printf("interrupt exception caught by thread [%d]\n",
83                 thr_self() );
84 }
```

ThreadOne will cause a SIGFPE signal to be synchronously generated when it performs the division by zero. Thus, the SIGFPE signal will be delivered to threadOne. If threadOne had masked the signal, then the signal would remain pending. ThreadTwo prints a standard message and then enters a sleep(10) function call. ThreadThree issues a thr_kill call to send a SIGINT signal to threadTwo.

Sample output from executing the thrkillExample program is given as:

```
creating threads
hello, world from threadOne [tid: 2]
divide by zero exception caught by thread [2]
hello, world from threadTwo [tid: 3]
hello, world from threadThree [tid: 4]
interrupt exception caught by thread [3]
thread two is now complete and exiting
interrupt exception caught by thread [4]
thread three is now complete and exiting
```

The sigaltstack Function

The sigaltstack function (*Figure 11.14*) is used to set, or get the signal alternate stack context. Depending on the implementation of the UNIX threads, this function may not be supported at the threads level. That is to say, this function may be available only at the LWP level. For this reason, it is recommended to avoid using the sigaltstack function unless writing a threads library.

The sigalstack function will define an alternate stack area on which signals are to be processed. If SS_DISABLE is not set, the alternate stack is enabled for the LWP for any signal for which the sigaction flag SA_ONSTACK has been set.

NAME:
        sigaltstack - Examine or modify the signal alternative stack context.

SYNOPSIS:
        #include <signal.h>
        int
        sigaltstack(const stack_t *ss, stack_t *oss)

Figure 11.14   sigaltstack() synopsis. [1]

[1] Printed with Permission of UNIX Systems Laboratories, Inc. All Rights Reserved.

12

Scheduling and Priorities

12.1   Process Scheduling: An Overview

From a historic perspective, processes existed very early in the UNIX operating system (*PDP-7 UNIX*) [RITC84]. The UNIX operating system viewed the process as the schedulable entity. This view allows the operating system to schedule processes for execution by multiplexing the processes onto the available CPUs.

The goals of the UNIX operating system's Time-Sharing policy are to allocate the CPU fairly among processes, maximize the throughput, reduce the response latency for interactive processes, and minimize the contention for kernel resources. In a time-sharing system the CPU is a critical resource and its use is carefully controlled to ensure that all processes will eventually make progress. This control is accomplished through a round-robin [CoKlF68], multilevel feedback scheduling policy [Henr84] [Bach86]. The process scheduler is responsible for allocating the CPU resources among contending processes and thus implicitly controls the order in which other scarce resources are acquired.

Through the Time-Sharing scheduling policy, each process has an assigned priority value. The operating system will adjust the priority value depending on specific criteria. The system maintains a series of priority queues, and each process is placed in a queue based on its current priority level.

The operating system allocates a time slice (*time quantum*), during which the highest priority RUNNABLE process can execute on the CPU. Upon expiration of the time slice, the operating system will preempt the process and place it at the end of the appropriate priority queue. The system then allocates another time slice and selects the next highest priority RUNNABLE process to execute.

The priority of a process executing in user mode is based on its recent CPU consumption. The priority of a process executing in kernel mode is fixed according to a priority argument to the sleep function. The Time-Sharing scheduler allows preemption of processes only while executing in user mode, or just prior to returning from kernel to user mode.

As part of the preemption process, the operating system will retain a copy of the state of the process. This information represents the *context* of a process. The process of saving the current process's state and loading a new process for execution is called a *context switch*. A change from user-level execution to kernel-level execution is not a context switch, but rather it is considered overhead in making a system call. When the process eventually becomes the highest priority RUNNABLE process, the operating system must restore the context such that the process will resume execution from the point at which it was preempted.

It was not until the UNIX SVR4 operating system that additional scheduling policies where incorporated into the base operating system. The scheduler code was separated into policy-dependent and policy-independent segments. When a context switch is to occur, the policy-independent scheduler code selects a process to run solely based on the priority (*without any knowledge of or bias toward a policy*). The dependent scheduler code determines the priority of a process, which ensures the goals of the particular scheduling policy are satisfied.

In multithreaded operating systems, the system scheduler will exploit the multiprocessor environment to take advantage of the extended process model. This result is accomplished by offering a dual-level scheduling abstraction.

The first scheduling abstraction is at the operating system level and encompasses the standard priority-based scheduling. The enhancement here is that the bound thread is now considered the schedulable entity. If the UNIX threads implementation provides multiplexed threads, then the underlying lightweight process is the schedulable entity. The multiplexed thread is mapped to an available LWP from the pool, and thus can be considered bound for the purposes of scheduling.[38]

As with previous releases of the operating system, multiple scheduling policies are available. From the operating system's perspective, there are two basic scheduling policies available: the Time-Sharing (TS) policy, and the fixed priority (FP) policy. The Solaris 2.x operating system offers a Real Time (RT) scheduling policy in lieu of the FP policy. A Fixed-Class (FC) priority scheduling policy is also available in UNIX SVR4.2 MPF.

The second level is in user-mode and provides for granular control over the scheduling of multiplexed threads. The advantage of user-level scheduling is that an application can control scheduling characteristics with a simple function call, rather than a trap [BALL91]. The user-level scheduling of UNIX threads is available in the UNIX SVR4.2 MPF. The UNIX Threads Interface provides the SCHED_FIFO and SCHED_RR Fixed-Priority scheduling policies, and the SCHED_TS and SCHED_OTHER Time-Sharing policies. The Solaris 2.3 operating system does not provide this extra layer of scheduling.

---

[38]Although some documentation states that the LWP is the schedulable entity, I have chosen the term *bound thread*. The distinction is that certain implementations of the UNIX Threads Interface may not use an underlying LWP model.

12.2   UNIX Process Scheduling and Control

The challenge in describing system scheduling is that the UNIX Threads Interface provides for bound and multiplexed threads without describing the implementation at the operating system level. When the threads are implemented directly at the UNIX kernel level, the kernel threads are considered the system schedulable units. In this context, a kernel thread is synonymous with a bound thread. If the implementation provides for multiplexed threads, then the threads are implemented at the user-level and mapped, according to a user-level scheduling algorithm, to a kernel-level thread. From the operating system's perspective, the kernel-level thread is the schedulable unit.

A UNIX threads implementation using an underlying LWP model at the kernel level can have a thread permanently bound to it. The system schedulable unit in this implementation is the LWP, and by implication, the bound thread. Multiplexed threads are mapped to an available LWP from a multiplexing LWP pool. It is the LWP that is considered the system schedulable unit, not the multiplexing thread. Once the user-level thread has been mapped, the system can schedule the LWP. The multiplexed thread may eventually be preempted and a different multiplexed thread could be subsequently mapped to this LWP.

There are several system calls that affect the schedulable unit. When the schedulable unit is a bound thread, the system call will affect that bound thread only. If, however, the schedulable unit is an LWP with a multiplexed thread, the system call affects the LWP, not the multiplexed thread. The distinction is subtle, but important. Caution must be exercised to ensure the desired schedulable unit is being effected. Altering the scheduling policy of an LWP in the multiplexing LWP pool, for example, could have catastrophic side effects.

The functions described in this section are based on an underlying LWP model, as provided by the UNIX SVR4.2 MPF porting base and provided in the Solaris 2.3 operating system. Your implementation may vary slightly. You should consult the accompanying manual pages for potential differences.

The priocntl Function

The priocntl (*see Figure 12.1*) system call provides the general programming interface to scheduling policies, and policy specific parameters for the schedulable unit. The priocntl call provides the capability to get information about the configured system scheduling policies, or to get or reset the policy or policy-specific parameters.

The major change to priocntl is that it now affects the LWP rather than the UNIX process. For single-threaded applications, the behavior is equivalent to the traditional UNIX process model, as there is only one thread and one LWP.

```
NAME:
       priocntl - Lightweight process scheduler control.

SYNOPSIS:
       #include <sys/types.h>
       #include <sys/priocntl.h>
       #include <sys/procset.h>
       #include <sys/fppriocntl.h>
       #include <sys/tspriocntl.h>

       long
       priocntl(idtype_t idtype, id_t id, int cmd, void *arg)

       long
       priocntlset(procset_t *psp, int cmd, void *arg)

       long
       priocntllist(lwpid_t *lwpid, int idcnt, int cmd, void
*arg)
```

Figure 12.1   priocntl synopsis. [1]

The LWPs affected by the call to priocntl are determined by the parameters idtype and id. The interpretation of the value specified by the idtype parameter has been updated to support the extended process model. The idtype values, along with a brief description, appear in Table 12.1.

The priocntl system call applies the command specified as parameter cmd to the LWPs given by the idtype and id parameters. The list of available commands, along with a brief definition, appear in Table 12.2.

The PC_GETCID and PC_GETCLINFO commands of the priocntl system call both use a pcinfo_t type data structure for the parameter arg. This data structure is defined to include the members:

```
       id_t          pc_cid;
       char          pc_clname[PC_CLNMSZ];
       long          pc_clinfo[PC_CLINFOSZ];
```

The PC_SETPARMS and PC_GETPARMS commands use a pcparms_t type data structure which includes the members:

```
       id_t          pc_cod;
       long          pc_clparms[PC_CLPARMSZ];
```

When a UNIX process is initially created by a fork1 or forkall system call, the initial LWP inherits the scheduling policy of the parent UNIX process's LWP that called fork. Similarly, the LWP resulting from a call to exec inherits the scheduling policy of the LWP that called the exec.

---

[1] Printed with Permission of UNIX Systems Laboratories, Inc. All Rights Reserved.

At the operating system level there are three scheduling policies available for application programs: the `Time-Sharing` (TS) policy; the `Fixed-Priority` (FP) policy[39]; and the `Fixed-Class` (FC) policy. In a typical environment, the `Time-Sharing` scheduling policy is used exclusively.

Table 12.1   The `priocntl idtype_t` Parameter Values [¶]

P_LWPID	The `priocntl` system call applies to a sibling lightweight process whose identifier is specified as parameter `id`.
P_PID	The `id` parameter is a UNIX process `pid`, and the `priocntl` system call applies to all lightweight processes within that UNIX Process.
P_PPID	The parameter `id` is a parent process ID. The `priocntl` system call applies to all lightweight processes within the specified parent UNIX process.
P_PGID	The parameter `id` is a process group ID. The `priocntl` system call applies to all lightweight processes in the specified process group.
P_SID	The parameter `id` is a session ID. The `priocntl` system call applies to all lightweight processes associated with the processes in the specified session.
P_CID	The `priocntl` system call applies to all of the lightweight processes currently in the scheduling class specified as parameter `id`.
P_UID	The `priocntl` system call applies to all lightweight processes that currently have the effective user ID specified as `id`.
P_GID	The `priocntl` system call applies to all lightweight processes that currently have the effective group ID specified as `id`.
P_ALL	The `priocntl` system call applies to all currently existing lightweight processes. The value of `id` is ignored.

---

[39]The `Real Time` (RT) policy has been renamed to the `Fixed-Priority` (FP) scheduling policy in UNIX `SVR4.2 MPF`. The various RT and `rt*` symbol names and prefixes will be changed to FP and `fp*` as appropriate. The old RT symbols are supported for compatibility. The `Solaris 2.2` operating system, however, continues to use the RT prefixes.

[¶] Printed with Permission of UNIX Systems Laboratories, Inc. All Rights Reserved.

Table 12.2   The priocntl() Commands [1]

PC_GETID	The parameter arg is a pointer to a pcinfo_t type data structure whose member, pc_clname, contains the name of a specific scheduling class. The PC_GETID command will return the class identifier (pc_cid), and the class attributes (pc_clinfo) for this named class. The format of the class attribute data is defined in the <sys/rtpriocntl.h> or <sys/tspriocntl.h> header files. Note that if arg is specified as a NULL pointer, then the priocntl system call returns the number of scheduling classes but no additional information.
PC_GETCLINFO	The parameter arg is a pointer to a pcinfo_t type data structure whose member, pc_cid, contains a class identifier. The PC_GETCLINFO command will return the corresponding class name (pc_clname) and class attributes (pc_clinfo) for this class Note that if arg is specified as a NULL pointer, then the priocntl system call returns the number of scheduling classes but no additional information.
PC_SETPARMS	The parameter arg is a pointer to a pcparms_t type data structure whose member pc_cid contains the class identifier of the scheduling class to be applied to the LWPs specified by the idtype and id parameters. The member pc_clparms contains the class-specific parameters to be used. If priocntl encounters an error for one or more of the target LWPs, it may or may not continue through the set of LWPs depending on the error.
PC_GETPARMS	The class-specific scheduling parameters of an LWP are returned in the pcparms_t type data structure pointed to by parameter arg. If the pc_cid member of this structure contains a valid class identifier, and a single LWP belonging to that class is given by the parameters idtype and id, then the scheduling parameters for that LWP are returned in the pc_clparms member of the data structure. When the idtype and id parameters specify a set of LWPs, then the scheduling parameters for a single LWP in the set (determined by the scheduling class implementation) are returned in the pc_clparms buffer. Finally, if the pc_cid is given as PC_CLNULL, and a single LWP is specified by the parameters idtype and id, then that LWP's scheduling class identifier is returned in pc_cid, and the scheduling class parameters are returned in the pc_clparms buffer.

Fixed-Priority Scheduling (UNIX SVR4.2 MPF),
Real Time Scheduling (Solaris 2.3)

The Fixed-Priority scheduling policy is provided for advanced applications requiring a finer control over scheduling. With the Fixed-Priority scheduling policy the schedulable unit will always execute at a fixed-priority value. The priority value is not adjusted by the operating system. Privilege is required for Fixed-Priority scheduling in order to discourage abuse.

The Fixed-Priority scheduling class (FP) of the UNIX SVR4.2 MPF operating system is similar to the Real Time scheduling class (RT) of the Solaris 2.3 operating system. The primary distinction is that the UNIX SVR4.2 MPF kernel has embedded preemption points, whereas the Solaris 2.x kernel can be preempted at 1 millisecond intervals [Ster93]. For the remainder of this section, both will be referred to as the FP scheduling policy.

The priorities for the FP class range from zero to an upper limit imposed by the installation. To determine the upper limit, use the priocntl system call with the PC_GETCID or PC_GETCLINFO command. Once a priority has been determined for an LWP in this class, the priority remains constant and is not altered by the operating system due to CPU usage. The priority value can be changed by an LWP with appropriate privilege, as defined by the priocntl system call.

The operating system scheduler maintains a series of queues, one per priority value of the FP class. All runnable LWPs in the FP class with the same priority value are placed on the same queue. The operating system scheduler selects an LWP from the highest priority nonempty queue for execution. The system scheduler uses a FIFO ordering for these queues such that the LWP at the front of the queue will be dispatched for execution first. An LWP is placed at the back of the priority queue when:

1. The LWP becomes runnable after being blocked on a condition, lock, or resource
2. The LWP changes to the FP scheduling policy
3. The LWP uses all of its time quantum
4. The LWP's priority is reset
5. The LWP is a newly created LWP with FP scheduling policy

When an LWP in the FP scheduling class is preempted by a higher priority LWP, the preempted LWP is placed at the front of the queue with the remainder of its time quantum. There are no provisions in the FP scheduling class to provide any implicit processor affinity or load-balancing mechanisms.

An interesting approach to solving the problem of priority inversion is described by [Ster93] who presents the notion of priority inheritance through which the lower-priority LWP inherits the priority of the waiting LWP. Upon releasing the lock, the LWP's original priority is restored.

Time-Sharing Scheduling (UNIX SVR4.2 MPF and SOLARIS 2.3)

The Time-Sharing scheduling class (TS) has not changed significantly for either the UNIX 4.2 MP operating system or the SunOS 5.2 operating system, with the exception that the LWP is now the schedulable unit.

The goal of the Time-Sharing scheduling policy is to allocate the CPU fairly among competing LWPs in the TS class. To this end, the operating system will adjust the priority of an LWP in the TS class based on CPU usage when executing in user mode, and based on a parameter to the sleep system call when executing in kernel mode. Thus, the priority value of the LWP is continually adjusted based on its most recent behavior.

The Time-Sharing policy is not required to, but is not prohibited from, using affinity or load-balancing techniques. The exact scheduling behavior may vary, depending on the implementation.

Priority inversion is not necessarily a problem for LWPs scheduled using the Time-Sharing policy. When an LWP of lower-priority is holding a lock required by an LWP with a higher priority, the lower priority LWP will ultimately have its priority raised as it becomes starved for CPU cycles.

Fixed-Class Scheduling (UNIX SVR4.2 MPF)

Fixed-Class scheduling class (FC) is similar to the Time-Sharing scheduling class. The distinction is that the operating system will not adjust the priority of an LWP in the Fixed-Class scheduling class based on its recent CPU usage. When an LWP enters this class, its priority remains constant except for potential adjustments while executing in kernel mode. There are no special privileges required for using this scheduling class. The Fixed -Class scheduling class differs from the Fixed-Priority scheduling class in that the you cannot change the allocated time quantum.

Gang Scheduling (UNIX SVR4.2 MPF)

The UNIX SVR4.2 MPF operating system is designed to provide a Gang scheduling class (GS), although the Novell Corporation's porting base does not yet provide the implementation. With Gang scheduling, also referred to as coscheduling, all runnable processes from the same application execute at the same time [FeRu90] [Oust82] [Jaco86] [Bart87]. At the end of the time slice, all running processes are preempted simultaneously, and all the processes of another application are then scheduled for execution. Upon rescheduling, all processes are attempted to be executed on the same processors.

This form of scheduling has the advantage of limiting the busy waiting associated with the use of shared resources. The disadvantage, however, is that there is a greater potential for cache inconsistency. Gang scheduling can also result in processor fragmentation. Consider, for example, a system with *n* processors. If application A requires *n -2* processors, then only those applications utilizing two or less processors can execute while application A is running.

In the Gang scheduling class, the application specifies a set of LWPs that should be run concurrently, assuming an appropriate number of available processors. The corresponding system priority value of an LWP in the gang is usually configured to be higher then those in the TS and FC classes, but lower than those in the FP class. Thus, FP LWPs run before GS LWPs, which run before TS LWPs.

The maximum size of the gang should not exceed the value of the tunable system parameter representing the maximum gang size. This maximum will prevent an application from taking over total control of the computer system. The maximum gang size tunable parameter should be less then the number of available processors. It should be noted, however, that there are no provisions to prevent a gang from exceeding this size.

A gang of LWPs will not be dispatched for execution until they can be dispatched together. When the appropriate number of processors becomes available, then the gang scheduler will allocate a time quantum (*determined by a tunable parameter*) and the gang will be dispatched. When the size of the gang exceeds the number of available processors, then the gang scheduler will attempt to dispatch the gang piecemeal.

An application program that requires a specific physical concurrency level must ensure the appropriate gang size is created. Simply creating a gang size less then the maximum gang size as defined by the tunable parameter is insufficient, as one or more processors may be taken off-line for various administrative duties.

When a single LWP in a dispatched gang blocks, the behavior of the remaining LWPs in the gang is specified by the application program. That is to say, when a member of the gang blocks, should all members of the gang be preempted, or should they be permitted to continue until the expiration of their time quantum, or until they exit? This behavior is determined by the priocntl PC_SETPARMS command. The priocntl commands PC_GETCID and PC_GETCLINFO both return the gang scheduling policy attributes in the pc_clinfo according to the format:

```
typedef struct gsinfo {
    int        gs_maxsz;    /* GS_MAXSZ tunable value      */
    ulong      gs_tqsecs;   /* time quantum seconds        */
    ulong      gs_tqnsecs;  /* additional nanoseconds in   *
                             * time quantum                */
} gsinfo_t;  ¶
```

The priocntl commands PC_SETPARMS and PC_GETPARMS both use a pc_clparms format of:

```
typedef struct gsparms {
    ulong       gs_flags;
} gsparms_t;  ¶
```

¶ Printed with Permission of UNIX Systems Laboratories, Inc. All Rights Reserved.

Note that in calling the `priocntl` system call with the `PC_SETPARMS` command, the LWPs identified through the `idtype` and `id` parameters will become a newly created gang of LWPs.

Currently, the only defined flag is the `GS_RUNTOGETHER` flag. If this flag is specified, then when one gang member is blocked, the remaining gang members are preempted. Otherwise, the remaining gang members would be permitted to continue until the expiration of their time interval, or until they terminated.

The processor_bind Function

The `processor_bind` function (*see Figure 12.2*) provides the application with a mechanism to bind and subsequently unbind a specified LWP or set of LWPs with a particular processor. This is necessary for those cases in which a particular device or kernel service is available from only a single processor. Multithreaded applications will not typically require the use of this function.

To bind an LWP or an LWP set to a particular processor, the real or effective user ID of the requesting LWP must match the real or saved user ID of the LWP being bound, or the requesting LWP must have appropriate privilege.

NAME:

    processor_bind - Bind an LWP to a specific processor.

SYNOPSIS:

```
#include <sys/types.h>
#include <sys/procset.h>
#include <sys/processor.h>

int
processor_bind(idtype_t idtype, id_t id, processorid_t
processorid,processorid_t *obind)
```

Figure 12.2   `processor_bind()` synopsis. [1]

The parameters `idtype` and `id` are used to identify the LWP or LWP set to be bound to the specified processor. The parameter `processorid` is the ID of the processor, or a special operation code, as described in Table 12.3. The parameter `obind`, if non NULL, is the address at which to store the previous binding for the LWP. When the parameter `processorid` is given as a nonnegative value, then it is interpreted as the identifier of a processor to which the specified LWPs are to be bound. A negative value for `processorid` applies special operations, as defined in Table 12.3.

Table 12.3   The `processor_bind idtype_t` and `id_t` Relationships [1]

processorid_t	idtype	Interpretation of parameter id
>= 0	P_LWPID	The parameter `id` is the identifier of an `LWP` within the same `UNIX` process as the requesting thread. The operation applies to this `LWP` only.
>=0	P_PID	The parameter `id` is the `UNIX` process `PID`. The operation applies to all `LWPs` within this `UNIX` process.
< 0	PBIND_NONE	Removes the current binding, if any, for the specified `LWP`.
< 0	PBIND_QUERY	Used in conjunction with `obind` to query the current binding of an `LWP`.

12.3   Setting the Scheduling Information

The `UNIX` Threads Interface provides an additional layer of scheduling for `UNIX` threads. Through this higher level scheduling abstraction, each `UNIX` thread has an associated scheduling policy and priority. Sibling threads of a `UNIX` process can execute under different scheduling policies. This provides granular scheduling control for sophisticated multithreaded applications.

To support the scheduling of `UNIX` threads, a separate threads scheduler may be supplied with the `UNIX` threads implementation. This scheduler executes in user mode. As such, the functionality of this scheduler, along with its supported scheduling policies, is unknown to the base operating system.

PROGRAMMER'S NOTE:

As noted in [ABLL91], the logical correctness of an application can be influenced by the use of multiplexed threads. That is to say, an application can be free of deadlocks under the assumption that all threads eventually make progress in the system. When a multiplexed thread blocks, however, so does the underlying `LWP`, thus rendering the `LWP` inaccessible for other multiplexed threads. An application can run out of `LWPs` even though there are `RUNNABLE` threads.

---

[1] Printed with Permission of UNIX Systems Laboratories, Inc. All Rights Reserved.

Table 12.4   Thread Scheduling Policies [1]

SCHED_TS	A Time-Sharing scheduling policy. Both bound and multiplexed threads can use SCHED_TS. Multiplexed threads must use the SCHED_TS or the SCHED_OTHER policy.
SCHED_FIFO	A Fixed-Priority scheduling policy. Only bound threads can use SCHED_FIFO. Threads scheduled under this policy run with an infinite time quantum.
SCHED_RR	A Fixed-Priority scheduling policy that utilizes a round-robin scheduling implementation. Only bound threads can use SCHED_RR. Threads scheduled under this policy run with the time quantum returned by thr_get_rr_interval.
SCHED_OTHER	An alias for SCHED_TS.

Through the UNIX threads scheduler, there are various scheduling policies available. These are described in Table 12.4. There is a restriction, however, that multiplexed threads must currently have a scheduling policy of SCHED_TS or SCHED_OTHER. Bound threads have greater flexibility with scheduling policies and may use any of the scheduling policies.

Time-Sharing Scheduling (UNIX SVR4.2 MPF)

The Time-Sharing UNIX threads scheduling policy (SCHED_TS) provides another layer of scheduling for UNIX threads. The definition of the SCHED_TS class states that no thread under the Time-Sharing policy will be dispatched if there are any threads in the RUNNABLE state under the SCHED_FIFO or SCHED_RR policies. The SCHED_TS class is synonymous with the SCHED_OTHER class.

Fixed-Priority FIFO Scheduling (UNIX SVR4.2 MPF)

The Fixed-Priority FIFO UNIX threads scheduling policy (SCHED_FIFO) permits a bound thread to be scheduled with an infinite time quantum. The priority value assigned by the application is mapped to an LWP running under the fixed-time priority (FP) policy with a global-priority value determined by the configuration.

[1] Printed with Permission of UNIX Systems Laboratories, Inc. All Rights Reserved.

Fixed-Priority Round-Robin Scheduling (UNIX SVR4.2 MPF)

The Fixed-Priority round-robin UNIX threads scheduling class (SCHED_RR) permits a bound thread to be scheduled with a finite time quantum. The priority value assigned by the application is mapped to an LWP running under the fixed-time priority (FP) policy with a global-priority value determined by the configuration. Upon expiration of the time quantum the UNIX thread is preempted in favor of running another LWP with higher, or equal system-priority value. The time quantum can be determined by calling the thr_get_rr_interval function.

> **PROGRAMMER'S NOTE:**
>
> The initial thread of a process inherits the scheduling policy of the LWP that called fork. The single LWP retained after an exec retains the policy of the LWP that called exec. [1]

Thread Scheduling Parameters API

The UNIX Threads Interface provides two functions available to modify the scheduling policy and scheduling parameters for UNIX threads. The thr_getscheduler() function reports the current policy and policy-specific parameters. The thr_setscheduler() function is used to establish a new scheduling policy.

These functions use the sched_param_t type data structure which contains the members:

```
        id_t        policy;
        long        policy_params[POLICY_PARAM_SZ];  [1]
```

The policy must be one of SCHED_RR, SCHED_FIFO, SCHED_TS, or SCHED_OTHER for bound threads; and SCHED_TS for multiplexed threads. Depending on the implementation, the policy_params member can be type-cast to a param structure corresponding to the specified policy.

Querying Scheduling Parameters (UNIX SVR4.2 MPF)

The thr_getscheduler function (*see Figure 12.3*) reports the scheduling policy and policy-specific parameters for a specified thread. There are no special privileges required to use this function.

The first argument, tid, is the identifier of the thread on which to report the scheduling information. The second argument, param, is a pointer to a sched_param_t type data structure that will be used to return the policy-specific parameters.

[1] Printed with Permission of UNIX Systems Laboratories, Inc. All Rights Reserved.

NAME:

      `thr_getscheduler` - Report scheduling policy and policy specific parameters.

SYNOPSIS:

```
#include <sys/types.h>
#include <thread.h>

int
thr_getscheduler(thread_t tid, sched_param_t *param)
```

Figure 12.3   `thr_getscheduler()` synopsis. [1]

Each of the available scheduling policies has structure describing its corresponding parameters. The scheduling policies and structure names are shown in Table 12.5. In the UNIX SVR4.2 MPF operating system, these structures include the member `prio`, which is of type int.

Table 12.5   Scheduling Policies and Parameter Structures. [1]

SCHED_TS	struct ts_param
SCHED_FIFO	struct fifo_param
SCHED_RR	struct rr_param

Setting Scheduling Parameters (UNIX SVR4.2 MPF)

The `thr_setscheduler` function (*Figure 12.4*) is a new interface for use by multithreaded applications needing to exercise control over their scheduling. This function can be used to define the scheduling policy and/or the scheduling policy parameters for the specified thread.

The first argument, `tid`, is the identifier of the thread to which the new scheduling policy will apply. The second argument, `param`, is a pointer to a `sched_param_t` type data structure initialized with the appropriate parameters for the policy being set.

Depending on the implementation, the scheduling policy can be one of those listed in Table 12.4. Most implementations will prohibit a multiplexed thread from using a policy other than SCHED_TS or SCHED_OTHER. The `thr_setscheduler()` function, however, can still be used to change the priority value of a multiplexed thread.

NAME:
>   thr_setscheduler - Administer thread scheduling policy.

SYNOPSIS:
```
#include <sys/types.h>
#include <thread.h>

int
thr_setscheduler(thread_t tid, const sched_param_t *param)
```

Figure 12.4   thr_setscheduler() synopsis. [1]

To set the scheduling policy or policy parameters, the real or effective user ID of the calling thread must match the real or saved ID of the target thread. Appropriate privilege is required to set the policy of any thread or process to any scheduling policy other then SCHED_TS.

PROGRAMMER'S NOTE:

The scheduling policy SCHED_OTHER is provided for POSIX compatibility, and may be implemented as a compile-time constant having the same value as SCHED_TS. The thr_setscheduler function provides equivalent functionality to the POSIX pthreads Draft 5 pthread_setscheduler and pthread_setprio interfaces, but does not treat sched_param_t as an opaque type. [1]

Threads using the SCHED_TS scheduling policy (*all multiplexed threads by implication*) have a priority ranging from zero to (MAXINT-1). To raise the priority value of a thread using the SCHED_TS scheduling policy requires appropriate privilege. The level of privilege may vary between implementations. As with any thread, however, the priority may be lowered without requiring special privileges.

Once a scheduling policy has been established for a bound thread, no additional privilege is required to change that thread's priority. That is to say, if the scheduling policy for a bound thread is changed to SCHED_RR or SCHED_FIFO, then no additional privilege is required to subsequently alter the thread's priority. When a bound thread has the SCHED_TS scheduling policy, however, additional privilege may be required to increase the priority value for the thread.

Certain implementations of thread scheduling use only 126 distinct priority queues. All threads with a priority value greater than 126 are placed in the same queue. Thus, the system scheduler must search this queue for the numerically highest priority value. For performance considerations it is better to keep the high range of priority values at 126 or lower.

PROGRAMMER'S NOTE:

It is strongly recommended to use the `thr_setscheduler` function instead of direct calls to `priocntl`.

Thread Priority API (UNIX SVR4.2 MPF and SOLARIS 2.3)

The `thr_getprio` function (*Figure 12.5*) returns the current priority value for the specified thread. The `thr_setprio` is used to adjust the priority value for a specified thread.

While it is possible to get or set a thread's priority value using the `thr_getscheduler` or `thr_setscheduler` functions, `thr_getprio` and `thr_setprio` provide a convenient shorthand for this purpose.

NAME:
       `thr_getprio` - Return a thread's current priority.
       `thr_setprio` - Set a thread's current priority.

SYNOPSIS:
```
#include <thread.h>

int
thr_getprio(thread_t tid, int *prio)

int
thr_setprio(thread_t tid, int prio)
```

Figure 12.5   `thr_getprio()` synopsis. [1]

The `thr_getprio` function accepts two parameters. The first is the identifier of the thread whose priority value is to be returned. The priority value is returned in the address pointed to by the second argument, `prio`.

The `thr_setprio` function also requires two parameters. The first is the identifier of the thread whose priority value is to be set. The second parameter, `prio`, is the desired priority value for this thread.

The priority value for a multiplexed thread can be set using the `thr_setprio` function without special permissions. Increasing the priority value for a multiplexed thread simply means that the specified thread will be multiplexed onto an LWP ahead of lower priority threads. This behavior

---

[1] Printed with Permission of UNIX Systems Laboratories, Inc. All Rights Reserved.

does not, however, imply that the multiplexed thread will execute more frequently compared to bound threads nor that the system will schedule the underlying LWP more frequently.

The priority value range for multiplexed threads is determined by the implementation, although any integral priority value is acceptable. Most implementations will provide separate scheduling queues for the priority value ranges 0 through 128. Higher priority value threads are all placed in the same queue, and the thread's scheduler must search this queue each time. Thus, keeping multiplexed thread priority values in the range of 0 through 128 may increase the performance of your application.

Bound threads are treated separately. A call to the thr_setprio function is translated into a call to the priocntl system call. Depending on the implementation, the specified priority value may be acceptable, or rejected with a EINVAL error condition being generated. Additionally, special privileges may be required to execute the underlying priocntl system call.

With bound threads, you can always lower the priority value, but may require special privileges to increase the priority. When the specified thread is using the SCHED_FIFO or SCHED_RR scheduling class, you can raise or lower the priority without special privileges. This is possible, since you must already have that privilege to set the scheduling policy for that thread. To change the priority value for bound threads using the SCHED_TS scheduling policy may also require privilege.

Yielding a Processor (UNIX SVR4.2 MPF and SOLARIS 2.3)

The thr_yield function (*Figure 12.6*) instructs the calling thread to yield the processor in favor of executing a thread with equal or greater priority value. When invoked, the calling thread's execution is temporarily suspended and the thread is transitioned to the RUNNABLE state. The thr_yield function causes the current thread to yield, and the associated LWP to schedule another thread.

The dispatching of a new thread to run after the calling thread has yielded is not specified. It is possible for the calling thread to be rescheduled immediately, even if other RUNNABLE threads exist. This situation will occur, for example, when the yielding thread's priority value is higher than the other RUNNABLE multiplexed threads.

```
NAME:
        thr_yield - Yield the processor.

SYNOPSIS:
        #include <thread.h>

        void
        thr_yield(void)
```

Figure 12.6   thr_yield() synopsis. [1]

If the calling thread is bound, then the LWP to which it is mapped will yield the processor. If there are other RUNNABLE threads in the system with higher priority values, then the system will dispatch those threads for execution.

Round-Robin Intervals (UNIX SVR4.2 MPF)

The thr_get_rr_interval function (*Figure 12.7*) is used to determine the system-imposed round-robin interval for the SCHED_RR scheduling policy. The parameter rr_time is a pointer to a timestruct_t type data structure, in which the default value used by the UNIX threads implementation will be returned.

```
NAME:
        thr_get_rr_interval - Determine system-imposed round-robin interval.

SYNOPSIS:
        #include <thread.h>

        void
        thr_get_rr_interval(timestruct_t *rr_time)
```

Figure 12.7   thr_get_rr_interval() synopsis. [1]

13

ADAM: A Dynamic Atom Manager

13.1   Introduction to ADAM

The complexity and size of software systems is continuing to grow as more demands are being placed on the application's functionality. The design of these software systems extends beyond algorithmic functionality and basic data structures [GSOS92]. To effectively engineer such complex software systems requires an architectural approach to system design, incorporating structural issues such as communication protocols, software partitioning, and synchronization.

The difficulty in using parallelism is in determining the software partitioning and scheduling of tasks in such a manner as to minimize the execution time [McRi89]. The ideal method to design an application is to separate the programmatic statement of an algorithm from the machine-dependent partitioning, mapping, and communication specifications [TDP89]. This would permit the machine-dependent partitions to change between hardware platforms while retaining the programmatic algorithms intact. Software partitioning permits developers to write and debug small, focused code segments rather than large, monolithic processes that live through many different computational stages [Spen92].

A partitioned code segment can be thought of as providing a discrete unit of work. An application program can incorporate several discrete units of work that collectively represent the capabilities of the application. A unit of work is a reusable asset that can be incorporated into other applications requiring the same discrete services.

This chapter presents the ADAM multithreaded software utility. ADAM is **A D**ynamic **A**tom **M**anager providing a higher level abstraction for designing and implementing multithreaded applications following software partitioning techniques. A partitioned code segment (a discrete unit of work) is represented as an *atom*. The unit of work is applied to a datum of the application by attaching the atom to the datum. ADAM will execute the unit of work associated with the atom as a separate thread within the application process. The value returned from this unit of work becomes the measured value of the atom.

As an example, consider a client-server application with a data structure to represent the server. On occasion, when the server is idle, we would like to perform some garbage-collection routine.

To appropriately determine the idle time, we need an algorithm to sample the CPU utilization at regular intervals. This could be accomplished by setting the interval timer and then catching the wake-up signal. This, however, influences the path of execution and represents a disjoint flow of control. Through the ADAM interface, we can simply create an atom called IDLE_TIME, and define a procedure to measure its value. When we attach the IDLE_TIME atom to the server data structure, ADAM will measure the value for us.

To use the ADAM interface, an application must invoke the ADAM manager. The application can create, attach, detach, and administer the available atoms. There are many instances where the ADAM interface will provide the high-level abstraction desired to assist in mulithreaded application development. ADAM does not apply to every application, but as you see the power offered through this interface, you will undoubtedly enjoy using it.

13.2   An Overview of ADAM

ADAM Objects

Through the ADAM interface, an application program can attach atoms to *objects*. An ADAM object is not the same entity, nor does it have the characteristics of objects, as used in object-oriented programming languages. An ADAM object is simply an entity through which application data can be referenced (*see Figure 13.1*). An ADAM object can be destroyed with no effect on its representative data.

Atom Definitions

Atoms are represented as *name/value* pairs. The atom name is determined when the atom is initially defined through the atomdef module. The basic components of an atom are shown in Table 13.2. Once defined, a named atom can be attached to an ADAM object. The attach process creates a separate copy of the atom for each object to which it is attached.

There are two basic types of atoms provided. An INTRINSIC atom's value is constant. A DERIVED atom's value is measured when the atom is attached to an object. To measure the value of a DERIVED atom, the ADAM manager will execute the atom's attach procedure. The returned value from the attach procedure will become the value of the atom. When the atom is subsequently detached from the object, the ADAM manager will execute the atom's detach procedure.

Both INTRINSIC and DERIVED atoms can have an associated constructor function and a destructor function. When the atom is initially attached to an object, ADAM will allocate a basic atom structure and will call the atom's constructor function. The constructor function allocates the storage for the atom's value. When the atom is subsequently detached from the object, ADAM will execute the destructor function to release the storage area.

Table 13.2.   Basic Components of an Atom Definition

type	Describes if the atom is INTRINSIC or DERIVED
constructor	Function to allocate storage for atom's value
destructor	Function to deallocate storage of atom's value
attach	Function to call when atom is attached to object
detach	Function to call when atom is detached
value	The default value for this atom

Atoms

In attaching a named atom to an object, the atom module will allocate the storage for the atom and associate it with the object. Once attached, the application can query the current value of the atom, and subsequently detach the atom from the object. Only one occurrence of a particular named atom can be attached to a single object.

The ADAM Module

A series of daemon threads are provided to administer the more rudimentary aspects of atom administration. When an atom is attached to an object there is a series of state transitions which must be completed.

The attach function must allocate the atom storage and transition the atom to the ATTACH state. The ADAM manager provides the Attacher, Binder, and Measurer daemon threads to take over from there. The atom state transitions appear in Figure 13.1. The threadLinks module is used to communicate messages between the daemon threads.

The attach function establishes the relationship between the object and the atom. It sends a message to the Attacher daemon thread to perform the remainder of the attachment. The Attacher thread receives the message and transitions the atom to the ATTACHING state.

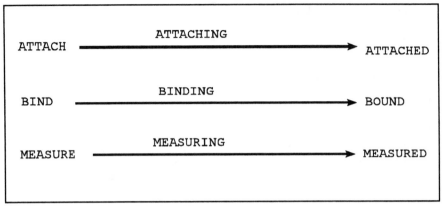

Figure 13.1   Atom state transitions.

The Attacher Daemon Thread

The `Attacher` daemon will transition the atom from the ATTACH to the ATTACHING state. If atom SETs are provided, they should be added here.[40] The atom will then transition to the ATTACHED state. The `Attacher` daemon will transition the atom to the BIND start state, and will notify the `Binder` daemon.

The Binder Daemon Thread

The `Binder` daemon will transition the atom from the BIND state to the BINDING state. It then invokes the atom's *constructor* function if defined. The atom will then transition from the BINDING state to the BOUND state.[41] The `Binder` daemon will transition the atom to the MEASURE state and will notify the `Measurer` daemon.

---

[40] The production version of ADAM supports attaching a group of atoms with a single call. The group of atoms are referred to as atom `sets`. The `file` atom set, for example, contains various atoms within the `set`, including file name, file content, file modification time, and so on. For the purposes of this book, however, atom `sets` are not presented. Contact Global Technologies Ltd., Inc. to obtain a production version of ADAM.

[41]   If additional atom types are to be provided, then the binding process should be responsible for binding the named atom to a particular type of entity (i.e., a VIRTUAL atom, FUNCTIONAL atom, or FILE atom).

The Measurer Daemon Thread

The `Measurer` daemon, as the name implies, is responsible for measuring the value of the atom. If a `NULL` atom value was specified on the `atom_f.attach` function call for an `INTRINSIC` atom, then the default value from the base atom definition will be used. For a `DERIVED` atom, however, the atom's `attach` procedure must be invoked as a separate thread. To support this, the `adam` module defines a function named `Procedure` to be used as the wrapper for calling the atom's `attach` procedure.

The Detacher Daemon Thread

The `Detacher` daemon is responsible for detaching an atom from a particular object. When the application calls the `atom_f.detach` function, the request is validated and the atom is marked for deletion. The actual detachment is handled by the `Detacher` daemon.

The Design of the ADAM Manager

The `ADAM` manager is implemented through a series of software modules. Each module has a descriptive header file and the module source code. The interface to the module is provided through a data structure, with pointers to the appropriate functions available to the application. Other functions within the module are local to that module and are not directly accessible to the application program. The `object` module, for example, provides the `object_f` data structure, with pointers to the `Create` and `Destroy` functions defined in the module source.

Extending the Functionality

There are various enhancements to the `ADAM` interface that can easily be made. First, the atoms are currently considered to be virtual in that they do not represent a permanent entity. Thus as a future enhancement, an atom could represent a particular entity with certain characteristics. We could, for example, define an atom to have a type of `FILE` to denote a `UNIX` file. A type of `FUNCTIONAL` could be used to denote the atom must be remeasured whenever it is referenced.

A natural extension of this module is to support `SET`s. An atom can represent a `SET` of atoms such that when the atom `SET` is attached to an object, all atoms within the `SET` are considered to be attached.

The support for dependencies between atoms is another feature that can be implemented. This would permit one atom to be dependent on a different atom's measure, or the time associated with that measure. Constraints are also a useful extension to this model. With constraints, we can apply certain that must be satisfied when the atom's value is measured. A variation of a constraint is the `TIME_CONSTRAINT` through which an atom's value is considered measured until the specified period expires. At that time, the value must be remeasured.

The ADAM Definitions

The `adamdef.h` header file (*Listing 13.1*) shows the common definitions used as the base for the ADAM interface. There are several type definitions and various constant values defined. This header file also includes other header files required for the compilation. These will be covered in the next several sections of this chapter.

Listing 13.1   *adamdef.h* -- The base ADAM header file.

```
 1 #if ! defined(ADAMDEF_H)
 2 #      define ADAMDEF_H
 3 #      include <synch.h>
 4 #      include "threadrw.h"
 5 #      include "threadLinks.h"
 6 #      include "state.h"
 7 #      include "threadQcond.h"
 8 #      include "comlink.h"
 9 #      include "mthreadLog.h"
10 #      include "object.h"
11
12 typedef unsigned long   set_t;
13 typedef unsigned long   attr_t;
14 typedef unsigned long   atomid_t;
15 /**** Define the types of data structures in use   ****/
16 #      define      OBJECT_TYPE 0x1
17 #      define      ATOM_TYPE   0x2
18 typedef      unsigned int      atomtype_t;
19 #      define      INTRINSIC       0x00000001
20 #      define      DERIVED         0x00000002
21 #      define      CONSTRUCTED     0x00000010
22 #      define      ALLOCATED       0x00000020
23 #      define      DEALLOCATE      0x00000040
24 #      define      ATTACH          0x00000010
25 #      define      ATTACHING       0x00000020
26 #      define      ATTACHED        0x00000040
27 #      define      BIND            0x00000100
28 #      define      BINDING         0x00000200
29 #      define      BOUND           0x00000400
30 #      define      MEASURE         0x00001000
31 #      define      MEASURING       0x00002000
32 #      define      MEASURED        0x00004000
33 #      define      CONSTRAIN       0x00010000
34 #      define      CONSTRAINING    0x00020000
```

Listing 13.1   *continued.*

```
#       define      CONSTRAINED      0x00040000
#       define      DETACH           0x00100000
#       include "adam.h"
#       include "atomdef.h"
#       include "atoms.h"
#       include "daemon.h"
#       include "message.h"
#endif
```

13.3   The ADAM Object Module

In Listing 13.2, object.h, the ADAM object is defined as an object_t type definition. The *identifier* is currently used to denote the allocated data structure as an object type. Additional functionality can be added here, such as the assignment of a unique identifier for each allocated object. The statevar member defines the current state of the object. The rwlock, as the name implies, is a reader/writer lock used to synchronize access to the object data structure. The data member is a pointer to the application's representative data. The atoms member is a link list of atoms currently attached to the object.

Listing 13.2   *object.h* -- The object module header file.

```
1 #if ! defined(OBJECT_H)
2 #       define OBJECT_H
3
4 typedef struct    _object      {
5       unsigned long       identifer;
6       statevar_t    statevar;
7       rwlock_t      *rwlock;
8       void          *data;
9       linkbase_t    *atoms;
10 } object_t;
11
12 typedef struct _object_f_t {
13       object_t      *(*create)(void *);
14       int           (*destroy)(object_t * );
15 } object_f_t;
16 extern object_f_t object_f;
17 #endif
```

The `Create()` function (*Listing 13.3*) accepts a single parameter depicting the application's data the created object is to represent. The application must reference this function through the `object_f.create()` function pointer. Atoms can be attached and detached from the ADAM object. When the object is no longer required, the application calls the `object_f.destroy()` function to deallocate the object structure. Creating and destroying an ADAM object has no effect on the application's representative data.

Listing 13.3   *object.c* -- The `object` module.

```
 1 #include <thread.h>
 2 #include <stdlib.h>
 3 #include <synch.h>
 4 #include <memory.h>
 5 #include <errno.h>
 6 #include "adamdef.h"
 7 static mutex_t ObjectMutex = { 0 };
 8 /***********************************************************
 9  *      Function Prototypes
10  ***********************************************************/
11 static      object_t    *Allocate(void);
12 static      object_t    *Create(void *);
13 static      int         Destroy(object_t *);
14 static      void        Deallocate(object_t *);
15
16 /***********************************************************
17  *      Create             FUNCTION
18  *
19  *      This function allocates and initializes an object_t type
20  *      structure. The object will be initialized with its data member
21  *      pointing to the specified application data.  The create
22  *      function returns a pointer to the allocated object structure
23  *      upon success, or NULL if an error occurrs.
24  ***********************************************************/
25 static object_t *
26 Create(void *data)
27 {
28         object_t  *object        = NULL;
29         int        errorCondition = 0;
30         threadLog_f.clearError();
31         object = Allocate();
32         if( object ) {
33                 object->data = data;
34
35
```

Listing 13.3 *continued.*

```
36
37                              /*****************************************
38                              *   CRITICAL SECTION     START
39                              *   We have to synchronize access to Adam.objects
40                              *   to ensure two or more threads do not
41                              *   initialize it concurrently.
42                              *****************************************/
43              mutex_lock( &ObjectMutex );
44              if( Adam.objects == NULL ) {
45                      Adam.objects = threadLink_f.create();
46                      if( Adam.objects == NULL ) {
47                              object_f.destroy(object);
48                              return(NULL);
49                      }
50              }
51              mutex_unlock( &ObjectMutex );
52                              /*****************************************
53                              *   CRITICAL SECTION     END
54                              *****************************************/
55                              /*****************************************
56                              *    Add the object to the list of allocated
57                              *    and initialized objects.
58                              *****************************************/
59              errorCondition=threadLink_f.add(Adam.objects, object);
60              if( errorCondition ) {
61                      Deallocate(object);
62                      threadLog_f.setError(errorCondition);
63                      return(NULL);
64              }
65      }
66      return( object );
67 }
68
69 /********************************************************************
70 *      Destroy              FUNCTION
71 *
72 *      The destroy function invalidates and deallocates the specified
73 *      object_t structure.
74 ********************************************************************/
75 static int
76 Destroy(object_t * object)
77 {
```

Listing 13.3   *continued.*

```
78
79      int     errorCondition = 0;
80      if( object == NULL )
81             return(EINVAL);
82                        /************************************************
83                         *     Lock the object's rwlock in write mode.
84                         ************************************************/
85      errorCondition = rw_wrlock(object->rwlock);
86      if( errorCondition )
87             return(errorCondition);
88                        /************************************************
89                         *     If the current state of the object is
90                         *     DEALLOCATE, then we are done.  So just
91                         *     return.
92                         ************************************************/
93      if( statevar_f.getstate(&object->statevar) & DEALLOCATE ) {
94             rw_unlock(object->rwlock);
95             return(0);
96      }
97                        /************************************************
98                         *     Remove the object from the Adam.objects list
99                         *     and transition the object to the DEALLOCATE
100                        *     state. We can then remove the write mode
101                        *     rwlock.
102                        ************************************************/
103     threadLink_f.delete(Adam.objects,object,NULL);
104     statevar_f.transition(&object->statevar,0,DEALLOCATE);
105     rw_unlock(object->rwlock);
106                       /************************************************
107                        *     Now lock the object's rwlock in read mode,
108                        *     and detach any currently attached atoms.
109                        ************************************************/
110     errorCondition = rw_rdlock(object->rwlock);
111     if( ! errorCondition ) {
112             threadLink_f.apply(object->atoms,atom_f.detach, object);
113             rw_unlock(object->rwlock);
114             threadrw_f.destroy(object->rwlock);
115             free(object);
116     }
117     return(errorCondition);
118 }
119
```

Listing 13.3   *continued.*

```
120
121 /********************************************************************
122  *      Define the object module interface
123  ********************************************************************/
124 object_f_t object_f = {
125       Create,
126       Destroy
127 };
128
129 /********************************************************************
130  *      Allocate     FUNCTION
131  *
132  *      The allocate function is local to the object module.  This
133  *      function returns a pointer to an allocated and initialized
134  *      object_t type structure.  On error, the function returns NULL
135  *      and calls threadLog to record the error condition.
136  ********************************************************************/
137 static object_t *
138 Allocate(void)
139 {
140       object_t  *object = NULL;
141       threadLog_f.clearError();
142       object = malloc(sizeof(object_t));
143
144       if( object != NULL ) {
145             memset(object,'\0', sizeof(object_t));
146             object->identifer = OBJECT_TYPE;
147             object->rwlock    = threadrw_f.create();
148             object->atoms     = threadLink_f.create();
149
150             if( object->rwlock == NULL || object->atoms == NULL )
151 {
152                   Deallocate(object);
153                   object = NULL;
154             }
155             statevar_f.transition(&object->statevar,0,ALLOCATED);
156       }
157       else
158             threadLog_f.setError(ENOMEM);
159
160       return(object);
161 }
162
```

Listing 13.3 *continued.*

```
162
163 /*******************************************************
164  *      Deallocate  FUNCTION
165  *
166  *      This function is local to the object module.  It will
167 release
168  *      the resources associated with the specified object.
169  *******************************************************/
170 static void
171 Deallocate( object_t *object)
172 {
173        if( object == NULL )
174              return;
175
176        if(! (statevar_f.getstate(&object->statevar) & ALLOCATED) )
177              return;
178        if( object->rwlock != NULL )
179              threadrw_f.destroy(object->rwlock);
180        if( object->atoms   != NULL )
181              threadLink_f.destroy( object->atoms );
182        free(object);
183        return;
184 }
```

In the ADAM object module, only the Create() and Destroy() functions are accessible by the application through the object_f structure. The scope of the Allocate() and Deallocate() functions are local to the object module.

The object_f.create() function call will allocate an object, initialize the object, and attach the object to the link list of objects maintained by the Adam.objects linkbase. If the function was called prior to initializing the ADAM manager, then a new linkbase will be created for the Adam.objects linked list. In a multithreaded application it is possible for multiple threads to call the object_f.create() function concurrently. To avoid a race condition, the test of the Adam.objects structure must be synchronized with a mutex lock. The Allocate() function will set the object's atoms linkbase and will also create the Reader-Writer lock dynamically through the threadrw module.

The Destroy() function is a bit more complex. To appropriately destroy an ADAM object, we must first detach all atoms currently attached to the object. To avoid a synchronization conflict, the Destroy() function will lock the object's rwlock for exclusive write. Once locked, we can check the current state of the object to see if it is currently being deallocated by another thread. In this case, the object's Reader-Writer lock can be removed and a successful status returned to the calling thread.

If the calling thread is to destroy the object, the thread must remove the object from the list of allocated objects, and transition the object to the DEALLOCATE state. The object can then be unlocked. Next, the object must be locked for read mode. We can now check for any attached atoms. For each atom currently attached to the object, the atom_f.detach() function must be called. If there were no atoms attached, then the Deallocate() function can be called. Otherwise, the object cannot be deallocated until all atoms have been detached. This is covered in the Section 13.5.

13.4   The Atom Definitions Module

The basic unit of the ADAM interface is the atom definition. The application program can define the characteristics of one or more atoms. The definition of the atom, however, does not cause the atom to be measured. It is only when the atom is attached to an object that the atom will be measured.

The atomdef module (*see Listings 13.3 and 13.4*) provides the application two functions for manipulating atom definitions. The atomdef_f.create() function is used to create an atom definition, while the atomdef_f.destroy() function will destroy the definition. The atomdef module's header file provides the atomdef_t structure type definition, and the atomdef_f_t function prototypes for the create and destroy functions.

Listing 13.4   *atomdef.h* -- The atom definition module header file.

```
1 #if !defined(ATOMDEF_H)
2 #     define ATOMDEF_H
3 typedef struct     _atomdef_t {
4       atomid_t    id;
5       atomtype_t  type;
6       unsigned long      referenceCount;
7       void         *defaultValue;
8       void         *(*constructor)(void);
9       void         *(*attach)(void*);
10      void         (*detach)(void*);
11      void         (*destructor)(void*);
12 }atomdef_t;
13 typedef struct _atomdef_t_f {
14      atomid_t    (*create)(atomtype_t, void*,
15                              void *(constructor)(void),
16                              void *(attach)(void*),
17                              void (detach)(void*),
18                              void (destructor)(void*));
19      int         (*destroy)(atomid_t);
20 }atomdef_t_f;
21 extern atomdef_t_f atomdef_f;
22 #endif
```

The `id` member of the `atomdef_t` type structure contains the unique identifier to reference this atom definition. The `type` field denotes if the atom's value is to be `INTRINSIC` or `DERIVED`. The `referenceCount` signifies the number of atoms with this identifier currently attached to objects. The `referenceCount` precludes the chances for an atom definition being destroyed while its definition is required. The `defaultValue` field, as the name implies, is a pointer to a default value to be used when the atom is attached to an object. The `constructor`, `attach`, `destructor`, and `detach` members will be set to the specified functions performing these services for the atom.

The `atomdef.c` source file contains five functions, only two of which are accessible by the application program. The remaining three functions are local to the `atomdef` module.

The `atomdef_f.create()` function contains parameters for most of the `atomdef_t` data structure initialization. When an `atomdef_t` type structure is successfully allocated and initialized, it will be added to the `Adam.atomdefs linkbase` for future reference. The `atomdef_f.create()` function will return a –1 on error, or the appropriate identifier for the allocated atom definition. The `threadLog` module is used to record any resulting error condition.

The `atomdef_f.destroy()` function uses the `threadLink_f.apply()` function to locate the specified atom definition. The first parameter to the `threadLink_f.apply()` function call specifies the `linkbase` to which the second parameter, function `Locate()`, should be applied. For each link in the `linkbase`, the `Locate()` function will be called, specifying the data value of the link, and the third parameter, which is `atomid`. The `Locate()` function is applied to each link's data value until the `Locate()` function returns a zero status value. A pointer to the data value causing the zero status is then returned to the calling thread. In this manner we can apply the `Locate()` function to find the appropriate data value reference in the `linkbase`.

The `threadLink_f.delete()` function will then be called to delete the atom definition from the `Adam.atomdefs linkbase`. The `Deallocate()` function is specified as the destructor function of the `threadLink_f.delete()` function call.

Listing 13.5   *atomdef.c* -- The `atom` definition source module.

```
 1 #include <stdlib.h>
 2 #include <errno.h>
 3 #include <memory.h>
 4 #include "adamdef.h"
 5
 6 /*******************************************************************
 7  *      Function Prototypes
 8  *******************************************************************/
 9 static       atomdef_t   *Allocate(void);
10 static       atomid_t     Create(atomtype_t, void *, void
11                                   *(constructor)(void),
```

Listing 13.5 *continued.*

```
12
13                                          void *(attach)(void *),
14                                          void (detach)(void *),
15                                          void (destructor)(void *));
16 static       int         Destroy(atomid_t);
17 static       int         Deallocate(void *);
18 static       int         Locate(void *,void *);
19
20
21 /***********************************************************************
22  * Create    FUNCTION
23  *
24  * This function will create a new atom described by the parameters.
25  * type, either INTRINSIC or DERIVED.
26  * defaultValue A defaultValue for the atom.
27  *      constructor  A constructor function to be called.
28  *                   when the atom is instantiated.
29  *      attach       An attach function to call to measure the
30  *                   value of the atom.
31  *      detach       A detach function to call when the atom
32  *                   is detached from the object.
33  *      destructor   A destructor function to call after the
34  *                   atom has been detached.
35  **********************************************************************/
36 static atomid_t
37 Create(atomtype_t type, void *defaultValue,
38        void *(constructor)(void),
39        void *(attach)(void *),
40        void  (detach)(void *),
41        void  (destructor)(void *))
42 {
43        atomdef_t    *atomdef    = NULL;
44        int           errorCondition = 0;
45
46        threadLog_f.clearError();
47
48                    /***********************************************
49                     *     The type parameter must be INTRINSIC or
50                     *     DERIVED.
51                     ***********************************************/
52        if( type != DERIVED && type != INTRINSIC )
53             errorCondition = EINVAL;
```

Listing 13.3   *continued.*

```
54                      /***********************************************
55                       *     DERIVED atoms require an attach procedure.
56                       ***********************************************/
57         else if( type == DERIVED  && attach == NULL )
58              errorCondition = EINVAL;
59                      /***********************************************
60                       *     INTRINSIC atoms cannot have an attach
61                       *     procedure.
62                       ***********************************************/
63         else if( type == INTRINSIC && attach != NULL )
64              errorCondition = EINVAL;
65         else   {
66              atomdef = Allocate();
67              if( atomdef == NULL)
68                   errorCondition = ENOMEM;
69
70         }
71                      /***********************************************
72                       *     If there are no errorConditions, then assign
73                       *     the values for the atom definition.
74                       ***********************************************/
75         if( ! errorCondition )   {
76              atomdef->type          |= type;
77              atomdef->defaultValue = defaultValue;
78              atomdef->constructor  = constructor;
79              atomdef->destructor   = destructor;
80              atomdef->attach       = attach;
81              atomdef->detach       = detach;
82                      /***********************************************
83                       *     Add this to the list of known definions.
84                       ***********************************************/
85              errorCondition=yhreadLink_f.add(Adam.atomdefs, atomdef);
86              if( ! errorCondition )
87                   atomdef->id = (atomid_t) atomdef;
88              else {
89                   Deallocate(atomdef);
90                   atomdef = NULL;
91              }
92         }
93         if( errorCondition )
94              threadLog_f.setError(errorCondition);
```

Listing 13.3 *continued.*

```
95
96          return(errorCondition? 0 : atomdef->id );
97 }
98
99 /********************************************************************
100  *   Destroy          FUNCTION
101  *
102  *   Invalidate the base atom definition with the specified atom id.
103  ********************************************************************/
104 static int
105 Destroy(atomid_t atomid)
106 {
107         int          errorCondition   = 0;
108         atomdef_t    *atomdef         = NULL;
109
110                     /**************************************************
111                      *    Locate the atom definition based on the
112                      *    specified atom identifier.
113                      **************************************************/
114
115         atomdef = (atomdef_t *)
116             threadLink_f.applySuccess(Adam.atomdefs,
117                                         Locate,(void *)atomid);
118
119                     /**************************************************
120                      *    If we found the atom definition, call the
121                      *    threadLink_f.delete function to remove the
122                      *    atom from the list, and then deallocate its
123                      *    definition.
124                      **************************************************/
125         if( atomdef != NULL )
126             errorCondition = threadLink_f.delete(Adam.atomdefs,
127                 atomdef,
128                 Deallocate);
129         else
130             errorCondition = ESRCH;
131         return(errorCondition);
132 }
133
134 /********************************************************************
135  *   Define the atomdef module interface
136  ********************************************************************/
```

Listing 13.3 *continued.*

```
137 atomdef_t_f atomdef_f = {
138        Create,
139        Destroy,
140 };
141 /****************************************************************
142  *     Allocate    FUNCTION
143  *
144  *     Allocate is local to the atomdef module.  This function will
145  *     allocate and initialize an atomdef_t structure.  A pointer to
146  *     the structure is returned.
147  ****************************************************************/
148 static atomdef_t *
149 Allocate(void)
150 {
151        atomdef_t    *atomdef;
152
153        threadLog_f.clearError();
154        atomdef = malloc(sizeof(atomdef_t));
155        if( atomdef != NULL ) {
156              memset(atomdef,'\0',sizeof(atomdef_t));
157              atomdef->type        = ALLOCATED;
158
159        }
160        else
161              threadLog_f.setError(ENOMEM);
162        return(atomdef);
163 }
164
165 /******************************************************************
166  *     Deallocate  FUNCTION
167  *
168  *     This function will release the memory associated with the
169  *     specified atomdef_t structure.
170  ******************************************************************/
171 static int
172 Deallocate(void *arg)
173 {
174        int        errorCondition = 0;
175
176        atomdef_t *atomdef        = arg;
177        if( atomdef == NULL  || ( ! (atomdef->type & ALLOCATED) ) )
178              errorCondition = EINVAL;
```

Listing 13.3 *continued.*

```
179
180        if( ! errorCondition )
181             free(atomdef);
182        return(errorCondition);
183 }
184
185 /*****************************************************************
186  *     Locate              FUNCTION
187  *
188  *     This function is local to the atomdef module.  It returns
189  *     zero when the arguments arg1 and arg2 have the same id value.
190  *     The Locate function is called by the threadLink_f.applySuccess
191  *     function.
192  *****************************************************************/
193 static int
194 Locate( void *arg1, void *arg2)
195 {
196        atomdef_t    *atomdef;
197        atomid_t      id;
198        atomdef = (atomdef_t *)arg1;
199        id      = (atomid_t)arg2;
200        if( atomdef->id == id )
201             return(0);
202        return(-1);
203 }
```

13.5   The Adam Module

The adam module provides the initialization and subsequent termination of the ADAM manager. The adam module consists of the adam.h header file and the adam.c source file (*see Listing 13.6 and 13.7*). The adam.h header file contains the adam_t type data structure definition, and the adam_f_t function prototypes for the module.

The adam_t type data structure contains several linkbases, a state variable denoting the current state of the ADAM manager, and a mutex to provide synchronization in the case of concurrent updates. The objects member is a linkbase for all objects dynamically allocated through the objects module. The atomdefs member is a linkbase for all atom definitions created through the atomdef module. Similarly, the atoms member is a linkbase for all atoms attached to objects through the atoms module. The atom_f_t structure defines the interfaces for the adam module.

The adam module contains two functions, both of which are available for use by the application program. The adam_f.initialize() function is used to start the ADAM manager and daemon threads. The adam_f.terminate() function terminates the execution of these daemon threads.

The declaration of the adam_t type structure will set its initial state to INITIALIZE. The adam_f.initialize() function will first attempt to transition the state from INITIALIZE to STARTING. If this fails, then an attempt is made for a state transition from TERMINATED to STARTING. If both cases fail, then a error condition is returned to the calling thread, since the ADAM manager is presumed to be already running. Alternatively, if there is no error condition, then the various ADAM daemons are started using the daemon_f.start.function() described in the daemon module section. Upon success, a state transition from STARTING to RUNNING is performed.

Listing 13.6   *adam.h* -- The adam module header file.

```
1 #if ! defined(ADAM_H)
2 #      define ADAM_H
3 typedef struct     _adam {
4       linkbase_t  *objects;
5       linkbase_t  *atomdefs;
6       linkbase_t  *atoms;
7       statevar_t   statevar;
8       mutex_t              mutex;
9 } adam_t;
10
11 typedef struct _adam_f {
12       int           (*initialize)(void);
13       int           (*terminate)(void);
14 } adam_f_t;
15
16 extern adam_t    Adam;
17 extern adam_f_t adam_f;
18 #endif
```

The adam_f.terminate() function will cause a state transition from RUNNING to TERMINATING. The terminate function will call the daemon_f.terminate.function() to terminate the currently executing daemon threads. When all daemon threads have successfully been terminated, a state transition from TERMINATING to TERMINATED is issued.

Listing 13.7   *adam.c* -- The adam source module.

```
1 #include "adamdef.h"
2 /****************************************************************
3 *      The adam_t type structure includes a linkbase for allocated
4 *      objects, a linkbase for the current atom definitions, and a
```

Listing 13.7 *continued.*

```
 5  *      linkbase for the current instantiated atoms.  Finally, it
 6  *      includes a state variable to denote the current run state.  We
 7  *      begin by initializing this structure.
 8  ******************************************************************/
 9 adam_t  Adam={ NULL, NULL,NULL,{ 0, INITIALIZE, { 0 } }, { 0 } };
10
11 /******************************************************************
12  *      Function Prototypes
13  ******************************************************************/
14 static int Initialize(void);
15 static int Terminate(void);
16
17 /******************************************************************
18  *   Initialize     FUNCTION
19  *
20  *   The adam_f.init() function is called to start the ADAM utility.
21  ******************************************************************/
22 static int
23 Initialize(void)
24 {
25      int    errorCondition;
26
27             /****************************************************
28              *      Transition the state of adam from INITIALIZE to
29              *      STARTING.  If there is an error condition, then
30              *      try transitioning from TERMINATED to STARTING.
31              *      This permits adam to be restarted within a
32              *      given application.
33              ****************************************************/
34      errorCondition = statevar_f.transition(&Adam.statevar,
35                                      INITIALIZE, STARTING);
36
37      if( errorCondition )
38          errorCondition = statevar_f.transition(&Adam.statevar,
39                                      TERMINATED,STARTING);
40
41      if ( ! errorCondition ) {
42             /****************************************************
43              *     Start the adam daemons.
44             ****************************************************/
```

Listing 13.7 *continued.*

```
45
46                    if(daemon_f.start.function( &daemon_f.attacher) == 0 &&
47                       daemon_f.start.function( &daemon_f.binder) == 0 &&
48                       daemon_f.start.function( &daemon_f.measurer) == 0 &&
49                       daemon_f.start.function( &daemon_f.detacher) == 0 )
50                    {
51                         /************************************************
52                          *    Now create the linkbases and transition to
53                          *    the RUNNING state.
54                          ***********************************************/
55                         Adam.atomdefs = threadLink_f.create();
56                         Adam.objects  = threadLink_f.create();
57                         Adam.atoms    = threadLink_f.create();
58                              errorCondition=
59                                   statevar_f.transition(&Adam.statevar,
60                                        STARTING, RUNNING);
61                    }
62               }
63          return( errorCondition );
64 }
65
66 /******************************************************************
67  *    Terminate      FUNCTION
68  *
69  *    The terminate function is called to terminate the ADAM utility.
70  ******************************************************************/
71 static int
72 Terminate(void)
73 {
74      int    errorCondition;
75                    /************************************************
76                     *    Transition the state of adam from RUNNING to
77                     *    TERMINATING.  If successful, terminate the
78                     *    adam daemons.
79                     ***********************************************/
80      errorCondition = statevar_f.transition(&Adam.statevar,
81                              RUNNING,TERMINATING);
82      if ( ! errorCondition ) {
83           daemon_f.terminate.function( &daemon_f.attacher);
84           daemon_f.terminate.function( &daemon_f.binder);
85           daemon_f.terminate.function( &daemon_f.measurer);
```

Listing 13.7 *continued.*

```
86
87                   errorCondition=statevar_f.transition(&Adam.statevar,
88                                   TERMINATING,TERMINATED);
89          }
90          return( errorCondition );
91 }
92
93 /**********************************************************************
94  *      Define the ADAM module interface.
95  **********************************************************************/
96 adam_f_t adam_f = {
97          Initialize,
98          Terminate
99 };
```

13.6   The Atoms Module

An atom is defined by the `atom_t` type definition in the `atoms.h` header file. The `id` member is a unique atom identifier. Each atom defined through the `atomdef` module is assigned a unique identifier. The `statevar` identifies the current state of the atom. The definition is a pointer to the base atom definition describing this atom. The remaining members are self-explanatory.

The `atoms` module (*see Listings 13.8 and 13.9*) offers three functions to the application program. The `attach` function is used to attach an atom to an object. The `detach` function performs the inverse operation. The `getValue` function will retrieve the current value of an atom.

Listing 13.8   atoms.h -- The atom module header file.

```
1 #if ! defined(ATOM_H)
2 #      define     ATOM_H
3
4 typedef struct     _atom {
5       atomid_t     id;
6       atomtype_t   type;
7       statevar_t   statevar;
8       atomdef_t    *definition;
9       void         *value;
10      object_t     *owner;
```

Listing 13.8   *continued.*

```
11        time_t               atime;
12        time_t               mtime;
13        linkbase_t   *constraints;
14        thread_t     tid;
15 } atom_t;
16 typedef struct _atom_f_t        {
17        int               (*attach)(object_t *,atomid_t, void *);
18        int               (*detach)(object_t *, atomid_t);
19        void              *(*getValue)(object_t *,atomid_t);
20 } atom_f_t;
21 extern atom_f_t atom_f;
22 #endif
```

The Attach function accepts three parameters: a pointer to the object, the identifier of the atom to attach, and an initial value for the atom. To guard against concurrent updates, the object's Reader-Writer lock must be locked in write mode. The object's atoms list is then searched to verify that the atom is not already attached to the object; otherwise, an error condition is reported.

The Attach function will then call the Create() function to allocate and initialize the atom. After transitioning the atom's state to the ATTACH state, the atom is added to the object's atoms linkbase. At this point we can unlock the write-mode lock currently held on the object.

If there were no errors encountered, a message structure is allocated and initialized to point to the current object and current atom. The last step is to push the message onto the Attacher() daemon's communication queue. (*The attacher is detailed in the next section.*)

The Detach function must also lock the object's Reader-Writer lock in write mode. Using the same call to the threadLink_f.apply function, the specified atom can be located. The threadLink_f.delete function is called to remove the atom from the object's atoms linkbase. The atom's state will transition to the DETACH state. A message is then allocated and initialized to the current object and atom being detached. Finally, the message is pushed onto the Detacher() daemon's communication queue.

The GetValue function is used to return the current measured value of an atom. The GetValue function will not return to the calling thread until the requested atom is in the MEASURED state.

Listing 13.9   *atoms.c -- The atom source module.*

```
1 #include <stdlib.h>
2 #include <errno.h>
3 #include <memory.h>
4 #include "adamdef.h"
5
```

Listing 13.9 *continued.*

```
 5 /*********************************************************************
 6  *      Function Prototypes
 7  *********************************************************************/
 8 static        atom_t  *Allocate(void);
 9 static        int      Attach(object_t *, atomid_t, void *);
10 static        atom_t *Create(atomid_t);
11 static        int      Deallocate(atom_t *);
12 static        int      Destroy(void *);
13 static        int      Detach(object_t *, atomid_t);
14 static        void    *GetValue(object_t *, atomid_t);
15 static        int      Locate(void *, void *);
16 /*********************************************************************
17  *   Attach          FUNCTION
18  *
19  *   The Attach function will attach a base atom (given by id) to the
20  *   specified object.  The default value of the atom is determined
21  *   as:
22  *           The default base atom value
23  *           The data parameter value (if non-NULL)
24  *           The value resulting from the Attach procedure
25  *********************************************************************/
26 static int
27 Attach(object_t *object, atomid_t id, void *data)
28 {
29       comqueue_t          *comqueue   = NULL;
30       int                 errorCondition = 0;
31       adamMessage_t       *message    = NULL;
32       atom_t              *atom       = NULL;
33                   /*********************************************
34                    *    Validate the object and obtain a write mode
35                    *    lock.
36                    *********************************************/
37       if( object == NULL )
38             errorCondition = EINVAL;
39       else
40             errorCondition = rw_wrlock(object->rwlock);
41       if( errorCondition )
42             return(errorCondition);
43                   /*********************************************
44                    *    Make sure the atom does not already exist in
45                    *    the scope of the object.
46                    *********************************************/
```

Listing 13.9   *continued.*

```
47          atom = (atom_t *)threadLink_f.applySuccess(object->atoms,
48                                          Locate,(void *)id);
49          if( atom != NULL ) {
50                  rw_unlock(object->rwlock);
51                  return(EEXIST);
52          }
53                  /**************************************************
54                   *      Create a new instance of the atom.
55                   **************************************************/
56          atom = Create(id);
57          if( atom == NULL ) {
58                  rw_unlock(object->rwlock);
59                  return(EINVAL);
60          }
61                  /**************************************************
62                   *      Set the default value of the atom based on the
63                   *      parameter "data."
64                   **************************************************/
65          atom->value = data;
66          atom->owner = object;
67                  /**************************************************
68                   *      Transition the atom to the ATTACH state.
69                   **************************************************/
70          statevar_f.transition(&atom->statevar, 0, ATTACH);
71                  /**************************************************
72                   *      Add the atom to the object's list of attached
73                   *      atoms and then unlock the rwlock.
74                   **************************************************/
75          errorCondition = threadLink_f.add(object->atoms, atom);
76          rw_unlock(object->rwlock);
77                  /**************************************************
78                   *      If everything went OK, allocate and initialize
79                   *      a message for use between the adam daemons.
80                   **************************************************/
81          if( ! errorCondition )  {
82                  message          = adamMessage_f.allocate();
83                  message->object = object;
84                  message->atom   = atom;
85                  comqueue         = daemon_f.attacher.comlink->comqueue;
86                  errorCondition  =
87                          threadQcond_f.qpush(comqueue->queue,message);
88          }
```

Listing 13.9 *continued.*

```
 89         else
 90             Destroy(atom);
 91         return(errorCondition);
 92 }
 93
 94 /*******************************************************************
 95  *   Detach          FUNCTION
 96  *
 97  *   The detach function will detach the atom (given by id) from the
 98  *   specified object.
 99  *******************************************************************/
100 static int
101 Detach(object_t *object, atomid_t id)
102 {
103         atom_t              *atom = NULL;
104         int                  errorCondition = 0;
105         adamMessage_t       *message = NULL;
106         comqueue_t          *comqueue = NULL;
107
108                /************************************************
109                 *     Validate the object and obtain a read mode
110                 *     rwlock.
111                 ************************************************/
112         if( object == NULL )
113             errorCondition = EINVAL;
114         else
115             errorCondition = rw_rdlock(object->rwlock);
116
117         if( errorCondition )
118             return(errorCondition);
119                /************************************************
120                 *     Locate the specified atom within the object.
121                 ************************************************/
122         atom = (atom_t *)threadLink_f.applySuccess(object->atoms,
123                                         Locate, (void *)id);
124                /************************************************
125                 *     Now delete the atom from the object's atom
126                 *     list.
127                 ************************************************/
128         if( atom != NULL )
129             errorCondition =
130                     threadLink_f.delete(object->atoms,atom,NULL);
```

Listing 13.9 *continued.*

```
131         else
132                 errorCondition = ESRCH;
133
134                 /*************************************************
135                  *      Transition the atom to the DETACH state.
136                  *      Create and initialize an adam message and send
137                  *      it to the detacher's comlink.
138                  *************************************************/
139         if( ! errorCondition ) {
140                 (void) statevar_f.transition(&atom->statevar, 0,
141                                                     DETACH);
142                 message = adamMessage_f.allocate();
143                 message->object = object;
144                 message->atom   = atom;
145                 comqueue = daemon_f.detacher.comlink->comqueue;
146                 errorCondition =
147                         threadQcond_f.qpush( comqueue->queue,
148                                                     message);
149         }
150
151         rw_unlock(object->rwlock );
152         return(errorCondition);
153 }
154
155 /*********************************************************************
156  *   GetValue        FUNCTION
157  *
158  *   The GetValue function returns the current MEASURED value of the
159  *   atom (given by id) in the specified object.  A pointer to the
160  *   value is returned to the calling thread.
161  *********************************************************************/
162 static void *
163 GetValue(object_t *object, atomid_t id)
164 {
165         atom_t      *atom      = NULL;
166         void        *data      = NULL;
167         state_t      state;
168
169         if( object == NULL ) {
170                 threadLog_f.setError(EINVAL);
171                 return(NULL);
172         }
```

Listing 13.9 *continued.*

```
173                    /***********************************************
174                    *     Locate the specified atom within the object.
175                    ***********************************************/
176        atom = (atom_t *)threadLink_f.applySuccess(object->atoms,
177                                            Locate, (void *)id);
178
179        if( atom == NULL )
180              return(NULL);
181                    /***********************************************
182                    *     We now need to increment its reference count.
183                    ***********************************************/
184        atom = threadLink_f.reference(object->atoms, (void *)atom);
185
186        if( atom == NULL )
187              return(NULL);
188
189              /***********************************************
190              *     While the current state of the atom is not
191              *     MEASURE, MEASURING, or MEASURED, then simply
192              *     yield the processor.
193              ***********************************************/
194        do    {
195              state = statevar_f.getstate(&atom->statevar);
196              if( state & (MEASURE|MEASURING|MEASURED))
197                    state = 0;
198              else
199                    thr_yield();
200        } while( state != 0 );
201
202              /***********************************************
203              *     While the state of the atom is MEASURE,
204              *     continue to yield the processor.
205              ***********************************************/
206        while((state=statevar_f.getstate(&atom->statevar))& MEASURE ){
207              thr_yield();
208        }
209
210              /***********************************************
211              *     If the state is now set to MEASURING, and this
212              *     is a DERIVED atom type, then wait for the
213              *     attribute's Attach procedure to complete.
214              ***********************************************/
```

Listing 13.9 *continued.*

```
215         if(((state=statevar_f.getstate(&atom->statevar)) & MEASURING)
216                   && (atom->type & DERIVED) )  {
217             thr_join(atom->tid,NULL,NULL);
218         }
219     else
220             /**************************************************
221             *     Otherwise, we must have an INTRINSIC atom type.
222             *     While the state of the atom is MEASURING,
223             *     continue to yield the processor.
224             **************************************************/
225             while((state=statevar_f.getstate(&atom->statevar))
226                   &MEASURING){
227                         thr_yield();
228             }
229             /**************************************************
230             *     If the current state of the atom is MEASURED,
231             *     then get a pointer to its value.  This will be
232             *     the value returned to the calling thread.  Note
233             *     that if the current state is not MEASURED, then
234             *     we have a critical error.
235             **************************************************/
236     if((state=statevar_f.getstate(&atom->statevar)) & MEASURED )
237             data = atom->value;
238     else
239             data = NULL;
240             /**************************************************
241             *     Now we can unreference the atom
242             **************************************************/
243     threadLink_f.unreference(object->atoms, (void *)atom);
244     return(data);
245 }
246
247 /*******************************************************************
248 *     Define the atom module interface.
249 *******************************************************************/
250 atom_f_t atom_f = {
251         Attach, Detach, GetValue,
252 };
253
```

Listing 13.9 *continued.*

```
254 /*******************************************************************
255  *    Create   FUNCTION
256  *
257  *    The create function will allocate and initialize an atom_t type
258  *    structure with the base definition of id.  This function is
259  *    local to the atom module.
260  *******************************************************************/
261 static atom_t *
262 Create(atomid_t id)
263 {
264         atom_t          *atom        = NULL;
265         atomdef_t       *atomdef     = NULL;
266
267         threadLog_f.clearError();
268         atomdef=(atomdef_t *)threadLink_f.applySuccess(Adam.atomdefs,
269                                            Locate,(void *) id);
270         if( atomdef == NULL )
271                 return(NULL);
272         atomdef = threadLink_f.reference(Adam.atomdefs,atomdef);
273         if( atomdef == NULL )
274                 return(NULL);
275         atom = Allocate();
276         if( atom != NULL ) {
277                 atom->id          = id;
278                 atom->definition = atomdef;
279                 atom->type        |= atom->definition->type;
280         }
281         else
282                 threadLink_f.unreference(Adam.atomdefs,atomdef);
283
284         return(atom);
285 }
286
287 /*******************************************************************
288  *    Destroy          FUNCTION
289  *
290  *    This function is local to the atom module.  It is called by
291  *    the Attach procedure when an error condition occurs.
292  *******************************************************************/
293 static int
294 Destroy(void *data)
```

Listing 13.9   *continued.*

```
295 {
296        int      errorCondition = 0;
297        atom_t *atom           = NULL;
298
299        atom = (atom_t *)data;
300        if( atom == NULL )
301                errorCondition = EINVAL;
302        else  {
303                errorCondition = threadLink_f.unreference(Adam.atomdefs,
304                    atom->definition);
305                if( (! errorCondition) && (atom->type & ALLOCATED) )
306                    Deallocate(atom);
307        }
308        return(errorCondition );
309 }
310
311 /****************************************************************
312  *   Allocate        FUNCTION
313  *
314  *   Allocate and initializes an atom_t type structure.
315  ****************************************************************/
316 static atom_t *
317 Allocate(void)
318 {
319        atom_t *atom = NULL;
320        threadLog_f.setError(0);
321        atom = malloc(sizeof(atom_t));
322        if( atom != NULL ) {
323                memset(atom,'\0',sizeof(atom_t));
324                atom->type = ALLOCATED;
325        }
326        else
327                threadLog_f.setError(ENOMEM);
328        return(atom);
329 }
330 /****************************************************************
331  *    Deallocate  FUNCTION
332  *
333  *    This function deallocates an atom_t type structure.
334  ****************************************************************/
```

Listing 13.9 *continued.*

```
335 static int
336 Deallocate(atom_t *atom)
337 {
338         int             errorCondition  = 0;
339
340         if( atom == NULL || ( ! atom->type & ALLOCATED) )
341                 errorCondition = EINVAL;
342         else
343                 free(atom);
344         return(errorCondition);
345 }
346
347 /*********************************************************************
348  *   Locate           FUNCTION
349  *
350  *   This function is used by the threadLink_f.applySuccess to
351  *   locate a specific atom within a list.  The function returns zero
352  *   when the atom specified as arg1 matches the id specified by
353  *   arg2.
354  *********************************************************************/
355 static int
356 Locate( void *arg1, void *arg2)
357 {
358         atom_t          *atom;
359         atomid_t        id;
360
361         atom = (atom_t *)arg1;
362         id   = (atomid_t)arg2;
363
364         if( atom->id == id )
365                 return(0);
366         return(-1);
367 }
```

13.7   The Daemon Module

When the ADAM manager is running, there are several daemon threads that are started to perform various tasks. The daemon threads are defined by the daemon module (*Listings 13.10 and 13.11*). The daemon_t type definition describes the components of the daemon structure. This includes a `name` component, a reference to its `function`, a state variable to denote the current state of the daemon, and a pointer to a `comlink_t` structure for communications.

The interfaces to the `daemon` module are defined by the `daemon_f_t` type structure. Of these interfaces, the `start` and `terminate` members are the general-purpose interfaces. The `attacher`, `binder`, `measurer`, `admin`, and `detacher` provide specific functionality toward the administration of ADAM.

Listing 13.10   *daemons.h* -- The ADAM `daemon` module header file.

```
 1 #if ! defined(DAEMON_H)
 2 #      define DAEMON_H
 3 #      define UNINITIALIZED    0x02
 4 #      define RESTARTABLE      0x04
 5 #      define CONTROL          0x08
 6 #      define ADAM_API         0x10
 7 #      define INITIALIZE       0x02
 8 #      define TERMINATED       0x04
 9 #      define STARTING         0x08
10 #      define RUNNING          0x10
11 #      define TERMINATING      0x20
12
13 typedef struct _function {
14      char          *name;
15      void          *(*function)(void *);
16      statevar_t    statevar;
17      unsigned int  control;
18      thread_t      tid;
19      comlink_t     *comlink;
20 } function_t;
21
22 typedef struct _daemon_t {
23      function_t    start;
24      function_t    terminate;
25      function_t    attacher;
26      function_t    binder;
27      function_t    measurer;
28      function_t    detacher;
29 } daemon_t;
30 extern daemon_t    daemon_f;
31 #endif
```

The `daemon` module offers two interfaces to control the execution of the daemon threads, and the definition of the five daemons. The `daemon_f.start()` function will lock the daemon's state variable to prevent concurrent updates. It then examines the daemon to determine if it must be initialized. If so, then a `comlink` must be allocated to communicate with this daemon.

When the daemon is started, it will always be the consumer on the `comlink`. Since the producer of the `comlink` is not executing as a separate thread, we can eliminate the producer component to minimize the memory requirements. If the daemon to be started is in the `INITIALIZE` or `TERMINATED` state, but its control variable denotes that the daemon is `RESTARTABLE`, then the `comlink_f.initialize()` function is called to establish the thread. Upon success, a state transition from the `INITIALIZE` or `TERMINATED` state to the `RUNNING` state is issued. The daemon's state variable is then unlocked.

The `daemon_f.terminate()` function simply sends a terminate message to the specified daemon thread. For this example, the termination function will send a message with a `NULL` object and `NULL` atom value. The daemon will then undergo a state transition from `RUNNING` to `TERMINATED`.

Listing 13.11   *daemons.c* -- The ADAM daemon source module.

```
1 #include <thread.h>
2 #include <synch.h>
3 #include <malloc.h>
4 #include <stdio.h>
5 #include <string.h>
6 #include <errno.h>
7 #include <unistd.h>
8 #include "adamdef.h"
9
10 /*****************************************************************
11  *      Function prototypes
12  *****************************************************************/
13 static      void   *Start(void *);
14 static      void   *Terminate(void *);
15 static      void   *Procedure(void *);
16 static      void   *Attacher(void * arg);
17 static      void   *Binder(void * arg);
18 static      void   *Measurer(void * arg);
19 static      void   *Detacher(void *arg);
20
21 /*****************************************************************
22  *   The start daemon is called to initialize an adam daemon given by
23  *   arg.
24  *****************************************************************/
```

Listing 13.11   *continued.*

```
25 static void *
26 Start( void * arg)
27 {
28         int          errorCondition = 0;
29         state_t      state          = 0;
30         function_t   *fptr;
31
32         fptr = (function_t *)arg;
33         if( fptr == NULL )
34               errorCondition = EINVAL;
35         else
36               errorCondition = statevar_f.lock(&fptr->statevar);
37
38         if( errorCondition )
39               return( (void *)errorCondition);
40
41         state = statevar_f.getstate( &fptr->statevar );
42
43               /******************************************************
44                *     If this is the first time we are starting the
45                *     daemon, then allocate a comlink for
46                *     communication with other daemons.
47                ******************************************************/
48         if( state & INITIALIZE)   {
49               fptr->comlink = comlink_f.allocate(USYNC_THREAD);
50               fptr->comlink->consumer->compoint->stackAddress= NULL;
51               fptr->comlink->consumer->compoint->stackSize    = 0;
52               fptr->comlink->consumer->compoint->startRoutine=
53                                            fptr->function;
54               fptr->comlink->consumer->compoint->flags = THR_DAEMON;
55               comthread_f.deallocate(fptr->comlink->producer);
56               fptr->comlink->producer = NULL;
57         }
58
59               /******************************************************
60                *     If this is the first time we are starting the
61                *     daemon, or if the daemon had terminated but is
62                *     restartable, then initialize its communication
63                *     link.
64                ******************************************************/
```

Listing 13.11   *continued.*

```
65          if( state & INITIALIZE ||
66              (state&TERMINATED  && (fptr->control & RESTARTABLE)) ) {
67                  errorCondition = comlink_f.initialize( fptr->comlink );
68                  if( ! errorCondition ) {
69                      errorCondition=statevar_f.transition(
70                                          &fptr->statevar,state, RUNNING);
71                  }
72          }
73          statevar_f.unlock( &fptr->statevar );
74          return( (void *)errorCondition );
75 }
76
77
78 /******************************************************************
79  *   Terminate        Function
80  *
81  *   The terminate function terminates the execution of the specified
82  *   daemon.  This is accomplished by sending a message to the
83  *   daemon.
84  ******************************************************************/
85 static void *
86 Terminate( void *arg )
87 {
88      int     errorCondition;
89      int     state;
90      function_t          *fptr;
91      adamMessage_t       *message     = NULL;
92      comqueue_t          *comqueue    = NULL;
93
94      fptr = (function_t *)arg;
95      if( fptr == NULL )
96              errorCondition = EINVAL;
97      else
98              errorCondition = statevar_f.lock(&fptr->statevar);
99
100     if( errorCondition )
101             return((void *)errorCondition);
102     state = statevar_f.getstate( &fptr->statevar);
```

Listing 13.11 *continued.*

```
103                 /************************************************
104                 *     if the daemon is currently in the RUNNING state
105                 *     then transition it to the TERMINATING state and
106                 *     send the TERMINATE message.
107                 ***********************************************/
108         if( state == RUNNING ) {
109                 errorCondition=statevar_f.transition(&fptr->statevar,
110                                         RUNNING, TERMINATING);
111
112                 if( ! errorCondition ) {
113                         message    = adamMessage_f.allocate();
114                         message->object = NULL;
115                         message->atom   = NULL;
116                         comqueue   = fptr->comlink->comqueue;
117                     errorCondition=threadQcond_f.qpush(comqueue->queue,
118                                 message);
119                 }
120         }
121         statevar_f.unlock( &fptr->statevar );
122         return((void *) errorCondition );
123 }
124 /*******************************************************************
125 *   Procedure      THREAD
126 *
127 *   The Procedure thread is called to execute the atom's attach
128 *   procedure.  The returned value from the attach procedure
129 *   becomes the value of the atom.
130 *******************************************************************/
131 static void *
132 Procedure(void *arg)
133 {
134         adamMessage_t *message        = NULL;
135         object_t       *object         = NULL;
136         atom_t         *atom           = NULL;
137         int             errorCondition = 0;
138
139         message = arg;
140         object  = message->object;
141         atom    = message->atom;
142         atom->value = (atom->definition->attach)(object);
```

Listing 13.11 *continued.*

```
143                          /**********************************************
144                          *      After the attach procedure has completed,
145                          *      transition the atom to the MEASURED state.
146                          **********************************************/
147          errorCondition = statevar_f.transition(&atom->statevar,
148                                               MEASURING,MEASURED);
149          thr_exit((void *)errorCondition);
150 }
151
152 /*****************************************************************************
153  *  Attacher        THREAD
154  *
155  *  The Attacher thread is responsible for attaching atoms to
156  *  objects. This thread executes as a daemon thread and waits for
157  *  messages from the atom_f.attach() function.  The message it
158  *  receives describes the object and the atom to be attached.  The
159  *  function will transition the atom from the ATTACH to the
160  *  ATTACHING state. If you wish to add   SET features, they should
161  *  be added after the atom enters the ATTACHING state.  The atom
162  *  then transitioned to the ATTACHED state.
163  *  Finally, the Attacher will initialize the atom with the
164  *  BIND state (note that this does not change the ATTACHED
165  *  state value).  The message is then sent to the Binder thread
166  *  thread to BIND the atom.  A NULL message atom and NULL message
167  *  object indicate that the  Attacher is to terminate.
168 *****************************************************************************/
169 static void *
170 Attacher(void * arg)
171 {
172          comqueue_t      *comqueue       = NULL;
173          unsigned int    runflag         = 1;
174          adamMessage_t   *message        = NULL;
175          atom_t          *atom           = NULL;
176          comqueue_t      *binderComqueue = NULL;
177          int              errorCondition = 0;
178
179          binderComqueue      = daemon_f.binder.comlink->comqueue;
180          comqueue = arg;
181
```

Listing 13.11   *continued.*

```
182        while(runflag) {
183             message = threadQcond_f.qpop( comqueue->queue);
184             if((message->atom==NULL)&&(message->object==NULL)) {
185                  runflag = 0;
186                  free(message);
187                  continue;
188             }
189             atom    = message->atom;
190             errorCondition = statevar_f.transition(&atom->statevar,
191                                          ATTACH, ATTACHING);
192             if( ! errorCondition )  {
193                  errorCondition = statevar_f.transition(
194                          &atom->statevar,ATTACHING, ATTACHED);
195             }
196             if( ! errorCondition ) {
197                  errorCondition = statevar_f.transition(
198                          &atom->statevar,0,BIND);
199             }
200             if( ! errorCondition ) {
201                  errorCondition = threadQcond_f.qpush(
202                          binderComqueue->queue,message);
203             }
204             if( errorCondition ) {
205                  threadLog_f.message("Attacher: error %d",
206                                        errorCondition);
207                  free(message);
208             }
209        }
210        thr_exit(NULL);
211 }
212
213 /****************************************************************
214 *  Binder        THREAD
215 *
216 *  The binder thread waits for messages from the Attacher daemon.
217 *  The message indicates the atom to be bound to the specified
218 *  object. This function will transition the atom from the BIND to
219 *  BINDING state.  The binder will call the atom's constructor
220 *  function, if defined, to allocate storage space for the atom's
```

Listing 13.11   *continued.*

```
221 *   value.  If you wish to add various Bound Types, the code should
222 *   be updated at this point. The atom is then initialized with the
223 *   MEASURE start state, and a message is sent to the Measurer
224 *   daemon.
225 ********************************************************************/
226 static void *
227 Binder(void * arg)
228 {
229     comqueue_t     *comqueue = NULL;
230     unsigned int    runflag  = 1;
231     adamMessage_t *message   = NULL;
232     atom_t         *atom     = NULL;
233     comqueue_t   *measurerComqueue= NULL;
234     int             errorCondition = 0;
235
236     measurerComqueue= daemon_f.measurer.comlink->comqueue;
237     comqueue = arg;
238     while(runflag) {
239             message = threadQcond_f.qpop( comqueue->queue);
240             if((message->atom == NULL) && (message->object == NULL))
241 {
242                     runflag = 0;
243                     free(message);
244             continue;
245             }
246             atom    = message->atom;
247             errorCondition = statevar_f.transition(&atom->statevar,
248                                                 BIND,BINDING);
249             if( atom->definition->constructor != NULL ) {
250                     atom->value = (atom->definition->constructor)();
251                     atom->type |= CONSTRUCTED;
252             }
253             /* Binding to various atom types can be added here. */
254             atom->atime = time(NULL);
255             if( ! errorCondition ) {
256                     errorCondition=statevar_f.transition(
257                             &atom->statevar,BINDING,BOUND);
258             }
259             if( ! errorCondition ) {
260                     errorCondition = statevar_f.transition(
261                             &atom->statevar, 0,MEASURE);
262             }
```

Listing 13.11 *continued.*

```
262              if( ! errorCondition ) {
263                   errorCondition = threadQcond_f.qpush(
264                             measurerComqueue->queue, message);
265              }
266              if( errorCondition ) {
267                   threadLog_f.message("Binder: error [%d]",
268                        errorCondition);
269                   free(message);
270              }
271         }
272         thr_exit(NULL);
273 }
274
275 /**************************************************************
276  *   Measurer        THREAD
277  *
278  *   The Measurer thread runs as a daemon thread, waiting for
279  *   messages from the Binder daemon.  Each message describes an
280  *   atom to be measured for a specific object.  This thread will
281  *   transition the atom from the MEASURE state to the MEASURING
282  *   state. If the atom value is NULL and the atom is an INTRINSIC
283  *   type, then its value will be set to the defaultValue for this
284  *   atom identifier. The atom will then transition to the MEASURED
285  *   state.  If the atom type is DERIVED, then a thread is created
286  *   to begin execution at the Procedure function (defined above),
287  *   to measure the value of the atom.   The atom will remain in
288  *   the MEASURING state. Finally, the Measurer thread will release
289  *   the storage space for with the message it just received.
290  **************************************************************/
291 static void *
292 Measurer(void * arg)
293 {
294         comqueue_t      *comqueue      = NULL;
295         unsigned int    runflag        = 1;
296         adamMessage_t   *message       = NULL;
297         atom_t          *atom          = NULL;
298         int             errorCondition= 0;
299
300         comqueue = arg;
301
302         while(runflag) {
```

Listing 13.11   *continued.*

```
303                    message = threadQcond_f.qpop( comqueue->queue);
304                    if((message->atom==NULL)&&(message->object==NULL)) {
305                            runflag = 0;
306                            free(message);
307                            continue;
308                    }
309                    atom    = message->atom;
310                    errorCondition=statevar_f.transition(&atom->statevar,
311                                              MEASURE,MEASURING);
312                    if( errorCondition ) {
313                            threadLog_f.message("Measurer: error [%d]",
314                                    errorCondition);
315                            free(message);
316                            continue;
317                    }
318                    if( atom->type & INTRINSIC ) {
319                            if( atom->value == NULL )
320                                    atom->value=atom->definition->defaultValue;
321                            errorCondition = statevar_f.transition(
322                                    &atom->statevar,MEASURING,MEASURED);
323
324                            free(message);
325                    }
326                    else if(atom->type & DERIVED ) {
327                       thr_create(NULL,0,Procedure,message,0,
328                                        &(atom->tid));
329                    }
330                    if( errorCondition )
331                            threadLog_f.message("Measurer: error [%d]",
332                                                    errorCondition);
333            }
334       thr_exit(NULL);
335 }
336
337 /*************************************************************
338 *  Detacher        THREAD
339 *
340 *  The Detacher thread reads messages from the atom_f.detach()
341 *  function.  Each message describes an atom to be detached from
```

Listing 13.11 *continued.*

```
342  *   an object.  Only MEASURED atoms will be detached.
343  *
344  *   If the Detacher thread reads a message and the atom is not in
345  *   the MEASURED state, the Detacher will simply push the message
346  *   onto the end of its communication queue.
347  *
348  *   If the atom to be detached has a Detach procedure associated
349  *   with it, then the Detacher will call this function.
350  *
351  *   If the atom has an associated destructor, then the destructor
352  *   will be called with a pointer to the atom's current value.
353  ***************************************************************/
354  static void *
355  Detacher(void *arg)
356  {
357          comqueue_t      *comqueue       = NULL;
358          unsigned int    runflag         = 1;
359          adamMessage_t   *message        = NULL;
360          object_t        *object         = NULL;
361          atom_t          *atom           = NULL;
362          int             errorCondition = 0;
363
364          comqueue = arg;
365          while(runflag) {
366                  message = threadQcond_f.qpop( comqueue->queue);
367                  if((message->atom==NULL)&&(message->object==NULL)) {
368                          runflag = 0;
369                          free(message);
370                          continue;
371                  }
372                  object  = message->object;
373                  atom    = message->atom;
374                  if(statevar_f.getstate(&atom->statevar) & MEASURED ) {
375                          if( atom->definition->detach != NULL )
376                                  (atom->definition->detach)(message);
377                          if( atom->definition->destructor != NULL)
378                                  (atom->definition->destructor)(atom->value);
379                          adamMessage_f.deallocate(message);
380                          if((statevar_f.getstate(&object->statevar)&
381  DEALLOCATE) &&(threadLink_f.removeFirst(object->atoms)==NULL)) {
382                                  threadrw_f.destroy(object->rwlock);
383                                  free(object);
```

Listing 13.11 *continued.*

```
384                            }
385                    }
386                else
387                        threadQcond_f.qpush(comqueue->queue,message);
388            }
389        thr_exit((void *)errorCondition);
390 }
391
392 daemon_t    daemon_f =
393 {
394 {"Start",     Start,     {0, INITIALIZE,{0} },ADAM_API,  0, NULL},
395 {"Terminate", Terminate,{0, INITIALIZE,{0} },ADAM_API,  0, NULL},
396 {"Attach",    Attacher,  {0, INITIALIZE,{0}},RESTARTABLE,0, NULL},
397 {"Bind",      Binder,    {0, INITIALIZE,{0}},RESTARTABLE,0, NULL},
398 {"Measure",   Measurer,  {0, INITIALIZE,{0}},RESTARTABLE,0, NULL},
399 {"Detacher",  Detacher, {0, INITIALIZE,{0} },RESTARTABLE,0, NULL}
400 };
```

The Attacher Daemon

The Attacher daemon monitors its comlink for messages. A message will contain the object and the atom to attach. The Attacher will transition the atom from the ATTACH state to the ATTACHING state. If atom sets are to be supported, they should be implemented at this point. The atom will then transition from the ATTACHING state to the ATTACHED state. Finally, the Attacher will transition the atom to the BIND state and push the message onto the binder daemon's communication queue.

The Binder Daemon

The Binder daemon reads messages from its communication queue and processes the messages accordingly. Each message is assumed to have an object and an associated atom that is to be bound. When a message is found, the atom's state will transition from the BIND state to the BINDING state. The process of binding an atom will cause the atom's constructor, if defined, to be invoked. A constructor function is used to allocate storage space for the atom's value. After the constructor has been called, the atom will transition from the BINDING state to the BOUND state. The Binder daemon will then push the message onto the Measurer daemon's communication queue.

The Measurer Daemon

The `Measurer` daemon is responsible for measuring the value of an atom. It reads messages from its communication queue containing the object and the atom to be measured. When a message is found, the atom will transition from the MEASURE state to the MEASURING state.

If the atom's type is INTRINSIC, and the atom was attached without an initial value, then the default value as defined by the atom definition will be used as the value for the atom. After the value has been determined, the atom will transition from the MEASURING state to the MEASURED state.

A DERIVED atom, however, must have its value measured by calling the atom's `attach` procedure. Although the `Measurer` could easily call the `attach` procedure directly, it is more advantageous to create a thread to execute the `attach` procedure. The local function, `Procedure`, is used as a wrapper to call the `attach` procedure. The `measurer` daemon does not change a DERIVED atom's state to MEASURED. Instead, this is handled by the `Procedure` function.

The Detacher Daemon

To minimize the functionality of the `Detacher` daemon, a simple constraint has been placed on the detach algorithm: Only MEASURED atoms can be detached. The `Detacher` reads messages from its communication's queue and attempts to detach the specified atom from its object. If the atom is not in the MEASURED state, then the message is simply pushed back onto the `Detacher`'s communication queue.

In detaching an atom, the `Detacher` will call the atom's `detach` procedure, if defined. The `Detacher` will pass the message to the `detach` procedure. Next, if the atom has a `destructor` function defined, then the `Detacher` will call the `destructor` passing the atom's value as the only argument.

Finally, if the object's state is DEALLOCATE and there are no additional atoms attached, then the `Detacher` daemon will deallocate the object's structure.

The Procedure Wrapper

The `Procedure` wrapper is a simple function to call the atom's `attach` procedure. The return value from the atom's `attach` procedure will be used as the value of the atom. After this function has been called, the atom will transition from the MEASURING state to the MEASURED state. The `procedure` thread then terminates.

13.8   The State Module

The state module provides several generic functions to manipulate a *state variable* in a multithreaded safe environment. A *state variable* defines the current state of an associated entity. In the ADAM software, state variables are applied to the objects, atoms, the Adam structure, and the daemons.

From the atom's perspective, there are different sets of states in which the atom can be. It can be, for example, in the ATTACHED state while also being in the BINDING state. In essence, the atom can belong to different state machines simultaneously. While we could use a different state variable for each state machine, it seemed prudent to share a single state variable for the various state machines. This will work provided that each state of all shared state machines has a unique state identifier.

A state variable is defined by the statevar_t type definition presented in the state.h header file (*Listings 13.12 and 13.13*). The state variable has a status member, denoting if the state variable has been dynamically allocated; a state member denoting the current state; and a recursive mutex to protect the state variable against concurrent updates.

The state module provides seven functions for the application program to administer and manipulate the state variable. The statevar_f_t type definition provides the interface.

Listing 13.12   *state.h* -- The state module header file.

```
1
2 #if ! defined(STATE_H)
3 #define STATE_H
4
5 typedef unsigned int     state_t;
6 typedef struct     _statevar    {
7       unsigned int   status;
8       state_t        state;
9       rmutex_t       rmutex;
10 } statevar_t;
11
12 typedef struct _statevar_f {
13      statevar_t *(*allocate)(void);
14      int         (*destroy)(statevar_t *statevar);
15      int         (*initialize)(statevar_t *,state_t);
16      int         (*lock)(statevar_t *);
17      int         (*unlock)(statevar_t *);
18      int         (*transition)(statevar_t *,state_t, state_t);
19      state_t     (*getstate)(statevar_t *);
```

Listing 3.12 *continued.*

```
20 } statevar_f_t;
21
22 extern statevar_f_t statevar_f;
23 #     define DYNAMIC    0x01  /*   status field value for
24 allocated
25                               *   state variables.
26                               */
27 #     define LOCKED     0x01  /*   state value LOCKED is reserved
28                               *   and used by the implementation.
29                               */
30 #endif
```

The state.c source file provides the functions for manipulating the state variable. The statevar_f.create() function dynamically allocates and initializes a statevar_t type data structure. The state variable can be used only between sibling threads. To extend the state module for use between UNIX processes, the state variable's recursive mutex must be initialized as a USYNC_PROCESS type mutex.

The statevar_f.destroy() function will deallocate a dynamically created statevar_t type structure. The function will call the rmutex_destroy() function to invalidate the recursive mutex. The state variable's memory is released.

The statevar_f.initialize() function is used to initialize the STATE of the state variable to the specified state. The statevar_f.initialize() function does not check the current state of the state variable. Instead, it simply locks the recursive mutex and sets the current state.

The statevar_f.lock() function will lock the state variable and set the state variable's current state to LOCKED. The function uses a bitwise-OR to set the state to LOCKED. This permits the state variable's state to hold the current state of several state machines.

The statevar_f.unlock() function will unlock the state variable and set the state variable's current state to UNLOCKED. Using bitwise operators, the statevar_f.unlock() function will eliminate the current LOCKED state value.

The statevar_f.transition() function will transition the state variable's state from the current state to a new state. The function uses bitwise operators to change the state of the state variable. The statevar_f.transition() function will not, however, permit a transition to the LOCKED state. A state variable can be locked only with the statevar_f.lock() function, and subsequently unlocked through the statevar_f.unlock() function.

The `statevar_f.getState()` function returns the current state of the state variable. Note that this function must lock the state variable prior to examining the current state. The `threadLog` module is used to record any error conditions.

Listing 13.13   state.c -- The `state` source module.

```
1 #include <synch.h>
2 #include <malloc.h>
3 #include <memory.h>
4 #include <errno.h>
5 #include "state.h"
6 #include "mthreadLog.h"
7
8 /*****************************************************************
9  *      Function Prototypes
10 *****************************************************************/
11 static        int          Destroy(statevar_t *);
12 static        int          Initialize(statevar_t *,state_t);
13 static        int          Lock(statevar_t *);
14 static        int          Unlock(statevar_t *);
15 static        int          Transition(statevar_t *,state_t,state_t);
16 static        statevar_t *Create(void);
17 static state_t           GetState(statevar_t *);
18
19 /*****************************************************************
20 *      Create        FUNCTION
21 *
22 *      Allocate and initialize a statevar_t type structure.
23 *****************************************************************/
24 static statevar_t *
25 Create(void)
26 {
27        statevar_t *statevar;
28        statevar = malloc(sizeof(statevar_t));
29        if( statevar ) {
30               memset(statevar,'\0',sizeof(statevar_t));
31               statevar->status = DYNAMIC;
32        }
33        return(statevar);
34 }
35
```

Listing 13.13 *continued.*

```
36 /*****************************************************************
37  *      Destroy              FUNCTION
38  *
39  *      Invalidate and release the resources associated with the
40  *      given state variable.
41  *****************************************************************/
42 static int
43 Destroy(statevar_t *statevar)
44 {
45         int    errorCondition;
46
47         if( statevar == NULL )
48                 errorCondition = EINVAL;
49         else {
50                 errorCondition = rmutex_destroy( &statevar->rmutex );
51                 if( ! errorCondition && statevar->status == DYNAMIC )
52                         free(statevar);
53         }
54         return(errorCondition);
55 }
56
57
58 /*****************************************************************
59  *      Initialize  FUNCTION
60  *
61  *      Initialize the given state variable to the specified state.
62  *****************************************************************/
63 static int
64 Initialize( statevar_t *statevar, const state_t state)
65 {
66         int    errorCondition;
67
68         if( statevar == NULL )
69                 errorCondition = EINVAL;
70
71         else
72                 errorCondition = statevar_f.lock( statevar );
73         if( ! errorCondition ) {
74                 statevar->state = state;
75                 (void) statevar_f.unlock( statevar );
76         }
```

Listing 13.13   *continued.*

```
77          return(errorCondition);
78 }
79
80 /****************************************************************
81  *    Lock      FUNCTION
82  *
83  *    This function will lock state variable's recursive mutex lock.
84  ****************************************************************/
85 static int
86 Lock( statevar_t *statevar)
87 {
88          int    errorCondition;
89
90          if( statevar == NULL )
91                  errorCondition = EINVAL;
92          else
93                  errorCondition = rmutex_lock( &statevar->rmutex);
94          if( ! errorCondition )
95                  statevar->state |= LOCKED;
96          return(errorCondition);
97 }
98
99 /****************************************************************
100  *    Unlock       FUNCTION
101  *
102  *    This function will unlock the state variable's recursive
103  *    mutex lock.
104  ****************************************************************/
105 static int
106 Unlock( statevar_t *statevar)
107 {
108          int    errorCondition;
109
110          if( statevar == NULL )
111                  errorCondition = EINVAL;
112          else
113                  errorCondition =  rmutex_unlock( &statevar->rmutex);
114          if( ! errorCondition )
115                  statevar->state &= ~LOCKED;
116          return(errorCondition);
117 }
```

Listing 13.13 *continued.*

```
118 /*****************************************************************
119 **
120  *      Transition  FUNCTION
121  *
122  *      This function will transition the given state variable from
123  *      the currentState to its newState.  The function will return
124  *      a zero value on success, or an appropriate error indication
125  *      value on failure.
126  *****************************************************************/
127 static int
128 Transition(statevar_t *statevar,state_t currentState,state_t
129 newState)
130 {
131         int    errorCondition;
132
133         if( statevar == NULL )
134                 errorCondition = EINVAL;
135         else
136                 errorCondition = statevar_f.lock(statevar);
137         if(  ! errorCondition ) {
138                 if( statevar->state & currentState ) {
139                         statevar->state &= ~currentState;
140                         statevar->state |= newState;
141                 }
142                 else if( currentState == 0 )
143                         statevar->state |= newState;
144                 else
145                         errorCondition = EINVAL;
146                 statevar_f.unlock(statevar);
147         }
148         return( errorCondition );
149 }
150
151 /*****************************************************************
152  *      GetState    FUNCTION
153  *      Return the current state of the state variable.
154  *****************************************************************/
155 static state_t
156 GetState( statevar_t *statevar)
157 {
158         state_t    state    = 0;
159         int    errorCondition = 0;
```

Listing 13.13 *continued.*

```
159          threadLog_f.clearError();
160          if( statevar == NULL ) {
161                  threadLog_f.setError(EINVAL);
162                  return(0);
163          }
164          errorCondition = statevar_f.lock(statevar);
165          if( ! errorCondition ) {
166                  state = statevar->state & (~LOCKED);
167                  errorCondition = statevar_f.unlock(statevar);
168          }
169          if( errorCondition )
170                  threadLog_f.setError(errorCondition);
171          return( state );
172 }
173
174 statevar_f_t  statevar_f = {
175          Create,
176          Destroy,
177          Initialize,
178          Lock,
179          Unlock,
180          Transition,
181          GetState
182 };
```

13.9   The Message Module

The message module (*see Listings 13.14 and 13.15*) provides the allocation and deallocation of the message_t type data structures used in communication between the various daemon threads. The message_t type data structure includes a pointer to an object, and a pointer to an atom. The operation to be applied is determined by the daemon receiving the message, and thus an opcode is not required as part of the message itself.

The message module assumes that all messages are dynamically allocated. Therefore, there is no requirement to check a status member for the ALLOCATED flag. Note that the message_f.allocate() function will call the threadLog module to record any error conditions.

Listing 13.14   *message.h* -- The `message` module header file.

```
1 #if ! defined(MESSAGE_H)
2 #      define MESSAGE_H
3
4 typedef struct _adamMessage_t {
5      object_t     *object;
6      atom_t       *atom;
7 } adamMessage_t;
8
9 typedef struct _adamMessage_f_t {
10     adamMessage_t     *(*allocate)(void);
11     int               (*deallocate)(adamMessage_t *);
12 } adamMessage_f_t;
13 extern adamMessage_f_t adamMessage_f;
14 #endif
```

Listing 13.15   *message.c* -- The `message` source module.

```
1 #include <stdlib.h>
2 #include <memory.h>
3 #include <errno.h>
4 #include "adamdef.h"
5
6 /*****************************************************************
7  *      Function Prototypes
8  *****************************************************************/
9 static        adamMessage_t     *Allocate(void);
10 static        int               Deallocate(adamMessage_t *);
11
12 /*****************************************************************
13  *   Allocate        FUNCTION
14  *
15  *   This function allocates and initializes an adamMessage_t type
16  *   structure. A pointer to the structure is returned on succcess;
17  *   otherwise a NULL value is returned and threadLog is called to
18  *   record the error.
19
20  *****************************************************************/
21 static adamMessage_t *
22 Allocate(void)
23 {
24     adamMessage_t   *message          = NULL;
```

Listing 13.15 *continued.*

```
24          threadLog_f.clearError();
25          message = malloc(sizeof(adamMessage_t));
26          if( message != NULL )
27                  memset(message,'\0',sizeof(adamMessage_t));
28          else
29                  threadLog_f.setError(ENOMEM);
30          return(message);
31 }
32
33 /********************************************************************
34  *      Deallocate   FUNCTION
35  *
36  *      This function deallocates an adamMessage_t structure.
37  ********************************************************************/
38 static int
39 Deallocate(adamMessage_t *message)
40 {
41          free(message);
42          return(0);
43 }
44
45 /********************************************************************
46  *      Define the adamMessage module.
47  ********************************************************************/
48 adamMessage_f_t adamMessage_f = {
49          Allocate,
50          Deallocate
51 };
```

13.10 ADAM Example

As an example of using the ADAM software utility, let us consider applying ADAM to the dirlist program presented in an earlier chapter. The dirlist program accepts zero or more arguments as directory names. The contents of each directory are then listed.

For this implementation we define two atoms: a directory listing atom (dirlistAtom) and an atom to represent the path name (pathnameAtom). We create one object per command-line argument, and attach the pathnameAtom and the dirlistAtom to the object.

An alternative design would have been to create an object whose data value is the path name. Using a pathnameAtom, however, provides additional flexibility for further enhancements to the application. The `adirlist.c` source file (*Listing 13.16*) shows the implementation of `dirlist` using the ADAM interface. In a generic sense, the algorithm used is given as:

```
initialize the ADAM interface
create an array of objects, one per command-line argument
define dirlist atom as DERIVED using
        attach with dirAtomAttach
        detach with unloadDirAtom
define pathname atom as INTRINSIC
for each command-line argument
        attach pathname atom to object (default value from
argv)
        attach the dirlist atom to the object
done
for each object
        get the value of the object's dirlist atom
        call printDirContents passing this value
        detach the dirlist atom from the object
        detach the pathname atom from the object
done
```

Note that the `dirlistAtom` definition uses the `dirAtomAttach` and the `unloadDirAtom` functions for the `attach` and `detach` procedures. This is required, since the ADAM interface will call the `attach` and `detach` procedures passing an `adamMessage_t` type data structure as the argument.

Listing 13.16   *adirlist.c* -- An ADAM version of the `dirlist` program.

```
 1 #include <thread.h>
 2 #include <stdio.h>
 3 #include <unistd.h>
 4 #include <string.h>
 5 #include <malloc.h>
 6 #include <dirent.h>
 7 #include "adamdef.h"
 8 #include "dircontent.h"
 9
10 static atomid_t    dirlistAtom;
11 static atomid_t    pathnameAtom;
12
```

Listing 13.16   *continued.*

```
13 /******************************************************************
14  *      Function Prototypes
15
16  ******************************************************************/
17 static void unloadDirAtom(void *);
18 static void *dirAtomAttach(void *);
19
20 /******************************************************************
21  *   PROGRAM         adirlist
22  *
23  *   Adirlist accepts one or more command-line arguments as
24  *   directory path names.  For each directory, adirlist generates
25  *   a listing of the directory's content.
26  *****************************************************************/
27 void *
28 main(int argc, char **argv)
29 {
30        object_t     **objectArray;
31        int          error = 0;
32        int          numpaths;
33        int          index;
34        void         *data    = NULL;
35
36             /************************************************
37              *     Initialize the adam module.
38              ************************************************/
39        error = adam_f.initialize();
40        if( error ) {
41            threadLog_f.message("Error: cannot start adam [%d]\n",
42                             error);
43            thr_exit((void *)1);
44        }
45
46
47             /************************************************
48              *     Define the directory listing atom as:
49              *          - A DERIVED atom
50              *          - Attach procedure is dirAtomAttach
51              *          - Aetach procedure is unloadDirAtom
52              ************************************************/
53        dirlistAtom=atomdef_f.create(DERIVED,NULL,NULL,
54                             dirAtomAttach,unloadDirAtom,NULL);
55
```

Listing 13.16 *continued.*

```
55          if( dirlistAtom == 0 ) {
56                  threadLog_f.message("dirlist atom definition failed");
57                  thr_exit((void *)1);
58          }
59
60                  /***************************************************
61                   *    Define the path name atom as an INTRINSIC atom.
62                   ***************************************************/
63          pathnameAtom =
64                  atomdef_f.create(INTRINSIC,NULL,NULL,NULL,NULL,NULL);
65
66          if( pathnameAtom == 0 ) {
67                  threadLog_f.message("pathname atom def failed");
68                  thr_exit((void *)1);
69          }
70                  /***************************************************
71                   *    Each command-line argument is a pathname to a
72                   *    directory that we are interested in.  We begin
73                   *    by establishing an array of object pointers
74                   *    (one for each command-line argument).
75                   ***************************************************/
76          numpaths = argc -1;
77          objectArray = (object_t **)
78                              malloc(sizeof(object_t)*numpaths);
79          for( index=0; index < numpaths; ++index ) {
80                  /***************************************************
81                   *    Create an object to represent the path name.
82                   ***************************************************/
83              objectArray[index] = object_f.create(NULL);
84
85                  /***************************************************
86                   *    Attach the pathnameAtom to the object and give
87                   *    it an initial value of the current command-line
88                   *    argument.
89                   ***************************************************/
90              error=atom_f.attach(objectArray[index],pathnameAtom,
91                                                      argv[index+1]);
92              if( error ) {
93                      threadLog_f.message("pathnameAtom failed[%d]\n",
94                          error);
95                      thr_exit((void *)1);
96              }
```

Listing 13.16 *continued.*

```
 97                     /**********************************************
 98                      *    Now attach the dirlistAtom to the object.
 99                      **********************************************/
100              error=atom_f.attach(objectArray[index],dirlistAtom,
101                             NULL);
102
103              if( error ) {
104                   threadLog_f.message("dirlistAtom failed [%d]\n",
105                        error);
106                   thr_exit((void *)1);
107              }
108         }
109
110      for( index=0; index< numpaths; ++index) {
111           data=atom_f.getValue( objectArray[index],
112                        dirlistAtom);
113           printDirContents( stderr, data );
114           atom_f.detach(objectArray[index], dirlistAtom);
115           atom_f.detach(objectArray[index], pathnameAtom);
116      }
117      thr_exit((void *)0);
118 }
119
120 /******************************************************************
121  *   dirAtomAttach ATTACH PROCEDURE
122  *
123  *   This function is the attach procedure for the dirlistAtom.
124  *   The dirAtomAttach procedure will get the value of the
125  *   path name associated with this object.  It then calls the
126  *   loadDirContents function to read the entries in the specified
127  *   directory.
128  ******************************************************************/
129 void *
130 dirAtomAttach(void *arg)
131 {
132      , object_t   *object;
133        void     *data;
134        object   = arg;
135
136        data   = atom_f.getValue(object,pathnameAtom);
137
138        if( data != NULL )  {
139             data = loadDirContents( data );
```

Listing 13.16 *continued.*

```
140        }
141        return(data);
142 }
143
144 /************************************************************
145 *     unloadDirAtom      DETACH PROCEDURE
146 *
147 *     This function is the dirlistAtom detach procedure.  When a
148 *     dirlistAtom is detached from an object, the ADAM module will
149 *     call the unloadDirAtom detach procedure with a pointer
150 *     to the message describing the object and the instance of the
151 *     atom being detached.
152 ************************************************************/
153 void
154 unloadDirAtom(void *arg)
155 {
156        atom_t          *atom;
157        adamMessage_t *message;
158        void            *data;
159
160        message = arg;
161        atom    = message->atom;
162        data    = atom->value;
163        unloadDirContents(data);
164 }
```

Compile adirlist program:

```
cc -D_REENTRANT -c -I${INSTALLROOT}/thread.d/example3.d\
           -I${INSTALLROOT}hdr dircontent.c
cc -D_REENTRANT -c -I${INSTALLROOT}/adam.d/hdr        \
        -I${INSTALLROOT}/hdr                          \
        -I${INSTALLROOT}/thread.d/example3.d          \
        adirlist.c
cc -D_REENTRANT adirlist.o                            \
     dircontent.o                                     \
     ${INSTALLROOT}/adam.d/atoms.d/atoms.o            \
     ${INSTALLROOT}/adam.d/atomdef.d/atomdef.o        \
     ${INSTALLROOT}/adam.d/daemons.d/daemon.o         \
     ${INSTALLROOT}/adam.d/adam.d/adam.o              \
     ${INSTALLROOT}/adam.d/objects.d/object.o         \
     ${INSTALLROOT}/adam.d/state.d/state.o            \
     ${INSTALLROOT}/adam.d/message.d/message.o        \
```

```
${INSTALLROOT}/lib/libtsync.a
-l thread    -o adirlist
```

13.11   Related Efforts

[EaZa93] describes a methodology called CHORES for support of functional parallelism. With this model, the chore is a collection of one or more atoms that constitute multiple applications of a single function. The atoms of a chore may have relationships maintained between them to denote dependencies. Alternatively, atoms may be denoted in a range such that a range of atoms may represent the chore. With such a range defined, the order of the atoms may be marked as initiation-ordered so that the atoms must be completed in a specific sequence. When a chore is to be completed, the atoms representing the chore are added to the chore queue. The chore system creates one worker thread per physical processor, and these worker threads will take an atom of work to complete from the chore queue. The execution continues until it is completed. This may result in more atoms being added to the chore queue.

In [GaRa91] two new constructs are proposed for concurrent programming. These are *handshake* and *unit*. A handshake is shared between multiple processors with one process being the master. Each process has a procedure-like interface with a handshake. When all of the participating processes call their handshake procedures, the shared handshake body is executed by the master. The unit is used to restrict the sequence of possible calls to various handshake procedures. Together, the handshake and unit form part of the Decomposed Petri Net (DPN) model. With this paradigm, there is a separation of concerns by separating computation objects and control objects. Computation objects are used to capture the computation aspects of the system, and do not concern themselves with synchronization. Control objects, written as units, specify the computation that is directly related to communications.

A description of applying an object-oriented database model to a scientific database is provided by [PrCo92]. Interrelationships between objects are described including:

```
generalization (is-a)
specialization (is-an-example-of)
aggregation    (is-a-part-of)
association    (is-related-to)
```

These interrelationships can be added to the ADAM interface at the atom level.

A generalized glossary of proposed terminology for temporal database concepts is provided in [JCGS92].

Asynchronous objects with CAUSE-REACTION specifications are described in [WeMe80]. This technique can be added to the ADAM interface for dependency handling between atoms. That is to say, an atom's measurement can be dependent on the evaluation of a different atom's measure, or on a user-defined event.

There are four steps required to reuse existing code as defined by [Oste92]: definition, retrieval, adaptation, and incorporation. [Oste92] presents an AI-based library system for software reuse called AIRS (*AI-based Reuse System*). This paper illuminates the issues for developing such a library.

APPENDIX A
Spin-Locks

This appendix provides an overview of the spin-lock synchronization primitive described in the UNIX System V Release for ES/MP Multi Processing Detailed Specifications.[43] Spin-locks are not included with the `Solaris 2.x` Software Developers Kit.

In its simplest form, a spin-lock is a particular form of a mutual exclusion lock. When a thread acquires the spin-lock, all other requesting threads spin in a loop, *busy waiting* for the lock to become available. This behavior contrasts sharply with the block-wait algorithms mentioned in the previous chapters.

Spin-locks are available for use between sibling threads of a UNIX process. A thread must not be preempted or blocked while holding the spin-lock. The spin-locks must be released by the thread prior to calling sleep, or sleep blocking on a synchronization operation.

PROGRAMMER'S NOTE:

Spin-locks should be used only on multiprocessor computers. The use of a spin-lock on a uniprocessor may deadlock an application. A thread will *busy wait* through its time quantum, waiting for the lock to be released. The owner of the lock does not have the potential to execute, however, until the busy waiting thread completes its time quantum.

The use of spin-locks in an application may cause lock contention. If this contention is high enough, then adding processors will offer no gain in the effective processing power [Bart87]. Note that all spin-lock function calls begin with a leading underscore in an attempt to highlight their use.

---

[43] Thread examples for the `Solaris 2.x` operating system can be found at `http://www.sun.com/sunsoft/Developer-products/sig/threads`.

A spin-lock is represented as a spin_t type data structure. The storage for the spin_t type data structure may be defined statically, or dynamically through a memory allocation function such as malloc. The _spin_init function initializes the spin-lock to the UNLOCKED state. The spin-lock can be used any number of times without having to be reinitialized.

The first argument to the _spin_init function (*Figure A.1*) is the address of the spin-lock to initialize. The second parameter, arg, is reserved for future use and should always be specified as NULL. The _spin_init function returns zero on success, or an appropriate error indication value.

NAME:

      _spin_init - Initialize a spin-lock to the unlocked state.

SYNOPSIS:

```
#include <synch.h>

int
_spin_init( spin_t *lock, void *arg);
```

Figure A.1   _spin_init() synopsis. [1]

To acquire a spin-lock, a thread must call the _spin_lock function (*see Figure A.2*). The only parameter to this function is the address of the spin_t type data structure to lock. The _spin_lock function will examine the current state of the spin-lock. If the spin-lock is in the LOCKED state, the _spin_lock function will enter a tight loop, continuously testing for the spin-lock to become available. When the spin-lock is available, the _spin_lock function will lock it and transition the lock to the LOCKED state. Once acquired, control is returned to the requesting thread.

PROGRAMMER'S NOTE:

Spin-lock operations are not recursive. If a thread has acquired a spin-lock and calls the _spin_lock function again for the same lock, the thread will deadlock. Note that a sibling thread could ultimately unlock the spin-lock.

The _spin_trylock function (*Figure A.2*) makes a single attempt to acquire the spin-lock. If the lock is currently held by a sibling thread, then control is immediately returned to the requesting thread with an EBUSY error indication value. In general, this operation is used when the resources

---

are exclusively held for such a short duration that releasing the process via a context switch may not be optimal.

NAME:

       `_spin_lock`   - Acquire a spin-lock.

       `_spin_trylock` - Make a single attempt to acquire a spin-lock.

SYNOPSIS:

```
#include <synch.h>

void _spin_lock( spin_t *lock )
void _spin_trylock( spin_t *lock)
```

Figure A.2   `_spin_lock()` synopsis. [1]

Once acquired, a thread can release a spin-lock by calling the `_spin_unlock` function (*see Figure A.3*). This function accepts as a single argument the address of the `spin_t` type data structure to be unlocked. The `_spin_unlock` function transitions the spin-lock to the UNLOCKED state.

PROGRAMMER'S NOTE:

The UNIX Threads Interface does not maintain a relationship between the thread that locked the spin-lock and the lock itself. If a sibling thread inadvertently calls the `_spin_unlock` function, the spin-lock will be released.

NAME:

       `_spin_unlock` - Release the lock previously acquired with _spin_lock or
                _spin_trylock.

SYNOPSIS:

```
#include <synch.h>

void
_spin_unlock( spin_t *lock)
```

Figure A.3   `_spin_unlock()` synopsis. [1]

The `_spin_destroy` function (*Figure A.4*) invalidates a spin-lock no longer required by the application. Once invalidated, the spin-lock cannot be used unless reinitialized with the `_spin_init` function.

NAME:

       `_spin_destroy` - Invalidate a spin-lock.

SYNOPSIS:

```
#include <synch.h>

int
_spin_destroy(spin_t *lock)
```

Figure A.4   `_spin_unlock()` synopsis. [1]

[1] Printed with Permission of UNIX Systems Laboratories, Inc. All Rights Reserved.

APPENDIX B
Spin-Type Barrier Locks

The UNIX System V Release for ES/MP Multi Processing Detailed Specifications includes the spin-type barrier synchronization primitive, but notes that the primitive will not be included in the SVID.[1] A brief discussion of the API is presented in this appendix.

The UNIX System V Release for ES/MP Multi Processing Detailed Specifications does not define the implementation requirements for the barrier synchronization primitive. When a thread arrives at a barrier, the implementation may cause the thread to sleep, waiting for the arrival of the participating threads. Alternatively, the implementation may cause the waiting thread to spin (busy-wait). Certain implementations may employ a combination of the two methods. There are no mechanisms available for the application to determine the underlying implementation.

Critical applications may require explicit use of a spin-type barrier for performance considerations. Spin-type barriers are available for use between sibling threads. The _barrier_spin_init function (*see Figure B.1*) initializes the spin-type barrier for count participating threads.

```
NAME:
        _barrier_spin_init   - Initialize a spin-type barrier.

SYNOPSIS:
        #include <synch.h>

        int
        _barrier_spin_init(barrier_spin_t *barrier,int count,void
*arg)
```

Figure B.1   _barrier_spin_init() synopsis. [1]

A participating thread executes the barrier by calling the _barrier_spin function (*see Figure B.2*). The calling thread will busy-wait until all participating threads have reached the barrier. When the last thread reaches the barrier, all of the threads are released, and the barrier is reset to its initial state.

[1] Printed with Permission of UNIX Systems Laboratories, Inc. All Rights Reserved.

NAME:

      `_barrier_spin` - Busy-wait at the barrier awaiting arrival of the participating.
threads

SYNOPSIS:

```
#include <synch.h>

int
_barrier_spin(barrier_spin_t *barrier)
```

Figure B.2   `_barrier_spin()` synopsis. [1]

A spin-type barrier is invalidate by calling the `_barrier_spin_destroy` function (*see Figure B.3*). This function will return a zero value to the calling thread if the barrier can be invalidated. If a sibling thread is currently waiting at the barrier, the function will return an EBUSY error value to the calling thread.

NAME:

      `_barrier_destroy` - Invalidate a spin-type barrier.

SYNOPSIS:

```
#include <synch.h>

int
_barrier_destroy(barrier_spin_t *barrier)
```

Figure B.3   `_barrier_destroy()` synopsis. [1]

---

[1] Printed with Permission of UNIX Systems Laboratories, Inc. All Rights Reserved.

APPENDIX C
UNIX SVR4.2 MP System Call Changes

This appendix provides a concise summary of changes to the UNIX SVR4.2 MP operating system calls in support of the extended process model. [1]

access(2)	Sibling threads share credentials, including UID and GID, and have the same access rights.
acct(2)	Accounting is enabled or disabled at the UNIX process level. Accounting records are written upon the termination of the UNIX process.
acl(2)	All security attributes are shared at the UNIX process level.
aclipc(2)	All security attributes are shared at the UNIX process level.
adjtime(2)	No change.
alarm(2)	The SIGALRM signal is sent to the bound thread that set the alarm. When the requesting thread is a multiplexed thread, then the SIGALRM signal is sent to the LWP that set the alarm.
brk(2) srbk(2)	Since the sibling threads of a UNIX process share the same address space, the change in allocated space affects all threads identically.
chdir(2)	Sibling threads share the same current directory. A change in the current directory affects all of the threads in the UNIX process.
chmod(2) fchmod(2)	Sibling threads share the same credentials and access rights.
chown(2)	Sibling threads share the same credentials and access rights.

[1] Printed with Permission of UNIX Systems Laboratories, Inc. All Rights Reserved.   363

chroot(2)	Sibling threads share the same root directory. The system call affects all sibling threads.
close(2)	Sibling threads share the same file descriptors. A close(2) issued by one thread closes the file descriptor for all sibling threads.
creat(2)	Sibling threads share the same file descriptors. The file descriptor returned by the creat(2) system call can be used by any sibling thread.
dup(2)	Sibling threads share the same file descriptors. The file descriptor returned by the creat(2) system call can be used by any sibling thread.
exec(2)	Only the bound thread calling exec(2) continues in the new image. When a multiplexed thread calls exec(2), then only the LWP to which the thread is bound continues in the new image.
_exit(2)	No change.
fcntl(2)	Sibling threads share the same file descriptors. The change affects all threads identically. File and record locks are based on pid, so do not restrain threads from manipulating segments locked by sibling threads. A new command, F_DUP2, has been added.
fork(2)	Fork has two flavors, fork1 and forkall. In both instances the created process is a duplicate of the creating UNIX process. With the forkall system call, the new UNIX process proceeds with the same number of bound threads (or LWPs). Alternatively, the fork1 system call proceeds with only the bound thread (or LWP) that issued the call.
fpathconf(2) pathconf(2)	No changes.
fsync(2)	No changes.
getcontext(2) setcontext(2)	A call to getcontext(2) returns the context of the requesting bound thread. When a multiplexed thread calls getcontext(2), then the context of the underlying LWP is returned. A call to setcontext(2) affects only the calling bound thread (or LWP).
getdents(2)	No changes.
getgroups(2) setgroups(2)	Sibling threads share the same credentials, thus there are no changes to these system calls.

getitimer(2) setitimer(2)	Interval timers are per bound thread (or LWP). A subsequent SIGALRM, SIGVTALRM, or SIGPROF will be posted to the bound thread (or LWP) that set the timers.
getmsg(2)	All sibling threads share the same streams. A bound thread (or LWP) will sleep independently while awaiting I/O.
getpid(2) getpgrp(2) getppid(2) getpgid(2)	All bound threads (or LWPs) share the same IDs.
getrlimit(2) getrlimit(2)	All bound threads (and LWPs) share the same resource limits.
getuid(2) geteuid(2) getgid(2) getegid(2)	No changes.
ioctl(2)	No changes.
kill(2)	The specified signal is delivered to exactly one of the sigwaiting or handling bound threads (or LWPs).
link(2)	No changes.
lseek(2)	Sibling threads share the same file descriptors and therefore the seek pointers. When a thread issues a lseek(2) system call on a file descriptor, all sibling threads see the resulting file pointer.
memcntl(2)	Sibling threads share the same address space. The results of the memcntl(2) system call affect all sibling threads.
mincore(2)	No changes.
mkdir(2)	No changes.
mknod(2)	No changes.
mmap(2)	Sibling threads share the same address space. The results of an mmap(2) system call affect all sibling threads.
mount(2)	No changes.
mprotect(2)	No changes.

msgctl(2) msgget(2) msgop(2) msgsnd(2) msgrcv(2)	Changes to message queues affect all sibling threads. Bound threads (or LWPs) sleep independently on message queue operations.
munmap(2)	Sibling threads share the same address space. The change affects all threads similarly.
nice(2)	Sibling threads do not share the same scheduling context. A call to nice(2) will bias only the priority of the calling bound thread (or LWP) by the specified value.
open(2)	Sibling threads share the same file descriptors. The new descriptor can be used by any sibling thread.
pause(2)	Only the bound thread (or LWP) calling pause(2) will wait.
pipe(2)	Sibling threads share the same file descriptors. The new file descriptors from pipe(2) can be used by any sibling.
plock(2)	Sibling threads share the same address space. The results of the plock(2) affect all sibling threads identically.
poll(2)	Sibling threads share the same file descriptors. All streams can be polled by any sibling thread.
priocntl(2) priocntlset(2)	Sibling threads do not share the same scheduling context. The results of priocntl(2) and priocntlset(2) may affect a single bound thread (or LWP), or all bound threads (or LWPs) of a UNIX process.
profil(2)	Profiling is per UNIX process.
ptrace(2)	The use of the ptrace(2) system call is to be replaced by the extended PROC file system functions.
putmsg(2)	Sibling threads share the same file descriptors. The results affect all sibling threads identically.
read(2)	Sibling threads share the same file descriptors. A read(2) of a file descriptor increments the file pointer for all sibling threads. Reads are considered atomic, and thus only one thread can be physically reading from the file descriptor at a time. The only exception to this is for the /proc address space I/O.
readlink(2)	No changes.

rename(2)	No changes.
rmdir(2)	No changes.
semctl(2) semget(2) semop(2)	Sibling threads share all semaphores, so the change affects all sibling threads identically. When issuing a semaphore operation, a bound thread (or LWP) sleeps independently of the siblings. It is advisable to use the new sema operations provided with the libsync.a library.
setpgid(2) setpgrp(2) setsid(2) setuid(2)	The change affects all sibling threads identically.
shmctl(2) shmget(2) shmop(2)	Sibling threads share the same address space, and thus the same shared memory segments. It is advisable to use the mmap(2) function in place of these system calls.
sigaction(2)	Sibling threads share the same disposition for a signal.
sigaltstack(2)	Alternate signal stacks are per bound thread (or LWP).
signal(2) sigset(2) sigignore(2)	Sibling threads share the same signal disposition.
sighold(2) sigrelse(2) sigpause(2) sigpending(2) sigprocmask(2)	These system calls affect only the requesting bound thread (or LWP).
sigsend(2) sigsendset(2)	Only one bound thread (or LWP) will receive the signal.
sigsuspend(2)	The sigsuspend(2) system call affects only the requesting bound thread (or LWP).
stat(2) lstat(2) fstat(2)	No changes.
statvfs(2) fstatvfs(2)	No changes.
stime(2)	No changes.
swapctl(2)	No changes.

[1] Printed with Permission of UNIX Systems Laboratories, Inc. All Rights Reserved.

`symlink(2)`	No changes.
`sync(2)`	No changes.
`sysfs(2)`	No changes.
`sysinfo(2)`	No changes.
`termios(2)`	Sibling threads share all file descriptors, and thus the changes affect all bound threads (or LWPs) identically.
`time(2)`	No changes.
`times(2)`	Returns the aggregate CPU time for all bound thread (and LWPs) of the UNIX Process.
`uadmin(2)`	No changes.
`ulimit(2)`	No changes.
`umask(2)`	Sibling threads share the same file-creation mask.
`umount(2)`	No changes.
`uname(2)`	No changes.
`unlink(2)`	The space occupied by the file is not released until all references to it have been closed.
`ustat(2)`	No changes.
`utime(2)`	All threads (and underlying LWPs) see the new file access and modification times immediately.
`vfork(2)`	The `vfork(2)` operation may fail if the requesting UNIX Process has more than one LWP. The calling LWP blocks until the child has exited or exec'd.

`wait(2)`
`waitid(2)`
`waitpid(2)`
	The thread (and its LWP) block. Sibling threads are not affected.

`write(2)`	The thread (and its LWP) block while waiting for the I/O request to complete. Sibling threads are not affected. Subsequent `write(2)` requests to a stream can be completed by different LWPs, but each operation is atomic except for `/proc` address space I/O.

APPENDIX D
Function Prototypes

This appendix presents the UNIX Threads API function prototypes, as described in the UNIX System V Release ES/MP Multi Processing Detailed Specifications from UNIX Systems Laboratories, Inc. A brief description of the functions along with their output and diagnostics are listed.

The UNIX Threads API is consistent between the UnixWare 2.x and Solaris 2.x operating systems. The synchronization API, however, is not consistent between the two operating system releases. The Solaris 2.x operating system, for example, does not provide the barrier synchronization primitive, nor does it provide spin-locks with the basic software developer's kit.[44]

The Threads API Function Prototypes [¶]

```
int
thr_continue(thread_t target_thread);
```

This function will resume the execution of the *target_thread*, which was previously suspended by thr_suspend. A zero value is returned on success.

Diagnostics:
ESRCH   The *target_thread* does not exist in the current process.

```
int
thr_create(void *stack_address, size_t stack_size,
           void *(*start_routine)(void *arg), void *arg, long
           flags, thread_t *new_thread);
```

On success, thr_create returns zero and sets the location pointed to by *new_thread* to the identifier of the created thread.

---

[44]   A version of a barrier lock will be available at the Sunsoft threads page: http://www.sun.com/sunsoft/Developer-products/sig/threads.

[¶] Printed with Permission of UNIX Systems Laboratories, Inc. All Rights Reserved.   369

Diagnostics:
      ENOMEM   There is insufficient memory to complete the operation.
      EINVAL   The *stack_size* is zero and *stack_address* is non NULL.
      EINVAL   The resulting *stack_size* is smaller than the system defined minimum.
      EINVAL   The *start_routine* is NULL.
      EAGAIN   A system-defined limit on the number of LWPs per real user-id would be exceeded.

```
void
thr_exit(void *status);
```

This function terminates the calling thread and establishes the exit value as status.

Diagnostics:
    None.

```
int
thr_getconcurrency(void);
```

This function returns the application-defined concurrency level for multiplexed threads. This is the value from the most recent thr_setconcurrency plus the number of calls to thr_create with the THR_NEW_LWP flag set. The return value does not necessarily reflect the number of LWPs in the pool.

Diagnostics:
    None.

```
int
thr_join(thread_t wait_for,thread_t *departed_thread,void **status);
```

On success, thr_join returns zero and sets the location pointed to by *departed_thread* to the identifier of the thread whose termination caused the join to complete. The thr_join function will set the location pointed to by *status* (if non-NULL) to the return status of that thread.

Diagnostics:
      ESRCH   There are no joinable (undetached) threads that can be found in the current process with identifier *wait_for*.
      EINVAL   There are no remaining threads that can be thr_join with.
      EDEADLK   The calling thread is attempting to thr_join for itself.

```
int
thr_keycreate(thread_key_t *key, void (*destructor)(void *value));
```

Returns the created thread-specific data `key`.

Diagnostics:
EAGAIN   The `key` name space is exhausted.
ENOMEM   There is insufficient memory to create the `key`.

```
int
thr_keydelete(thread_key_t *key);
```

Delete the specified `key` calling the destructor associated with `key` for each thread that has storage allocated under `key`.

Diagnostics:
EINVAL   The `key` is invalid.

```
int
thr_kill(thread_t tid, int sig);
```

On success, `thr_kill` returns zero. This function is the thread analog of `kill`. The thread to which the signal is to be sent is specified by `tid`; the signal that is to be sent is specified by `sig` and is either 0 or a value from the list given in `signal(4)`.

Diagnostics:
EINVAL   The value of `sig` is not a valid signal number, or is SIGLWP or SIGWAITING.
ESRCH   No thread can be found in the current process with identity `tid`.

```
int
thr_getspecific(thread_key_t key, void **value);
```

Return the thread-specific data associated with `key` in the address pointed to by `value`.

Diagnostics:
EINVAL   The key value is invalid.

```
size_t
thr_minstack();
```

This function returns the aligned minimum stack size, as enforced by the implementation.
Diagnostics:
None.

```
thread_t
thr_self(void);
```

This function returns the identifier of the calling thread.

Diagnostics:
None.

```
int
thr_setconcurrency( int new_level);
```

Set the requested degree of concurrency to *new_level*.

Diagnostics:

EAGAIN   A system resource limit would have been exceeded by using the requested value in the implementation's algorithm. LWPs created up to the failed _lwp_create will not be killed but will continue to exist. Because the change of concurrency level is not synchronous with the call to thr_setconcurrency, this condition is unlikely to be detected.

EINVAL   The value of *new_level* is negative.

```
int
thr_setspecific(thread_key_t key, void *value);
```

This function will establish the thread-specific data for the specified *key*.

Diagnostics:

EINVAL   The key value is invalid.

ENOMEM   There is insufficient memory available to establish the binding.

```
int
thr_sigsetmask(int how, const sigset_t *set, sigset_t *oset);
```

On success, thr_sigsetmask returns zero. This function changes or examines the thread's signal mask.

Diagnostics:

EINVAL   The value of how is not equal to one of the defined values.

```
int
thr_suspend(thread_t target_thread);
```

This function will suspend the target_thread's execution. A value of zero is returned on success.

Diagnostics:
  ESRCH   No thread can be found in the current process with identity
                     target_thread.

The Barrier Synchronization Primitive [1]

```
int
_barrier_spin( barrier_spin_t *barrier);
```

The calling thread will spin-wait at the specified barrier until all participating threads have
reached the barrier. On success, a zero value is returned to the calling thread. Note that
this is available through the UNIX System V Release for ES/MP Multi Processing
Detailed Specifications.

Diagnostics:
  EINVAL   An invalid argument was specified.

```
int
_barrier_spin_destroy( barrier_spin_t *barrier);
```

Invalidate the spin-wait type barrier pointed to by *barrier*. On success, a zero value is
returned to the calling thread. Note that this is available through the UNIX System V
Release for ES/MP Multi Processing Detailed Specifications.

Diagnostics:
  EINVAL   An invalid argument was specified.
  EBUSY   The barrier is currently referenced by other threads.

```
int
_barrier_spin_init( barrier_spin_t *barrier, int count, void *arg);
```

Initialize a spin-wait type barrier for use between *count* sibling threads. On success, a
zero value is returned to the calling thread. Note that this is available through the UNIX
System V Release for ES/MP Multi Processing Detailed Specifications.

Diagnostics:
  EINVAL   An invalid argument was specified.

```
int
barrier_destroy( barrier_t *barrier);
```

Invalidate the barrier pointed to by *barrier*. On success, a zero value is returned to the
calling thread. Note that this is available through the UNIX System V Release for ES/MP
Multi Processing Detailed Specifications.

Diagnostics:
  EINVAL   An invalid argument was specified.
  EBUSY   The barrier is currently referenced by other threads.

[1] Printed with Permission of UNIX Systems Laboratories, Inc. All Rights Reserved.

```
int
barrier_init( barrier_t *barrier, int count, int type, void *arg);
```

Initialize the barrier pointed to by *barrier* for *count* threads. A USYNC_THREAD *type* is for use between sibling threads, while a USYNC_PROCESS *type* is for use between UNIX processes. On success, a zero value is returned.

Diagnostics:
EINVAL	An invalid argument was specified.
EBUSY	The barrier is currently referrenced by other threads.

```
int
barrier_wait( barrier_t *barrier);
```

The calling thread is blocked at the barrier until all count threads have arrived. (The count is specified during the barrier initialization). On success, a zero value is returned to the calling thread.

Diagnostics:
EINVAL	An invalid argument was specified.

The Condition Variable Synchronization Primitive ¶

```
int
cond_broadcast( cond_t *cond );
```

This function will wake up all threads waiting on the condition variable pointed to by *cond*. On success, a zero value is returned to the calling thread.

Diagnostics:
EINVAL	An invalid argument was specified.

```
int
cond_destroy( cond_t *cond );
```

Invalidate the condition variable pointed to by *cond*. On success, a zero value is returned to the calling thread.

Diagnostics:
EINVAL	An invalid argument was specified.
EBUSY	Other threads are currently waiting on the condition variable.

```
int
cond_init( cond_t *cond, int type, void *arg);
```

> Initialize the condition variable pointed to by *cond*. A USYNC_THREAD type is for use between sibling threads, while a USYNC_PROCESS type is for use between UNIX processes. On success, a zero value is returned.

> Diagnostics:
> > EINVAL   An invalid argument was specified.

```
int
cond_signal( cond_t *cond );
```

> This function will wake up a single thread, if one exists, waiting on the condition variable pointed to by *cond*. On success, a zero value is returned to the calling thread.

> Diagnostics:
> > EINVAL   An invalid argument was specified.

```
int
cond_timedwait( cond_t *cond, mutex_t *mutex, timestruc_t *abstime);
```

> The calling thread will wait at most *abstime* time for the occurrence of a condition at the condition variable pointed to by the *cond* parameter. On success, a zero value is returned to the calling thread.

> Diagnostics:
> > EINVAL   An invalid argument was specified.
> > ETIME   The time specified by abstime has expired.
> > EINTR   The operation was interrupted by a signal to the calling thread, or a forkall().

```
int
cond_wait( cond_t *cond, mutex_t *mutex);
```

> The calling thread will wait for the occurrence of a condition at the condition variable pointed to by the *cond* parameter. On success, a zero value is returned to the calling thread.

> Diagnostics:
> > EINVAL   An invalid argument was specified.
> > EINTR   The operation was interrupted by a signal to the calling thread, or a forkall().

The Mutex Synchronization Primitive ¶

```
int
mutex_destroy(mutex_t *mutex);
```

> Invalidate the mutex pointed to by *mutex*, and release all implementation-dependent allocated resources. On success, a zero value is returned to the calling thread.
>
> Diagnostics:
> > EINVAL   An invalid argument was specified.
> > EBUSY   The mutex is currently locked by another thread.

```
int
mutex_init( mutex_t *mutex, int type, void *arg);
```

> The state of the mutex is initialized to UNLOCKED. A USYNC_THREAD *type* is for use between sibling threads, while a USYNC_PROCESS *type* is for use between UNIX processes. On success, a zero value is returned.
>
> Diagnostics:
> > EINVAL   An invalid argument was specified.

```
int
mutex_lock( mutex_t *mutex);
```

> Acquire the mutex pointed to by *mutex*, transitioning it from the UNLOCKED to the LOCKED state. On success, a zero value is returned to the calling thread.
>
> Diagnostics:
> > EINVAL   An invalid argument was specified.

```
int
mutex_trylock( mutex_t *mutex);
```

> A single attempt is made to acquire the mutex pointed to by *mutex*. On success, a zero value is returned to the calling thread.
>
> Diagnostics:
> > EINVAL   An invalid argument was specified.
> > EBUSY   The specified mutex is currently in the LOCKED state.

```
int
mutex_unlock(mutex_t *mutex);
```

> This function will unlock the mutex pointed to by *mutex*. On success, this function will return a zero value to the calling thread.
> Diagnostics:
> > EINVAL   An invalid argument was specified.

¶ Printed with Permission of UNIX Systems Laboratories, Inc. All Rights Reserved.

The Recursive Mutex Synchronization Primitive [1]

```
int
rmutex_destroy( rmutex_t *rmutex );
```

Invalidate the recursive mutex found at the location pointed to by *rmutex*. This may include freeing any dyanmically allocated resources associated with the `rmutex`. On success, a zero value is returned to the calling thread.

Diagnostics:
EINVAL   An invalid argument was specified.
EBUSY   The *rmutex* is currently in the locked state.

```
int
rmutex_init(rmutex_t *rmutex, int type, void *arg);
```

Initialize the recursive mutex pointed to by *rmutex*. The initialized rmutex will be for use between sibling threads if *type* is USYNC_THREAD, or for use between UNIX processes if *type* is USYNC_PROCESS. On success, a zero value is returned to the calling thread.

Diagnostics:
EINVAL   An invalid argument was specified.

```
int
rmutex_lock( rmutex_t *rmutex);
```

This function acquires the recursive mutual exclusion lock pointed to by *rmutex*. On success, a zero value is returned to the calling thread.

Diagnostics:
EINVAL   An invalid argument was specified.

```
int
rmutex_trylock( rmutex_t *rmutex);
```

This function makes a single attempt to acquire the recursive mutual exclusion lock pointed to by *rmutex*. On success, a zero value is returned to the calling thread.

Diagnostics:
EBUSY   The *rmutex* is already locked by another thread.
EINVAL   An invalid argument was specified.

```
int
rmutex_unlock( rmutex_t *rmutex);
```

Unlock the recursive mutex pointed to by *rmutex*. On success, a zero value is returned to the calling thread.

---

[1] Printed with Permission of UNIX Systems Laboratories, Inc. All Rights Reserved.

Diagnostics:
    EINVAL   An invalid argument was specified.
    EACCES   The requesting thread did not previously lock the *rmutex*.

The Reader-Writer Lock Synchronization Primitive [1]

```
int
rwlock_destroy( rwlock_t *lock);
```

Invalidate the reader-writer lock pointed to by parameter *lock*. On success, a zero value is returned to the calling thread.

Diagnostics:
    EINVAL   An invalid argument was specified.
    EBUSY   The reader-writer lock is currently locked.

```
int
rwlock_init(rwlock_t *rwlock, int type, void *arg);
```

Initialize the reader-writer lock pointed to by *rwlock* to the unlocked state. If *type* is USYNC_THREAD, then the *rwlock* will be used between sibling threads. A *type* of USYNC_PROCESS indicates the *rwlock* will be used between disjoint processes. On success, a zero value is returned to the calling thread.

Diagnostics:
    EINVAL   An invalid argument was specified.
    EBUSY   The lock pointed to by *rwlock* is currently in the locked state.

```
int
rw_rdlock(rwlock_t *lock);
```

Acquire a read-mode lock on the reader-writer lock pointed to by *lock*. On success, a zero value is retured to the calling thread.

Diagnostics:
    EINVAL   An invalid argument was specified.

```
int
rw_wrlock( rwlock_t *lock);
```

Acquire a write-mode lock on the reader-writer lock pointed to by *lock*. On success, a zero value is returned to the calling thread.

Diagnostics:
    EINVAL   An invalid argument was specified.

```
int
rw_tryrdlock(rwlock_t *lock);
```

This function will make a single attempt to acquire a read-mode lock on the reader-writer lock pointed to by *lock*. On success, a zero value is returned to the calling thread.

Diagnostics:

EINVAL	An invalid argument was specified.
EBUSY	The reader-writer lock is already locked by another thread.

```
int
rw_trywrlock(rwlock_t *lock);
```

This function will make a single attempt to acquire a write-mode lock on the reader-writer lock pointed to by *lock*. On success, a zero value is returned to the calling thread.

Diagnostics:

EINVAL	An invalid argument was specified.
EBUSY	The reader-writer lock is already locked by another thread.

```
int
rw_unlock( rwlock_t *lock);
```

This function releases a lock acquired by a previous call to `rw_rdlock`, `rw_wrlock`, `rw_tryrdlock`, or `rw_trywrlock`. On success, a zero value is returned to the calling thread.

Diagnostics:

EINVAL	An invalid argument was specified.
ENOLCK	The reader-writer lock pointed to by parameter *lock* is currently not locked.

The Semaphore Synchronization Primitive [1]

```
int
sema_destroy(sema_t *sema);
```

Invalidate the semaphore pointed to by *sema*. On success, a zero value is returned to the calling thread.

Diagnostics:

EINVAL	An invalid argument was specified.
EBUSY:	The semaphore is currently locked.

---

[1] Printed with Permission of UNIX Systems Laboratories, Inc. All Rights Reserved.

```
int
sema_init(sema_t *sema, int sema_count, int type, void *arg);
```

Initialize the semaphore pointed to by *sema* for use with count resources. If *type* is USYNC_THREAD, then the semaphore will be used between sibling threads. A *type* of USYNC_PROCESS indicates the semaphore will be used between disjoint processes. On success, a zero value is returned to the calling thread.

Diagnostics:
EINVAL   An invalid argument was specified.

```
int
sema_post(sema_t *sema);
```

Release a lock associated with the semaphore pointed to by *sema*. On success, a zero value is returned to the calling thread.

Diagnostics:
EINVAL   An invalid argument was specified.

```
int
sema_trywait(sema_t *sema);
```

The calling thread will make a single attempt to acquire the semaphore pointed to by *sema*. On success, a zero value is returned to the calling thread.

Diagnostics:
EINVAL   An invalid argument was specified.
EBUSY   The semaphore could not be acquired.

```
int
sema_wait(sema_t *sema);
```

The calling thread will wait to acquire the semaphore pointed to by *sema*. On success, a zero value is returned to the calling thread.

Diagnostics:
EINVAL   An invalid argument was specified.
EINTR   The sema_wait was interrupted by a signal to the calling thread, or a forkall().

The Spin-Lock Synchronization Primitive ¶

```
int
_spin_init( spin_t *lock, void *arg);
```

The spin-lock pointed to by *lock* is initialized to the UNLOCKED state.

Diagnostics:
    EINVAL   An invalid argument was specified.

```
int
_spin_lock( spin_t *lock);
```

This function will lock the spin-lock pointed to by *lock*. If the lock is currently held by another thread, the calling thread will loop until the lock can be acquired. The spin-lock will transition to the LOCKED state.

```
int
_spin_trylock( spin_t *lock);
```

This function will make a single attempt to lock the spin-lock pointed to by *lock*.

Diagnostics:
    EBUSY   The requested spin-lock is currently locked by another thread.

```
int
_spin_unlock( spin_t *lock);
```

This function will unlock the spin-lock pointed to by *lock*. The spin-lock will transition to the UNLOCKED state.

```
int
_spin_destroy( spin_t *lock);
```

This function will invalidate the spin-lock to by *lock*.

Diagnostics:
    EINVAL   An invalid argument was specified
    EBUSY   The spin-lock is currently in the LOCKED state.

APPENDIX E
Reentrant Libraries

In a multithreaded application all functions must be designed to be Multithreaded Safe (MT-Safe). There are three categories of problems causing a function to be nonreentrant in a multithreaded environment [Kuce89]:

1. Function uses a global variable
2. Function uses statically defined variable
3. Function call is replace as inline code (i.e., macro)

In prior releases of the libc library, functions were permitted to use global data, static data, and even to return data in statically allocated buffers. This was possible, since the scope of the data was limited to the traditional UNIX process.

Shared libraries also did not pose a problem. Even though each UNIX process could reference the same functions from the shared library, only the text sections were actually shared. The data sections were allocated on a per-UNIX-process basis.

In the extended UNIX-process model, however, each UNIX process can have numerous threads of control. Although each thread has its own user-level stack, these sibling threads share the same UNIX-process address space. The implication herein is that the user-level stack ensures only per-thread storage for automatic variables, not for global or static variables. Thus, global and static variables can be altered by any sibling thread.

Other functions in libc use static data for maintaining state between invocations. This includes functions such as lfind and lsearch. The malloc family of functions also uses certain global and static variables.

Another challenge in providing an MT-Safe version of libc is that certain implementations replace specific function calls with inline code. Macros are often used as a replacement for function calls, for performance considerations. Several of the stdio functions, such as the getc and putc functions, are prime candidates for this behavior.

In general terms there are three basic approaches for providing reentrant functions. The first is to provide a separate reentrant version of the function. A typical implementation may rename the function with an _r suffix, as in `localtime_r`. The disadvantage to this approach is that the code using this function must be updated to reflect the appropriate reentrant function. This approach may also result in changes to the parameter list as well.

The second is to use thread-specific data in place of static and/or global data. In making a function reentrant by implementing thread-specific data, the function will allocate the necessary storage on a per-thread basis. This ensures the uniqueness of storage for threads, and precludes sibling threads from interfering with the data. The primary advantage to this approach is that the existing API remains unchanged. The disadvantages include (1) performance cost of allocating buffers; and (2) having buffers remain until explicitly released.

The third method is to use synchronization primitives to control the access to these functions. There are two types of synchronization that can be applied. The application process can provide external locks, or the function can use internal locks.

External synchronization locks become the responsibility of the application process. This places an additional burden on the application programmer to ensure that locks are acquired, and subsequently released around all nonreentrant functions. This is the equivalent of:

```
mutex_lock( &localtimeMutex );
localtime();
mutex_unlock( &localtimeMutex);
```

The primary benefit is that the nonreentrant function does not require changes. Thus the function can be used with a single threaded application as is, or with a multithreaded application providing the appropriate synchronization. The disadvantage is that the application programmer must ensure the appropriate synchronization is provided. There is also the problem of using static data returned by the function. The application program would need to acquire the lock, and hold the lock while the data is to be used.

The use of internal locks within a function are generally considered the best approach. Here, the function guards against unwanted concurrency by applying a synchronization primitive. The advantage to this approach is that the library API remains consistent, and the application program need not be modified. The disadvantage is that in many cases the lock will be uncontested, and thus the cost of acquiring and releasing the lock is overhead.

The granularity of internal lock placement can be coarse-grained, in that the function immediately acquires the lock and holds the lock until it completes. An alternative is for the function to acquire the lock only during its critical section. In designing the reentrant function, you may find it advantageous to use a macro definition for the lock acquisition and subsequent release.

APPENDIX F
The Kawalec Algorithm

To address the need for minimizing the cost of acquiring a lock, there are various approaches frequently used. Many of these approaches, however, are nonportable. In any event, the strategy is the same: If there are no threads waiting on the lock, then inherit the lock and continue. Otherwise, wait for the lock to become available.

The test for the lock could be implemented in assembly language using an `asm` statement, or implemented in C, providing your system offers a test-and-set operation. The use of `asm` statements in your C code may preclude certain forms of optimization, which could have an adverse impact on performance.

An alternative strategy is to develop separate assembly language functions to perform the LOCK and UNLOCK operations. The rationale is that if a LOCK function call must wait for the lock to become available, then the overhead of calling the function should not have a significant performance impact, since the thread must wait, anyhow. If the lock is immediately available, then you simply pay the cost of a function call.

Using the Kawalec algorithm [Kawa89], we can implement a simple test and set operation to avoid a `mutex_lock` function call when the lock is uncontested. With the Kawalec algorithm, the mutex lock is paired with a integer counter variable to denote the number of threads currently waiting on the LOCK (*Listing F.1*). The counter is initialized to a –1 value to denote the LOCK is initially unused. A zero value for the counter simply means that a single thread has locked the resource. When the counter value is greater then 0, then the LOCK is contested.

Listing F.1   *LOCK.h.* -- `lock` definitions header file.

```
1 typedef struct {
2       int    contentionCounter;
3       mutex_t mutex;
4 } lock_t;
```

Listing F.2   *Lock.s.* -- LOCK() and UNLOCK() assembly source file.

```
 1          .file Lock.s
 2          .version    "01.01"
 3          .type LOCK,@function
 4          .text
 5          .globl      LOCK
 6          .align      16
 7 LOCK:
 8          movl        4(%esp),%edx
 9          incl        (%edx)
10          je          .GOTIT
11          leal        4(%edx),%eax
12          pushl %eax
13          call        mutex_lock
14          addl        $4,%esp
15 .GOTIT:
16          xorl        %eax,%eax
17          ret
18          .align      4
19          .size LOCK,.-LOCK
20          .type UNLOCK,@function
21          .text
22          .globl      UNLOCK
23          .align      16
24 UNLOCK:
25          movl        4(%esp),%ecx
26          decl        (%ecx)
27          jl          .RELESD
28          leal        4(%ecx),%eax
29          pushl %eax
30          call        mutex_unlock
31          addl        $4,%esp
32 .RELESD:
33          xorl        %eax,%eax
34          ret
35          .align      4
36          .size UNLOCK,.-UNLOCK
```

To acquire a LOCK, the LOCK function must increment the LOCK's contention counter and examine its current value. If the value is zero, then the LOCK is acquired. A value greater then zero denotes that the LOCK is currently held by another thread, and thus the requesting thread must wait for the LOCK to become available. The LOCK operation would therefore call the mutex_lock function to wait for the lock.

Listing F.3   *clock.c* -- Sample C source using LOCK functions.

```
 1 #include <thread.h>
 2 #include <synch.h>
 3 #include "lock.h"
 4
 5 lock_t Lock = { -1, { 0 } };
 6
 7 void
 8 main()
 9 {
10        int    i;
11
12        for(i=0; i < 100000; ++i ) {
13                LOCK( &Lock );
14                UNLOCK( &Lock );
15        }
16        thr_exit(0);
17 }
```

Listing F.4   *mlock.c* -- Equivalent C source using mutex locks.

```
 1 #include <thread.h>
 2 #include <synch.h>
 3
 4 mutex_t mutex = { 0 };
 5
 6 main()
 7 {
 8        int    i;
 9
10        for(i=0; i < 100000; ++i ) {
11                mutex_lock( &mutex );
12                mutex_unlock( &mutex );
13        }
14        thr_exit(0);
15 }
```

After a thread has completed its critical section, the thread must call the UNLOCK function. This will decrement the LOCK's contention counter value. If the decremented value is greater than or equal to the value 0, then a sibling thread is waiting on the LOCK. The UNLOCK operation must therefore call the mutex_unlock function to release the LOCK.

The Kawalec algorithm will work only for those cases in which the increment and the decrement operations are considered atomic. The result of these operations must set the status registers such that an assembly language jump operation can be performed. The algorithm is not guaranteed to work using the C language since the increment, and/or the decrement could be followed by a compare instruction. The assembly language listing for mutex-type LOCK and UNLOCK functions using the Kawalec algorithm appears in Listing F.2.

Even though the call to LOCK and UNLOCK are function calls and thus will incur a certain amount of overhead, the performance gain is approximately 50 percent on a uniprocessor Gateway 2000 running UNIX SVR4.2 MP TLP5. Consider the two programs in Listing F.3 and Listing F.4. The execution times for these two programs appear in Listing F.5.

Listing F.5 Output of `mlock` and `clock` time trials.

$ time mlock	
real	0m0.33s
user	0m0.31s
sys	0m0.02s
$ time clock	
real	0m0.14s
user	0m0.12s
sys	0m0.02s

From a practical standpoint, the LOCK and UNLOCK functions should be modified to return an error indication value, presumably the return value of a `mutex_lock` or `mutex_unlock` function call.

Bibliography

[ABDGLS89]   Aral, Z.; J. Bloom; T. Doeppner; I. Gertner; A. Langerman; G. Schaffer. 1989. "Variable-Weight Processes with Flexible Shared Resources," *Conference Proceedings 1989 Winter USENIX Technical Conference*, pp. 405-413, San Diego, CA.

[ABLL91]   Anderson, T.; B. Bershad; E. Lazowska; H. Levy. 1991. "Scheduler Activations: Effective Kernel Support for the User-Level Management of Parallelism," *ACM Transactions on Computer Systems*, Vol 9 No 2, pp. 175-198.

[ATT86a]   AT&T. 1986. *Concepts of UNIX System Internals*. AT&T Systems Training Center, version 2.00, pp. 2-4.

[ATT91a]   AT&T. 1991. *UNIX System V Release V Internals*, AT&T Systems Training Center, Course Notes.

[Atwo76]   Atwood, J.W. 1976. "Concurrency in Operating Systems," *Computer*, v9 n10, pp. 18- 26.

[Bach84]   Bach, M.; S. Buroff. 1984. "A Multiprocessor UNIX Operating System," *USENIX 1984 Summer Conference Proceedings*, pp. 174-177.

[Bach86]   Bach, Maurice. 1986. *The Design of the UNIX Operating System*. Prentice Hall, Englewood Cliffs, NJ.

[BALL91]   Bershad, B.; T. Anderson; E. Lazowska; H. Levy. 1991. "User-Level Interprocess Communication for Shared Memory Multiprocessors," *ACM Transactions on Computer Systems*, v9 n2, pp. 175-198.

[Bart87]   Barton, J.M. 1987. "Can UNIX Take the Plunge?" *UNIX Review*, v5 n10, pp. 59-67.

[BaWa88]   Barton, J.; J. Wagner. 1988. "Beyond Threads: Resource Sharing in UNIX," *USENIX Winter Conference*, Dallas, TX, pp. 259-266.

[Beck84]   Beck, R.; R. Kasten. 1984. "Multiprocessing with UNIX," *Systems and Software*, October 1984.

[BeOi87]   Beck, R.; D. Olien. 1987. "A Parallel Programming Process Model," *USENIX Technical Conference*, Washington, D.C., pp. 83-103.

[Birr89]   Birrell, A. 1989. *An Introduction to Programming with Threads*, A White Paper, Digital Equipment Corporation, pp. 1-35.

[CALL89]   Chase, J.; F. Amador; E. Lazowska; H. Levy; R. Littlefield. 1989. "The Amber System: Parallel Programming on a Network of Multiprocessors," *ACM Operating Systems Review*, v23 n5, pp. 147-158.

[CaVa92]   Catchings, B; M. Van Name. 1992. "Multiprocessing: What's the point?" *Corporate Computing*, v1 n1, pp. 139.

[CBBC91]   Campbell, M.; R. Barton; J. Browning; D. Cervenka; B. Curry; T. Davis; T. Edmonds; R. Holt; J. Slice; T. Smith; and R. Wescott. 1991. "The Parallelization of UNIX System V Release 4.0," *USENIX Conference Proceedings*, Dallas TX, pp. 307-323.

[CGT88]   Cooprider, L; R. Gurwitz; T. Teixeira. 1988. "Support for Tightly Coupled Processors," UNIX Review, v6 n5, pp. 72-75.

[ChMi81]   Chandy, K.M.; J. Misra. 1981. "Asynchronous Distributed Simulation via a Sequence of Parallel Computations," *Communications of the ACM*, v24 n4.

[CoDo88]   Coulouris, G.; J. Dollimore. 1988. *Distributed Systems Concepts and Design.* Addison-Wesley Publishers, Ltd., ISBN 0-201-18059-6.

[CoKl68]   Coffman, E.; L. Kleinrock. 1968. "Computer Scheduling Methods and Their Countermeasures," *Spring Joint Computer Conference*, 1968.

[Cox92]   Cox, Dr. William. 1992. "Why Multiprocessing?" *UNIX Vision*, A Publication of Unix System Laboratories, Fall 1992, pp. 18-21.

[Davi83]   Davis, W. 1983. *Operating Systems: A Systematic View, 2nd Edition*, Addison-Wesley Publishing, pp. 95-104.

[Deit90]   Deitel, H.M. 1990. *An Introduction to Operating Systems, 2nd Edition*, Addison-Wesley Publishing, pp. 73-183, ISBN 0-201-18038-3.

[DiIy91]   Dimpsey, R.T.; R.K. Iyer. 1991. "Performance Prediction and Tuning on a Multiprocessor," *18th Annual International Symposium on Computer Architecture Conference Proceedings*, pp. 190-199. Toronto, Canada.

[Dijk65]   Dijkstra, E.W. 1965. "Solution of a Problem in Concurrent Programming Control," *Communications of the ACM*, v8 n9, September, 1965. pp. 569.

[EaZa93]   Eager, D.; J. Zahorjan. 1993. "CHORES: Enhanced Run-Time Support for Shared Memory Parallel Computing," *ACM Transaction on Computer Systems*, v11 n1, pp. 1-32.

[EKBF92]   Eykholt, J.R.; S.R. Kleiman; S. Barton; R. Faulkner; A. Shicalingiah; M. Smith; D. Stein; J. Voll; M. Weeks; D. Williams. 1992. "Beyond Multiprocessing ... Multithreading the SunOS Kernel," *Summer '92 USENIX*, San Antonio, TX.

[FeRu90]   Feitelson, D; L. Rudolph. 1990. "Distributed Hierarchical Control for Parallel Processing," *IEEE Computer*, v 23 n 5, May 1990, pp. 65-77.

[Fren86]   Frenkel, K. 1986. "Evaluating Two Massively Parallel Machines," *Communications of the ACM*, v29 n8, pp. 752-759.

[GaPe]   Gajski, D; J.Peir. " Essential Issues in Multiprocessor Systems," *Computer*, v18 n6, pp. 9-27.

[GaRa91]   Garg, V.; C. Ramamoorthy. 1991. "ConC: A Language for Concurrent Programming," *Computer Languages*, v16, n1, Pergamon Press, pp. 5-18.

[GeNa90]   Gehani, Narain H. 1990. "Working in Concurrent C," *UNIX Review*, v7 n5, pp. 60-70.

[Gibs92]   Gibson, S. "How Multiple Threads Work in the Computing Environment," *Infoworld*, v14 n12, p. 35.

[Gosc91]   Goscinski, A. 1991. *Distributed Operating Systems: The Logical Design*. Addison-Wesley Publishing, ISBN 0-201-41704-9.

[GSOS92]   Garlan, D.; M. Shaw; C. Okasaki; C. Scott; R. Swonger. 1992. *Experience with a Course on Architectures for Software Systems Part 1: Course Description*. Carnegie Mellon University, Publication: CMU-CS-92-176.

[HaCo88]   Hamilton, G.; D. Conde. "An Experimental Symmetric Multiprocessor Ultrix Kernel," *USENIX Winter Conference*, February 9-12, 1988, Dallas TX, pp. 283-290.

[Harp82]   Harper, M. E. 1982. "Mutual Exclusion within Both Software and Hardware Driven Kernel Primitives," *ACM Operating Systems Review*, October, 1982, v16 n4, pp. 60-68.

[Henr84]   Henry, G.J. 1984. "The Fair Share Scheduler," *AT&T Bell Laboratories Technical Journal*, v. 63 n. 8 part 2, pp. 1845-1857.

[Issa91]   Issarny, V. 1991. "An Exception Handling Model for Parallel Programming and Its Verification," *Proceedings of the ACM SIGSOFT '91 Conference on Software for Critical Systems*, New Orleans, LA, December 4-6, 1991, pp. 92-100.

[Jaco86]   Jacobs, H. 1986. "A User-Tunable Multiprocessor Scheduler," *USENIX Conference Proceedings*, Winter 1986.

[JCGS92]   Jensen, C.; J. Clifford; S. Gadia; A. Segev; R. Snodgrass. 1992. "A Glossary of Temporal Database Concepts," *ACM SIGMOD Record*, v21, n3, September 1992, pp. 35-43.

[JoJo91c]   Jolitz, W.; L. Jolitz. 1991. "Porting UNIX to the 386: The Basic Kernel, Part II," *Dr. Dobbs Journal*, v16 n10, p. 60.

[Kris95]   Krishnamurthy, Balachander. 1995. *Practical Reusable UNIX Software*. John Wiley & Sons, Inc., New York, NY.

[Kuce89]   Kucera, J. 1989. "Making libc Suitable for Use by Parallel Programs," *USENIX Workshop Proceedings on Experiences with Distributed and Multiprocessor Systems*, Ft. Lauderdale FL, pp. 145-152.

[Lamp77]   Lamport, L. 1977. "Proving the Correctness of Multiprocess Programs," *IEEE Transactions on Software engineering*, v SE-3 n3, pp. 125-143.

[Litt92]   Littman, J. 1992. "Applying Threads," *USENIX Technical Conference Proceedings*, Winter 1992, San Francisco CA, pp. 209-221.

[Mart84]   Martin, R. L. 1984. "The UNIX System: Preface," *AT&T Bell Laboratories Technical Journal*, v63 n8, Part 2, pp. 1571-1572.

[McRi89]   McGregor, J.; Riehl, A. 1989. "Support For Multiprocessing," *Communications of the ACM*, v32 n9, pp. 1063-1065.

[McSw89]   McJones, P.; G. Swart. 1989. " Evolving the UNIX System Interface to Support Multithreaded Programs," *1989 Winter USENIX Technical Conference*, San Diego CA, pp. 393-405.

[MKOI85]   Murakami, K; T. Kakuta; R. Onai; N. Ito. "Research on Parallel Machine Architectures for Fifth Generation Computer Systems," *Computer*, v18 n6, pp. 76-92.

[MSLM91]   Marsh, B.; M. Scott; T. LeBlanc; E. Markatos. 1991. "First-Class User-Level Threads," *In Proceedings of the 13th ACM Symposium on Opertaing Systems Principles*, Asilomar Conference Center, v25 n5, Pacific Grove, GA, pp. 110-121.

[Muel93]   Mueller, F. 1993. "A Library Implementation of POSIX Threads Under UNIX," *Winter USENIX*, San Diego, CA, pp. 29-41.

[MuTa85]   Mullender, S.; A. Tanenbaum. 1985. "A Distributed File Service Based on Optimistic Concurrency Control," *Proceedings of the 10th Symposium on Operating Systems Principles*, ACM, v19 n5, pp. 51-62.

[Oste92]   Ostertag, E; J. Hendler; R. Diaz; C. Braun. 1992. "Computing Similarity in a Reuse Library System: An AI-Based Approach, " *ACM Transactions on Software Engineering and Methodology*, v1. n3., pp. 205-228.

[Oust82]   Ousterhout, J. 1982. "Scheduling Techniques for Concurrent Systems," 3rd International Conference on Distributed Computing Systems, pp. 23-30.

[Phil78]   Phillips, J.; M. Burke; GS Wilson. 1978. "Threaded Code for Laboratory Computers," *Software Practice and Experience*, v8, pp. 257-263.

[PKBS91]   Powell, M.; S. Kleiman; S. Barton; D. Shah; D. Stein; M. Weeks. 1991. "Sun OS 5.0 Multithreaded Architecture," *Usenix Winter Conference*, Dallas TX, pp. 65-79.

[RaRo81]   Rashid, R.; G. Robertson. 1981. "ACCENT: A Communication-Oriented Network Operating Sytem Kernel," *Proceedings of the 8th ACM Symposium on Operating System Principles*, December 1981, pp. 64-75.

[Rash86]   Rashid, R. 1986. "Threads of a New System," *UNIX Review*, pp. 37-49.

[Ritc78]   Ritchie, D. 1978. "The UNIX Time-Sharing System: A Retrospective," *The Bell System Technical Journal*, v57 n6, pp. 1947-1969.

[Ritc84]   Ritchie, D. 1984. "The Evolution of the UNIX Time-Sharing System," *AT&T Bell Laboratories Technical Journal*, v63, n8, pp. 1577-1593.

[Schn85]   Schneck, P.; D. Austin; S. Squires; J. Lehmann; D. Mizell; K. Wallgren. 1985. "Parallel Processor Programs in the Federal Government," *Computer*, v18 n6, pp. 43-56.

[Shat84]   Shatz, S.M. 1984. "Communication Mechanisms for Programming Distributed Systems," *Computer*, v17, n6, pp. 21-28.

[Spen92]   Spencer, G. 1992. "Multiprocessing in Transition," *SunWorld*,   v5 n9,   pp. 96-102.

[Ster93]   Stern, H. 1993. "Process Scheduling in SunOS 5.x," *Sun Technical Bulletin*, September 1993, pp. 2.1 - 2.14.

[StSh92]   Stein, D.; D. Shah. 1992. "Implementing Lightweight Threads," *Summer '92 USENIX*, San Antonio, TX.

[SunM91]   Sun Microsytems. 1991. "SPARCsystem(TM) 600MP New Technology for Flexibility, Scalability, and Growth," *Technical White Paper*, Sun Microsystems, Inc., Mountain View, CA.

[SunM92]   Sun Microsystems. 1992. "Multiprocessing Technology: A Primer," *Software Technical Bulletin*, March 1992, pp. 2.1-2.17.

[TDP89]   Terrano, A.; S. Dunn; J. Peters. 1989. "Using an Architectural Knowledge Base to Generate Code for Parallel Computers," *Communications of the ACM*, v32 n9, pp. 1065-1073.

[Test86]   Test, J. 1986. "Concentrix - A UNIX for the Alliant Multiprocessor," *Usenix Conference Proceedings*, January 1986.

[Thom78]   Thompson, K. 1978. "UNIX Time-Sharing System: UNIX Implementation," *The Bell System Technical Journal*, v57 n6, pp. 1931-1946.

[Thom79]   Thomas, R.H. 1979. "A Majority Consensus Approach to Concurrency Control," ACM Transactions on Database Systems, v4, pp. 180-209.

[WeMe80]   Wettstein, Prof. H.; Dr. G. Merbeth. 1980. "The Concept of Asynchronization," *ACM Operating System Review*, v. 14 n. 4, October 1990, pp.50-70

[WeSm83]   Wegner, P; S. A. Smolka. 1983.   "Processes, Tasks, and Monitors: A Comparitive Study of Concurrent Programming Primatives," *IEEE Transactions on Software Engineering*, vol SE-9, n 4, pp. 446-462.

INDEX